Gabriele Koehler, Alberto D. Cimadamore, Fadia Kiwan,
Pedro Manuel Monreal Gonzalez (Eds.)

**The Politics of Social Inclusion:
Bridging Knowledge and Policies
Towards Social Change**

About CROP

CROP, the Comparative Research Programme on Poverty, was initiated in 1992, and the CROP Secretariat was officially opened in June 1993 by the Director General of UNESCO, Dr Frederico Mayor. The CROP network comprises scholars engaged in poverty-related research across a variety of academic disciplines and has been coordinated by the CROP Secretariat at the University of Bergen, Norway.

The CROP series on *International Studies in Poverty Research* presents expert research and essential analyses of different aspects of poverty worldwide. By promoting a fuller understanding of the nature, extent, depth, distribution, trends, causes and effects of poverty, this series has contributed to knowledge concerning the reduction and eradication of poverty at global, regional, national and local levels.

From CROP to GRIP

After a process of re-thinking CROP, 2019 marked the beginning of a transition from CROP to GRIP – the Global Research Programme on Inequality. GRIP is a radically interdisciplinary research programme that views inequality as both a fundamental challenge to human well-being and as an impediment to achieving the ambitions of the 2030 Agenda. It aims to facilitate collaboration across disciplines and knowledge systems to promote critical, diverse and inter-disciplinary research on inequality. GRIP will continue to build on the successful collaboration between the University of Bergen and the International Science Council that was developed through thep former Comparative Research Programme on Poverty.

For more information contact:

GRIP Secretariat
Faculty of Social Sciences
University of Bergen
PO Box 7802
5020 Bergen, Norway.

E-mail: gripinequality@uib.no
Web: www.gripinequality.org

For more information about CROP and previous publications in this series, please visit www.crop.org.

Gabriele Koehler, Alberto D. Cimadamore, Fadia Kiwan,
Pedro Manuel Monreal Gonzalez (Eds.)

THE POLITICS OF SOCIAL INCLUSION: BRIDGING KNOWLEDGE AND POLICIES TOWARDS SOCIAL CHANGE

Bibliografische Information der Deutschen Nationalbibliothek
Die Deutsche Nationalbibliothek verzeichnet diese Publikation in der Deutschen Nationalbibliografie; detaillierte bibliografische Daten sind im Internet über http://dnb.d-nb.de abrufbar.

Bibliographic information published by the Deutsche Nationalbibliothek
Die Deutsche Nationalbibliothek lists this publication in the Deutsche Nationalbibliografie; detailed bibliographic data are available in the Internet at http://dnb.d-nb.de.

Published in 2020 by the United Nations Educational, Scientific and Cultural Organization, 7, place de Fontenoy, 75352 Paris 07 SP. France, the Comparative Research Programme on Poverty (CROP), University of Bergen, PO Box 7800, N- 5020 Bergen, Norway, and *ibidem* Press, Stuttgart, Germany.

ISBN 978-3-8382-1333-0

© UNESCO / CROP / *ibidem* Press

This publication is available in Open Access under the Attribution-ShareAlike 3.0 IGO (CC-BY-SA 3.0 IGO) license (http://creative-commons.org/licenses/by-sa/3.0/igo/). By using the content of this publication, the users accept to be bound by the terms of use of the UNESCO Open Access Repository (http://www.unesco.org/open-access/terms-use-ccbysa-en).

The designations employed and the presentation of material throughout this publication do not imply the expression of any opinion whatsoever on the part of UNESCO concerning the legal status of any country, territory, city or area or of its authorities, or concerning the delimitation of its frontiers or boundaries.

The ideas and opinions expressed in this publication are those of the authors; they are not necessarily those of UNESCO and do not commit the Organization.

Typeset: Tatiana Jourja
Cover picture: ID 32994791 © Robertosch | Dreamstime.com

Printed in the EU

Figures, tables and boxes

Figures
2.1	Baseline: net primary school attendance, by wealth and gender	64
2.2	Excluding poor girls yet attaining the goal	65
2.3	Equitable approach to targeting	66
6.1	Social transformation and social growth	144
6.2	Growth rates, Jamaica, Haiti, and Latin America and the Caribbean, 2005–15	148
9.1	Kathputli Colony as a vibrant community, 2014	242
9.2	Kathputli Redevelopment Plan	243
9.3	Redevelopment of the Kathputli Colony, 2018	244

Tables
2.1	Policy intervention	60
6.1	Basic socio-economic data for selected countries and the region	146
6.2	Profile of poor and non-poor children in Jamaica	147
6.3	Gender participation indicators in Jamaica and Haiti	149
6.4	Economic and human impacts of selected storm events on Jamaica	150
6.5	Effects of natural disasters on Haiti	151
9.1	Urban sector policies in India	239
12.1	South Asia – selected national indicators	314
12.2	Multidimensional poverty index (MPI) across social groups, India	323
12.3	Poverty ratio by social groups, India, 2011–12	323
12.4	Intersectional inequalities: hunger and nutrition outcomes for women in India	324
12.5	Inequalities in education in India	325
12.6	Gender inequalities in India: drop-out rates by school grade	326
12.7	Unequal access to water and sanitation for all	326
12.8	Crimes against Dalit women	328
12.9	Crimes against SCs registered under the Prevention of Atrocities Act	329
12.10	Overview: selected public policy programmes in South Asia	331
12.11	The 5-Rs framework for social inclusion	340

Boxes
6.1	Facts about poverty in Haiti	145
6.2	Some issues identified by residents in three urban poor communities	154
6.3	Features of social exclusion in Haiti	155
6.4	A teacher's account of school violence in Haiti	156
6.5	Education as a liberating force from social exclusion in Jamaica	157
11.1	Dulare	296
11.2	Sureshi	298
11.3	Ramnaresh	299
11.4	Nahid	300
11.5	Somvati	304

Acronyms and abbreviations

ACHR	Asian Coalition for Housing Rights
ADB	Asian Development Bank
APVVU	Andhra Pradesh Vyvasaya Vruthidarula Union
BJP	Bhartiya Janata Party
BNA	Basic Needs Approach
BSP	Bahujan Samaj Party
CBO	community-based organizations
CEDAW	International Convention on the Eradication of all forms of Discrimination against Women
CEE	Centre for the Economics of Education
CERD	International Convention on the Elimination of All Forms of Racial Discrimination
CPRC	Chronic Poverty Research Centre
CRPD	International Convention on the Rights of Persons with Disabilities
CROP	Comparative Research Programme on Poverty
CSEI	Centre for Social Equity and Inclusion
DDA	Delhi Development Authority
DFID	(UK) Department for International Development
FAO	Food and Agriculture Organization of the United Nations
GPI	gender parity index
HDA	human development approach
HDI	Human Development Index
IAY	Indira Awas Yojna
IDS	Institute of Development Studies
IIEP	UNESCO International Institute for Educational Planning
IILS	International Institute for Labour Studies
ILGI	informal local governance institution
ILO	International Labour Organization
IOM	International Organization for Migration
ISC	could be a mistake
ISSC	International Social Science Council
JNNURM	Jawaharlal Nehru National Urban Renewal Mission
KCC	Kampala City Council
KCCA	Kampala Capital City Authority
MDG	Millennium Development Goal
MGNREGA	Mahatma Gandhi National Rural Employment Guarantee Act
MHUPA	Ministry of Housing and Urban Poverty Alleviation (India)
MOST	Management of Social Transformations
NBER	(US) National Bureau of Economic Research
NCDHR	National Campaign on Dalit Human Rights
NGO	non-governmental organization
NPEP	National Poverty Eradication Programme
NSDFU	National Slum Dwellers Federation of Uganda

Acronyms and abbreviations

OBC	other backward castes
OHCHR	Office of the High Commissioner for Human Rights
OPP	Orangi Pilot Project
PATH	Programme of Advancement through Health and Education
PCI	Planning Commission of India
RAY	Rajiv Awas Yojana
SC	Scheduled Castes
SDG	Sustainable Development Goal
SDI	Slum/Shack Dwellers International
SES	socio-economic status
SIDS	Small Island Developing States
SP	Samajwadi Party
SRS	Slum Redevelopment Scheme
ST	Scheduled Tribes
UDHR	Universal Declaration of Human Rights
UiB	University of Bergen
UNDESA	UN Department of Economic and Social Affairs
UNDP	UN Development Programme
UNDRIP	UN Declaration on the Rights of Indigenous Peoples
UNICEF	UN Children's Fund
UNRISD	UN Research Institute for Social Development
UPA	United Progressive Alliance
WHO	World Health Organization

Acknowledgements

This book has its origin in an international workshop organized by the Comparative Research Programme on Poverty (CROP) of the International Social Science Council (now the International Science Council (ISC)) and the University of Bergen (UiB), and UNESCO's Management of Social Transformations Programme (MOST), held at the UNESCO Headquarters in Paris on 6–7 July 2017.

The editors would like to express sincere thanks to the CROP Secretariat, the contributing authors, UNESCO, the International Science Council and the University of Bergen for all their support. A special thank you also to Katja Hujo (UNRISD) for critical insights, and to John Crowley, Jakob Horstmann, Sonja Keller and Maria Sollohub for steering the process.

Contents

List of figures, tables and boxes

List of acronyms and abbreviations

Acknowledgements

Part I: Conceptual understandings of social inclusion............. 11

Chapter 1. The politics of social inclusion: introduction *(Gabriele Koehler, Alberto D. Cimadamore, Fadia Kiwan and Pedro Monreal Gonzalez)*.. 13

Chapter 2. Overcoming social exclusion in education: reflections on policy challenges *(Enrique Delamonica)*...................... 41

Chapter 3. Social exclusion and the relational elements of poverty *(Paul Spicker)*.. 81

Chapter 4. Policies without politics: the exclusion of power dynamics in the construction of 'sustainable development' *(Juan Telleria)*.. 99

Part II: The politics of social exclusion and policies for inclusion 115

Chapter 5. An alternative reading of the concept of 'inclusion': the Bolivian concept of 'community with quality of life' *(Nelson Antequera Durán)*... *117*

Chapter 6. Social growth and social transformation: experiences from the Caribbean *(Aldrie Henry-Lee)*........................... *137*

Chapter 7. Critical and propositional urban planning: the co-production approach in Kampala *(Gilbert Siame)*................... *167*

Chapter 8. Between control and compassion: the politics of neighbourhood community services in urban China *(Judith Audin)*.. *195*

Contents

CHAPTER 9. The right to centrality and discursive articulations: a case of city planning policies in Delhi (*Ashok Kumar*) *223*

CHAPTER 10. Undermining the SDGs: informality, patronage and the politics of inclusion in Mumbai (*Joop de Wit*) *255*

CHAPTER 11. Politics of caste-based exclusion: poverty alleviation schemes in rural India (*Rachel Kurian and Deepak Singh*) *283*

CHAPTER 12. Transformations necessary to 'leave no one behind': social exclusion in South Asia (*Gabriele Koehler and Annie Namala*) *313*

Notes on the contributors *353*

Part I
Conceptual understandings of social inclusion

CHAPTER 1
THE POLITICS OF SOCIAL INCLUSION: INTRODUCTION

Gabriele Koehler, Alberto D. Cimadamore, Fadia Kiwan and Pedro Monreal Gonzalez

A. The rationale for a volume on the politics of inclusion

Academics, policy-makers, civil society and concerned citizens across the planet are alarmed by the persistence of global poverty, the intensity of social exclusion and increasing inequalities. Multidimensional poverty continues to affect half of humanity. Inequality has reached unprecedented levels: according to Oxfam's analysis, for example, in 2018, 26 people owned the same wealth as the 3.8 billion people who make up the poorest half of humanity (Oxfam, 2019; also see Piketty, 2014; UNRISD, 2018). Climate change impact and armed conflicts are wiping out many human development achievements of the past decades, frequently exacerbating existing patterns of social exclusion.

To redress the dystopian situation, the international community adopted the 2030 Agenda for Sustainable Development – Transforming our World (United Nations, 2015), the Paris Agreement on Climate Change (UNFCCC, 2015), and designed a new urban agenda (UN Habitat, 2016). All of these have in common a commitment to norms and principles of social inclusion – promising to 'end poverty and hunger in all their forms and dimensions' and to 'leave no one behind'. Leaving no one behind has been understood in a universalist and rights-based interpretation as including all people on the planet in sustainable and just societies. That would indeed be transformative of the dominant socio-economic orders, which have been reproducing and cementing poverty, inequality and social exclusion throughout history.

The status quo to be transformed is maintained by power relations which need to be addressed in order to produce sustainable economic, social, ecological and political inclusion for all. However, the structural transformations that would be required to unseat the dynamics of poverty, inequalities and exclusion are far less addressed, and do not feature expressly in the normative texts. Besides, the concept of inclusion is not defined, and therefore it is not possible to measure or evaluate progress toward the achievement of this goal, which is central to the general ambition to 'leave no one behind'. In short, power relations tend to be ignored or overlooked in domestic and multilateral policy debates (UNRISD, 2016), and the absence of a clear understanding of what social inclusion means articulates the problematic on which this book intends to focus.

This volume was therefore conceived to address the power relations that both sustain and transform social orders marked by social exclusion, and to advance the understanding of the *politics* of social inclusion.

The collective construction of this understanding began with an international workshop held at UNESCO Headquarters, followed up in collaborative work between the editors and authors. This introductory chapter intends to synthesize and reflect on this process of collaborative knowledge production while advancing useful knowledge on the politics of inclusion. In order to do that, we first track social inclusion deliberations from two critical vantage points – first, that of academic discussions which generally analyze the phenomenon of social exclusion, and second, from the discussion of social inclusion as it has informed debates and agenda-setting at the United Nations and related multilateral bodies, and at the European Commission. We then provide an overview of the two sections of the volume and their chapters. In closing, we sketch out a possible way forward regarding the research and policy nexus, trying to avoid jargon and unnecessary complexities to reach beyond the academic community.

B. Defining and understanding exclusion, inclusion and their political dimensions

Social inclusion presupposes in our view the realization of human rights, as laid out in the Universal Declaration of Human Rights (UDHR), and the UN Covenants on Economic, Social and Cultural Rights, and Political and Civil Rights. This general understanding needs of course to be contextualized within national and subnational legal orders that articulate states and societies around notions of justice which are not normally realized. The high levels of poverty and inequality are indicative of the structural violation of human, social, economic and cultural rights observed in many societies. In this view, social exclusion implies the denial to members of society of their basic human, political, social and economic rights guaranteed in international, national and subnational constitutions and legal orders. Rights are not realized for many reasons, principally because the excluded and the poor have limited or no access to the institutions of justice, and therefore are usually powerless in systems structurally biased against them. In this general context, the politics of inclusion refers to the power relations evolving within historical forms of states and international relations where asymmetrical economic, social and political orders tend to exclude large segments of the population (Cimadamore, 2008; UNRISD, 2018).

As we can see below and throughout the volume, this view is not necessarily shared by those who tend to focus narrowly on notions of inclusion as merely concerning inclusion in labour markets or social protection measures. The transformational challenge is complex in itself. It is even more so when we depart from a situation where there is no clear consensus on what inclusion is, how it is measured, what the targets are, and the means and policies to reach them. This volume can only deal with some aspects of the enormous analytical and policy puzzle that needs to be solved – at the latest – by 2030 if we wish to remain true to the commitments of the UN Agenda for Sustainable Development (United Nations, 2015) and other multilateral normative frameworks. Nevertheless, the book might at least selectively contribute with a number of insights to stimulate debates and research agendas aimed at addressing the problematic of social inclusion in the era of the Sustainable Development Goals (SDGs). In order to situate these insights in a broader discourse, there is a need to scan some relevant understandings of exclusion and inclusion (Delamonica, Chapter 2), and their interface and overlappings with poverty (see Spicker, Chapter 3). We therefore begin by sketching the evolution of these and other related concepts. This may serve to assess the pool of policies for social inclusion derived from different schools of thought and political ideologies, so as to contribute to an analysis of the *politics* of social inclusion.

Social exclusion/inclusion in the academic literature

The concept of social exclusion has analytical and political implications. Analytically, it can be traced to various strands in social and political literature focusing mainly on the causes and consequences of the systematic marginalization of individuals and communities from decent work, socio-economic security and equitable access to public services.

As suggested before, socially, economically and politically, processes of exclusion undermine social justice in societies where constitutional rights and obligations set the parameters of the relationships among all components of the state. In this sense, policies of social inclusion aim to redress and overcome those unbalances and asymmetries produced by the lack of realization of those basic human, social, economic and cultural rights that constitute the pillars of state and societal orders.

However, in mainstream discussions the concept of exclusion is often attributed to and refers to the work of the French social worker René Lenoir. His treatise on the excluded from the 1970s does not define the term social exclusion, but instead is an empirical enquiry into the situation of people challenged by difficult economic, social or health circumstances in the 1960s and early 1970s in France (Lenoir, 1974). Such focus on discussions in 1970s Europe somehow ignores or minimizes the fact that the social sciences have at least since the nineteenth century had a customary concern with issues of social exclusion, originally identified as 'marginalization', and that processes of social exclusion have been a major analytical theme in the global South for many decades.

For instance, Karl Marx's 'reserve army' provides the centrepiece of an explanation that situates marginalization as a structural phenomenon endemic to capitalism and the related processes of exclusion and poverty. Conversely, neoclassical economics used the term 'residuum' (Marshall, 1925) in a different political vein, ascribing exclusion to personal character flaws or cultural resistance, such as 'poor physique and feeble will, with no enterprise, no courage, no hope and scarcely any self-respect, whom misery drives to work for lower wages than the same work gets in the country' (Marshall, 1925, pp. 142–51).

Social sciences in Latin America and the Caribbean during the 1960s and 1970s focused on marginality (*marginalidad*) in the context of the modernization process. This referred to those segments of the population that were sidelined from the dynamics of modernization that took place in the region in the first half of the twentieth century. The main analytical (and political) proposition was that this part of the population needed to be integrated into the process of modernization, since marginality indicated a transitory phenomenon located between traditional societies and modern societies (Pérez Sáinz, 2012; Nun, 1969).

Authors like Janice Perlman conducted a thorough analysis of the different approaches to marginality in the context of the theory of modernization, and developed a critical assessment. Her main argument was that the approach of marginality was based in a model of equilibrium of social integration in which relations among all social actors were seen as mutually beneficial. Her critique can be summarized as the idea that:

> it is perfectly possible to have a stable system biased towards the benefit of some actors precisely because there is exploitation, explicit or implicit, of other actors. The exploited groups are not marginalized. On the contrary, they are integrated into the system, operating as a vital component of the system. That is, integration does not necessarily imply reciprocity.
> (Perlman, 1976; and also see Pérez Sáinz, 2012)

Nor does integration necessarily imply progress towards a more just social inclusion. In a similar vein, it is argued that the operation of basic markets (labour, capital, credit, land, knowledge) necessitates the disempowerment of certain social groups, and when the access to social citizenship is not guaranteed, primary exclusion turns into social exclusion (Mora Salas, 2004; Pérez Sáinz and Mora Salas, 2006).

This assessment tallies with approaches from/about Asia that build on the notion of participatory exclusion (Agarwal, 2001) or adverse incorporation (Hickey and Du Toit 2007) – forms of inclusion that are detrimental to the community concerned.

Concerning Asia, the literature looks at social exclusion generically and analytically. Amartya Sen, for example, was one of the first to raise the issue for the region: his work on gender-based exclusion – resulting in millions of 'missing women' in South Asia – was seminal (Sen, 1990). Sen noted a 'specific type of social exclusion that – particularly from basic education and elementary social opportunities – plagues the economies of West and South Asia' (Sen, 2000, p. 31). His work on identity-based exclusions and the need to strengthen capabilities informed an entire literature, both academic research and empirical studies, including surveys commissioned and conducted for or by civil society, human rights bodies and development agencies.[1] Power is constituent in social exclusion, and many of the Asian theoreticians have formulated this in various ways. Amartya Sen understands social exclusion as a relational issue, in terms of how individuals relate to each other; this is constituent for his conceptualization of the issue (Sen, 2000). For Arundhati Roy (2014), social exclusion is embedded in political structures and contestations. At the empirical level, the relationality – in the sense of political oppression – becomes manifest

---

1 The Asian Development Bank (ADB), for example, picked up the social exclusion concept after the Asian financial crisis of 1997/98.

in the field work presented in this volume, and in the global survey done elsewhere by Deborah Rogers and Balint Balázs (2016).

Horizontal exclusion and the exclusion–poverty nexus

A related strand of social exclusion discourse is that of the different vectors or processes of social exclusion, and their interface, sometimes described as intersecting inequalities (Kabeer, 2010) or intersecting forms of discrimination and clustered deprivations (Bennett, 2006; Razavi and Hassim, 2007; Razavi, 2016; UN Women, 2018). Clustered deprivations, for example, refer to the process whereby 'deprivations ... co-produce and "cluster" together, so that deprivation in one area is accompanied by deprivation in another' (UN Women, 2018, p. 139). Poverty, understood as a lack of access to resources, tends to be 'strongly correlated with many other forms of deprivation, including ... education, health and well-being' (UN Women, 2018 p. 139). Similarly, inequality is experienced not only among individuals but among groups defined by class, gender, ethnic condition and territory, among other factors (Pérez Sáinz and Mora Salas, 2009). The operation of 'basic markets' is determined not only by power dynamics of class but also by those other factors, resulting in diverse possibilities of unequal distribution of the surplus, which could be different by country and period.

Most analysts agree that gender-based exclusion is overarching. It takes the form of political and social oppression, discrimination and economic marginalization of women and sexual minorities. It is frequently expressed in outright violence against women. It affects all income and sociocultural groups: women in all societies, classes, and ethnic and faith communities are at a structural and deeply embedded disadvantage. It exacerbates the other vectors of exclusion and marginalization, and is cross-cutting and hence definitive. However, women are not a minority, so the processes and dynamics of exclusion are different from those affecting other identity groups.

Gender-based exclusion is often exacerbated by ethnicity-based and racist forms of exclusion, including caste systems. All are based on entrenched hierarchies and asymmetrical power relations (Kabeer, 2010; Rogers and Balázs, 2016; World Bank, 2013). Vectors and outcomes of exclusion can also be categorized by other forms of identity. These comprise economic factors such as socio-economic and employment status, and coverage by social protection/social security systems; sociocultural factors, such as gender and sexual orientation, age, health status, including physical and mental challenges, or educational status, language and ethnicity, faith, and a person's cultural identity; geophysical factors such as shelter quality, urban or rural location, topography and accessibility of one's home; and political factors such as citizenship status, migrant or refugee status, and access to the justice system. Silver (1995), Levitas (2006) and Delamonica (see Chapter 2) among others have developed or discussed similarly comprehensive lists.

One concern of this volume is the relationships and the intersections between poverty and the many vectors of social exclusion. The notion of poverty has been researched for quite some time, primarily in the form of income poverty, and not necessarily correlated to social exclusion (see Spicker, Chapter 3, for a comprehensive overview). One early analysis of the systemic connection between poverty and exclusion, using a different terminology, was provided by Galtung (1969): social structures oppress individuals and communities by ethnicity, gender, age, income, class and other factors. Seemingly hidden structural violence is a cemented feature across all societies, leading to income poverty. Many countries and communities in addition suffer from open, manifest violence as the most extreme form of social exclusion. In the same vein, Paul Spicker (in Chapter 3) emphasizes the political and relational dimensions of exclusion and poverty.

The concept of multidimensional poverty has been introduced as a criterion in the targets of the 2030 Agenda and its SDG goals (goal 1.2). Progress in conceptualizing and measuring poverty in a multidimensional way (using the Human Development Index (HDI), the Multidimensional Poverty Index (MPI) and so on) (Alkire et al., 2015) has been quite significant. At the same time, the study of causes and consequences of absolute and relative poverty in different historical contexts has become more differentiated, making structural, socio-economic, political and institutional aspects more visible. Ethical and legal approaches to poverty production and eradication not only add to the notion of relative deprivation but also subsume the normative approach based on the principle of citizenship implied in the exclusion/inclusion conceptualization.

In sum, there is now an agreement in academic discourse that social exclusion is related to the genesis and the re-production of poverty and is an expression of power relations; that a relational, power-aware concept is needed to understand multidimensional poverty; and that a wide set of 'inclusion policies' is required if we genuinely want to achieve poverty eradication, and this in all relevant dimensions, not just income poverty. However, with respect to inclusion policy approaches, the academic literature limits itself to rather general and generic recommendations, mainly (but not exclusively) because of the lack of agreement on its definition and indicators. This volume is therefore also an attempt to offer some policy options.

The main strands of the conceptual problematic in UN discourse

Parallel to academic research, a number of UN and UN-related bodies have also contributed to the discourse on social inclusion and exclusion. At UNESCO (2012), issues directly relevant to 'social inclusion' were prominent in the MOST (Management of Social Transformations) Programme even before the concept was formally incorporated into the terminology of UNESCO and the UN system. Over the past twenty years, UNESCO contributed to the production of knowledge relevant to social inclusion, and integrated the concept into programmatic work, notably in the sector of education, including an Intersectoral Programme on Poverty Eradication which situated poverty as a human rights issue. Following this tradition, the MOST Programme aims to serve as a bridge from evidence-based knowledge from social sciences research to decision-making in public policy. Its purpose is to enhance the capacities of governments to manage multidimensional crises, to restore and consolidate stability, and to achieve justice and peace. This was in fact the general frame of reference for the 2017 International workshop organized by the Comparative Research Programme on Poverty – CROP (ISSC/UiB) and MOST (held at UNESCO Headquarters in Paris on 6–7 July 2017) – which was the origin of this volume. By selecting 'politics of social inclusion' as a metatopic and partnering with CROP as a scientific international network, the MOST intergovernmental body intends to produce and disseminate more comprehensive knowledge about exclusion and inclusion, as well as to make an impact in the policy debate oriented to 'leave no one behind'.

Previous efforts to advance on the conceptual clarification of social exclusion and inclusion as well as their complex interrelationships with poverty reached one of its peaks in the 1995 with the publication of the seminal study by the International Labour Organization (ILO) International Institute for Labour Studies (IILS) (Rodgers et al., 1995). It was a milestone since it aimed to 'deconstruct' the usage of the term in European policy debates and to 'fashion a notion of social exclusion which is not Eurocentric but relevant globally, in a wide variety of country-settings'. It was a reaction to the policy debates that took place in Western Europe on the 'emerging patterns of social disadvantage, particularly associated with long-term unemployment'. Within this framework, the ILO volume highlights that social exclusion refers to marginalization from society through economic deprivation and social isolation, as well as fragmentation of social relations and breakdown of social cohesion (Gore and Figueiredo, 1997). That study also aimed 'to clarify the interrelationships between poverty and social exclusion and to assess the potential usefulness of this latter approach for anti-poverty strategies' (Gore and Figueiredo, 1997, p. 3).

The context in which the debate emerges is a relevant background to assess its political and analytical strengths. The increasing relevance of employment/unemployment in European political debates, along with the political inconvenience that poverty implies for politicians and other decision-makers who cannot properly deal with it, contributed to promoting the use of exclusion/inclusion as a 'euphemism'. Certainly, the research on poverty was relatively more advanced at that time, and there were ways to not only define it but also measure it with more precision. However, perhaps the intention was to produce or develop not an analytical concept but a political one. In this regard, Else Øyen (1997) concluded in a chapter of a study for IILS that social exclusion and social inclusion are political rather than analytical concepts. In her view, politicians found the concept of poverty 'too loaded' so they moved towards the concepts of social exclusion/inclusion.

Other UN and UN-related sites of social inclusion/exclusion discourse include the UN Research Institute for Social Development (UNRISD), the UN Department of Economic and Social Affairs (UNDESA), and the World Bank. UNRISD has been seminal with respect to examining gender-based exclusions (e.g. UNRISD, 2005, 2016). The UNDESA Expert Group on 'Creating an Inclusive Society' was decisive for the emergence and further refinement of the concept of social inclusion, in particular for the intensification of its use within the UN system and beyond.[2] The World Bank has commissioned much country-level research on social exclusion/inclusion over the past decade, and published a comprehensive global study on social inclusion. Analytically, that study defines social inclusion 'as the process of improving the ability, opportunity, and dignity of people, disadvantaged on the basis of their identity, to take part in

---

[2] UNDESA organized three Expert Group meetings between 2007 and 2009 in Paris, Helsinki and Accra.

society' (World Bank, 2013, p. 4). With respect to policy-making, it defines social inclusion 'as the process of improving the terms for individuals and groups to take part in society' (World Bank, 2013, p. 3). It discusses the roles of both intersecting identities and power, and offers a compendium of policy responses, arguing the case for cross-cutting approaches across policy domains (World Bank, 2013, pp. 229 ff), which tallies with the findings of many of the chapters in this volume that policies for inclusion need to be multilayered and multipronged. ILO and the International Organization for Migration (IOM) have also produced country-level and regional studies on social exclusion processes and their impact on poverty (e.g. ILO, 2005).

Social inclusion in UN development agendas

In the context of formulating UN development agendas, the concepts of social inclusion and social integration have been intertwined or used interchangeably. Social integration, paired with the concept of social exclusion, first appeared in the UN Copenhagen Summit on Social Development in 1995 (United Nations 1995). UNESCO and ILO had played significant roles in the intellectual debates leading up to the Summit.

The Social Summit emphasized the concept of an 'inclusive society', defined as a society 'in which every individual, each with rights and responsibilities, has an active role to play'. The policy-related concept was that of 'social integration', defined in the documents of the Summit as:

> with full respect for the dignity of each individual, the common good, pluralism and diversity, non-violence and solidarity, as well as their ability to participate in social, cultural, economic and political life, encompasses all aspects of social development and all policies. It requires the protection of the weak, as well as the right to differ, to create and to innovate. It calls for a sound economic environment, as well as for cultures based on freedom and responsibility. It also calls for the full involvement of both the State and civil society.
> (United Nations, 1995, Point 2 of the Programme of Action)

It does not, however, call into question the imbalances in power between states, civil society, communities and individuals.

The analytical preference for the concept of social inclusion seems to be based on tactical considerations: 'Social inclusion is also often more easily accepted as a policy goal, as it clearly eliminates a connotation of assimilation that some associate with the term "integration" – not all individuals and/or groups in societies are eager to be "integrated" into mainstream society, but all strive to be included' (UNDESA, 2009). For example, in the Millennium Development Goals (MDG) Roadmap (United Nations, 2001), the policy-related concept of integration was used only in the – important but rather narrow – context of reintegrating ex-combatants into their communities.

Curiously, the concept of social inclusion and policy proposals of social integration did not feature in the first two of the United Nations' two poverty eradication decades, which were the direct political follow-up to the Copenhagen Summit, nor did they play a role in the Millennium Declaration (United Nations, 2000). However, in the formal call for the International Day for the Eradication of Poverty 2018, UNDESA states that 'Government policies alone cannot create the social inclusion that is fundamental to reaching those left furthest behind and overcoming poverty in all its dimensions.'[3]

In global intergovernmental UN debates, social inclusion resurfaced as a key concept in the UN 2030 Agenda for Sustainable Development and its SDGs (United Nations, 2015). 'Sustainable development recognizes that eradicating poverty in all its forms and dimensions, combating inequality within and among countries, preserving the planet, creating sustained, inclusive and sustainable economic growth and fostering social inclusion are linked to each other and are interdependent' (United Nations, 2015, article 13). The aspiration of social inclusion is present in many of the goals, such as the – perhaps central – goal of addressing inequality within and among countries (Goal 10) and the goal on empowering women and achieving gender equality (Goal 5). Inclusiveness is a driving notion with regard to making cities and human settlements inclusive, safe, resilient and sustainable (Goal 11), and with regard to promoting peaceful and inclusive societies for sustainable development, providing access to justice for all, and building effective, accountable and inclusive institutions at all levels (Goal 16). More visibly, it is intrinsically link to the motto of 'leaving no one behind'.

---

3   www.un.org/development/desa/socialperspectiveondevelopment/international-day-for-the-eradication-of-poverty-homepage/2018-2.html. 'Social inclusion' was missing in previous DESA documents on the Third Decade, for instance, the 'Message on the occasion of the Inter-Agency Expert Group Meeting in support of the Implementation of the Third United Nations Decade for the Eradication of Poverty (2018–2027)', 18 April 2018, did not mention social inclusion or social exclusion: www.un.org/development/desa/statements/mr-liu/2018/04/iaeg-on-eradication-of-poverty.html

Inclusiveness informs many of the goals, even when social inclusion is not the concept used. Thus, there is a call to ensure universal access to sexual and reproductive health-care services (target 3.7), to universal health coverage (3.8), and the commitment to inclusive and equitable quality education and promoting lifelong learning opportunities for all (Goal 4). Goals and targets concerning water and sanitation (Goal 6) and access to affordable, reliable, sustainable and modern energy for all (Goal 7) speak of access 'for all'.[4] Many of the indicators recommended to Member States to measure progress (United Nations, 2017) are to be disaggregated by factors such as gender, age, location (rural/urban), indigeneity, and living with a disability. Such data could help reveal differential outcomes, for example in poverty and hunger eradication, owing to social exclusion.[5]

Interestingly, the goals around sustainable economic growth, full and productive employment and decent work for all (SDG 8) and sustainable industrialization (SDG 9) are explicitly designated under an inclusiveness agenda.[6]

In sum, while the 2030 Agenda recognizes and gives importance to social inclusion via several of the SDGs, it addresses neither the definition problematic nor the *politics* of exclusion/inclusion. The lack of structural analysis (UNRISD, 2016; Koehler, 2017) and diagnosis about the causes and most effective solutions needed to achieve the goals are perhaps one of the main barriers to fulfilling the promise to 'leave no one behind'. Something similar can be said about the Agenda's avoidance of clearly identifying the causes of poverty, hunger and inequality, which need to be tackled in order to achieve the agreed objective and targets. There is but one – redeeming – sentence, in the Agenda's section outlining the current situation, which does acknowledge the connection: 'Billions of our citizens continue to live in poverty and are denied a life of dignity. There are rising inequalities within and among countries. There are enormous

---

4   All UN agencies/funds and programmes and UN country team have been asked to (re-)design their work on the basis of leaving no one behind (UN CEB, 2017).
5   On the complexity of meaningful and available data see UN IAEG-SDGs (2018), which classifies SDG-relevant indicators into those that conceptually clear, have an internationally established methodology, and data are regularly produced ('tier one'); those that are conceptually clear, have an internationally established methodology, but data are not regularly produced ('tier two'); and those where no internationally established methodology or standards are yet available for the indicator ('tier three').
6   As these particular SDGs do jar with the notions of sustainability and planetary boundaries that inform the rest of the Agenda, this has been met by analytical and political misgivings in some academic and CSO circles.

disparities of opportunity, wealth and *power*' (United Nations, 2015, para 14, emphasis the authors). This is not however expanded, and therefore the 'elephant in the room' continued to be undercover even in the most ambitious agenda the international community has ever had.

This is the place to remind readers that in terms of policy advice, the UN multilateral discussions beyond the development agenda-setting over time have provided a series of normative frameworks to address exclusion. For example, ethnicity-based exclusion is addressed by the International Convention on the Elimination of All Forms of Racial Discrimination (CERD) of 1965. With respect to gender-based exclusion, the international community adopted early the Convention on the Eradication of all forms of Discrimination against Women (CEDAW) (1979), and complemented it later with the Beijing Platform of Action (1995), as normative frameworks intended to inform national legislation and policy-making on women and girl children's rights. CEDAW is binding on those states that have ratified it. Another inclusion framework is the UN Convention on the Rights of Persons with Disabilities (CRPD), adopted in 2006. The Declaration on the Rights of Indigenous Peoples (UNDRIP), adopted in 2007, while not binding, has become influential in recent years.

Social inclusion in EU debates

In terms of regional debates on inclusion, the European Union Summit in Lisbon in 2000 turned to the promotion of social inclusion, and provided some clues to assess the nature of the concept. The concept of social inclusion replaced poverty as the guiding concept for policies in the European Union. Social exclusion here refers to patterns of systematic social disadvantage associated with long-term unemployment: in other words, being excluded from the workforce and the labour market (Levitas, 2006). EU member states are in this context required to develop plans for combating social exclusion, based on the open method of coordination (European Council, 2000). The method applied basically consists of common objectives agreed at EU level which in due course need to be achieved at country levels. This encompasses facilitating employment and access to resources, rights, goods and services; preventing exclusion; and helping the most vulnerable. These objectives need to be operationalized, and adequate modes of measurement are to be developed from a common understanding of the concept of social exclusion/inclusion. The dominant European discourse revolves around a set of indicators

The politics of social inclusion: introduction

prepared by the EU Social Protection Committee (in October 2001) and endorsed by the Laeken European Council (in December 2001).

The lack of decent work is, however, just one of the many dimensions of social exclusion. This narrow approach has consequences for its definition, its measurement – and notably for policies, hollowing out both the resonance of the notion of poverty, and the need for complex and sophisticated policy-making to address all aspects and the power dimensions of social exclusion processes and outcomes. Nevertheless, Europe is the region where the conceptual and political debate is more nuanced, although overlappings and the lack of a clear definition of the boundaries between social exclusion and poverty persist even in those EU departments that are following up the process (see for instance Ireland, 2016).

C. What does this volume offer?

As outlined above, the overarching aspiration of the 2030 Agenda is to leave no one behind, and more concretely to eradicate absolute poverty by 2030 (SDG 1), ensure gender equality (SDG 5), overcome inequalities (SDG 10), and build peaceful and inclusive societies (SDG 16). There is also an orientation to inclusive cities (SDG 11). Yet, as the conceptual analyses and case studies compiled in this volume almost unanimously conclude, power relations bias, weaken, undermine or even pervert policy measures conceived to achieve such social justice and inclusion outcomes. Social exclusion is systemic (see Spicker, Chapter 3, Delamonica, Chapter 2 and Telleria, Chapter 4) – it is part of an encompassing socio-economic and political structure. Within its structural character, it is complex, playing out in different ways from the interpersonal (see Durán, Chapter 5 and Audin, Chapter 8) to the level of policy choices and their implementation (Kumar, Chapter 9; Kurian and Singh, Chapter 11). On the top of that, there are evident conceptual problems related to definition and operationalization which need to be addressed as a first step towards adequate systems of measurement and monitoring.

In the first section of the volume on concepts, key themes are based around conceptualization issues, and notably on how power plays out in the politics of social exclusion. Delamonica, for example, offers a detailed discussion of understandings and definitions of social exclusion, discrimination and related concepts. The varied terminology used to explain the phenomenon of social exclusion is associated with different explanatory patterns regarding the causes and consequences of inequality. analyzes of social exclusion processes display different approaches across various disciplines, with economics, sociology and the legal sciences having divergent views on the drivers of exclusion and on the most effective policy responses. These varied approaches both present analytical challenges and affect policy choices. Unravelling the differentiations is important to assure clarity over the exact aspired form and coverage of inclusion policy (see Delamonica, Chapter 2).

That leads to a core theme of the volume – the politics of social inclusion as a relational issue characterized by dominance and power (also relational concepts themselves). As Spicker puts it when focusing on poverty and its relationships with exclusion, 'Poverty is at root a relational concept, which can only be understood by locating the experience of poor people in the social and economic situation where they are found', and 'exclusion, a concept which is self-evidently relational, come(s) closer to the idea of poverty than much of the academic literature on poverty in itself, offering a way to escape from the limitations of conventional models of poverty'. As a history of poverty and of social exclusion discourses shows, 'conventional discussions of poverty treat the concept in a narrow and limited way, as if it could be understood solely in terms of income, resources, capabilities or the circumstances of individuals. Poverty consists in a set of relationships, not a state of being that can be treated in isolation from the society and networks of relationships that people experience' (Spicker, Chapter 3). Conversely, and more helpfully, 'the idea of exclusion is rooted in a relational understanding of people's circumstances', so that 'discussions of exclusion come closer to the idea of poverty than much of the literature on poverty in itself, offering a way to escape from the limitations of the academic analysis of poverty' (again see Chapter 3).

The bridge chapter between the conceptual and the suite of case studies problematizes the UN discourse on development agendas. Telleria argues that 'the UN has failed to reflect on the power relations that have shaped the unequal international order'. Telleria's critique is that the UN development agendas – understood as various multilateral agreements, most recently the Millennium Agenda and the 2030 Agenda – tackle 'political issue(s) in technical terms – by promoting supposedly neutral win–win policies intended to improve everyone's life'. They therefore 'exclude ... alternative perspectives on the causes and possible solutions of underdevelopment, poverty and inequality. As a consequence of this exclusion, the Millennium Declaration and the Agenda for Sustainable Development promote policies without politics: they propose courses of action without holding a plural and inclusionary political debate' (Telleria, Chapter 4). The obliviousness to power relations, and the need for policies that tackle hierarchies, dominance and power head on, is recognized as a central weakness of the 2030 Agenda. This is an important finding not just to illustrate the limitations of UN intergovernmental agenda-setting; it applies similarly to national policy-making that purports to advance social inclusion – but without addressing entrenched power hierarchies.

The second section of the volume presents case studies from a wide range of countries. They offer unsettling insights from practice.

The first level of these findings relates to personal and community-level processes of exclusion. In Bolivia, for example, the '*Vivir bien*' philosophy is an alternative paradigm of development based on a pluralist vision and a promised respect of indigenous or peasant communities and their choices, which addresses the issues of inclusion and exclusion. Implementation of the '*Vivir bien*' model has however 'been erratic and partial' (Antequera Durán, Chapter 5). Despite a number of transformations that took place in Bolivia during past years with positive impact on socio-economic outcomes, income poverty owing to a lack of decent employment persists, making it difficult for adults to balance their roles as the primary carers for their family, and as providers of the family's material basis. This is seen as the main driver of dysfunctional families, in turn generating societal exclusion. Fieldwork in La Paz, for example, reveals that 'poverty, exclusion and inequality result in the progressive deterioration of social relationships, negatively influencing affective ties and notions of identity'. Antequera Durán therefore makes the case that national and local governments should emphasize conditions for the strengthening the community if we wish to genuinely overcome social exclusion.

A similar nexus is documented in case studies from urban communities in two Caribbean countries, Jamaica and Haiti. Patriarchy, poverty and the lack of employment, arduous access to health facilities, and the slum location itself generate extreme forms of violence at the interpersonal level. The processes of economic and social exclusion in turn recreate violence (Henry-Lee, Chapter 6). Physical violence and destruction of personal property are also reported in case studies from two villages in India (Kurian and Singh, Chapter 11).

In many of the country experiences presented, hierarchical power relations perpetuate deeply embedded processes of social exclusion at the community level. The processes of social exclusion are complex and multilayered. Gender is the overarching vector of exclusion in all the case studies, regardless of the geographic location. It is 'interlocking and cumulative' (Kurian and Singh), exacerbating all other drivers of exclusion. Caste (Kurian and Singh; Koehler and Namala, Chapter 12; Kumar, Chapter 9; de Wit, Chapter 10), ethnicity (Henry-Lee, Chapter 6; Antequera Durán), location (Audin, Chapter 8; Henry-Lee; Kumar; de Wit), as well as ability, age and migrant status (Audin, Kumar) are the other social exclusion determinants revealed in the case studies. In India and other parts of South Asia, exclusion of communities runs along combined lines of patriarchy and caste (de Wit, Kumar, Kurian and Singh, Koehler and Namala).

These each have an inbuilt interface with income poverty (Spicker, Delamonica, Koehler and Namala, Henry-Lee) and with cultural poverty (Antequera Durán). The case studies moreover illustrate that social exclusion is relational – determined by interactions which are subject to power asymmetries and hierarchical stratification. As a result, dominant groups, to their own benefit, divert public resources or extract personal resources, exclude people from income-earning opportunities or access to social services, and exert violence against disadvantaged groups, based on 'socio-religious and cultural practices' (Kurian and Singh).

A second level of findings from the case studies underpins the critical point that national or local-level policies reveal a systemic disconnect. For example, caste-based exclusionary practices such as untouchability undermine poverty alleviation schemes in rural India, as illustrated in the research of Kurian and Singh: 'in spite of progressive legislations, schemes, central monitoring system and a pro-Dalit political party in power, there has been no significant change in the livelihood options' in the villages they studied. They add that 'local power relations revealed the limitations of laws and policies as instruments for changing the lives of people who function in different social fields associated with informal, hidden rules that are often stronger and where compliance is enforced face-to-face, at microlevel' (Kurian and Singh, Chapter 11).

The research from Bolivia, Jamaica and Haiti, and the studies from India reconfirm that disadvantaged communities are excluded, or adversely included, on grounds of ethnicity, income and political affiliations (Antequera Durán, Henry-Lee, de Wit). Garrison communities in Jamaica for example were political enclaves built to secure votes after independence, but they have become 'characterized by chronic poverty, social exclusion, violence and misery' and a systematic lack of access to quality education (Henry-Lee). In the case of urban planning outcomes in Delhi, women are the most affected, losing their employment opportunities, and facing additional mobility restrictions. In addition, those displaced are migrants from other states in India, engaged in the informal sector, who have no networks into local power centres (Kumar).

Indeed, a number of the cases summarize field work in urban or village settings. Urban slum dwellers see their rights violated in processes of city planning; this is the case in cities in Jamaica and Haiti, in Uganda and in India (de Wit; Kumar; Henry-Lee; Siame, Chapter 7). In China, social work is caught in the tension between providing support to disadvantaged citizens and controlling their access to social assistance, and even being complicit in the razing of their settlements or imposing family planning (Audin, Chapter 8).

The volume's concentration on the local level is important for two reasons. The local environment is where individuals and communities experience exclusion or inclusion – be it adverse or empowering – and can coalesce to organize and fight for the realization of their rights. Kumar illustrates how spatial exclusions cause and perpetuate deprivation, with seemingly inclusionary planning policies ending up in multiple exclusions. In his study, public–private partnerships in Delhi resulted in the 'displacement of citizens from one place to another' and 'also exclusion from work, particularly for poor women'. One conceptual notion in this connection is the right to centrality – the right to the urban (Kumar, based on Henri Lefebvre) – which encompasses rights to social services, infrastructure, and – extremely importantly – the right to decent and secure housing. This plane of discussion, second, interfaces with SDG11 which of itself was a major innovation in the evolution of UN development agendas – the recognition of space as constituting a key area for human dignity, identity, well-being, and hence policy-making as well as collective action.

As mentioned earlier, the UN Agenda for Sustainable Development devotes an entire goal to cities and human settlements. Target 11.3 deserves quoting: 'By 2030, enhance inclusive and sustainable urbanization and capacity for participatory, integrated and sustainable human settlement planning and management in all countries.' Many of the targets are about housing, transport systems and public spaces for all, with a special emphasis on disadvantaged groups. Likewise, the New Urban Agenda (UN Habitat, 2016) seeks 'to promote inclusivity and ensure that all inhabitants, of present and future generations, without discrimination of any kind, are able to inhabit and produce just, safe, healthy, accessible, affordable, resilient and sustainable cities and human settlements to foster prosperity and quality of life for all' (article 11). This outcome document commits to leaving no one behind, ending poverty and ensuring environmental sustainability (article 14), and calls for the participation of all actors. The field work presented in this volume illustrates the urgency of living up to the promises of the 2030 and New Urban agendas.

In addition, findings from the volume strengthen the thesis that processes of social exclusion are reinforced by a lack of democracy. In Mumbai, 'patronage democracy', observed in the slums, 'malfunctions for the poor as it neither gives them real voice nor helps towards uniform pro-poor services and policies' (de Wit, Chapter 10). It also isolates citizens, as they seek support through vertical relationships with powerful players in the community, rather than coalescing for collective action in horizontal relationships. In several cases, individuals and communities witness impunity for violations of their rights, despite legal provisions in place (Kurian and Singh, Chapter 11).

In urban China, residents' committees are in charge of implementing public policies, such as the urban registry system, family planning and birth control policies, as well as social assistance programmes. They are also tasked with organizing sociocultural activities, or mediating conflicts among neighbours. This is a broad and invasive remit, demonstrating an understanding of social inclusion that is opposed to the empowering notions of social inclusion that characterize the academic literature or UN normative frameworks.[7] Audin (in Chapter 8), based on ethnographic work in Beijing and Chongqing, highlights the challenges that social workers face. On the one hand, they are assigned to enforce public policies regarding access to social assistance in cases of disability or unemployment, or compliance with family planning laws. The community-level social work also controls residents and serves to exclude rural migrants who until recently had no residence rights in cities, co-opting neighbours into scrutinizing entitlements to social assistance or public housing. On the other hand, they have, and do internalize, a responsibility for social care work, designed to help the 'weak and vulnerable groups' in each neighbourhood. Their roles hence oscillate between a conveyer of state control of the family and the individual, and social work for social inclusion. While not characterized as such, this constitutes a

---

7 On recent political developments in China, see Strittmatter (2018).

form of adverse inclusion, also experienced in other settings, such as is apparent in the Mumbai case (de Wit, Chapter 10).

On a third level, many of the examples showcased in the volume illustrate the impact of global processes. They reveal the socio-economic impact of neoliberal policies, a topic not often elaborated in the context of social exclusion research. Public services – access to social services and basic urban infrastructure such as drinking water and sanitation, and garbage collection – have been dismantled and privatized. This seems to be the case even in the context of the state-party form of governance in China. In Mumbai, the 'local state has shrunk, with services increasingly provided by the private sector, so that poor people are squeezed between reduced public services and costly private ones. In contrast, private sector firms benefited much: they have a strong voice in governance, while financing and influencing politician's election campaigns' (de Wit). In several situations, incorporation into the system is 'adverse' – against the objective interest of the individual or community concerned.

Harking back to the overarching question of power relations in the multilateral context (Telleria, Chapter 4), an important observation is that exclusions at the personal or community level are mirrored by exclusionary politics affecting nation-states. As Henry-Lee argues for the Small Island Developing States (SIDS), they are marginalized systematically by the functionings of international monetary policy, international trade and development assistance. Despite commitments to consider the special geo-climatic challenges that SIDS face through dedicated programmes of action, the international power hierarchy plays out to the detriment of these smaller countries (Henry-Lee, Chapter 6).

The logical insights are twofold. Firstly, remedies need to be sophisticated if they are to overcome poverty and social exclusion, and lead to genuine transformation at the personal, the socio-economic and the political levels. Thus, the politics of social inclusion need to be multipronged, multidisciplinary and multilayered. Secondly, they need to tackle power relations. This position is shared by all the contributing authors, even when they come from diverse disciplines and schools of thought. What the volume contributes here is glimmers of hope.

At the conceptual level, it shows the connections between poverty and exclusionary processes which create and reinforce poverty. As Spicker puts it, 'discussions of exclusion come closer to the idea of poverty than much of the literature on poverty in itself, offering a way to escape from the limitations of the academic analysis of poverty'. There is a need for a 'distinct view of society, based on networks of social solidarity' (Spicker), echoed in other chapters of the volume (de Wit, Kurian and Singh, Antequera Durán, Siame). There are indeed many instances of collective action for policy change.

In the policy approaches reviewed, there is an agreement that inclusion policy needs to be based on the ethics of social solidarity (Spicker). It needs to be genuinely participatory and empower the excluded (Kumar, Siame, de Wit). As Antequera Durán argues on the basis of the UN Development Programme (UNDP) *Human Development Report* (2016, p. 8), for the marginalized and deprived, collective agency can be more powerful than individual agency; an individual is unlikely to achieve much alone, and power may be realized only through collective action.

Policy action also needs to be multipronged (Kurian and Singh, Koehler and Namala), as follows from the analysis that social exclusion operates at so many levels. One example is community urban planning processes in Kampala, where urban slum dwellers created civic movements and partnered with local stakeholders to achieve gains in inclusive urban development: 'mechanisms have included use of boycotts, protests, propositions of alternative city development pathways, negotiations, and the introduction of leadership structures that seek to lead and not to be led by city officials and politicians' (Siame). Siame argues for a 'co-production' approach in urban planning: by 'consciously and cautiously engaging with issues of deep difference, diversity, livelihoods, a weak state and a divided civil society, co-production ... crafts a normative position that attempts to address social justice and equity issues'.

Another approach was developed by civil society in India, advocating a five-layered approach to social inclusion (Koehler and Namala), which may serve to overcome the shortcomings in the policy responses in place in many countries in South Asia, where there is also a long history of attempts to overcome some forms of exclusion, notably gender discrimination and violence, and caste-based exclusion. This is especially important because of the many policies in place at the government level (see overview tables in Kumar and in Koehler and Namala), which have insufficient traction or are undermined by lack of political will and financial resources, coupled with the effects of power hierarchies at the local level.

Completing the circle which started from the aspirations of the UN Agenda for Sustainable Development and its goals around inclusion is a reference to related UN processes which can be drawn upon to claim and promote social justice. Established human rights soft law, such as the UDHR, and the many conventions on gender and other vectors of inclusion, can provide 'policy anchors' (Koehler and Namala) to achieve social inclusion and reach the vision of the 2030 Agenda to leave no one behind.

D. The way forward: the research and policy nexus

The remit of CROP and of UNESCO, and of the engaged academic community more broadly, is to produce meaningful knowledge to inform policy. For instance, the 2016 Report on challenging inequalities by the International Social Science Council (ISSC) (CROP's mother institution), UNESCO and the Institute of Development Studies (IDS) identifies as its first priority to 'increase support for knowledge production about inequality, and processes of social inclusion and exclusion' (ISSC et al., 2016, p. 31), and makes an unequivocal case for the production of social science research on inequality and elucidating how transformative pathways greater equality (pp. 274, 277). Similarly, the International Conference on Humanities held in Liege, Belgium from 6–12 August 2017[8] reiterated the responsibility of scientific research for achieving good governance by highlighting the relevance of interdisciplinary research and the fundamental contribution of the humanities in general.

This volume is an effort to create such a constructive bridge from research and analysis to policy formulation and implementation, and its critical reflection. Thus, an overarching question is how the principle of social inclusion can be transferred from the normative commitment of abolishing social exclusion and eradicating poverty, into policies that address the asymmetrical power relationships that create the different forms of exclusion. How can we address the processes in which the terms of inclusion are adverse, disempowering and inequitable? Would an approach focusing on the politics of inclusion be politically more relevant than approaches based on poverty eradication, and the commitment to leave no one behind, as advanced by the UN Agenda 2030?

This volume exposes relevant issues that need to be solved for the international community to move forward in the effective implementation of politics promoting social inclusion. First of all, it is indispensable to clarify what social inclusion is, identify indicators to

---

8   A joint initiative of UNESCO and the Association of Philosophy and the Humanities.

measure it, and then agree on feasible mechanisms to assess progress toward the achievement of inclusion-related SDGs. Second, there is an overarching conclusion in this volume around the recognition of the decisive role of power relations and of intersectionality, which creates and recreates social, political and economic exclusion. Effective policies on social inclusion should therefore depart from that fact of social life.

These are key findings that are supported by this volume and in previous contributions. To produce usable knowledge and ideas for transformative policies is a systematic task that requires long-term support – at national and international levels – by the agencies responsible for the implementation of policies to achieve the SDGs. Such support also needs to include the follow-up and monitoring processes indispensable to making the necessary adjustments during the process that ends in 2030.

This volume is a modest contribution towards that end. We intended to generate questions, problematize a complex issue and provide a few provisional answers articulating different views, perspectives, cases and disciplines in a collective process to produce meaningful knowledge. As usual, there are shortfalls that do not impede progress but encourage further research and discussion.

References

Agarwal, B. 2001. Participatory exclusions, community forestry, and gender: an analysis for South Asia and a conceptual framework. *World Development,* Vol. 29(10), pp. 1623–48.

Alkire, S., Foster, J., Seth, S., Santos, M. E., Roche, M. and Ballon, P. 2015. Multidimensional poverty measurement and analysis: chapter 6 – normative choices in measurement design, Oxford Poverty and Human Development Initiative (OPHI) working paper. https://ophi.org.uk/multidimensional-poverty-measurement-and-analysis-chapter-6-normative-choices-in-measurement-design/ (Accessed 7 March 2019.)

Atkinson, A. B., Marlier, E. and Nolan, B. 2004. Indicators and targets for social inclusion in the European Union. *Journal of Common Market Studies* vol. 42, pp. 47–75.

Bennett, L. 2006. *Unequal Citizens: Gender, Caste and Ethnic Exclusion in Nepal.* Washington DC and London, World Bank and UK Department for International Development (DFID). http://documents.worldbank.org/curated/en/745031468324021366/pdf/379660v20WP0Un-00Box0361508B0PUBLIC0.pdf. (Accessed 28 May 2017.)

Cimadamore, A. 2008. Las políticas de producción de pobreza: construyendo enfoques teóricos integrados. A. Cimadamore and A. Cattani (eds), *Producción de pobreza y desigualdad en América Latina*. Bogotá, Siglo del Hombre Ed.

Cimadamore, A., Koehler, G. and Pogge, T. (eds). 2016. *Poverty and the Millennium Development Goals: A critical look forward.* London, Zed and CROP. http://bora.uib.no/bitstream/handle/1956/15276/Cimadamore%20et%20al%20MDGs%20text%20with%20cover.pdf?sequence=1&isAllowed=y (Accessed 7 March 2019.)

European Council. 2000. Fight against poverty and social exclusion – definition of appropriate objectives. Brussels, 30 November. http://ec.europa.eu/employment_social/soc-prot/soc-incl/approb_en.pdf (Accessed 7 March 2019.)

Galtung, J. 1969. Violence, peace, and peace research. *Journal of Peace Research*, Vol. 6, No. 3, pp. 167–91.

Gore, C. and Figueiredo, J. B. (eds). 1997. Introduction. *Social Exclusion and Anti-Poverty Policy: A debate.* Research Series 110. Geneva, ILO.

Hickey, S. and du Toit, A. 2007. Adverse incorporation, social exclusion and chronic poverty, Working Paper 81. Manchester, UK, Chronic Poverty Research Centre (CPRC).

ILO. 2005. Indigenous Peoples, Poverty Reduction and Conflict in Nepal. Geneva, ILO. www.ilo.org/wcmsp5/groups/public/---ed_norm/---normes/documents/publication/wcms_100554.pdf (Accessed 4 April 2019.)

Ireland. 2016. *Social Inclusion Monitor 2014*. Dublin, Department of Social Protection.

ISSC, IDS and UNESCO. 2016. Challenging inequalities: pathways to a just world. *World Social Science Report*. http://unesdoc.unesco.org/images/0024/002458/245825e.pdf (Accessed 7 March 2019.)

Kabeer, N. 2010. Can the MDGs provide a pathway to social justice? The challenges of intersecting inequalities. Brighton, UK, Institute of Development Studies (IDS). www.ids.ac.uk/files/dmfile/MDGreportwebsiteu2WC.pdf (Accessed 21 October 2018.)

Koehler, G. 2017. The 2030 Agenda and eradicating poverty: new horizons for global social policy? *Global Social Policy,* Vol. 17(2), pp. 1–7.

Lenoir, R. 1974. *Les exclus : un Français sur dix*. Paris, Editions du Seuil.

Levitas, R. 2006. The concept and measurement of social exclusion. C. Pantazis, D. Gordon and R. Levitas (eds), *Poverty and Social Exclusion in Britain*. Bristol, UK, Policy Press.

Marshall, A. 1925. Where to house the London poor. *Contemporary Review*, February 1884; repr. in A. C. Pigou (ed.), *Memorials of Alfred Marshall*, London, Macmillan, pp. 42–51.

Mora Salas, M. 2004. Desigualdad social: ¿nuevos enfoques, viejos dilemas? M. Mora Salas, J. p. Pérez Sáinz and F. Cortés (eds), *Desigualdad social en América Latina. Viejos problemas, nuevos debates.* Cuaderno de Ciencias Sociales, No. 131, San José, Costa Rica, Faculdad Latinoamericana de Ciencias Sociales (FLACSO).

Nun, J. 1969. Superpoblación relativa, ejército industrial de reserva y masa marginal, *Revista Latinoamericana de Sociología,* Vol. 5, No. 2, pp. 178–236.

Oliveira, F. de. 1981. *A economia brasileira: crítica à razão dualista.* Petrópolis, Brazil, Vozes and Brazilian Center for Analysis and Planning (CEBRAP).

Oxfam. 2019. Public good or private wealth, briefing paper, January. https://oxfamilibrary.openrepository.com/bitstream/handle/10546/620599/bp-public-good-or-private-wealth-210119-summ-en.pdf (Accessed 7 March 2019.)

Øyen, E. 1997. The contradictory concepts of social exclusion and social inclusion. C. Gore and J. B. Figueiredo (eds), *Social Exclusion and Anti-Poverty Policy: A debate.* Research Series 110. Geneva, ILO.

Pérez Sáinz, J. P. 2012. Una propuesta crítica para abordar las carencias materiales en América Latina. J. P. Pérez Sáinz (ed.), *Sociedades fracturadas: la exclusión social en Centroamérica.* San José, FLACSO.

Pérez Sáinz, J. P. and Mora Salas, M. 2006. Exclusión social, desigualdades y excedente laboral. Reflexiones analíticas sobre América Latina, *Revista Mexicana de Sociología,* Vol. 68, No. 3, pp. 431–465.

–––. 2009. Excedente económico y persistencia de desigualdades en América Latina. *Revista Mexicana de Sociología,* Vol. 71, No. 3, pp. 411–451.

Perlman, J. E. 1976. *The Myth of Marginality: Urban poverty and politics in Rio do Janeiro* Berkeley, Calif., University of California Press.

Piketty, T. 2014. *Capital in the Twenty-First Century.* Boston, Mass., Harvard University Press.

Razavi, S. 2016. The 2030 Agenda: challenges of implementation to attain gender equality and women's rights. *Gender and Development,* Vol. 24, No. 1, pp. 25–41.

Razavi, S. and Hassim, S. (eds). 2007. *Gender and Social Policy in a Global Context: Uncovering the gendered structure of 'the social'.* London, Palgrave Macmillan, and Geneva, UNRISD.

Rodgers, G., Gore, C. and Figueiredo, J. (eds). 1995. *Social Exclusion: Rhetoric, reality, responses.* Geneva, ILO-IILS.

Rogers, D. S. and Balázs, B. 2016. The view from deprivation: poverty, inequality and the distribution of wealth. A. Cimadamore, G. Koehler and T. Pogge (eds), *Poverty and the Millennium Development Goals: A critical look forward.* London, Zed and CROP.

Roy, A. 2014. The doctor and the saint. Preface to B. R. Ambedkar. *The Annihilation of Caste.* London and New York, Verso.

Sen, A. 1990. More than 100 million women are missing. *New York Review of Books,* 20 December. www.nybooks.com/articles/1990/12/20/more-than-100-million-women-are-missing/ (Accessed 24 March 2019.)

———. 2000. Social exclusion: concept, application, and scrutiny, paper No. 1, June. Manila, ADB Office of Environment and Social Development. https://think-asia.org/bitstream/handle/11540/2339/social-exclusion.pdf?sequence=1 (Accessed 10 April 2019.)

Silver, H. 1995. Reconceptualizing social disadvantage: three paradigms of social exclusion. G. Rodgers, C. Gore and J. Figueiredo (eds), *Social Exclusion: Rhetoric, reality, responses.* Geneva, ILO-IILS, pp. 57–80.

Strittmatter, K. 2018. *Die Neuerfindung der Diktatur.* Munich, Germany, Piper.

UNESCO. 2012. Social Inclusion, Social Transformations, Social Innovation. Consultations of the Director-General with Member States. Paris, France. www.unesco.org/new/fileadmin/MULTIMEDIA/HQ/BPI/EPA/images/media_services/Director-General/ConceptNoteSocialInclusionSocialTransformationsSocialInnovationEN.pdf (Accessed 4 April 2019.)

United Nations. 1995. Programme of Action of the World Summit for Social Development - A/CONF.166/9 Chapter I, Annex II. www.un.org/en/development/desa/population/migration/generalassembly/docs/globalcompact/A_CONF.166_9_PoA.pdf (Accessed 4 April 2019.)

———. 2000. United Nations Millennium Declaration. Resolution adopted by the General Assembly A/55/L.2. New York, United Nations. www.un.org/millennium/declaration/ares552e.htm (Accessed 10 April 2019.)

———. 2001. Road map towards the implementation of the United Nations Millennium Declaration. Report of the Secretary-General. A/56/326. United Nations General Assembly. www.un.org/documents/ga/docs/56/a56326.pdf (Accessed 10 April 2019.)

———. 2015. *Transforming Our World. The 2030 agenda for sustainable development.* A/RES/70/1. New York, United Nations. https://sustainabledevelopment.un.org/content/documents/21252030%20Agenda%20for%20Sustainable%20Development%20web.pdf (Accessed 10 April 2019.)

———. 2017. Work of the Statistical Commission pertaining to the 2030 Agenda for Sustainable Development. Resolution adopted by the General Assembly on 6 July 2017, A/RES/71/313. New York, United Nations. https://undocs.org/A/RES/71/313 (Accessed 22 January 2019.)

UN CEB (Chief Executives Board).2017. *Leaving No One Behind: Equality and non-discrimination at the heart of sustainable development. A Shared United Nations system framework for action.* New York, United Nations.

UN IAEG-SDGs. 2018. *Tier Classification for Global SDG Indicators,* 31 December. New York, United Nations. https://unstats.un.org/sdgs/files/Tier%20Classification%20of%20SDG%20Indicators_31%20December%202018_web.pdf (Accessed 22 January 2019.)

UN Women. 2018. *Turning Promises into Action: Gender equality in the 2030 Agenda for Sustainable Development*. New York, UN Women.

UNDESA. 2009. *Creating an Inclusive Society*. New York, UNDESA. http://undesadspd.org/ExpertGroupMeetingsPanelDiscussions/MoreExpertGroupMeetings/PracticalStrategiestoPromoteSocialIntegration.aspx (Accessed 4 April 2019.)

---. 2018. *Promoting Inclusion Through Social Protection: Report on the World Social Situation 2018*. www.un.org/development/desa/dspd/wp-content/uploads/sites/22/2018/04/Cover-RWSS2018-ExecuiveSummary.png (Accessed 21 October 2018.)

UNDP. 2016. *Human Development Report 2016: Human development for everyone*. New York, UNDP. http://hdr.undp.org/sites/default/files/2016_human_development_report.pdf (Accessed 7 March 2019.)

UNFCCC. 2015. Paris Agreement on Climate Change. https://unfccc.int/sites/default/files/english_paris_agreement.pdf (accessed 24 March 2019)

UNRISD. 2005. *Gender Equality. Striving for Justice in an Unequal World*. Geneva, UNRISD. http://www.unrisd.org/80256B3C005BCCF9/httpNetITFramePDF?ReadForm&parentunid=E0CCDA6F0D-9651CFC1256FB1004AA6E8&parentdoctype=documentauxiliarypage&netitpath=80256B3C005BCCF9/(httpAuxPages)/E0CCDA6F0D9651CFC1256FB1004AA6E8/$file/GE_01prelims.pdf (Accessed 24 March 2019.)

--------. 2016. *Policy Innovations for Transformative Change: Implementing the 2030 Agenda for Sustainable Development*. Geneva, UNRISD. www.unrisd.org/80256B3C005BCCF9/(httpPublications)/92AF5072673F-924DC125804C0044F396?OpenDocument (Accessed 21 October 2018.)

---. 2018. Overcoming Inequalities in a Fractured World: Between Elite Power and Social Mobilization: Call for papers. www.unrisd.org/80256B3C005BD6AB/(httpEvents)/845A4834BECE32D-3C12582FD004389A9?OpenDocument (Accessed 21 October 2018.)

World Bank. 2013. *Inclusion Matters. The foundation for shared prosperity*. Washington DC, World Bank. http://siteresources.worldbank.org/EXTSOCIALDEVELOPMENT/Resources/244362-1265299949041/6766328-1329943729735/8460924-1381272444276/InclusionMatters_AdvanceEdition.pdf (Accessed 7 March 2019.)

UN Conventions and declarations

United Nations. 1965. International Convention on the Elimination of All Forms of Racial Discrimination (CERD). www.ohchr.org/EN/ProfessionalInterest/Pages/CERD.aspx (Accessed 7 March 2019.)

The politics of social inclusion: introduction

---. 1979. UN Convention on the Eradication of all forms of Discrimination against Women (CEDAW). www.un.org/womenwatch/daw/cedaw/text/econvention.htm (Accessed 7 March 2019.)

---. 2006. Convention on the Rights of Persons with Disabilities (CRPD). www.un.org/development/desa/disabilities/convention-on-the-rights-of-persons-with-disabilities.html (Accessed 7 March 2019.)

---. 2007. UN Declaration on the Rights of Indigenous Peoples (DRIP). www.un.org/development/desa/indigenouspeoples/declaration-on-the-rights-of-indigenous-peoples.html (Accessed 7 March 2019.)

---. 2015*a*. Paris Agreement (under the UN Framework Convention on Climate Change). https://unfccc.int/sites/default/files/english_paris_agreement.pdf (Accessed 11 November 2018.)

---. 2015*b*. Transforming our world: the 2030 Agenda for Sustainable Development. Resolution adopted by the General Assembly on 25 September 2015. A/RES/70/1. www.un.org/ga/search/view_doc.asp?symbol=A/RES/70/1&Lang=E (Accessed 7 March 2019.)

UN Habitat. 2016. *New Urban Agenda*. http://habitat3.org/wp-content/uploads/NUA-English.pdf (Accessed 25 January 2019.)

Chapter 2
OVERCOMING SOCIAL EXCLUSION IN EDUCATION: REFLECTIONS ON POLICY CHALLENGES

Enrique Delamonica

A. Introduction

At the World Conference on Education for All held in Jomtien in 1990 (UNESCO, 1990), countries agreed to realize universal basic education by the year 2000. They renewed this pledge at the World Summit for Children in New York (UNICEF, 1990) and the World Summit for Social Development (United Nations, 1995*a*). However, given the failure to accomplish this goal, countries re-established it under the Millennium Development Goals (MDGs) in 2000 (United Nations, 2000). In 2015, having failed again to achieve education for all, they included it in the Agenda 2030 for Sustainable Development (United Nations, 2015).

Section B of this chapter summarizes and explains concepts and interpretations of social inclusion and exclusion across disciplines. Section C discusses policies to avoid children being excluded from the education system. The premise is that an economic, sociological or legal perspective alone could not provide all the answers to fully address the plight of millions of children denied their right to education. The various approaches provide dissimilar recommendations. For instance, economists would argue for more funds, while lawyers would request changing a law, and sociologists would campaign for cultural change. While all these recommendations are reasonable, none of them are sufficient by themselves. They need to be integrated to encourage and achieve an education system for all. This integration should take place at the level of specific policy recommendations.

Nevertheless, within the international policy debates on how best to ensure universal basic education, this chapter shows that the assessment of specific policy recommendations is not contingent on the discipline being used. The same policy measure (for instance, mandatory uniforms) may be prescribed and criticized by lawyers, sociologists or economists, based on their disciplinary views. A discipline does not unequivocally determine policy recommendations. There is debate within each discipline, and as much divergence within disciplines as across them.

B. Disparities and social exclusion: different concepts across disciplines and empirical evidence

Discrimination, inequality, inequity, exclusion

In order to better understand the causes and consequences of inequality, it is useful to understand its many dimensions. A challenge is created by the varied terminology used to explain the (same?) phenomenon: discrimination, inequality, marginalization, inequity, social exclusion and disparity. The words 'unreached', 'disadvantaged' and 'vulnerable' are also used. Moreover, these words have specific meaning in certain disciplines. In this section, this terminology is explored in order to ascertain the many dimensions of inequality and inequity.

Inequality and inequity

First, a distinction needs to be made between inequity and inequality. While the latter refers to a quantitative difference (for instance, a person is taller than another one), inequity refers to a difference which is deemed unfair and avoidable[9] (such as women earning less than men for the same job and given the same qualifications).

Thus, in economics, when dealing with income, the terminology most commonly used is about inequality. For instance, the Gini, Theil, Palma and Vast Majority are indices of income inequality (Atkinson, 1983; Atkinson and Bourguignon, 2015; Cornia, 2004; Deaton, 1997; Salverda et al., 2009; Shaikh and Ragab, 2008; Shaw et al., 2007). Although implicitly (sometimes explicitly) authors using and analysing these indices prefer a more egalitarian income distribution than the

---

9   Therborn (2006) makes conceptually the same distinction, calling them 'difference' and 'inequality' respectively.

one they observe, they still concentrate on the purely descriptive aspect of equality, without infusing the moral aspect of equity.[10]

These indices deal with the whole distribution or the extremes. They describe income distribution. However, distribution of property is much less analyzed. While some authors (Agarwal, 1994; Nell, 1998; Piketty, 2014; Shaikh, 2016, 2017; Wolff, 2007, 2010) have explored empirically and theoretically the distribution of wealth and assets as well as the impact of rents and financial flows on the instability of income distribution and gender dynamics, most economists do not pay attention to these issues.[11]

In addition, most economists are aware of (and often cite) Rawls (1971) and his principle of justice. However, rarely do they venture into discussing which levels of income inequality are acceptable or which magnitude of income redistribution should be achieved (or how!). On the contrary, their main tool for assessing policy changes, Pareto efficiency, is intrinsically biased towards the status quo. Simply put, Pareto's efficiency principle says that a change that improves somebody's standing without diminishing somebody else's is efficient. In other words, efficiency is reached in a situation where it is not possible to improve anybody's standing without diminishing somebody else's. This means that a change that benefits 99 per cent of the population but diminishes, even if not by much, the standing of the 1 per cent would not be considered efficient.

Besides measuring income distribution, individuals or households are also grouped or ranked in order to assess the distribution of non-income outcomes or attributes, such as the levels of education and morbidity. This leads to SES (socio-economic status) rankings and analyzes of inequalities. In addition, concentration indices can be constructed.[12]

---

10 Most professional and academic economists rarely dare to venture into ethical discussions (Hirschman, 1982, Myrdal, 1953, and Sen, 1988, being iconic exceptions). They prefer to dwell on the instrumental aspects of inequality, for instance its impact on economic growth or democracy (IMF, 2011; Stiglitz, 2012; Welch, 1999).

11 Nor, usually, do they pay attention to causes of the inequalities/inequities such as hierarchical structures, exploitation or exclusion/discrimination (Therborn, 2006).

12 A Gini coefficient compares the actual income distribution (described in a Lorenz curve) with the hypothetical one under strict equal distribution. The Lorenz curve correlates the share of income to income-based groups (ranked from lowest to highest). A concentration index (Wagstaff et al., 1989) compares income (or other socio-economic characteristics) with other outcomes (school attainment, disability-adjusted life years (DALYs) and so on). Although it is possible to construct a pseudo Gini coefficient of education outcomes (Thomas et al., 2001),

In this literature, it is common to find the expression 'disparity'. It is often used as a synonym of inequality, relating to non-income outcomes.

Gender, and whether women have (or should have) the same opportunities and outcomes as men, also can be considered a dimension of inequality and inequity. Clearly, gender differentials fall under the rubric of horizontal inequalities or suspect grounds for discrimination (see below).[13]

Horizontal and vertical equity

Another important dimension in the analysis of inequality concerns horizontal and vertical inequality (Langer and Stewart, 2007; Stewart, 2001; Stewart et al., 2005; Tilly, 1998). The former refers to differences among groups that cannot be ranked. For instance, there is no intrinsic reason to rank either an urban or rural area ahead of the other one. Contrariwise, when individuals are grouped in terms of income or education level, there is a clear natural way in which to order or rank them from highest to lowest. When such ordering is possible, vertical equality is used. It should be noticed however, that in the public health literature (Braveman and Gruskin, 2003; Macinko and Starfield, 2002; UNICEF, 2011; Wagstaff et al., 1991), horizontal and vertical equality has a completely different interpretation. It refers to the equal treatment of equals (horizontal) and unequal treatment of unequal situations (vertical). This is similar to the legal principle of equality (see below).

Equality of outcomes and opportunities

In addition, a seemingly fundamental distinction is often made between equality of outcomes and equality of opportunities (Arneson, 1989; Cohen, 1989; Dworkin, 1981; Phillips, 2004; Sen

---

this would prevent the analysis of the impact of socio-economic characteristics on educational opportunities (Chakraborty, 2009).

13 The report of the 1995 Beijing Conference on Women (United Nations, 1996) recorded the points raised by the various government delegations; Buss (1998) and Swiebel (2015) provide further background and analysis. Some governments argued that differences between women and men were acceptable if they were caused by intrinsic aspects of 'womanhood'. Restricting women's advancement (concomitant with women's need for 'protection') was defended under the rubric of equity. The response was that no difference could or should be considered fair. Strict equality between men and women ought to be the goal. Thus, the term 'gender equality' is the one commonly used.

and Hawthorne, 1985). The latter are supposed to help with the former. However, 'forcing' equality of outcomes is often perceived as too difficult if not impossible. Besides impractical, it is deemed unfair and counterproductive. The policies or legislation required to ensure equal outcomes across the whole population could be too expensive or 'stifling'.[14] On the other hand, equality of opportunity is often characterized in a positive light because it is seen as a fair way to ensure a level playing field for everyone (Roemer, 1998; World Bank, 2006). If they ended up in different positions later on (unequal outcomes), so the argument goes, it would be because the successful deserve their success while those left behind do not – as they all started with the same opportunities.

However, seemingly neutral ways to allow every member of society an equal opportunity can actually be very unfair. They do not take into account that people do not all start out with the same clean slate and at the same time.

That is the reason why equality of opportunities, unless they can be ensured in absolutely all aspects of the individual, is not sufficient to ensure fair results in terms of outcomes – even if they are a bit unequal (Chang, 2011; Palma, 2011; Swift, 2001). Education provides a good example: even if all children have access to schooling, not all schools are of the same quality (some have better teachers, infrastructure or learning materials).[15] Even if all schools were identical, children's family backgrounds and contacts (social capital) are not the same, thus their chances of success later in life are not the same. The result is that equality of outcomes is needed to achieve equal opportunities. This would seem a paradoxical result only under the assumption there is a fundamental distinction between equality of opportunities and of outcomes – they are intertwined, resulting in inequalities being replicated across generations (Breen and Jonsson, 2005; Erikson and Goldthorpe, 1992; Sano, 2000; Vandemoortele, forthcoming).

---

14 This is not the place to unravel all the (incorrect) assumptions in this type of argument.
15 Moreover, this distribution is not random. It is associated with other disparities (such as urban or rural location, or parents' socio-economic status). While there is a 35-years-long debate about the Heyneman–Loxley effect (about the relative importance of school quality and family characteristics in children's achievement), there is no debate concerning the unequal distribution of school quality (Baker et al., 2002; Chudgar and Luschei, 2009; Gameron and Long, 2007; Heyneman, 2015; Heyneman and Loxley, 1983; Smaali, 2015; Zumbach, 2010).

Poverty, inequality, and vulnerability

Even within the poverty discussions, issues of inequality do appear, for instance when estimating relative poverty (when the poverty line is not based on the absolute[16] cost of a minimum basket of goods and services everybody should be able to afford, but on the distance to the average income in the country) (Desai, 1986; Laderchi et al., 2003). When estimating absolute monetary poverty (based on the poverty line) the incidence of poverty can be estimated as well as the depth and severity of poverty, which illustrate income distribution among the poor (Blackwood and Lynch, 1994; Foster et al., 1984; Sen, 1976).

Since the Sustainable Development Goals (SDGs) were agreed, multidimensional poverty has been recognized as important too.[17] A general misconception is that multidimensional assessment can only capture the level of incidence. However, depth and severity can also be estimated for multidimensional poverty (Alkire and Foster, 2011; Delamonica and Minujín, 2007; ECLAC-UNICEF, 2010).[18]

Another concept usually discussed in the literature is 'vulnerability' and 'the vulnerable'. Vulnerability refers to a situation where two elements are combined. One is the risk of being affected by a threat (such as loss of income, flooding or sickness) and the other is the capacity to cope with it or its effects (Aday, 2001). Thus, clearly vulnerability is always defined in relation to something. However, 'the vulnerable' are often used as category of people without specifying to what they are vulnerable.[19] Unfortunately, this is a conceptual

---

16 Sometimes 'absolute poverty' is misinterpreted as a 'very low' poverty line. The so-called 'international' poverty line ('a dollar a day') is thought to measure absolute poverty. However, the line is not equivalent to the cost of living in the vast majority of countries. Consequently, it does not actually measure the incidence of poverty, in most countries (Deaton, 2003, 2010; Pogge and Reddy, 2006; Reddy and Minoiu, 2007; Vandemoortele, 2002). As a result, the World Bank estimates monetary poverty for different countries at 'a dollar a day', 'three dollars a day', and 'five dollars a day' (World Bank, 2018).

17 The grounding of multidimensional poverty in human rights (Hunt et al., 2002; OHCHR, 2012; UNICEF, 2007a), in other words the thesis that the dimensions of deprivation included in its measurement are or should be based on denial of rights constitutive of poverty (not all human rights), is often missed. The relationship between the right to a minimum standard of living (United Nations, 1948) and monetary poverty is even more often forgotten. Lister (2004) and Redmond (2014) propose additional dimensions, not based on constitutive rights.

18 Albeit with slightly more complex calculations.

19 Sometimes this is done for stylistic purposes and the context makes it obvious which vulnerability is being discussed. Nevertheless, mostly this is not the case.

mistake.[20] All human beings are vulnerable to many things. Moreover, all human beings are vulnerable to different risks along the life cycle. Given the different nature of these risks, vulnerabilities are incommensurable.[21]

In addition, when discussing a specific risk, it should be borne in mind that not all persons are equally vulnerable to it. The reason is that vulnerability combines the exposure to risk with the capacity to cope with it (or its consequences). Thus, individuals with more resources (financial, social capital, physical resilience and so on) can cope better with risks (Mechanic and Tanner, 2007). Inequities are present in relation to vulnerability (although not often analyzed) as richer groups may have more options to cope with risks.[22] In summary, although there is a relationship between poverty and vulnerability, the two concepts are clearly distinct.

Social exclusion

Besides vulnerability, poverty, inequality and inequities, there is social exclusion. Social exclusion happens when a group is not allowed to fully enjoy the benefits of participation in society (economic, social, political, cultural or their combination). The concept of social exclusion originated[23] in France in the 1970s (Lenoir, 1974). It arose partly to describe a situation where lack of income or material resources is not a major issue (because those without earned income are protected via social security, unemployment benefits and other welfare state programmes), yet particular groups of people are not able to partake in the same activities (political, cultural or economic) as the rest of the population.

---

20 According to Vladeck (2007), 'The concept of "vulnerable populations" is an artificial portmanteau, the use of which arises more from the pressures for euphemism in the discussion of health policy and health services than from any intellectual power inherent in the concept.' Regarding its use in economic policy-making, Alston (2018) says it 'is an amorphous and open-ended concept that is rarely given fixed policy content'.
21 For instance, it is not possible to measure whether being vulnerable to a heart attack is more or less significant than being vulnerable to becoming unemployed.
22 For example, while everybody is equally at risk of getting wet when it rains (rain does not discriminate where it falls), richer individuals can protect themselves better from the rain (through stronger houses, avoiding low land areas prone to floods, and so on).
23 Sen (2000) lucidly traces earlier origins in his analysis of what social exclusion brings in terms of understanding the nature and causes of poverty and new policy insights.

The concept has not been without its critics. For instance, it has been criticized as unclear and not grounded in theory, and for hiding or distorting underlying drivers of inequalities and inequities (Daly and Silver, 2008; Levitas, 2004; Oyen, 1997). It has also been connected with the capabilities approach,[24] and its similarities and differences with poverty analysis have been extensively compared (Chakravarty and D'Ambrosio, 2006; Duffy, 2005; Petmesidou and Papatheodorou, 2006). In this vein, a major issue is that poverty, in the sense of actual measurable deprivations, ends up being hidden under the concept of social exclusion, which is rightly much broader.[25] However, its being broader does not mean it completely encapsulates poverty. A group (such as the elderly or an ethnic minority) can be excluded (culturally, socially or politically) yet be wealthy. Nor does it mean that social exclusion is the only cause of poverty, or that poverty itself may lead to social exclusion.[26]

Two types of multidimensional social exclusion exist. At one level of analysis, individuals or groups can be excluded from political participation, markets (economic exclusion), society or culture (Kabeer, 2000). At another level of analysis, excluded groups are identified. A remarkable list is provided by Silver (1994).[27] An interesting aspect in her list is the role of age-related categories.[28] Another issue is that

---

24 One way to understand the relationship among these concepts is to think of three stages in the development of poverty analysis. The first stage is centred on monetary poverty, while the second one brings in multidimensional poverty, and the third stage encompasses non-material deprivations (such as some capabilities, exclusion, subjective poverty and time poverty). Similarly, Therborn (2006) describes inequities in terms of (material) resources, other vital dimensions (such as health), and relational (existential) dimensions.

25 This is the case for both monetary and multidimensional poverty. (On the relationship between poverty and human rights, see above.)

26 For instance, being excluded from the labour or credit markets may itself be grounded on discrimination (perhaps gender or ethnic), on monetary poverty (parents' income, own income shortfall), or on multidimensional poverty (e.g. if lack of education becomes a barrier owing to the perceived risk by creditors). Rather than linear causal paths, there are synergetic connections among the various phenomena. Moreover, social exclusion could be wide, deep and/or concentrated (Levitas et al., 2007), resulting in interesting measurement issues (Burchardt et al., 2002).

27 As in other similar lists, populations displaced because of wars and armed conflicts are not included because of the nation-state focus of the discussion. This complicates both politics and policy-making.

28 Also, as in the case of vulnerability, the long list captures almost the whole population (women, young people and so on). Nobody is exempt from eventually falling under some of those categories. A similar list (grouped into seven categories) is provided by Percy-Smith (2000).

there may be strong correlations between some of the categories (for instance, the low paid, poor, unemployed, unskilled and illiterate) and that social exclusion may be exacerbated by a combination of factors.[29]

However, there are connections between the two levels of analysis. For instance, being excluded from labour markets (perceived at the level of analysis of what people are excluded from) may lead to other deprivations and exclusion, such as needing but not receiving social assistance (which belong in the discussion of which people are excluded).

Moreover, the picture emanating from the list is one in which the situation of individuals is not static. During a life span, they may find themselves moving into and out of some of these categories.[30] Furthermore, at any point in time, individuals may be closer or further from total exclusion/inclusion (for many of the dimensions of exclusion there is a range of levels or degrees of inclusion, not a clear-cut dichotomy in the sense of being in or out). Combining the many dimensions, and the fact that along each dimension there is a range or degree of exclusion,[31] leads to the categorization of a great many people in a grey area, being partially included and partially excluded (Oyen, 1997).

One salient aspect of this debate is the recognition there are 'good' and 'bad' ways to be included. It can be said that a poor peasant is very much included (and is a crucial player) in feudal society, but in starkly unfavourable conditions (Agarwal, 2001; Streeten, 1997).[32]

There is also active and passive exclusion (Sen, 2000; Popay et al., 2008). The latter (as in the case of legal/formal equality that allows substantive inequality to exist) is unintentional, while the former is done explicitly and on purpose (and sometimes coded, even in law).

---

29 This is closely related to the concept of intersectionality of discrimination (discussed below).
30 However, this does not apply to all categories. The list includes axes of discrimination (women or ethnic minorities) which people cannot change (see below) and of disparities which could change (such as intra-urban; the fact that urban–rural is not mentioned is probably owing to the focus on industrialized societies).
31 The idea of degrees of exclusion is also associated with constitutive exclusion, which is bad in itself, and instrumental exclusion, which is not necessarily bad in itself but leads to other instances of exclusion (Sen, 2000). This is similar to the distinction between constitutive and instrumental rights in the human rights approach to poverty (Hunt et al., 2002). As in that literature, some aspects of exclusion (ranging from nil to total exclusion) can be simultaneously both constitutive and instrumental.
32 Tokenism, the presence of a representative of an excluded group, without any real voice or vote, is also an example of bad inclusion.

Clearly, given the interactions among levels, different degrees in the continuum from exclusion to inclusion, and various dimensions or axes of exclusion, there is a dynamic social process of exclusion (Estivill, 2003).[33] However, analytically social exclusion could be understood as more than just the process. It could also be the structure (of types and degrees of exclusion) resulting from such process (Byrne, 2010). This structure is maintained through time, and often reproduced intergenerationally (Bäckman and Nilsson, 2011; Halleröd and Bask, 2008; Hobcraft, 2007; Peruzzi, 2013).[34]

Thus, there are at least three ways of analysing the process of exclusion and inclusion. One is based on the sense of belonging to a shared culture and social bonds of solidarity. Another is based on interactions among individuals. The interactions are based on differentiation of roles and are perceived as fair. However, when there is no freedom or only limited opportunities to move from one type of interaction to another one (or from one role to another one), exclusion is present. A final one concentrates on providing cultural and economic support and (quasi) homogeneity within the closed group of the included ones.[35]

Although the focus of this chapter is on social inclusion, it is useful to briefly delve into economic and political exclusion too, as the three are intertwined.[36] Economic inclusion affects three main aspects: income, production and recognition. Political exclusion is tied to the idea of a territory from which people may be excluded[37] (which is

---

[33] This could even be the result of 'including' certain groups through the process of modernization/globalization: Grinspun (1997).

[34] Other authors have linked monetary poverty during childhood (in toto or analysing spells of different duration) to income as adults, as well as the well-being of the individual as a child or later in life (Case and Paxson, 2006; Brooks-Gunn and Duncan, 1997; Duncan et al., 1994; Gregg and Machin, 1999). Also, there is research linking non-material deprivations during childhood and later in life (Blanden et al., 2010; Forrest and Riley, 2004). However, these studies are not about social exclusion per se. In addition, many of the positive effects of investing in (all) children, which improves their circumstances, do not 'correct' for other sources of disparity and exclusion precisely because everybody benefits (Barnett and Belfield, 2006; Blossfeld and Shavit, 1993). This is similar to the criticism of substantive legal equality, which fails to actually transform into a proper egalitarian situation (see below).

[35] Silver (1994) labels these approaches the solidarity, specialization and monopoly paradigms respectively, and associates them with political traditions (French republicanism, individual liberalism, and social democracy).

[36] They are also related to Marshall's civil, political and socio-economic rights (Marshall, 1950).

[37] Silver (1997) also recognizes that social and political inclusion (involving migrants, asylum seekers, international human rights treatises) has an

linked to the definition of state) as well as regions of exclusion within a particular country (Silver, 1997). Social exclusion is mainly relational, referring both to the relationship of individuals and groups[38] within communities, and the relationship between individuals and groups, and the state (Bhalla and Lapeyre, 1995).

In all these aspects (economic, social and political exclusion; the three types of process driving exclusion; the different degrees along the continuum of exclusion; the different layers of analysis; and the multiple dimensions of excluded groups), it is worth remembering that the situation is never static (at least not over the long term). When the situation changes, there may be many causes. One of them may actually be that the excluded act as agents of change (Rodgers, 1997). This may be in part owing to differences and inequalities within excluded groups which could result in (diverse and competing) leadership in claiming redress and ways to be included.[39]

Thus, clearly, exclusion is different from differentiation, and not to be confused with inequality (Silver, 1994). Permeability of boundaries across groups, membership to the group being freely chosen, and the absence of extra-ordinary benefits or advantages (social, economic or political) based on the distinction or differentiation among groups would determine whether the differentiation is perceived as fair, or unfair and consequently leading to exclusion (Silver, 1994). The distinction between difference and differentiation, thus, is similar to the one between inequality and inequity.

Obviously, then, there are analytical and normative dimensions in the social exclusion debate. This allows us to better understand the processes (and resulting structures) of social exclusion, distinguish between social exclusion and other phenomena or problems (which may be related or associated with exclusion, although conflating them would be counterproductive), and to design ways to combat social exclusion.

---

international dimension (and an impact on struggles for inclusion and political alliances). On trans-boundary politics, see also Chalmers (1993) and Keck and Sikkink (1998).

38 Group dynamics of social exclusion may entail discrimination (see below on defining discrimination against groups) or they can be associated with social capital and its critiques (Arrow, 1999; Bourdieu, 1986; Coleman, 1990; Solow, 1999).

39 It may also be connected to the point about people being excluded for different 'reasons' (such as because they belong, or seem to belong, to different excluded groups). This is similar to the issues of intersectionality of discrimination and identity (see above) which may thus imply different affiliations and (potential) allies in their struggles.

Overcoming social exclusion in education

Inequality and discrimination

In legal analysis, there a several interpretations of equality. Among them we can find (based on ethics and moral philosophy) the idea that all human beings have 'equal worth and dignity'. In terms of political rights, most modern constitutions declare rights in terms of equal participation and representation of all citizens in government. Equality is also often linked to non-discrimination (Donnelly, 2003; Fredman, 2005; Holtmaat, 2013; Koukoulis-Spiliotopoulos, 2008).

However, the two concepts are again different. Discrimination refers to a situation in which a group of people suffer from unequal treatment or outcomes compared with other groups based on characteristics which people cannot change without altering who they are (either because change is not possible or because it would impinge on their personal dignity and identity[40]). In other words, it is about to which identity they are ascribed and whether a person wishes to assume or reject that ascribed identity.

Thus, a central concept in discrimination law is the idea of a 'discrimination ground' (European Union, 2011; Fredman, 2011). This defines the group that is being discriminated against, such as women, ethnic minorities, people with disabilities or homosexuals. In international and national legislation, legal documents and court sentences, these 'discrimination grounds' are called 'suspect', meaning that in principle, when unequal treatment or differential outcomes are observed, it is assumed discrimination is at play (Fredman, 2011).

It is important not to victimize these groups (which would be disempowering and take away their agency[41]). Essentialism should also be avoided (as when individuals belong to, and identify with, different groups). Anti-discrimination law also protects those who 'seem' to belong to these groups, regardless of whether they actually belong to the group or not.[42] Nevertheless, as the aim of anti-discrimination legislation is to avoid oppression, and it is clear some people are oppressed (in terms of the effects on their life opportunities), and these persons share some common characteristics, it is possible to use

---

40 This applies in terms of both 'being it' and 'living it' (Hendriks, 2010; Waaldijk and Bonini-Baraldi, 2006) as well as 'by association' (which would apply if mothers of disabled children were discriminated against in the labour market: Karagiorgi, 2014). Moreover, these characteristics result in a series of disadvantages raging from everyday slights through lack of opportunities to political powerlessness, which define people's 'place in society' or status in the social hierarchy (Balkin, 1997; McColgan, 2014; Young, 2001).
41 As discussed above for social inclusion.
42 This applies for instance to people of mixed ancestry.

anti-discrimination law to protect them without necessarily agreeing on a constraining or artificial (essentialist) classification[43] (McColgan, 2014).

In legislation and legal practice, the attempt is to list and cover all discrimination grounds (sex, religion and so on) and some aspects (fields) of human activity throughout the life cycle (participation in labour markets, schools, pensions). This could be done by setting up an explicit (closed) list, by leaving it open-ended (allowing the courts to assess which groups to protect as cases come up), or by an in–between solution in which there is a list but the list is portrayed as examples without precluding the possibility of adding further categories (Fredman, 2011). However, as non-discrimination law has evolved through the last few decades, some legislation has had a narrower focus than other pieces of legislation. This has entailed quite precise rules tailored to specific discriminatory behaviour (such as unequal outcomes) and kinds of discrimination (on different suspect grounds) impacting various aspect of the law (private labour markets, civil employment, contracts, property and so on). As a result, there are different levels of protection for different groups[44] for different issues.

Thus, non-discrimination laws prohibit, among other actions, any form of distinction or differential which cannot be justified.[45] Also, any disadvantaged status or outcome caused by unequal treatment (directly or indirectly[46]), exclusion, disrespectful behaviour towards any group (in other words, harassment, including calls to harassment),

---

43 This also explains why court cases, although brought by an individual, apply to the whole group.

44 Another issue with the definition of groups is determining when people are sufficiently 'alike' or belong (or not) to a group and consequently there are grounds to suspect discrimination. Elements like immutability, a history of disadvantage, and constituting a clear and distinct minority have been proposed, all the while recognizing there are political considerations (and struggles) in defining and applying these criteria (Fredman, 2011; Young, 2001). In developing countries there is a further complication when the group historically disadvantaged and disempowered is the majoritarian one (demographically speaking).

45 However, legislation, and even jurisprudence, sometimes leaves room for ambiguity about the precise definitions and contours of 'justified' (for instance, over what is known as a genuine occupational requirement) resulting in lack of 'real legal certainty' (Howard, 2010; Otto et al., 2008; Waaldijk and Bonini-Baraldi, 2006).

46 Indirect discrimination occurs when a disadvantage or adverse impact is the result of a seemingly neutral provision which disproportionally affects a group (on purpose or as a result of unintended consequences). For instance, an employment requirement of formal education is discriminatory when minority students cannot access such education, and a pension that excludes part-time workers could be discriminatory if the excluded are primarily female and their

or systematic or structural exclusion are outlawed (Cook and Cusack, 2011; Holtmaat, 2013).

As equality and non-discrimination are different, it is important to dwell on the characteristics or principles of equality in legal thinking. Three of them are relevant in this context: equality before the law, equality as fairness (or consistency), and equal opportunities (Fredman, 2011).

In terms of the principle of equality before the law, political and citizenship rights as well as freedoms are established explicitly for all citizens in most modern constitutions. Moreover, equality before the law ensures that everybody is treated equally in the court proceedings (whether a pauper or the prime minister). In a way this is a very individualistic conceptualization of equality.[47]

Nevertheless, while in principle all laws are made for everybody, there may be circumstances in which laws could and should make distinctions between groups of people in order to achieve fairness or consistency. For instance, the right to free education can reasonably be limited to children under 18, and the right to vote to citizens aged over 18.

This general principle of equality as consistency has roots in Aristotle's proposition that there should be equal treatment of equals and unequal treatment of unequals in proportion to their inequality[48] (Holtmaat and Naber, 2011; Tobler, 2014). This principle applies both to law-making and to the application of legal rules.[49] Thus, the principle of equality does not strictly prohibit differential treatment (Cook and Cusack, 2011). It does emphasize that such differences in treatment cannot occur if they are arbitrary, inconsistent, irrational or unfair.

Consequently, policies and rules that deal with groups of citizens differently should be assessed to find out whether equal or unequal cases deserve and/or are benefiting from equal or unequal treatment.

---

part-time status reflects socially imposed stereotypes, expectations and time constraints (Loenen, 2000).

47 A consequence of this individualism is that it becomes hard to address issues of structural discrimination (in which there is no clear-cut perpetrator), and partly as a result of this, to obtain legal redress.

48 And, as mentioned above, is replicated in the public health discourse.

49 However, there is a hidden risk related to the question of equality compared with whom. All too often the (implicit) comparator is a male (or ethnic majority) standard. This may lead to conformism and oppression (Fredman, 2011; MacKinnon, 1987). Thus, there is a debate about whether laws and jurisprudence actually suppress women or could be a vehicle for empowerment and liberation (Travers, 2010).

For example, visually impaired children may need books in Braille in order to learn to read, thus it would be reasonable to provide them (even it means a higher per-pupil cost than for other children). However, limiting visually impaired persons' right to vote would not be justifiable.

Given the pervasive and historical discrimination against certain groups, legislation sometimes offers guarantees of equal opportunities to historically discriminated groups in order to achieve equal opportunities or equal rights.[50] These are known as (temporary) special measures (Holtmaat and Naber, 2011).[51] While some ought to be temporary in nature (for instance, to redress past discrimination[52]), some of them should be permanent (such as those designed to overcome permanent disadvantages).

In addition, there is the combination of effects, or intersectionality of discrimination (Crenshaw, 1989). Analysing the impact of gender and race-based anti-discrimination legal outcomes, Crenshaw claims that in the United States black women are marginalized and invisible because their situation cannot be interpreted as the sum of gender and ethnic discrimination. While in some cases their plight is similar to that of black men, on other occasions it is similar to that of white women, and in yet other cases it is completely different from either of the other two groups.

In other words, in an additive or union approach, the concurrent presence of various dimensions of discrimination could compound or aggravate the situation (Kabeer, 2016). However, intersectionality means that the presence of one of the other dimensions may not be a problem. The problem is when both are present, and the problem is idiosyncratic in the sense that if both dimensions are problematic in and of themselves, their joint presence is a different problem, not a combination of the problems.

---

50   In a way, this is a recognition that equal treatment laws (see below) may unintentionally maintain or allow the reproduction of discrimination. This is similar to the notion of active and passive exclusion.
51   In some contexts they are also called affirmative action, positive actions, positive discrimination or reverse discrimination. Regardless of the label, they involve eradicating discrimination, promoting inclusion, outreach programmes, preferential treatment and redefining merit (McColgan, 2014; McCrudden, 1986).
52   Which is insidious and overcomes individual choices or merit (McColgan, 2014; Phillips, 2004).

Formal and substantive legal equality

Another important dimension or axis of debate concerning equality is the distinction between formal and substantive equality (Arnardóttir, 2007; Holtmaat and Tobler, 2005). As discussed above, equal cases should be treated equally, and all people have equal rights. This aspect of the principle of equality as consistency is classified as formal equality.

However, equality could be considered as encompassing more than this 'procedural' aspect. It includes also equality in terms of practical results in people's lives. This aspect would be substantive equality.[53]

The separation of formal and substantive equality leads to practical implications. The formal approach results in 'negative' legal norms (banning certain types of discriminatory behaviour or activities). A substantive equity perspective results in 'positive' norms (Holtmaat and Tobler, 2005). It is also understood that 'positive' norms may not necessarily turn an unequal situation around quickly, thus the concept of progressive realization.[54]

Nevertheless, even addressing substantive inequality may not be sufficient when discrimination is systematic, present society-wide, entrenched in culture, and reproduced by economic, power and everyday relationships, dynamics and interactions. Consequently, a 'different' kind of law (and concomitantly policy) is needed to absorb and surpass formal and substantive equality.[55] It addresses structural discrimination by examining how legal systems, social patterns, cultural practices and religious views reproduce discrimination.

---

53 The distinction between formal and substantive equality is similar to (but certainly not the same as) the one between opportunities and outcomes.

54 Progressive realization, while recognizing the limits to achieve equality (such as budgetary or personnel resources constraints to provide all the required services or support) and that reaching it may take time, is not an excuse to delay efforts. Plans, milestones and time-bound targets should guide progressive realization. According to the Limburg Principles (UN Commission on Human Rights, 1986) and General Comment Number 3 of the UN Commission on Economic, Social and Cultural Rights (1990), retrogressive measures should be avoided. (This is the non-regression principle, of no going back or revising standards of protection already achieved.) Moreover, while progressive realization is acceptable for substantial equality, it is not for formal equality, which can and should be immediately addressed through legislation.

55 Besides these three levels, there are four dimensions of substantive equality (Fredman, 2011): disadvantage associated with status or out-groups (redistribution), dignity and respect (recognition), accommodating differences (rather than forcing everybody to conform to dominant norms), and participation (which is associated with belonging and social inclusion).

Unfortunately, sometimes equal treatment laws (both formal and substantive) contribute to or allow certain types of discrimination or dominance to continue.[56] This 'different' type of law unpacks these mechanisms, thus going beyond substantive and formal equality by addressing structural inequality (Holtmaat, 2004). In other words, formal equality may produce equality at low levels of achievement for everybody, substantive equality may lift everybody but maintain/reproduce stereotypes and disadvantages (for instance, women may receive equal pay for equal work, and high wages too, but still be limited to certain professions), and structural equality addresses these repressive stereotypes and norms.

By way of intermediate conclusion

In summary, there are many dimensions of inequalities, exclusion and discrimination. Some of them are related (and measured) to income distribution, different types of income (from labour or property), and other aspects of socio-economic status. Some of these dimensions are described as horizontal and vertical, outcomes and opportunities, affecting individual or groups, or formal and substantive. In spite of all these difference, three areas of commonality exist:

i) A distinction ought to be made between inequity and inequality. In other words, some distinctions or differences or levels of inequalities are acceptable while other are not because they are perceived as avoidable, unfair or unjust.

ii) Disparities are multilayered: they cover different aspects such as income and assets, different principles of equity, injurious and 'positive' discrimination, equality and discrimination, and diverse fields of life.

iii) The axes of disparities, or suspect grounds of discrimination, or social cleavages of exclusion are similar (involving gender, ethnic/religious minorities, disabled people, geography and other factors). These are the ones often referred to as dimensions of inequities/inequalities.

Moreover, it is clear that these axes are not independent of each other. This interdependence can be twofold. From one perspective, some of the different dimensions are the result of another one (for

---

56 This is similar to the point discussed above about active and passive social exclusion.

instance, rural disadvantage resulting from ethnic discrimination). There may be synergetic feedback loops or simple causality across dimensions depending on specific temporal and locational circumstances. The second perspective is intersectionality. Either way, the various perspectives are needed to assess specific policies because solutions are not discipline-specific. This is shown for the case of education in the next section.

C. Universal primary education: policies for social inclusion

In the national and international policy debates focused on how to attain universal education, two layers of policy recommendations are present. One deals with generalities (including to increase public budget allocations, allow community participation and so on) which are not education specific. Other recommendations are tailored precisely for education systems (hiring more female teachers, using the native language as the means of instruction, providing appropriate water and sanitation in schools, distributing free books and learning materials, and so on[57]). They are discussed below.

Within these debates, the disciplinary frameworks in Section B influence the policy recommendations (or criticisms of certain polices) of different authors, but do not determine them (Brock-Utne, 2000; Chimombo, 2005; Hallak, 1991). For instance, when dealing with social exclusion/inclusion, the core of the analysis and the arguments is about the impact (intended but also very often unintended) of the policies on various groups, and the interaction among these groups (Unterhalter, 2007; Unterhalter and North, 2017). Diverse opinions, partly based on an appreciation of the most relevant impact or the perspective of different groups, lead to a rich within-discipline policy debate.[58]

Thus, there is as much (if not more) divergence of opinions within each realm as between realms. The following examples illustrate some of these debates. Admittedly, this is not an exhaustive review, just a sampling to buttress the point.

---

[57] Inter-Agency Commission for the World Conference on Education for All (1990), UNGEI (2010) and World Bank (2011) are examples of documents that address both types of policy recommendation.
[58] As Calavita (2010) shows, human rights arguments can be made to either promote or block social inclusion.

Inter- and intra-disciplinary education policy interventions

In this section, five policy interventions are analyzed. It is shown that the same intervention or policy proposal can be supported or criticized within each disciplinary approach – economic (barriers), social (exclusion) and legal (discrimination). While some of the topics are related to specific human rights conventions (such as on disability or gender discrimination), other ones are part and parcel of the standard debates within education policy (for instance, on different school curricula in urban and rural areas, or mandatory uniforms). The fifth one (bilingual or minority language schooling) squarely straddles both categories. However, this distinction is a bit too facile. All the issues can be grounded on human rights (or an economic or social exclusion perspective).

In summarily describing the 'for' and 'against' positions for each proposed policy intervention under the perspectives from Section B, no attempt is made to cover the whole literature and to pinpoint exactly which author makes each argument *(Table 2.1)*. Most writers and documents touch upon several of them simultaneously (Tomasevski, 2001, 2004, 2006; UNESCO, 2000, 2009, 2010, 2014, 2015).[59] In addition, some arguments are absent, such as the impact of uniforms on learning achievement (as the focus of this chapter is on attendance) or different schedules or multi-grade teaching in rural and urban settings (in order to concentrate on the substance of education). Moreover, the arguments are not articulated or classified in the literature as presented here, where an attempt to distil them has been made.

---

59 Nevertheless, for each topic, a few illustrative or particularly interesting references are mentioned.

Overcoming social exclusion in education

Table 2.1 Policy intervention

Mandatory school uniforms[60]

	For	Against
Economic	They can help families save on clothing.	They represent a barrier to access if families cannot afford them.
Social	They are empowering. Children from richer families do not show off their wealth through clothing.	They imply excluding children who cannot afford them (although this is not identity-based so it cannot be called discrimination).
Legal	Rules should apply equally for everybody.	They may lead to a clash between uniforms and religious attire (for instance, preventing the use of hijab).

Different standards for rural schools[61]

	For	Against
Economic	Their cost is lower (than higher standard, urban schools).	Different textbooks and additional training increases cost resulting in inefficiency (cost per pupil is 'too high' in rural areas).
Social	Rural schools will be more appropriate to existing traditions and pedagogical needs of rural children.	They institutionalize the differences between urban and rural populations, preventing schools from becoming a tool for social and cultural change.
Legal	It is part of progressive realization (eventually rural schools will be comparable to urban ones, lower quality is only temporary).	Rural children are discriminated against and receive lower-quality education than urban children.

---

60 Brunsma (2006) and Brunsma and Rockquemore (1998) provided interesting evidence but only for the US context.
61 Atchoarena and Gasperini (2003), Kannapel (2000), Alderuccio (2010), Westbrook et al. (2013).

Using native language in primary schools[62]

	For	Against
Economic	It would save parents' resources by eliminating the need to teach children a second language.	Books and other learning materials will be costlier. Children not fluent in the dominant language will have difficulty finding jobs when they grow up.
Social	It would promote values of diversity and tolerance.	It would perpetuate exclusion.
Legal	It addresses historical discrimination/oppression against certain groups through an affirmative action type of intervention.	Not all children use the same native language.

Hiring female teachers[63]

	For	Against
Economic	Cheaper teachers will represent a saving in the public budget.	Female teachers may be condemned to dead-end jobs.
Social	It promotes girls' enrolment through role models of inclusion. It may be an opportunity for a first formal, non-farm job for many young women.	Women get relegated to stereotypical jobs.
Legal	It addresses structural gender stereotypes. It could be affirmative action.	Gender-based hiring is discriminatory.

---

62 Ball (2010), Durnnian (2007), Young (2009).
63 Aikman and Unterhalter (2005), Glick (2008), Herz and Sperling (2004), Unterhalter and Aikman (2007).

Special accommodation for children with disabilities[64]

	For	Against
Economic	It taps the 'lost brains' of children who otherwise would have missed schooling.	Special accommodation is costly. For (some) learning disabilities, it does not 'pay'.
Social	It is good for other children to learn and accept differences.	Children may be singled out, feeling they do not 'fit'.
Legal	Children have a right to education, even if there is a 'low' rate of return.	It may violate the right to special education (and appropriate care which may be undermined if children are forced into 'regular' classrooms).

Some of the arguments are similar across the examples (for instance, affirmative action when hiring female teachers or using minority language as medium of instruction). In some cases, across disciplines the arguments and counter-arguments are the same but using different words/conceptual frameworks (dead-end jobs and stereotypical jobs in the case of female teachers).

In summary, there is debate within each discipline and more divergence within disciplines than across them. Thus, a combined model is needed.

Where do we go from here? A combined model based on equity

In this section, an attempt is made to bridge these various approaches (combining the elements of the many dimensions of exclusion, inequity and discrimination discussed in Section B). Analytically, using the perspectives jointly provides a more complete picture of the options and tools available for policy-makers searching to answer the dilemmas described in the previous subsection, and for ways to improve educational opportunities for all the children in their countries (address social inclusion in education, eliminate discrimination, include all children in good-quality schools, and eventually also in society). This approach may also be helpful to either avoid duplication of efforts or avoid setting policies in each realm that contradict or cancel each other out. [65]

---

64 Fulcher (1989), UNESCO (1994), UNICEF (2007b).
65 Moreover, Pfeffer (2012) provides evidence that quality of education is correlated to equality of access to education.

The proposal is based on values (ensuring social inclusion and equity) which are paramount and may override (pseudo-) scientific approaches. This is similar to how Ganimian and Murnane (2014) and Murnane and Nelson (2005) avoid policy-making driven by 'technocratic' evidence.

A usual starting point to analyze policies is efficiency. However, the traditional understanding of efficiency, as discussed above, is inherently biased against redistribution. Thus, in order to deal with the dilemmas mentioned in the previous section, it is proposed to make the impact on equity and social inclusion[66] central among the criteria used to choose different courses of action.

When using equity as a driving criterion, it should be remembered that the concept is multilayered and multidimensional. All aspects should be addressed. Fortunately, the axes of analysis across approaches, as was discussed above, are very similar.[67]

Thus, all layers should be considered, as in **Table 2.1**. Moreover, looking at all of them simultaneously does not mean they are added or combined in an index. Each one is analyzed on its own terms (although as was also discussed above, some are similar across disciplines). Only by considering all of them (and their direct and indirect impacts) simultaneously is it possible to fully understand the situation, and consequently arrive at better solutions.[68]

Progressive realization also has to be part of the analysis and the solution. This means the proposals should include clear guidance on how, over time, social inclusion will be achieved and discrimination avoided.

A practical application could be when targets cannot be set to 100 per cent coverage. This is quite common (depending on initial conditions, and other factors), in particular within short periods of time (3 to 5 years). Thus, planning matrices, quantifiable targets, planning instruments and the like systematically set coverage targets that fall short of 100. This is labelled as 'realistic'. Very often, it is indeed realistic. However, it should be clear that eventually (under progressive realization) universality will or ought to be achieved.

---

66 It was mentioned above that not all forms of social inclusion are necessarily good. Obviously, only good social inclusion is the aim to be pursued.
67 It is important, in this context to consider intersectionality explicitly, the theoretical possibility that addressing one dimension may lead to retrogression in another one (which obviously should be avoided, as discussed earlier), and other unintended consequences.
68 'Better' solutions, of course, can only be defined in terms of a clear objective. In this case, 'better' means a more cost-effective, faster and more long-lasting impact on ensuring all children participating in high-quality education.

Overcoming social exclusion in education

From an equity perspective, once we have accepted that during a given programming cycle 100 per cent will not be achieved, the important issue is to assess the various ways to achieve a less than 100 per cent target – because not all of them are equitable.

The data in *Figure 2.1* are close to the net primary school attendance in many developing countries. While the national average is 70 per cent, there are both wealth (represented in quintiles) and gender disparities. Richer children (both boys and girls) are more likely than poorer ones to attend school. At any wealth level, boys are more likely to attend school than girls, with widening gaps among the poorest children.

Figure 2.1 Baseline: net primary school attendance, by wealth and gender

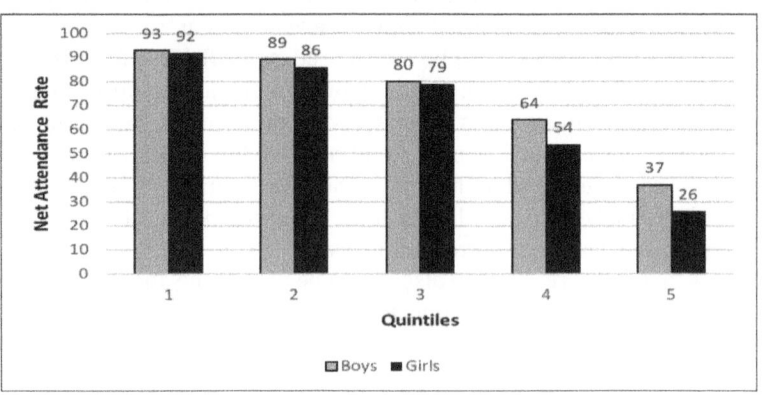

For reference: Boys national average 72.6, girls national average 67.4, gender parity ratio 1.08.

Let us assume it is desired to increase the national average school attendance by 10 percentage points (from 70 to 80 per cent). As mentioned above, this could be realistic and perfectly acceptable.

However, the other side of the coin of aiming to reach 80 per cent is an acceptance that 20 per cent will continue to be excluded. Thus, second, criteria need to be established for which groups will be asked to wait to achieve coverage (under the assumption that the 20 per cent not covered initially will be covered in ensuing planning cycles, following the progressive realization approach).

Criteria are important because 80 per cent coverage could be achieved by providing either for the most disadvantaged groups or for the better-off. In *Figure 2.2*, a situation where rich boys are the main (almost only) beneficiaries of the increase in school attendance is depicted.

Figure 2.2. Excluding poor girls yet attaining the goal

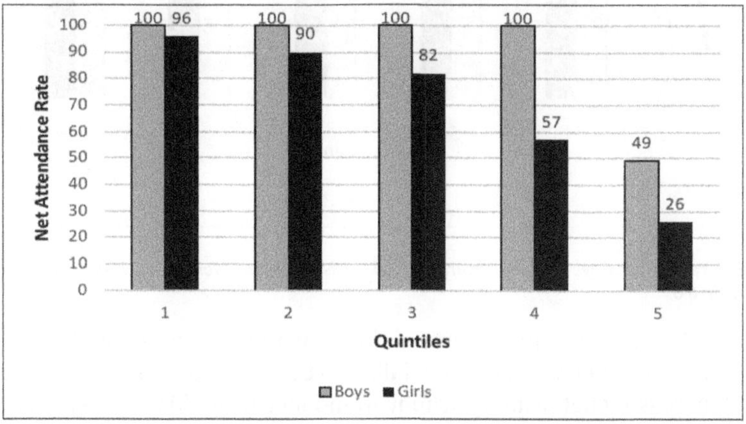

[Bar chart showing Net Attendance Rate by Quintiles:
- Quintile 1: Boys 100, Girls 96
- Quintile 2: Boys 100, Girls 90
- Quintile 3: Boys 100, Girls 82
- Quintile 4: Boys 100, Girls 57
- Quintile 5: Boys 49, Girls 26]

For reference: Boys national average 89.8, girls national average 70.2, gender parity ratio 1.28.

Clearly, in this situation inequities have increased (the gender parity index, GPI, goes from 1.08 to 1.28, so attendance among boys ends up being 28 per cent higher than for girls instead of only 8 per cent higher). Yet, monitoring the planned targets, everything is on track. The goal of reaching net primary school attendance of 80 per cent is achieved.

Contrast this situation to the case where the focus is on increasing school attendance among poor girls. The result is shown in *Figure 2.3*.

Figure 2.3. Equitable approach to targeting

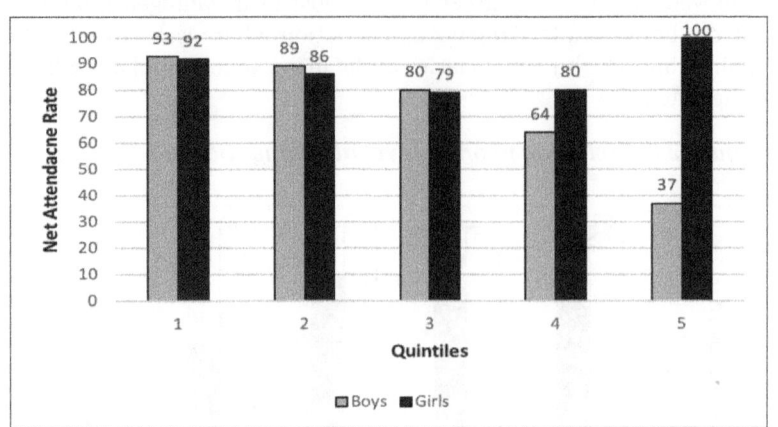

For reference: Boys national average 72.6, girls national average 87.4, gender parity ratio 0.8.

The equity implications of these two approaches could not be more different (with a GPI that falls to 0.8). Yet in both cases, the target of increasing net primary school attendance from 70 to 80 per cent is reached.

The conclusion is simple. An overall target of 80 per cent is not sufficient if the objective of the plan is to reach the most disadvantaged. It leaves the door open to exclusion, inequity and discrimination.

There are at least two ways to solve this issue. One is to set targets for the (most) disadvantaged group *and not for the school-age population as a whole*. In this case, if the objective is to address gender disparities, the target should be to increase girls' attendance from 67.4 to 87.4 per cent. This increase (which would still leave some girls out) would attain the objective of 80 per cent for the country as whole.

An alternative is to specify targets that measure equity. For instance, in the base line, the GPI is 1.08. However, in the second scenario it is 1.28. Thus, the target could be to increase net primary school attendance from 70 to 80 per cent *without increasing the GPI*. Or, alternatively, reduce the GPI from 1.08 to 1.02. In this case, it is important to keep the national target, because a reduction in the GPI may occur if boys' attendance declines more than it declines among girls, which is obviously undesirable.

These approaches could be combined. The exact specification would depend on the criteria chosen to identify disadvantaged groups (for instance girls, rural dwellers, the poor, the disabled). National targets could be set for the whole population, as well as for some subgroups and for different measures of inequity (GPI, wealth quintiles, absolute and relative gaps, geographic disparities and so on). Depending on subgroups and the measurable impact of disparity, the analysis at the start of Section C could be used to address the various drivers of inequality, discrimination and exclusion, and the interventions (mother tongue instruction, integration of disabled children, female teachers and so on).

D. Conclusions

Based on the analysis of inequity, social exclusion and discrimination, a proposal for guiding policy which transcends disciplines is offered in this chapter. It brings equity to the fore of the selection criteria for proposing and choosing policy interventions.

As a way forward, in terms of ensuring education for all children, it is recognized that there are context-specific degrees and levels of disparities along the various dimensions of social exclusion and discrimination. Thus, it is important to measure and assess the situation (the problem) and the probable outcomes of alternative policy options, to decide which one works (or could work). However, this leads to a fundamental question: for what does it work?

In order to answer this question there have to be clear objectives. The objectives have to be based on principles. The principle is to ensure social inclusion of all children in the education system.

Nevertheless, it has been argued in this chapter that this is easier said than done. This is partly because social exclusion is multidimensional, and partly because different disciplines approach issues of social exclusion, discrimination and inequity in different ways. However, two elements come to our rescue.

One of them is that despite methodological, lexical and philosophical differences across disciplines, there is a strong convergence in terms of the main axes of exclusion (inequity and discrimination). This simplifies the empirical analysis of the problem.

The other element, extensively documented in Section C, is that (often) there is more disagreement within disciplines than across them. Thus, there is a need for a multidisciplinary and collaborative approach in the analysis of both the causes of the problem and the likely impact of the proposed alternative solutions.

Practical examples of the types of debate, in terms of specific policy proposals in the education sector, were analyzed. They illustrate the type of assessment that is needed to consider alternatives and confront the trade-offs when assessing possible outcomes. In each case, this was done by providing inputs from the various disciplines. Moreover, it was shown that these inputs converge across disciplines by proving additional arguments for (or against) specific interventions.

As a final step, a practical way to plan for social inclusion and equity in the expansion of education coverage was introduced through a simple numerical example. Thus, putting equity at the core of policy-making and combining perspectives from diverse disciplines is not only desirable, it is possible, in order to promote social inclusion in education – as one fundamental goal in the Agenda for Sustainable Development.

References

Aday, L. A. 2001. *At Risk in America. The health and health care needs of vulnerable populations in the United States*, 2nd edn. San Francisco, Calif., Jossey-Bass.

Agarwal, B. 1994. *A Field of One's Own: Gender and land rights in South Asia.* Cambridge, Cambridge University Press.

---. 2001. Participatory exclusions, community forestry, and gender: an analysis for South Asia and a conceptual framework. *World Development*, Vol. 29, No. 10, pp. 1623–48.

Aikman, S. and Unterhalter, E. 2005. *Beyond Access: Transforming policy and practice for gender equality in education.* Oxford, Oxfam GB.

Alderuccio, M. C. 2010. An investigation of global/local dynamics of curriculum transformation in sub-Saharan Africa with special reference to the republic of Mozambique. *Compare*, Vol. 40, No. 6, pp. 727–39.

Alkire, S. and Foster, J. 2011. Counting and multidimensional poverty measurement. *Journal of Public Economics*, Vol. 95, Nos 7–8, pp. 476--87.

Alston, P. 2018. Report of the special rapporteur on extreme poverty and human rights to the Human Rights Council of the UN General Assembly, A/HRC/38/33. New York, United Nations.

Arnardóttir, O. M. 2007. Non-discrimination in international and European law: towards substantive models. *Nordisk Tidsskrift for Menneskerettigheter*, Vol. 25, No. 2, pp. 140–57.

Arneson, R. 1989. Equality and equality of opportunity for welfare. *Philosophical Studies*, No. 56, pp. 77–93.

Arrow, K. J. 1999. Observations on social capital. P. Dasgupta and I. Serageldin (eds), *Social Capital: A multifaceted perspective.* Washington DC, World Bank.

Atchoarena, D. and Gasperini, L. (eds). 2003. *Education for Rural Development: Towards new policy responses.* Rome and Paris, Food and Agriculture Organization of the United Nations (FAO) and UNESCO International Institute for Educational Planning (IIEP).

Atkinson, A. B. 1983. *The Economics of Inequality*, 2nd edn. Oxford, Clarendon Press.

Atkinson, A. B. and Bourguignon, F. (eds). 2015. *Handbook of Income Distribution*, Vol. 2. Amsterdam, Elsevier.

Bäckman, O. and Nilsson, A, 2011. Pathways to social exclusion – a life course study. *European Sociological Review*, Vol. 2, No. 1, pp. 107–23.

Baker, D. P., Goesling, B. and LeTendre, G. K. 2002. Socioeconomic status, school quality, and national economic development: a cross-national analysis of the 'Heyneman-Loxley' effect on mathematics and science achievement. *Comparative Education Review,* Vol. 46, No. 3, pp. 291–312.

Ball, J. 2010. Enhancing learning of children from diverse language backgrounds: mother tongue-based bilingual or multilingual education in early childhood and early primary school years, presentation to UNESCO International Symposium on Translation and Cultural Mediation, Paris.

Balkin, J. 1997. The constitution of status. *Yale Law Journal*, No. 106.

Bardach, E. 2012. *A Practical Guide for Policy Analysis. The eightfold path to more effective problem solving*, 4th edn. London, Sage.

Barnett, W. S. and Belfield, C. R. 2006. Early childhood development and social mobility. *The Future of Children*, Vol. 6, No. 2, pp. 73–98.

Bennell, p. 1996. Using and abusing rates of return: a critique of the World Bank's 1995 education sector review. *International Journal of Educational Development*, Vol. 16, No. 3.

Bhalla, A. and Lapeyre, F. 1995. Towards an analytical and operational framework, mimeo. Geneva, IILS.

Blackwood, D. L. and Lynch, R. G. 1994. The measurement of inequality and poverty: a policy maker's guide to the literature. *World Development*, Vol. 22, No. 4, pp. 567–78.

Blanden, J., Machin, S., Murphy, R. and Tominey, E. 2010. *Research on the Intergenerational Links in the Every Child Matters Outcomes*, Special Report 005. London, Centre for the Economics of Education (CEE).

Blossfeld, H.-P. and Shavit, Y. 1993. *Persistent Inequality: Changing educational attainment in thirteen countries.* Boulder, Colo., Westview Press.

Bourdieu, P. 1986. Forms of capital. J. G. Richardson (ed.), *Handbook of Theory and Research for the Sociology of Education*. Westport, Conn., Greenwood Press.

Braveman, P. and Gruskin, S. 2003. Defining equity in health. *Journal of Epidemiology and Community Health*, No. 57, pp. 254–8.

Breen, R. and Jonsson, J. O. 2005. Inequality of opportunity in comparative perspective: recent research on educational attainment and social mobility. *Annual Review of Sociology*, No. 31, pp. 223–43.

Brock-Utne, B. 2000. *Whose Education for All. The recolonization of the African mind.* New York, Falmer Press.
Brooks-Gunn, J. and Duncan, G. J. 1997. The effects of poverty on children. *The Future of Children,* Vol. 7, No. 2.
Brunsma, D. L. 2006. School uniform policies in public schools. *Principal* (Jan./Feb.), pp. 50–3.
Brunsma, D. L. and Rockquemore, K. A. 1998. Effects of student uniforms on attendance, behavior problems, substance abuse, and academic achievement. *Journal of Educational Research,* Vol. 92, No. 1, pp. 53–62.
Burchardt, T., Le Grand, J. and Piachaud, D. 2002. Degrees of exclusion: developing a dynamic, multidimensional measure. J. Hills, J. Le Grand and D. Piachaud (eds), *Understanding Social Exclusion.* Oxford, Oxford University Press.
Buss, D. 1998. Robes, relics and rights: the Vatican and the Beijing Conference on Women. *Social and Legal Studies,* Vol. 7, Issue 3, pp. 339–63.
Byrne, D. 2010. *Social Exclusion,* 2nd edn. Milton Keynes, UK, Open University Press.
Calavita, K. 2010. *Invitation to Law and Society: An introduction to the study of real law.* Chicago, Ill., University of Chicago Press.
Carnoy, M. 2000. *Globalization and Educational Reform: What planners need to know.* Paris, IIEP.
Case, A. and Paxson, C. 2006. Children's health and social mobility. *The Future of Children,* Vol. 16, No. 2, pp. 151–73.
Chakraborty, A. 2009. Inequality in non-income dimensions, presentation at Conference on Employment, Growth, and Poverty Reduction in Developing Countries in Honor of Professor Azizur Rahman Khan, 27–28 March, University of Massachusetts at Amherst, USA.
Chakravarty, S. R. and D'Ambrosio, C. 2006. The measurement of social exclusion. *Review of Income and Wealth,* Vol. 52, No. 3, pp. 377–98.
Chalmers, D. 1993. Internationalized domestic politics in Latin America: the institutional role of internationally based actors, mimeo. New York, Columbia University.
Chang, H.-J. 2011. *23 Things They Don't Tell You about Capitalism.* New York, Bloomsbury.
Chimombo, J. p. G. 2005. Issues in basic education in developing countries: an exploration of policy options for improved delivery. *Journal of International Cooperation in Education,* Vol. 8, No. 1, pp. 129–52.
Chudgar, A. and Luschei, T. F. 2009. National income, income inequality, and the importance of schools: a hierarchical cross-national comparison. *American Education Research Journal,* Vol. 46, No. 3, pp. 626–58.
Cohen, G. A. 1989. On the currency of egalitarian justice. *Ethics,* No. 99, pp. 906–44.
Coleman, J. 1990. *Foundations of Social Theory.* Cambridge, Mass., Harvard University Press.

Cook, R. and Cusack, S. 2011 *Gender Stereotyping: Transnational legal perspectives.* Philadelphia, Penn., University of Pennsylvania Press.

Cornia, G. A. (ed.). 2004. *Inequality, Growth, and Poverty in an Era of Liberalization and Globalization.* Oxford, Oxford University Press.

Crenshaw, K. 1989. Demarginalizing the intersection of race and sex: a black feminist critique of antidiscrimination doctrine, feminist theory and antiracist politics, paper for University of Chicago Legal Forum 1989, Feminism in the Law: Theory, Practice and Criticism. Chicago, Ill., University of Chicago Law School.

Daly, M. and Silver, H. 2008. Social exclusion and social capital: a comparison and critique. *Theory and Society,* Vol. 37, No. 6, pp. 537–66.

Deaton, A. 1997. *The Analysis of Household Surveys.* Baltimore, Md., Johns Hopkins University Press.

---. 2003. How to monitor poverty for the Millennium Development Goals. *Journal of Human Development*, Vol. 4, No. 3.

---. 2010. Price indexes, inequality, and the measurement of world poverty. *American Economic Review*, Vol. 100, No. 1, pp. 5–34.

Delamonica, E. and Minujín, A. 2007. Incidence, depth and severity of children in poverty. *Social Indicators Research*, Vol. 82, No. 2, pp. 361–74.

Desai, M. 1986. Drawing the line: on defining the poverty threshold. p. Golding (ed.), *Excluding the Poor.* London, Child Poverty Action Group.

Donnelly, J. 2003. *Universal Human Rights in Theory and Practice*, 2nd edn. Ithaca, N.Y., Cornell University Press.

Duffy, K. 2005. *Social Exclusion and Human Dignity in Europe.* Strasbourg, France, Council of Europe.

Duncan, G. J., Brooks-Gunn, J. and Kato Klebanov, P. 1994. Economic deprivation and early childhood development. *Child Development*, Vol. 65, No. 2, pp. 296–318.

Durnnian, T. 2007. *Mother Language First.* Dhaka, Save the Children Fund.

Dworkin, R. 1981. What is equality? Part 1: Equality of welfare. *Philosophy and Public Affairs*, No. 10, pp. 185–246.

ECLAC-UNICEF. 2010. Pobreza infantil en América Latina y el Caribe. Santiago de Chile, ECLAC.

Erikson, R. and Goldthorpe, J. H. 1992. *The Constant Flux: A study of class mobility in industrial societies.* Oxford, Clarendon Press.

Estivill, J. 2003. *Concepts and Strategies for Combating Social Exclusion.* Geneva, ILO.

European Union. 2011. *Handbook on European Non-Discrimination Law.* Strasbourg, France, European Court of Human Rights – Council of Europe.

Forrest, C. B. and Riley, A. W. 2004. Childhood origins of adult health: a basis for a life course health policy. *Health Affairs*, Vol. 23, No. 5, pp. 155–64.

Foster, J., Greer, J. and Thorbecke, E. 1984. A class of decomposable poverty measures. *Econometrica*, Vol. 52, No. 3. (May, 1984), pp. 761–766.

Fredman, S. 2005. Changing the norm: positive duties in equal treatment legislation. *Maastricht Journal of European and Comparative Law*, Vol. 12, No. 4, pp. 369–97.
———. 2011. *Discrimination Law*, 3nd edn. Oxford, Oxford University Press.
Fulcher, G. 1989. *Disabling Policies? A comparative approach to education policy and disability*. London, Routledge.
Gameron, A. and Long, D. 2007. Equality of educational opportunity: a 40 year retrospective. R. Teese, S. Lamb and M. Duru-Bellat (eds), *International Studies in Educational Inequality, Theory and Policy*. Dordrecht, Netherlands, Springer.
Ganimian, A. and Murnane, R. 2014. Improving educational outcomes in developing countries: lessons from rigorous impact evaluations, Working Paper 20284. Cambridge, Mass., National Bureau of Economic Research (NBER).
Glick, P. 2008. What policies will reduce gender schooling gaps in developing countries: evidence and interpretation. *World Development*, Vol. 36, Issue 9, pp. 1623–46.
Gregg, P. and Machin, S. 1999. Childhood disadvantage and success or failure in the labour market. D. Blanchflower and R. Freeman (eds), *Youth Employment and Joblessness in Advanced Countries*. Cambridge, Mass., NBER.
Grinspun, Al. 1997. Policy implications of a social exclusion approach: an overview. C. Gore and J. B. Figueiredo (eds), *Social Exclusion and Anti-Poverty Policy: A debate*. Geneva, IILS.
Hallak, J. 1991. *Education for All: High expectation or false hopes*, IIEP contributions No. 3. Paris, UNESCO.
Halleröd, B. and Bask, M. 2008. Accumulation of welfare problems in a longitudinal perspective. *Social Indicators Research*, No. 288, pp. 311–27.
Hendriks, A. 2010. The UN Disability Convention and (multiple) discrimination: should EU non-discrimination law be modelled accordingly? L. Waddington and G. Quinn (eds), *European Yearbook of Disability Law*, Vol. 2, Antwerp, Belgium, Intersentia.
Herz, B. and Sperling, G. B. 2004. *What Works in Girls' Education*. New York, Council on Foreign Relations.
Heyneman, S. 2015. The H/L effect: three decades of debate. S. McGrath and Qung Gu (eds), *Routledge International Handbook on Education and Development*. Oxford, Routledge.
Heyneman, S. and Loxley, W. A. 1983. The effect of primary school quality on academic achievement across twenty-nine high cost and low income countries. *American Journal of Sociology*, Vol. 88, pp. 162–98.
Hirschman, A. O. 1982. Rival interpretations of market society: civilizing, destructive or feeble?' *Journal of Economic Literature*, Vol. 20, No. 4, pp. 1463–1484.
Hobcraft, J. 2007. Child development, the life course, and social exclusion: are the frameworks used in the UK relevant for developing countries? Working Paper 72. Manchester, UK, Chronic Poverty Research Centre.

Holtmaat, R. 2004. *Towards Different Law and Policy. The significance of Article 5a CEDAW for the elimination of structural gender discrimination*. Doetinchem, Netherlands, Reed Business Information.
---. 2013. The CEDAW: a holistic approach to women's equality and freedom. A. Hellum and H. S. Aase (eds), *Women's Human Rights: CEDAW in international, regional, and national law*. Cambridge, Cambridge University Press.
Holtmaat, R. and Naber, J. 2011. *Women's Human Rights and Culture: From deadlock to dialogue*. Antwerp, Belgium, Intersentia.
Holtmaat, R. and Tobler, C. 2005. CEDAW and the European Union's policy in the field of combating gender discrimination. *Maastricht Journal of European and Comparative Law*, Vol. 12, No. 4, pp. 399–425.
Howard, E. 2010. *The EU Race Directive: Developing the protection against racial discrimination within the EU*. London, Routledge.
Hunt, P., Osmani, S. and Nowak, M. 2002. *Draft Guidelines: A human rights approach to poverty reduction strategies*. Geneva, Office of the High Commissioner for Human Rights.
Inter-Agency Commission for the World Conference on Education for All. 1990. *Meeting Basic Learning Needs: A vision for the 1990s*, Background Document for the World Conference on Education for All, Jomtien. New York, UNICEF.
IMF (International Monetary Fund). 2011. All for one: why inequality throws us off balance. *Finance and Development*, Vol. 48, No. 3, pp. 6–29.
Kabeer, N. 2000. Social exclusion, poverty and discrimination: towards an analytical framework. *IDS Bulletin*, Vol. 31, No. 4.
---. 2016. 'Leaving no one behind': the challenge of intersecting inequalities. *World Social Science Report*. Paris, UNESCO and ISSC.
Kannapel, P. J. 2000. Standards-based reform and rural school improvement: finding the middle ground. *Journal of Research in Rural Education*, Vol. 16, No. 3, pp. 202–8.
Karagiorgi, C. 2014. The concept of discrimination by association and its application in the EU Member States. *European Anti-Discrimination Law Review*, Issue 18, pp. 25–36.
Keck, M. and Sikkink, K. 1998. *Activists Beyond Borders: Advocacy networks in international politics*. Ithaca, N.Y., Cornell University Press.
King, C. S. (ed.). 1983. *The Words of Martin Luther King*. New York, New Market Press.
Koukoulis-Spiliotopoulos, S. 2008. The limits of cultural traditions. *Annuaire international des Droits de l'Homme*, Vol. 3, pp. 411–43.
Laderchi, C., Saith, R. and Stewart, F. 2003. Does it matter that we don't agree on the definition of poverty? A comparison of four approaches, Working Paper 107. Oxford, Queen Elizabeth House, University of Oxford.
Langer, A. and Stewart, F. 2007. Macro adjustment policies and horizontal inequalities, Working Paper 158. Oxford, Queen Elizabeth House, University of Oxford.

Lauglo, J. 1996. Banking on education and the uses of research: A critique of World Bank priorities and strategies for education. *International Journal of Educational Development*, 1996, Vol. 16(3), pp. 221–233.

Lenoir, R. 1974. *Les exclus : un Français sur dix*. Paris, Editions du Seuil.

Levitas, R. 2004. The concept of social exclusion and the new 'Durkheimian' hegemony. *Critical Social Policy,* Vol. 16, No. 46, pp. 5–20.

Levitas, R., Pantazis, C., Fahmy, E., Gordon, D., Lloyd, E. and Patsios, D. 2007. The multi-dimensional analysis of social exclusion, mimeo. Bristol, Department of Sociology and School for Social Policy, Townsend Centre for the International Study of Poverty and Bristol Institute for Public Affairs, University of Bristol.

Lister, R. 2004. *Poverty*. Cambridge, Polity Press.

Loenen, T. 2000. Indirect discrimination as a vehicle for change. *Australian Journal of Human Rights*, Vol. 6, No. 2, pp. 77–100.

Macinko, J. A. and Starfield, B. 2002. Annotated bibliography on equity in health, 1980–2001. *International Journal for Equity in Health*, Vol. 1, No. 1.

MacKinnon, C. 1987. *Feminism Unmodified*. Cambridge, Mass., Harvard University Press.

Marshall, T. H. 1950. *Citizenship and Social Class and Other Essays*. Cambridge, Cambridge University Press.

McColgan, A. 2014. *Discrimination, Equality and the Law*. Oxford, Hart.

McCrudden, C. 1986. Rethinking positive action. *Industrial Law Journal*, Vol. 15(4), pp. 219–243.

Mechanic, D. and Tanner, J. 2007. Vulnerable people, groups, and populations: societal view. *Health Affairs*, Vol. 26, No. 5, pp. 1220–30.

Murnane, R. and Nelson, R. R. 2005. Improving the performance of the education sector: the valuable, challenging, and limited role of random assignment evaluations, Working Paper 11846. Cambridge, Mass., NBER.

Myrdal, G. 1953. *The Political Element in the Development of Economic Theory*. London, Routledge & Kegan Paul.

Nell, E. 1998. *The General Theory of Transformational Growth: Keynes after Sraffa*. Cambridge, Cambridge University Press.

OHCHR (Office of the High Commissioner for Human Rights). 2012. *Guiding Principles on Extreme Poverty and Human Rights*. Geneva, OHCHR

Otto, J., Stoter, W. S. R. and Arnscheidt, J. 2008. Lawmaking for development explorations into the theory and practice of international legislative projects. J. Arnscheidt, B. van Rooij and J. Otto (eds), *Using Legislative Theory to Improve Law and Development Projects*. Leiden, Netherlands, Leiden University Press.

Oyen, E. 1997. The contradictory concepts of social exclusion and social inclusion. C. Gore and J. B. Figueiredo (eds), *Social Exclusion and Anti-Poverty Policy: A debate*. Geneva, IILS.

Palma, J. G. 2011. Homogeneous middles vs. heterogeneous tails, and the end of the 'inverted-u': it's all about the share of the rich. *Development and Change*, Vol. 42, No. 1, pp. 87–153.

Percy-Smith, J. 2000. *Policy Responses to Social Exclusion: Towards inclusion?* Oxford, Oxford University Press.

Peruzzi, A. 2013. From childhood deprivation to adult social exclusion, CLS Cohort Studies Working paper 2013/5. London, Centre for Longitudinal Studies, University of London.

Petmesidou, M. and Papatheodorou, C. 2006. *Poverty and Social Deprivation in the Mediterranean Area*. London, Zed.

Pfeffer, F. T. 2012. Equality and quality in education, Research Report 12-774. Ann Arbor, Mich., Population Studies Center, Institute for Social Research, University of Michigan.

Phillips, A. 2004. Defending equality of outcome. *Journal of Political Philosophy*, Vol. 12, No. 1, pp. 1–19.

Piketty, T. 2014. *Capital in the Twenty-First Century*. Cambridge, Mass., Harvard University Press.

Pogge, T. and Reddy, S. 2006. Unknown: extent, distribution and trend of global income poverty. *Economic and Political Weekly*, Vol. 41, No. 22, pp. 2241–7.

Popay, J., Escorel, S., Hernández, M., Johnston, H., Mathieson, J. and Rispel, L. 2008. *Understanding and Tackling Social Exclusion*, Final Report to the WHO Commission on Social Determinants of Health from the Social Exclusion Knowledge Network. Lancaster, UK, Social Exclusion Knowledge Network.

Rawls, J. 1971. *A Theory of Justice*. Cambridge, Mass., Harvard University Press.

Reddy, S. and Minoiu, C. 2007. Has poverty really fallen? *Review of Income and Wealth*, Vol. 53, No. 3, pp. 484–502.

Redmond, G. 2014. Poverty and social exclusion. A. Ben-Arieh, F. Casas, I. Frønes, and J. Korbin (eds), *Handbook of Child Well-Being*. Dordrecht, Netherlands, Springer.

Rodgers, G. 1997. Labour market exclusions and the roles of social actors. C. Gore and J.B. Figueiredo (eds), *Social Exclusion and Anti-Poverty Policy: A debate*. Geneva, IILS.

Roemer, J. E. 1998. *Equality of Opportunity*. Cambridge, Mass., Harvard University Press.

Salverda, W., Nolan, B. and Smeeding, T. M. (eds). 2009. *The Oxford Handbook of Economic Inequality*. Oxford, Oxford University Press.

Samoff, J. 1996. Which priorities and strategies for education?' *International Journal of Educational Development*, Vol. 16, No. 3, pp. 249–271.

Sano, H.-O. 2000. Development and human rights: the necessary but partial integration of human rights and development. *Human Rights Quarterly*, No. 22, pp. 734–52.

Sen, A. K. 1976. Poverty: an ordinal approach to measurement. *Econometrica*, pp. 219–31.

---. 1988. *Ethics and Economics.* Oxford, Oxford University Press.
---. 2000. Social exclusion: concept, application, and scrutiny, Social Development Papers No. 1, Manila, Office of Environment and Social Development, Asian Development Bank (ADB).
Sen, A. and Hawthorne, G. 1985. *The Standard of Living*, Tanner Lectures in Human Values. Cambridge, Cambridge University Press.
Shaikh, A. 2016. *Capitalism: Competition, conflict, crises.* New York, Oxford University Press.
---. 2017. Income distribution, econophysics and Piketty. *Review of Political Economy*, Vol. 29 Issue 1, pp. 18–29.
Shaikh, A. and Ragab, A. 2008. The vast majority income (VMI): a new measure of global inequality, Policy Research Brief No. 7. Brasilia, International Poverty Centre.
Shaw, M., Galobardes, B., Lawlor, D. A., Lynch, J., Wheeler, B. and Smith, G. D. (eds). 2007. *The Handbook of Inequality and Socioeconomic Position: Concepts and measures.* Bristol, UK, Policy Press.
Silver, H. 1994. Social exclusion and social solidarity: three paradigms, Discussion Paper No. 69. Geneva, IILS.
---. 1997. Poverty, exclusion and citizenship rights. C. Gore and J. B. Figueiredo (eds), *Social Exclusion and Anti-Poverty Policy: A debate.* Geneva, IILS.
Smaali Bouhlila, D. 2015. The Heyneman–Loxley effect revisited in the Middle East and North Africa: analysis using TIMSS 2007 database. *International Journal of Educational Development*, Vol. 42, pp. 85–95.
Solow, R. 1999. Notes on social capital and economic performance. P. Dasgupta and I. Serageldin (eds), *Social Capital: A multifaceted perspective.* Washington DC, World Bank.
Stewart, F. 2001. Horizontal Inequalities: a neglected dimension of development, Annual Lecture 5. Helsinki, UN University World Institute for Development Research (WIDER).
Stewart, F., Brown, G. K. and Mancini, L. 2005. Why horizontal inequalities matter: some implications for measurement, Working Paper No. 19. Oxford, Centre for Research on Inequality, Human Security and Ethnicity (CRISE), University of Oxford.
Stiglitz, J. 2012. *The Price of Inequality.* London, Allen Lane.
Streeten, P. 1997. Some reflections on social exclusion. C. Gore and J. B. Figueiredo (eds), *Social Exclusion and Anti-Poverty Policy: A debate.* Geneva, IILS.
Swiebel, J. 2015. Recognizing gender and sexuality at the United Nations. Habemus gender! Déconstruction d'une riposte religieuse', *Sextant (Revue de la structure de recherche interdisciplinaire sur le genre et la sexualité)*, No. 31, pp. 25-41. Editions de l'Université de Bruxelles.
Swift, A. 2001. *Political Philosophy: A beginners' guide for students and politicians.* Cambridge, Polity Press.
Therborn, G. 2006. Meaning, mechanisms, patterns, and forces: an introduction. G. Therborn (ed.), *Inequalities in the World.* London, Verso.

Thomas, V., Wang, Y. and Fan, X. 2001. Measuring education inequality: Gini coefficients of education, Policy Research Working Paper 2525. Washington DC, World Bank.

Tilly, C. 1998. Durable Inequality. Los Angeles, Calif. and London, University of California Press.

Tobler, C. 2014. Equality and non-discrimination under the ECHR and EU law: a comparison focusing on discrimination against LGBTI persons. *Zeitschrift für ausländisches öffentliches Recht und Völkerrecht*, Vol. 74, No. 3, pp. 521–61.

Tomasevski, K. 2001. Human Rights Obligations: Making education available, accessible, acceptable, and adaptable, Right to Education Primers, No. 3. Gothenburg, Sweden, Novum Grafiske AB for Swedish International Development Cooperation Agency.

---. 2004. Manual on Rights-Based Education: Global human rights requirements made simple. Bangkok, UNESCO.

---. 2006. Human Rights Obligations in Education. The 4-A Scheme. Nijmegen, Netherlands, Wolf Legal.

Travers, M. 2010. *Understanding Law and Society*. New York, Routledge.

United Nations. 1948. *Universal Declaration of Human Rights*. New York, United Nations.

---. 1995a. *Copenhagen Declaration on Social Development*, A/CONF.166/9. New York, United Nations.

---. 1995b. *Beijing Declaration and Platform of Action, adopted at the Fourth World Conference on Women*. New York, United Nations.

---. 1996. *Report of the Fourth World Conference on Women*, A.CONF.177/20/Rev.1. New York, United Nations.

---. 2000. *United Nations Millennium Declaration. Resolution adopted by the General Assembly* A/55/L.2. United Nations New York. www.un.org/millennium/declaration/ares552e.htm (Accessed 10 April 2019.)

---. 2015. *Transforming Our World. The 2030 agenda for sustainable development*, A/RES/70/1. New York, United Nations. https://sustainabledevelopment.un.org/content/documents/21252030%20Agenda%20for%20Sustainable%20Development%20web.pdf (Accessed 10 April 2019.)

---. 2017. *Work of the Statistical Commission.*

UN Commission on Human Rights. 1986. Note verbale dated 5 December 1986 from the Permanent Mission of the Netherlands to the United Nations Office at Geneva addressed to the Centre for Human Rights ('Limburg Principles'), 8 January 1987, E/CN.4/1987/17. www.refworld.org/docid/48abd5790.html (Accessed 14 January 2018.)

UN Committee on Economic, Social, and Cultural Rights. 1990. General comment No. 3. The nature of states parties' obligations (art. 2, para. 1, of the Covenant). Geneva, UN Committee on Economic, Social, and Cultural Rights.

UNESCO. 1990. *World Declaration on Education for All*. Paris, UNESCO.
———. 1994. *The Salamanca Statement and Framework for Action on Special Needs Education*. Paris, UNESCO.
———. 2000. *The Dakar Framework Education For All: Meeting our collective commitments*. Paris, UNESCO.
———. 2009. *EFA Global Monitoring Report 2009. Overcoming inequality: why governance matters*. Paris, UNESCO.
———.2010. *EFA Global Monitoring Report 2010. Reaching the marginalized*. Paris, UNESCO.
———. 2014. *EFA Global Monitoring Report 2013/14. Teaching and Learning: Achieving quality for all*. Paris, UNESCO.
———. 2015. *EFA Global Monitoring Report 2015. Education For All 2000–2015: Achievements and challenges*. Paris, UNESCO.
UNGEI (UN Girls' Education Initiative). 2010. *UNGEI at 10: A Journey to Gender Equality in Education*. New York, UN Children's Fund (UNICEF).
UNICEF. 1990. World Declaration on the Survival, Protection and Development of Children. New York, UNICEF.
———. 2007a. *Global Study on Child Poverty and Disparities*. New York: UNICEF Global Policy Section, Division of Policy and Planning.
———. 2007b. *Promoting the Rights of Children with Disabilities*, Innocenti Digest No. 13. Florence, Italy, UNICEF Innocenti Research Centre.
———. 2011. *Training Handbook on the Equity Focus in Programmes*. New York, UNICEF.
Unterhalter, E. 2007. *Gender, Schooling and Global Social Justice*. London, Routledge.
Unterhalter, E. and Aikman, S. 2007. *Practising Gender Equality in Education*. Oxford, Oxfam GB.
Unterhalter, E. and North, A. 2017. *Education, Poverty and Global Goals for Gender Equality: How people make policy happen*. London, Routledge.
Vandemoortele, J. 2002. Are we really reducing global poverty? P. Townsend and D. Gordon (eds), *World Poverty: New policies to defeat an old enemy*. Bristol, UK, Policy Press.
———. forthcoming. Framing social protection within the context of growing inequality.
Vladeck, B. C. 2007. How useful is 'vulnerable' as a concept? *Health Affairs*, Vol. 26, No. 5, pp. 1231–4.
Wagstaff, A., van Doorslaer, E. and Paci, P. 1989. Equity in the finance and delivery of health care: some tentative cross-country comparisons. *Oxford Review of Economic Policy*, Vol. 5, No. 1, pp. 89–112.
Wagstaff, A., Paci, P. and van Doorslaer, E. 1991. On the measurement of inequalities in health. *Social Science and Medicine,* No. 33, pp. 545–57.
Waaldijk, K. and Bonini-Baraldi, M. 2006. *Sexual Orientation Discrimination in the European Union: National laws and the Employment Equality Directive*. The Hague, Asser Press.
Welch, F. 1999. In defense of inequality. *American Economic Review*, Vol. 89, No. 2, pp. 1–17.

Westbrook, J., Durrani, N., Brown, R., Orr, D., Pryor, J., Boddy, J. and Salvi, F. 2013. *Pedagogy, Curriculum, Teaching Practices and Teacher Education in Developing Countries*, Final Report. Education Rigorous Literature Review. London, DFID.

Wolff, E. 2007. Recent trends in household wealth in the United States: rising debt and the middle-class squeeze, Working Paper No. 502. Annandale-on-Hudson, N.Y., Levy Economics Institute of Bard College.

---. 2010. Recent trends in household wealth in the United States: rising debt and the middle-class squeeze – an update to 2007, Working Paper No. 589. Annandale-on-Hudson, N.Y., Levy Economics Institute of Bard College.

World Bank. 2006. World Development Report 2006: Equity and Development. Washington DC, World Bank.

---. 2011. World Bank Education Strategy 2020. Washington DC, World Bank.

---. 2018. Poverty and Shared Prosperity: Piecing together the poverty puzzle. Washington DC, World Bank. www.worldbank.org/en/publication/poverty-and-shared-prosperity (Accessed 10 April 2019.)

World Health Organization (WHO) and World Bank. 2011. World Report on Disability. Geneva, WHO.

Young, C. 2009. Mother tongue education in multilingual settings: quality education for all, paper for 8th International Conference on Language and Development, in Language and development: Sociocultural issues and challenges. Denpasar, Trustees of the Language & Development Conferences (LDC 8). www.langdevconferences. org/publications. html (Accessed 10 March 2019.)

Young, I. M. 2001. Equality of whom? Social groups and judgements of injustice. Journal of Political Philosophy, Vol. 9, No. 2, pp. 1–18.

Zumbach, D. 2010. The 'Heyneman-Loxley effect' in sub-Saharan Africa: school quality, socioeconomic status and national economic development. https://ssrn.com/abstract=1815463 (Accessed 10 March 2019.)

CHAPTER 3
SOCIAL EXCLUSION AND THE RELATIONAL ELEMENTS OF POVERTY

Paul Spicker

Introduction: poverty as a multifaceted concept

Poverty refers to a wide range of interrelated issues, but it has often been interpreted in a very narrow academic framework. Robert Chambers comments:

> 'Poverty' is used in two main senses: in its first, common usage in development, it is a broad, blanket word used to refer to the whole spectrum of deprivation and ill-being; in its second usage, poverty has a narrow technical definition for purposes of measurement and comparison. In the words of one authority, '... "poverty" has to be given scientifically acceptable universal meaning and measurement.' Poverty is then defined as low income, as it is reported, recorded and analyzed, or often as low consumption, which is easier to measure. This is the normal meaning of poverty among economists, and is used for measuring poverty lines, for comparing groups and regions, and often for assessing progress or backsliding .... The classic pattern in erudite analysis is to start with a recognition that poverty is much more than income or consumption but then to allow what has been measured to take over and dominate.
>
> (Chambers, 1995, pp. 179–80)

In previous work developed in conjunction with CROP, I have identified twelve clusters of meaning associated with the concept of poverty (Spicker, 2007). There are understandings of poverty that relate to *material conditions*:

o the lack of specific goods and items, such as housing, fuel, or food
o a pattern or 'web' of deprivation, where people have multiple deprivations, or may be frequently deprived, even if the precise circumstances they are in vary
o a generally low standard of living, which refers to a general experience rather than specific deprivations.

Some clusters of meaning are based in *economic circumstances*:

o a lack of resources, such as low income or limited assets

Social exclusion and the relational elements of poverty

- o an 'economic distance' from the rest of the population, or a degree of inequality, which means that people are denied access to the resources that others can buy
- o class – variously understood as an economic status, or relationship to production and the labour market – which means that people are consistently likely to be disadvantaged or deprived.

Several other concepts relate to *social relationships*:
- o poverty as dependency on financial support and state benefits
- o poverty as a set of social roles, low status and social dishonour – the idea of the 'underclass' is an extreme example
- o the problem of exclusion, where people are denied access to essential resources because they are left out, shut out or pushed out
- o lack of basic security: the Wresinski report argued that insecurity or precariousness amount to poverty when they affect several spheres of a person's life, when they are persistent and when they affect people's ability to assume responsibilities and to exercise their rights (Wresinski, 1987, p. 6)
- o a lack of entitlement, in the sense that poor people do not have the rights to access and use resources that others can; the concept is linked by Sen and Nussbaum to a lack of capabilities (Sen, 1981; Nussbaum, 2006).

Underlying many, if not most, of the ideas is the position of poverty as *a moral evaluation*, referring to severe hardship or a situation that is morally unacceptable. That also implies some moral obligation to take action – which is why so many commentators want to deny that a condition might even be described as poverty.

Poverty as a relational concept

Poverty is sometimes described as a 'relative' concept. Poverty is relative when its character and nature change with the society where it takes place. This might mean any of four rather different things. First, relative poverty might mean that poverty is defined socially – that the minimum standards that apply in a society are different in different places. In Amartya Sen's work, the commodities through which capabilities are realized are different in different societies (Sen, 1999); so, for example, the 'capability' of transport can be realized in different places by different commodities such as a bicycle, a car or a boat. What counts as food or shelter depends not just on social preference, but a complex system of rules; so there are societies where building a squatter shack is almost impossible, and others where it is the norm. Second, relative poverty might mean that the concept of poverty is socially constructed: Peter Townsend took poverty to refer to the expectations, patterns of behaviour and customs that are accepted in a society (Townsend, 1979). Third, relative poverty might mean that the standards that can be used are particular, rather than universal – that is, they depend on the specific social context where they are applied. For Martin Ravallion, poverty is a moving target: the idea of 'relative' poverty simply applies different, more liberal standards than absolute tests might do (Ravallion, 2016). The fourth view is comparative: poverty is relative because it depends on a comparison between those who are poor and those who are not. That is assumed in the use of relative income standards.

The claim that poverty is *relational* begins from a different set of premises. Social issues are relational when they consist of relationships with other people. Membership of a family or citizenship of a nation is relational. The issues of class and gender are relational. Some of these issues overlap with 'identity', but it is possible to have an identity – such as religious belief, ethnic identity or political conviction – without that defining any associated relationships, and conversely to have certain sorts of relationship – caring, financial dependency or employment – without necessarily accepting an identity as a result.

There is a literature that interprets 'relational issues' in terms of the causes of poverty – arguing, for example, that poverty is structural in its origins. Frances Fox Piven puts it in this way:

> The concept of 'relational poverty' implies a theory or theories about causality. In contrast to prevalent understandings which root economic hardships in the deficits of individuals or families or subcultures, the theory asserts that poverty is best explained by patterns of human relationships, and by the social institutions that organise those relationships. And in contrast to understandings that ascribe hardship to the consequences of social exclusion or isolation, it asserts that poverty is importantly the result of the different terms and conditions on which people are included in social life.
>
> (Piven, 2018, p. ix)

The argument I want to make here goes some way beyond that. Poverty is not just a product of its relational elements; it is in itself a description of social relations. Lister comes nearest to this position, with what she calls the 'relational-symbolic' aspects of poverty. The 'symbolic' aspects, like stigma, humiliation and low self-esteem, occur when people react to poverty by fixing labels on it (Lister, 2004, p. 8). Her argument is still, however, that poverty is 'mediated and interpreted' through social relationships. The case being made here that poverty is actually made up of such relationships.

Most of the competing understandings of poverty outlined here are directly concerned with relationships. Five of the twelve sets of meaning I have outlined are explicitly concerned with social relationships – that is, the position of poor people in relation to other people. Dependency, low status and exclusion are all relationships; lack of basic security and lack of entitlement describe a constellation of such relationships. Class is another relational concept; and moral judgement depends on, and implies, social obligations, rights and responsibilities. That leaves five further clusters of meaning where the relational elements may not be immediately obvious:

- o the lack of specific goods and items
- o the web of deprivation
- o a low standard of living
- o a lack of resources
- o economic distance, which is a comparative lack of resources; strictly speaking, it is relative rather than relational.

Poverty depends on relationships with other people, not just in the obvious and direct ways – in the social, economic and political relationships that emerge in the discussions of the subject – but in those categories too.

The argument is clearest when we focus on money. Money does not have an intrinsic value; it is relative in its nature. That statement goes beyond the familiar point about purchasing power, that prices differ in different places. Money determines how resources are shared, and its value depends substantially on other people. That in turn has implications for resources. The most basic reason why some people are unable to eat, Sen tells us, is that they lack entitlements to the food that is there (1981). Where there are shortages, people with more money are able to outbid people with less; so richer people get the use of housing and land, and exclude poorer people from it. There are 'positional goods', such as education or living in more salubrious areas, where the relative worth of a good is determined by what other people have (Hirsch, 1976). Money is a way of representing relationships, and access to goods, resources and amenities is a reflection of the same relationships.

Conventional welfare economics, and formalized models of social justice such as Rawls's, have been marred by adherence to the misconceived idea of 'Pareto efficiency', the assumption that welfare for all can be said to be increased if at least one person is better off (Sugden, 1981; Kaplow and Shavell, 2001, pp. 281–7; Spicker, 2013). The idea is widely accepted. Despite that acceptance, it is plainly wrong. It is basic economics that prices reflect demand as well as supply – the value of the money that one person has depends on the money that other people have. If some people gain income and others do not, it devalues the income that the others have. The issues of scarcity and allocation even affect money in itself. Davala and colleagues argue:

> In Indian villages, power relations over many generations have solidified conditions of contrived scarcity, generating a rent-based distribution system in which the weaker sections cannot escape. Being a comparatively efficient medium of exchange, money is the most important scarce commodity. It thus has a high price, and those who possess it can exploit those who do not.
>
> (Davala et al., 2015, p. 48)

Money is not just relative, then, it is relational: that is to say, it expresses, intrinsically, something about the relationship between different actors in a set of social transactions. Wherever material deprivation is expressed in terms of monetary resources, it is being expressed as a relationship to others.

The idea of economic distance already has a social dimension. The four other clusters of meaning associated with resources and deprivation – the lack of specific goods and items, the web of deprivation, the low standard of living and lack of resources – might be applied to people living in isolation from society – the struggle for existence. In so far as that is possible, it implies that the terms are not exclusively relational. However, all four are also relational in some respects: both the web of deprivation and a low standard of living call for consideration of relative purchasing power, while the lack of resources, lack of specific goods and economic distance are as much about entitlements as they are about goods. It follows that all the understandings of poverty considered in this chapter can be understood in relational terms. When that is done, the distinction between resource-based and relational definitions collapses.

Relative and comparative concepts are not enough to capture what is being said here. There are at least two sides to every relationship. If the concept of poverty is relational, the character of those relationships cannot be determined simply by knowing things about the person in isolation. That is important for poverty, because so much poverty research does consider poor people as if poverty was an isolated state of being, capable of being described separately from world around it: income thresholds, calorific intakes and asset frameworks are illustrative. It follows, too, that poverty cannot be understood as if it was a definable state of being, determined by the things that people do nor do not have. Much of the literature depends on a common fallacy, that there is a clear and decisive threshold below which people can be said to be poor, and above which they are not poor. So, at the same time as Townsend argued for a 'thoroughgoing' relativism (1979, p. 33), and protested against any idea of poverty as being about a crude minimum, he also accepted the idea that there was an effective threshold: 'individual, families and groups in the population can be said to be in poverty when ... their resources are so seriously below those commanded by the average individual of family that they are, in effect, excluded from ordinary living patterns, customs and activities' (Townsend, 1979, p. 31). If poverty is relational, rather than a description of a state of being, there is no such threshold.

Lawson and Ellwood write that 'Relational poverty scholars counter poverty studies' predominant emphasis on measuring, benchmarking and individualizing poverty through structural analysis of the constitution and reproduction of poverty' (2018, p. 6). The argument in this chapter is constitutive rather than causal – considering what poverty is, rather than why it happens. There is more than one understanding of poverty, just as there is more than one understanding of what constitutes other relational concepts such as class or citizenship. The objection to an exclusively individualized analysis is, however, fundamental. Any attempt to 'bracket off' the concept of poverty from its relational elements – treating deprivation as if it were wholly about the things people actually have – closes off consideration of entitlements, relative purchasing power, access to resources or basic security. The relational elements are only part of the constellation of factors, but leaving them out strips the resources and goods of their social context and economic meaning. Poverty – like class, citizenship or power – is a relational concept.

Social exclusion

The UN 2030 Agenda for Sustainable Development (United Nations, 2015) is strongly focused on the eradication of poverty, but poverty is not the only issue it considers. There are frequent references in the Agenda to the process of social inclusion, both in general terms – peaceful and inclusive societies, inclusive and sustained economic growth, a 'socially inclusive world' – and in more specific contexts, such as calls for inclusive education, financial inclusion or inclusive cities. 'Creating sustained, inclusive and sustainable economic growth and fostering social inclusion are linked to each other and are interdependent' (United Nations, 2015, para. 13). Goals 8 and 9 of the Sustainable Development Goals propose 'sustained, inclusive and sustainable economic growth' and aim to 'promote inclusive and sustainable industrialization'.

The idea that policy should be 'inclusive' might seem, on the face of the matter, to mean only that policy should be widely beneficial. Discussions of 'inclusive growth', for example, have suggested that the criterion will be met if growth is guided to bring people into the economic system; if it leads to a more favourable distribution to people on low incomes; or if growth has inclusive outcomes, improving the situation of poor people both within and beyond the economic system itself (Klasen, 2017). The idea of inclusion is a relative newcomer to the field of anti-poverty policy, and it has been the subject of some confusion; the vocabulary associated with exclusion and inclusion has been applied indiscriminately to a wide range of topics, including inequality, discrimination and pathological accounts of poverty, which are only tenuously linked with the concept. The idea of exclusion developed in France, in the absence of a political discourse about poverty, and it did so in terms which are immediately and directly relational.

The starting point for the concept is neither exclusion nor inclusion in itself, but a fundamental idea which defines them both: the idea of solidarity. The language of solidarity has been part of French social policy since at least the 1830s (long before Durkheim, who reinterpreted the idea for his own purposes). The Napoleonic Code refers to solidarity in the sense of mutual financial obligations, but the term gradually came to have a broader meaning, referring to mutual obligations of all kinds: the Académie Française noted in 1835 that the term 'sometimes refers, in ordinary language, to mutual responsibility, which is established between two or several people. Solidarity binds us together' (Zoll, 1998, p. 2). The term came to feature in French political discourse through the writings of Leroux and Renaud in the 1840s, which was also probably the period when it began to influence Catholic social teaching. Before the end of the nineteenth century, solidarity had come to be the centrepiece of a political movement, 'solidarism' (Bourgeois, 1897).

Solidarity does not mean here, as it might in other countries, common identity and group action. Mutual responsibility is the glue that holds society together. People are born into the solidarities of family and community; national solidarity is built from a complex, diverse set of more immediate or local solidarities. If solidarity only referred to such obligations, however, many people would be left out. Catholic social teaching has sought to modify and extend the sense of responsibility associated with solidarity, covering 'the good of all and of each individual, because we are all really responsible for each other' (John Paul II, 1987). If there is a tension in the idea of solidarity in France, it lies between a narrower concept of solidarity as mutualism, and solidarity as a general responsibility for others.

When the French system of social security was developed, the idea of solidarity was taken to be its core principle: the first article of the Code of Social Security declares that 'the organization of social security is founded on the principle of national solidarity'. The main mechanism chosen to do this was the *régime général*, an attempt to 'generalize' the system by the progressive extension of solidarity to those who are not otherwise covered by mutualized networks. Pierre Laroque, often thought of as the founder of the system, explained:

> Every country, after the war, had the same preoccupations but each responded to them according to its history, and on the basis of the institutions which then existed. We wanted to remain faithful to the French tradition of syndicalism and mutuality. At the same time, we wanted to put in place a unified system, applying to every worker, and to being to all salaried workers, by contrast with social insurance schemes. That corresponded, too, to the movement of solidarity one felt at that time.
> (interview in *Le Monde* 1985, quoted in Chatagner, 1993)

The central problem with that strategy is a common flaw in mutualism; it can only extend so far. The *régime général* continued to expand until the early 1970s, by which time virtually everyone was covered who might be covered by it; and that left out those who were not employed or unable to contribute. The realization that generalization was not going to be enough led to a major change in the direction of policy. This was the situation at the time of René Lenoir's watershed book, *Les exclus : un Français sur dix* (Lenoir, 1974). That book found a word for the people who were not covered by solidaristic arrangements: the excluded. Exclusion referred, in the first place, to people who were left out. The use of the term was rapidly extended, however, to cover other circumstances – and in particular, the circumstances of those who were excluded by design, or shut out, and those who were socially rejected, or pushed out. Already, by the mid-1990s, Palier and Bonoli were complaining that the term seemed to refer to everything – 'poverty, long-term unemployment, public housing, urban problems, various handicaps, AIDS, racism, immigration etc.' (Palier and Bonoli, 1995, p. 682). It was no less true to suggest that the term might also be taken to apply to people with lifestyles that were disapproved of: 'marginality' might mean that people were badly integrated into social processes, but it might also mean that they were deviant. Lenoir himself referred repeatedly to the excluded as *inadaptés*, a word with unfortunate implications that in English might be rendered as 'maladjusted' or 'misfits'; but the better-judged title produced the term that stuck.

People who were excluded had to be brought in to networks of solidarity, or 'inserted' into society. The first use of the term 'insertion' was probably the introduction of the *Allocation d'insertion* for young workers in 1972; it was used again in the law covering disabilities in 1975. It became a major element of social policy with the introduction in 1988 of the *Revenu minimum d'insertion* (RMI), which extended provision to millions of people who were not otherwise covered by the benefits system. (The RMI was subsequently replaced by the *Revenu de solidarité active*.)

This is the background to the adoption of the term more generally in the European Union. The UK government had been critical, for its own reasons, of the use of the term 'poverty'; the European Commission, and the French speaking DG5 in particular, had an alternative discourse to hand. A resolution was passed in 1989 to commit to 'combatting social exclusion' (European Communities, 1989). The Tiemann Report of 1993 gave a fabulously cavalier justification for the switch: 'Poverty is a complex phenomenon, which cannot be defined solely in terms of low income levels. Consequently, the European Community and several of its Member States instead emphasize "social exclusion"' (European Communities ESC, 1993).

In other words, if poverty is too complicated to make sense of, we might as well take on an idea which is even more complicated. Much of this was a response to the objections that the UK government had raised to the idea of 'poverty', but they were no more taken with the idea of exclusion than they had been with arguments about poverty:

> It is very doubtful whether the idea ... of an integration plan for all the excluded is practical, not least because there is no generally accepted definition of social exclusion, let alone reliable evidence about the most effective way to tackle its causes.
>
> (European Commission, 1994, p. 268)

The Commission's approach was based on developing services incrementally, gradually extending coverage, and the insertion of those who are excluded (Chassard, 1992), all described in terms of the promotion of solidarity (European Commission, 1992). In other words, it followed the path laid by French social policy. That belies the idea that exclusion had come to mean nothing at all. As a sophisticated, developed discourse and social model, it clearly justified, and was associated with, a range of concepts and policy actions distinct from the pre-eminent models of responding to poverty.

Poverty and exclusion

The overlap between the concepts of exclusion and poverty is direct and substantial. People write of exclusion when they mean poverty, and poverty when they mean exclusion. For example, Peter Townsend's *Poverty in the United Kingdom* explicitly (and perhaps innocently) describes poverty, terms of exclusion from social activity: 'Their resources are so seriously below those commanded by the average individual or family that they are, in effect, excluded from ordinary living patterns, customs and activities' (1979: 32). However, the advocates of a stronger focus on exclusion have often sought to claim that the idea of exclusion offers insights that a focus on poverty cannot.

> When we talk about social exclusion, we are acknowledging that the problem is no longer simply one of inequity between the top and bottom of the social scale (up/down) but also one of the distance within society between those who are active members and those who are forced towards the fringes (in/out). We are also highlighting the effects of the way society is developing and the concomitant risk of social disintegration and, finally, we are affirming that, for both the persons concerned and the society itself, this is a process of change and not a set of fixed and static situations.
> (European Commission, 1993a, p. 43)

If poverty was to be construed exclusively as an absolute, resource-based concept, and exclusion as a relational one, this might have made some sense. If poverty is relational, the theoretical distinction collapses – as the discussion collapses in practice. The literature on poverty has long been concerned with relational issues and complex inequalities, such as gender, race and disability. Issues of social development and integration have been recurring themes in debates about social support – consider, for example, the focus of the US 'War on Poverty' or material about 'dangerous classes' (Morris, 1994). The dynamics of poverty have not always been given the attention they deserve, but they have been examined in a series of studies (see e.g. Leisering and Walker, 1988; Cellini et al., 2008).

Exclusion is not necessarily equivalent to poverty. Some forms of exclusion take a different form from the issues of deprivation and lack of welfare that have played such a large part in discussions of poverty. There are aspects of exclusion that are distinct from the idea of poverty – relationships where people are socially rejected (for example through the stigma of disability or mental illness) or shut out (through religion, ethnicity or nationality). Conversely, groups who have consistently low status and relationships of disadvantage – relationships of gender and caste are illustrative – are not necessarily excluded.

With that said, the idea of exclusion is centred on relational issues. That means, in my view, that discussions of exclusion have come nearer to capturing the elusive character of poverty than much of the literature on poverty itself. The discourse of exclusion avoids some of the limitations imposed by a restrictive interpretation of poverty as a lack of resources, and it offers a way to escape from the limitations of the conventional model. The European Commission justified its distinctions between exclusion and poverty in these terms:

> The concept of social exclusion is a dynamic one, referring both to processes and consequent situations. ... More clearly than the concept of poverty, understood far too often as referring exclusively to income, it also states out the multidimensional nature of the mechanisms whereby individuals and groups are excluded from taking part in the social exchanges, from the component practices and rights of social integration and of identity. Social exclusion does not only mean insufficient income, and it even goes beyond participation in working life: it is felt and shown in the fields of housing, education, health and access to services .... Social exclusion is thus a multidimensional phenomenon stemming from inadequacies or weaknesses in the services offered and policies pursued in these various policy areas. ... such insufficiencies and weaknesses often combine to affect both people and regions via cumulative and interdependent processes of such a nature that it would be futile to try to combat exclusion by tackling only one of its dimensions and ignoring, for example – de jure or de facto – the essential role played by housing or health in any integration process. Social exclusion affects not just individuals who have suffered serious setbacks, but also groups, particularly in urban and rural areas, subject to discrimination and segregation or victims of the weakening of the

> traditional forms of social relations. More generally, by highlighting the risks of cracks appearing in the social fabric, it suggests something more than social inequality and, concomitantly, carries with it the risk of a two-tier or fragmented society.
>
> (European Commission, 1992, p. 8)

There is scarcely a word about exclusion in this passage that could not have been said about contemporary understandings of poverty, and that illustrates the general point, that exclusion has come to be the principal way in which the relational elements of poverty are discussed.

International approaches

The idea of social exclusion went from France to Europe, and from Europe to the international organizations. Bhalla and Lapeyre (1999) argued persuasively for the extension of the arguments to developing countries in the 1990s; they developed arguments centring on economic, social and political inclusion. A well-informed ILO report approached the idea with some reservations, while seeming to welcome its 'polyvalence and fluidity': 'It is becoming increasingly clear that the concept of exclusion complements that of poverty, which has also been enriched by its dynamic, structural and multidimensional profile' (Estivill, 2003, p. 115). The work of Tony Atkinson and his colleagues on indicators of exclusion was initially done for the European Union (Atkinson et al., 2002), and subsequently extended to the United Nations (Atkinson and Marlier, 2010). For the United Nations, 'social exclusion describes a state in which individuals are unable to participate fully in economic, social, political and cultural life, as well as the process leading to and sustaining such a state' (UNDESA, 2016, p. 18).

Taking this at face value, we can identify three problems with that formulation. In the first place, it assumes that exclusion is experienced by individuals, rather than groups. Second, it suggests that those individuals might be excluded from 'cultural life'. That is possibly clumsily expressed, because cultural exclusion is primarily an issue for people from minority cultures, and as such it is experienced by groups. Third, the UN definition describes social exclusion as a 'state of being' rather than a set of relationships – the same problem as conventional characterizations of poverty.

Beyond the definition itself, however, the UN approach seems to shift the argument to new ground. The key point is in the report's title:

Leaving No One Behind. This is a different approach from the French, or European, idea of generalization, or progressively extending solidarity. The model of exclusion I have been describing is communitarian, not universal (see Rasmussen, 1990). It does not guarantee that everyone will be included, but depends on negotiating inclusion and developing solidarity between the excluded or marginalized person and the groups and networks that have left that person out. Solidarity can be exclusive as well as inclusive; it identifies out-groups as well as in-groups. It can also be inegalitarian. The UN approach offers a way of avoiding those weaknesses. Their interest in inclusion has developed at a time when, however belatedly, there is also increasing interest in the relevance of human rights to poverty. The *Guiding Principles on Extreme Poverty and Human Rights* (United Nations, 2012) emphasize dignity, autonomy and empowerment. Some of the specifics relate to capabilities – shelter, water and nutrition among them – but most are about social relationships: among others, dignity, security, legal status, protection from abuse and violence, participation in cultural activities and public services. Combining universal rights with social inclusion develops a stronger concept than either has previously provided on its own.

Goals and targets

Emphasizing poverty as a relational concept does not mean that we have to go back on existing measures and programmes and start again. It does mean that we need to reinterpret what we have. We have a growing number of instruments intended to describe the conditions of poverty, to report the extent of exclusion and examine the outcomes of policies. Indicators are not measures: as the word implies, they indicate, and we look for signs and confirmatory indicators rather than true and accurate measures of an unknowable core.

To some extent, the SDGs have already taken these issues into account. The SDGs are sprinkled liberally with references both to material deprivation and to issues of inequality. There some elements in the actions relating to people's capabilities that are not directly relational – good health, clean water and sanitation, and clean energy – but everything else is. Hunger and famines, we know from Amartya Sen's work, are the product of lack of entitlement, rather than lack of food. Health care and education are a matter of social organization. Affordability, consumption and production are relative issues.

Recognizing the relational elements of poverty cannot solve all the problems. Poverty is still a complex, multi-headed beast. Ravallion

(2016) has been critical of 'mash-ups' of the figures – they lack the severe elegance that economists like to see in a concept. Whenever multidimensional indexes are constructed, there tends be a process of selection. On one hand, items that are too closely correlated or 'multicollinear' tend to be dropped, because they carry with them a risk of double-counting. On the other, items that seem not be correlated at all are also dropped, on the basis that they do not seem to be describing the phenomenon that is to be studied. (For example, the Index of Multiple Deprivation in the United Kingdom has dropped housing factors, because they are poorly correlated with other indicators of deprivation.) For a study of relationships of poverty, there are more dangers in the latter issue than in the former. Dropping facets that do not tally mathematically runs the risk of excluding issues that matter to people.

The relationships that need to be considered go far beyond economic issues. Poverty is a matter of material, social, economic and political relationships, and for the indicators to be most useful, they need to point in all these directions. There are already many available indicators along these lines, such as the Multidimensional Poverty Index, the Human Development Index and the Access to Nutrition Index. Indicators of inequality – the Gini, the GEI, or indices of health inequalities – are no less relevant, because inequality is itself a relational concept. We need to stop thinking of this range as covering the secondary implications of poverty, and start thinking of it as the stuff of poverty.

Conclusion: poverty and policy

This chapter does not of itself have major implications for policy. Its purpose is, rather, to help the theoretical representation of poverty catch up with the changes that have already taken place in the way that social scientists, agencies and practitioners understand and approach the subject. Twenty years ago, Peter Townsend and many of the leading social scientists in the field published an international declaration, to the effect that 'Poverty is primarily an income- or resource-driven concept. ... SCIENTIFIC PROGRESS can be made if material deprivation is also distinguished from both social deprivation and social exclusion' (Townsend et al., 1997, quoted in Gordon and Townsend, 2000). In the intervening period, the understanding of poverty has changed almost beyond recognition. The complex, multidimensional elements of the subject are widely recognized. The arguments about the social definition and construction of the terms were then hotly debated;

now it is rare to see them seriously questioned. The importance of engagement, and empowering research, has been firmly established. The importance of social exclusion, originally developed as a distinct discourse, has merged with discussions of poverty. New methods of assessing and gauging poverty, such as the Multidimensional Poverty Index and the development of indicators of social exclusion for the European Union, have become commonplace.

However, identifying poverty as a relational concept must have implications for the selection and development of new policies in the future. There are many strategies for responding to poverty: they include poor relief, provision for contingencies where people may be poor, indicator targeting, strategic or 'key' intervention, prevention and comprehensive welfare programmes. Policies which have a limited range – focusing narrowly on resources, ignoring dynamic processes or defining arbitrary thresholds – can still have a beneficial effect. We do not have to understand a topic to have an impact on it, but, in a complex environment, the impact might not be what we expect. For example, conditional cash transfers have had benefits that probably have nothing to do with the conditionality they impose (Hanlon et al., 2010); economic growth has delivered a limited but proportionate impact on the condition of the poor (Dollar and Kraay, 2000); while marketization, though conceived as an anti-poverty policy, has had very mixed effects (World Bank, 1994). Keynes once argued that even war and earthquakes might still be beneficial, if we could not think of a better way to do things (1936, p. 129). However, if we want policies to be more effective, it makes sense to think about what we are doing; and to do that, we need to look more directly at the relational aspects of poverty. If we want to understand why participation, gender-based policies, local ownership of policies and partnership-based strategies have made such a difference to poverty, we need to come to terms with their relational impact. Ignoring the relational elements of poverty can only impede efforts to make a significant and lasting difference to the circumstances of the poor.

References

Atkinson, A., Cantillon, B., Marlier, E. and Nolan, B. 2002. *Social Indicators. The EU and social inclusion.* Oxford, Oxford University Press.

Atkinson, A. and Marlier, E. 2010. *Analysing and Measuring Social Inclusion in a Global Context.* New York, United Nations.

Bhalla, A. and Lapeyre F. 1999. *Poverty and Exclusion in a Global World.* Basingstoke, Hants, Macmillan.

Bourgeois, L. 1897. *Solidarité.* Paris, Armand Colin.

Cellini, S., McKernan, S. M. and Ratcliffe, C. 2008. The dynamics of poverty in the United States: a review of data, methods, and findings. *Journal of Policy Analysis and Management*, Vol. 27, Issue 3, pp. 577–605.

Chambers, R. 1995. Poverty and rural livelihoods: whose reality counts? *Environment and Urbanization*, Vol. 7, No. 1, pp. 173–204.

Chassard, Y. and Quintin, O. 1992. Social protection in the European Community: towards a convergence of policies. *International Social Security Review*, Vol. 45, Nos 1–2, pp. 91–108.

Chatagner, F. 1993. *La protection sociale.* Paris, Le Monde-Editions.

Davala, S., Jhabvala, R., Standing, G. and Mehta, S. 2015. *Basic Income: A transformative policy for India.* London, Bloomsbury.

Dollar, D. and Kraay A. 2000. Growth is good for the poor, Policy Research Working Paper WPS2587. Washington DC, World Bank. http://documents.worldbank.org/curated/en/419351468782165950/Growth-is-good-for-the-poor (Accessed 11 March 2019.)

Estivill, J. 2003. *Concepts and Strategies for Combating Social Exclusion*, Geneva, ILO. http://www.ilo.org/public/english/protection/socsec/step/download/96p1.pdf

European Communities. 1989. *Official Journal of the European Communities.* 89/C277/01. Luxembourg, European Communities.

European Communities ESC (Economic and Social Committee). 1993. Opinion on social exclusion. *Official Journal of the European Communities*, 93/C 352/13. Luxembourg, European Communities.

European Commission. 1992. *Towards a Europe of Solidarity*, Com (2) 542 final. Brussels, European Commission.

---. 1993. *Medium Term Action Programme to Control Exclusion and Promote Solidarity*, COM(93) 435. Brussels, European Commission.

---. 1994. *European Social Policy: A way forward for the Union*, White Paper, COM(94) 333 final. vol 2. Brussels, European Commission.

Gordon, D. and Townsend p. 2000. *Breadline Europe.* Bristol, UK, Policy Press.

Hanlon, J., Barrientos, A. and Hulme, D. 2010. *Just Give Money to the Poor.* Sterling Va., Kumarian Press.

Hirsch, F. 1976. *Social Limits to Growth*, Cambridge, Mass., Harvard University Press.

John Paul II, Pope. 1987. *Sollicitudo rei socialis.* Vatican, Catholic Church.

Kaplow, L. and Shavell, S. 2001. Any non-welfarist method of policy assessment violates the Pareto principle. *Journal of Political Economy*, Vol. 109, No. 2, pp. 281–7.

Keynes, J. M. 1936. *The General Theory of Employment, Interest and Money*, London, Macmillan.

Klasen, S. 2017. Measuring and monitoring inclusive growth in developing and advancing economies. C. Deeming and p. Smyth (eds), *Reframing Global Social Policy: Social investment for sustainable and inclusive growth*. Bristol, UK, Policy Press.

Lawson, V. and Elwood, S. 2018. *Relational Poverty Politics*. Athens, Ga., University of Georgia Press.

Leisering, L. and Walker, R. (eds). 1988. *The Dynamics of Modern Society*. Bristol, UK, Policy Press.

Lenoir, R. 1974. *Les exclus : un Français sur dix*, Paris, Editions du Seuil.

Lister, R. 2004. *Poverty*, Cambridge, Polity.

Morris, L. 1994. *Dangerous Classes. The underclass and social citizenship*. London, Routledge.

Nussbaum, M. 2006. Poverty and human functioning: capabilities as fundamental entitlements. D. Grusky and R. Kanbur (eds), *Poverty and Inequality*. Stanford, Calif., Stanford University Press.

Palier, B. and Bonoli, G. 1995. Entre Bismarck et Beveridge. *Revue Française de Science Politique*, Vol. 45, No. 4, pp. 668–699.

Piven, F. 2018. Introduction. V. Lawson and S. Elwood (eds), *Relational Poverty Politics*. Athens, Ga., University of Georgia Press.

Rasmussen, D. 1990. *Universalism versus communitarianism*. Cambridge, Mass., MIT Press.

Ravallion, M. 2016.*The Economics of Poverty*. Oxford, Oxford University Press.

Sen, A. 1981. *Poverty and Famines: An essay on entitlement and deprivation*. Oxford, Clarendon Press.

---. 1999. *Commodities and Capabilities*. Oxford, Oxford University Press.

Spicker, P. 2007. Definitions of poverty: twelve clusters of meaning. P. Spicker, S. Alvarez Leguizamon and D. Gordon (eds), *Poverty: An international glossary*. London, Zed Books.

---. 2013. *Reclaiming Individualism*. Bristol, Policy Press.

Sugden, R. 1981. *The Political Economy of Public Choice*. Oxford, Martin Robertson.

Townsend, P. 1979. *Poverty in the United Kingdom*. Harmondsworth, UK, Penguin.

United Nations. 2012. *Guiding Principles on Extreme Poverty and Human Rights*. Geneva, Office of the UN High Commissioner on Human Rights. www.ohchr.org/Documents/Publications/OHCHR_ExtremePovertyandHumanRights_EN.pdf (Accessed 11 March 2019.)

--- 2015. *Transforming our World: the 2030 agenda for sustainable development,* A/RES/70/1. New York, United Nations. https://sustainabledevelopment.un.org/content/documents/21252030%20Agenda%20for%20Sustainable%20Development%20web.pdf (Accessed 10 April 2019.)

--- 2017. Work of the Statistical Commission.

UNDESA. 2016. *Leaving No One Behind.* ST/ESA/362. New York, United Nations,

World Bank. 1994. *Adjustment in Africa: Reforms, results and the road ahead.* Washington DC, World Bank.

Wresinski, J. 1987. Grande pauvreté et précarité économique et sociale. *Journal officiel de la République française,* 1987 Vol., No. 6. www.lecese.fr/sites/default/files/pdf/Rapports/1987/Rapport-WRESINSKI.pdf (Accessed 11 March 2019.)

Zoll, R. 1998. Le défi de la solidarité organique. *Sociologie et sociétés*, Vol. 30, No. 2, pp. 1–10.

Chapter 4
POLICIES WITHOUT POLITICS: THE EXCLUSION OF POWER DYNAMICS IN THE CONSTRUCTION OF 'SUSTAINABLE DEVELOPMENT'

Juan Telleria

Introduction: a global agreement that fully benefits all?

The 2030 UN Agenda for Sustainable Development (United Nations, 2015) explicitly affirms that it is a global agreement 'of the people, by the people, and for the people' (Art. 52), 'for the full benefit of all' (Art. 5). Such a strong statement awakens the attention of any critical reader. Is there any political, economic or social formula capable of solving everyone's needs and claims in a way that all interests and principles are equally respected, at least on a basic level? Or is it, instead, a discursive formula intended to present a concrete specific and partial political, economic and social equation as neutral, universal and equally beneficial for everyone? This chapter proposes a re-reading of the UN development agenda intended to answer this question.

This critical re-reading focuses on the implicit philosophical and theoretical premises of the UN development agenda and its content – the seventeen Sustainable Development Goals (SDGs) and their 169 targets. It also includes in the analysis the Millennium Declaration of 2000 (United Nations, 2000). I refer to the 2030 Agenda and the Millennium Declaration jointly as the UN development agenda. The chapter examines essential assumptions and reflects on the limitations that they imply for a proper understanding of complex development dynamics in a multipolar and diverse world. To do so, I draw on the work of Ernesto Laclau and Chantal Mouffe. The critical reflections of these authors about essentialist approaches to social issues offer an adequate theoretical framework to answer the questions above.

The chapter has three parts. Part A explains the theoretical framework that guides the critical analysis throughout the chapter. More precisely, I explain two different ways to theorize and understand social issues, the essentialist and the antagonistic. Part B analyzes the UN development agenda and shows that it addresses social issues following an essentialist approach. Drawing on Laclau and Mouffe's thought, Part C reflects on the limitations of the UN development agenda to properly grasp development issues and tackle them in practice. Finally, the conclusion notes the necessity to find alternative approaches to better understand development issues in a changing, multipolar world.

A. Essentialist and antagonistic approaches to social issues

This section explains Laclau and Mouffe's theoretical framework, which guides the critical analysis of the UN development agenda in Part B. To do so, I pose three theoretical questions – What is 'society'? What is a social subject? How do social subjects organize coexistence? – and I answer them departing from two different ways to understand social and political issues: the essentialist approach, which Laclau and Mouffe criticize; and the antagonistic one, which these authors defend. The contrast between these two approaches offers insights and thoughts that enable a critical analysis of the UN development agenda.

What is 'society'? Essentialism versus antagonism

According to Mouffe, democracy and diversity create societies in which the markers of certainty are dissolved (Laclau, 2007, p. 100; Mouffe, 200, p. 18). Rational argumentation replaces the will of God or the decisions of an authoritative figure – such as a dictator. Hence, there is no law, decision or institution 'whose foundations cannot be called into question' (Lefort, quoted in Laclau and Mouffe, 2014, p. 170). Laclau and Mouffe differentiate two general ways to theoretically overcome such lack of certainty, depending on how society is philosophically conceptualized.

On the one hand, we find *an essentialist understanding of society*, which (explicitly or implicitly) assumes the existence of some kind of essential characteristic present in every member of that society. Uncertainty is overcome by positing a philosophical or anthropological universal certainty – such as a specific rational ability, the will to freedom, specific rights or some concrete cultural elements. Since such essential traits are universal (present in every member), every social subject is basically equal to some extent. The posited essential characteristic establishes a solid foundation to define what society is. In other words, such essence is understood as 'a privileged point of access to "the truth"' and certainty (Laclau and Mouffe, 2014, p. 175).

From this perspective, society is *the realm in which essentially equal subjects coexist.*

On the other hand, we find *an antagonistic understanding of society*. Instead of overcoming uncertainty by positing an essential certainty, this approach accepts uncertainty and contingency as constitutive elements of society. From this perspective, there is no essential, universal and foundational element that would offer privileged access to the truth. Hence, there is no essence that can define social beings and society as such. On the contrary, society is understood to be *the realm in which essentially different subjects coexist.* These general and abstract answers to the first question lead us to the second one.

What is a social subject? Identity and power

Who 'dwells' in the thing we call 'society'? The answer depends on the perspective we choose. From an essentialist approach, the posited essential certainty defines (constitutes) the identity of every social being. If – as contemporary democratic liberal theory does, for example Habermas and Rawls – 'rationality' and 'the will to freedom' are the posited essential, universal characteristics of every individual, a social subject could be defined as 'a rational individual who seeks to enlarge their freedom'. Accordingly, society and social issues are theorized starting from such definition, and every member of society is, at the most basic level, equal.

It is important to highlight that, from this perspective, the constitution of a social subject requires two consecutive steps (consecutive not necessarily in terms of time, but in theoretical terms). *First,* the identity of the social subject is defined: the subject knows what its essential and universal principles and objectives are. *Then,* and only then, the subject opens itself to others and interacts with other social subjects. First, the essence emerges; then social bonds are created. Following the example above, contemporary democratic liberal theory assumes that (first) every individual is a rational being who aims for freedom and who (then) seeks to establish agreements to protect their most essential needs (this is the social contract). The (theoretical) existence of these consecutive steps is necessary to understand how power is conceptualized from an essentialist perspective. Since the first step is internal to the subject, no power dynamics are considered as influencing this process. Only when the subject interacts with others do power dynamics appear. Power is conceptualized as an external relation between two preconstituted subjects.

For Laclau and Mouffe, these two steps are only one: the social subject *is constituted through power relations*. The lack of certainty – the lack of an essential, universal element – impedes the autonomous, inner constitution of basically equal subjects. Society is assumed to be the realm in which coexist different groups with different historical interests, motivations, principles and aims. Accordingly, each social subject (individual or group) constitutes its identity by contrasting these elements – interests, motivations and so on – with others. For example, labour unions are not preconstituted groups existing in the social realm that *then* struggle against other social subjects with different (opposing) interests – the bourgeoisie, capital, the owners and so on. Rather, labour unions are created – are constituted as such – *because* other groups with different interests emerge, and *because* they confront each other through power relations. Unions can thus only be understood through their conflictual, power-laden relationships with other groups.

Accordingly, power is not – as the essentialist perspective assumes – an external relationship between pre-constituted agents that negotiate with other preconstituted agents on the basis of their common essence. Rather, *power is constitutive of social relations* (Mouffe, 2009, p. 99): each agent is constituted by these social – conflictual, antagonistic, power-laden – relations:

> Power should not be conceived as an external relation taking place between two preconstituted identities, but rather as constituting the identities themselves. Since any political order is the expression ... of a specific pattern of power relations, political practice cannot be envisaged as simply representing the interests of preconstituted identities, but as constituting those identities themselves.
>
> (Mouffe, 2009, p. 100)

Again, the contrast between both perspectives takes us to a new question.

How do social subjects organize coexistence? Consensus and politics

Since the essentialist approach assumes that an essential trait makes every social being basically equal, coexistence is theoretically constructed over such a shared characteristic. Although each social subject may have a partly different idea of what a good life is, a consensus might be achieved by invoking such a universal, essential trait. This agreement would represent a win–win solution that, to some extent, benefits all (Laclau and Mouffe, 2014, p. xv). As mentioned above, Mouffe affirms that this is the case of Rawls's and Habermas's work, which is based on 'the rationalist belief in the availability of a universal consensus based on reason' (Mouffe, 2013, p. 3).

Two aspects result from this position. First, it is assumed that such a hypothetical consensus would virtually end social conflicts. As every subject shares a universal essential trait that constitutes their identity, this perspective assumes that there is a specific social order – a specific set of institutions, principles, norms and so on – that fulfils every subject's basic and fundamental claims. Attaining such an order implies – at least on a virtual, theoretical level – reaching a stage where harmony, stability and peace reign. Fukuyama's 'End of History' thesis plainly represents this belief. Second, the definition of a social agreement (a consensus) implies that, once the terms of such an agreement are established, its implementation is a technical (not a political) issue. That is, from that moment on, the debate is about *how to* manage the means and resources to realize the terms of the agreement, not about *what is* the desired aim.

It can be argued that the debate before the agreement is political. However, such political debate would be determined by the universal essential characteristic assumed to be the constitutive element of social subjects. In other words, the debate would be limited since the very essential characteristic shared by every member in the debate would implicitly define the desired end. For example, contemporary democratic liberal theory starts from the *essence* defined above – rational, free individuals – and accordingly defines *the end* as a peaceful, stable society with rational institutions that channel and end conflict, where every member can enjoy a free life while respecting other individuals' freedom. The essential basis implicitly defines the end; and achieving the end means the full realization of the essential basis.

Since, in the antagonistic approach, pluralism and contingency are taken to be constitutive at the conceptual level of the very nature of modern societies (Mouffe, 2009, pp. 9, 19), this perspective posits that there is no basis for a consensus that equally benefits all. The coexistence of diverse social subjects with diverse ideas of what a good life is – different interests, motivations, principles and aims – implies the existence of tensions that can never be fully overcome, but must instead be constantly negotiated in different ways (Mouffe, 2009, p. 5). No agreement can generate a harmonious, stable and peaceful situation: on the contrary, every social order is understood as the result of the conflicting relations and power-laden negotiations between social subjects. That is, every order is the precarious stabilization and consolidation of certain power relations that imply domination dynamics that exclude other possible orders (Mouffe, 2009, p. 104). Hence, the essentialist rational consensus proposed by contemporary liberal democracy theories 'cannot exist' (Mouffe, 2009, p.104). Mouffe concludes:

> When we envisage democratic politics from such an anti-essentialist perspective, we can begin to understand that, for democracy to exist, no social agent should be able to claim any mastery of the foundation of society. This signifies that the relation between social agents becomes more democratic only as far as they accept the particularity and the limitation of their claims .... The democratic society cannot be conceived any more as a society that would have realized the dream of a perfect harmony in social relations.
>
> (Mouffe, 2009, pp. 21-2)

As a result, society, in its antagonistic dimension, is a field in which the creation of an order 'always results from a decision which excludes other possibilities and for which one should never refuse to bear responsibility by invoking the commands of general rules or principles', as liberal theory does (Mouffe, 2009, p. 105). Following Laclau and Mouffe, only by accepting that social life is characterized by antagonistic relations, and by acknowledging that every order benefits some groups to the detriment of others (Mouffe, 2009, p. 136) can we understand *the political as choosing – an exercise of decision – between different (conflicting) alternatives.*

> Political questions are not mere technical issues to be solved by experts. Proper political questions always involve decisions that require making a choice between conflicting alternatives. The political in its antagonistic dimension cannot be made to disappear by simply denying it or wishing it away.
>
> (Mouffe, 2013, pp. 3-4)

From an antagonistic perspective, society is not a neutral terrain in which win–win solutions favour everyone and problems are merely technical (Laclau and Mouffe, 2014, p. xv). On the contrary, it is a terrain where every decision has political consequences, since it systematically benefits the interests and aims of some at the expense of others.

B. The essentialist tenets of the UN development agenda

The following paragraphs analyze the UN development agenda, drawing on the insights and theoretical elements highlighted in Part A. The analysis shows that the Millennium Declaration and the 2030 Agenda plainly reproduce the essentialist understanding of the social, since their legitimacy relies on the assumption of a specific truth; they are portrayed as a universal agreement (consensus) that benefits all; and they reproduce the essentialist understanding of the constitution of identities and power relations.

Development and essentialism

Both the Millennium Declaration and the 2030 Agenda propose practices to tackle social issues such as poverty, exclusion and inequality. Therefore, both documents rely implicitly on an understanding of human beings and social interactions. How do these two documents deal with the lack of certainty that, for Mouffe, is characteristic of plural, diverse, democratic contexts? To overcome such lack of certainty, the UN development agenda invokes *the principles and purposes of the UN Charter as the essential elements* that sustain and legitimize its universalist discourse. The agenda assumes first, that these principles and purposes 'have proved timeless and universal' (United Nations, 2000, Art. 3), and second, that they are the '*indispensable foundations* of a more peaceful, prosperous and just world' (United Nations, 2000, Art. 1, emphasis added). Accordingly, these principles are considered to be '*essential* to international relations in the twenty-first century' (United Nations, 2000, Art. 6, emphasis added), and the United Nations 'the most universal and most representative organization in the world' (United Nations, 2000, Art. 6).

In order to reassert this solid and essential foundation, the 2030 Agenda compares the development agenda with the creation of the United Nations: Article 49 explains that 'seventy years ago, an earlier generation of world leaders came together to create the United Nations', and Article 50 states that 'today we are also taking a decision of great historic significance'.

A universal consensus

Starting from this essential foundation, the UN development agenda argues that win–win solutions that equally benefit all (consensus) can fulfil the interests of every group and create a harmonious society: 'We will implement the Agenda *for the full benefit of all*, for today's generation and for future generations' (United Nations, 2015, Art. 18, emphasis added). Likewise, the signatories of the UN agenda state their aim to 'create a shared future, based upon our common humanity' (United Nations, 2000, Art. 5); to promote 'a culture of peace and dialogue among all civilizations' (United Nations, 2000, Art. 6); to 'implement this Agenda through a revitalised ... spirit of strengthened global solidarity' (United Nations, 2015, Preamble) and to 'embark on this great collective journey [and] pledge that no one will be left behind' (United Nations, 2015, Art. 4). In this way, the world would get to a peaceful and harmonious stage: 'We envisage a world free of poverty, hunger, disease and want, where all life can thrive. We envisage a world free of fear and violence' (United Nations, 2015, Art. 7).

The consensus – the universal agreement – is represented in the Millennium Declaration and 2030 Agenda as a universal 'we' which encompasses all of humanity – what Ziai calls 'a Self (we) which comprises the entire human race' (2016, p. 162). The Millennium Declaration and the 2030 Agenda both start by affirming that 'We, the Heads of State and Government' gather to support the agenda. The 2030 Agenda is very explicit in its constitution of the universal 'we' – recalling again the constitutive moment of the present international political order:[69]

> 'We the Peoples' are the celebrated opening words of the UN Charter. It is 'We the Peoples' who are embarking today on the road to 2030. Our journey will involve Governments as well as Parliaments, the UN system and other international institutions, local authorities, indigenous peoples, civil society, business and the private sector, the scientific and academic community – and all people. Millions have already engaged with, and will own, this Agenda. It is an Agenda of the people, by the people, and for the people – and this, we believe, will ensure its success
>
> (United Nations, 2015, Art. 52)

Thus, the UN development agenda's success relies on the essential assumption that it is a universal consensus owned by the universal 'we' – an agenda 'accepted by all countries' that 'involve(s) the entire world' (United Nations, 2015, Art. 5).

---

[69] For a more extensive analysis of the use of 'we' in the UN development agenda, see Telleria (2018).

The international arena

The UN development agenda recognizes the importance of globalization in the interconnectedness of societies (for example, the Millennium Declaration Art. 5 and 2030 Agenda Art. 15). However, its focus is still on nation states – especially in terms of responsibility and accountability. By doing this, the agenda echoes the essentialist understanding of social agents explained in Part A.

First, the agenda reproduces what Ziai calls a 'methodological nationalism [which] sees each country as a kind of container unrelated to others' (Ziai, 2016, pp. 220–1). Development problems are primarily a national issue. Saith explains that this perspective was strengthened by the UN 'Financing for Development' meeting held in Monterrey, Mexico in 2002:

> Here the US unveiled and established the so-called Monterrey Consensus which effectively and firmly embedded the MDG implementation process within the mainstream neoliberal strategic and policy framework, significantly emphasizing the responsibility of the poor countries themselves in addressing their development agendas, making external assistance contingent on such efforts, and at the same time heavily underscoring the role of the private sector in the development process.
>
> (Saith, 2006, p. 1170)

Indeed, the sixth point of the Monterrey Consensus states that 'each country has primary responsibility for its own economic and social development, and the role of national policies and development strategies cannot be overemphasized'. This new emphasis was plainly adopted in the 2030 Agenda: 'we recognize that each country has primary responsibility for its own economic and social development' (United Nations, 2015, Art. 41). In this way, development is primarily defined as an internal, national issue that *constitutes the identity of each country*: developed, underdeveloped, developing, poor, rich and so on.

Only after this constitutive step – once the individual identity of each country has been defined – do countries open themselves to the international realm. The Millennium Declaration, for example, states that 'we recognize that, *in addition* to our separate responsibilities to our individual societies, we have a collective responsibility to uphold the principles of human dignity, equality and equity at the global level' (United Nations, 2000, Art. 2, emphasis added).

In this way, the essentialist understanding of social subjects and relations is reproduced. Subjects – countries in the international arena – are first constituted on the basis of a shared essential characteristic: the will to develop within the principles and purposes of the UN Charter. Then, depending on such identity, they play a different role within global power structures: some provide resources, others receive resources; some account for social and economic problems within their borders, others do not; some did well in the past and accordingly offer help, others did wrong in the past and need help. As a consequence, power dynamics promoting or impeding development are clearly divided in two groups: internal – those happening within the borders of a country – and external – those happening in the global realm. We can conclude Part B by saying that, as mentioned above, the UN development agenda reproduces the essentialist tenets described in Part A. Part C critically analyzes these tenets, and their consequences, drawing on Laclau and Mouffe's work.

C. A critical re-reading of the UN development agenda

Practically the entire academic work of both Laclau and Mouffe was directed at examining the contradictions and limitations of the essentialist approach with respect to social and political issues. For that reason, their critical reflections – laid out in Part A – offer a theoretical framework to critically reflect on the Millennium Declaration and Agenda 2030 in order to conclude the analysis.

Essentialism and exclusion

Laclau and Mouffe explain that when a political discourse states that its positions are neutral, and that the actual order is beneficial for all and can fulfil everyone's interests and motivations, such a position avoids (and conceals) the political issue: deciding between conflicting alternatives. This constitutes what Mouffe calls 'the paradox of liberalism'. Through this paradox, a political discourse 'eliminate(s) its adversaries while remaining neutral' (Mouffe, 2009, p. 31). In other words, it pretends to include everyone but implicitly excludes alternative political positions.

By affirming that 'it is "We the Peoples" who are embarking today on the road to 2030' and that the UN development agenda is 'of the people, by the people, and for the people' (United Nations, 2015, Art. 52), the agenda reproduces the liberal paradox. It explicitly portrays its positions as a universal agreement, which is inclusive, neutral and beneficial for everyone. However, it thereby impedes the emergence and expression of alternative proposals, and consequently limits the political debate. For example, an agenda 'guided by the purposes and principles of the Charter of the United Nations' (Agenda 2030, Art. 10) *systematically excludes* any political position that would challenge the political limits agreed by the most powerful countries during the second half of the twentieth century.[70] In some cases, such exclusion even generates contradictions within the UN agenda. For example, Article 30 of the Millennium Declaration affirms that 'a comprehensive reform of the Security Council in all its aspects' is necessary to achieve the objectives of the development agenda. However, since the Security Council is one of the key agreements between the most powerful countries to stabilize the post-Second World War international order, that claim was later plainly excluded: the Security Council is not even mentioned in the Millennium Development Goals a year later (2001) or in Agenda 2030 in 2015; moreover, the Security Council has not been substantially reformed since the publication of the Millennium Declaration.

In other cases, exclusion affects alternative diagnostics on global development issues, alternative economic perspectives and analytical approaches, and alternative methodologies to implement and assess the strategy (Briant, 2017; Pogge and Sengupta, 2015; Stewart, 2015). Mouffe concludes that 'Once the very idea of an alternative to the existing configuration of power disappears, what disappears also is the very possibility of a legitimate form of expression for the resistances against the dominant power relations. The status quo has become naturalized and made into the way "things really are"' (2009, p. 5).

In this way, the UN development agenda implicitly presents the institutionalization of a concrete (post-Second World War) structure of power relations as the single alternative within which poverty and underdevelopment can be overcome (Amin, 2006; Ziai, 2011). In other words, this is what Mouffe defines as 'the ever present temptation existing in democratic societies to naturalize its frontiers and essentialize its identities' (2009, p. 105).

---

70 For a longer explanation of this idea, see Telleria (2018).

The implementation of the agreement through technical decisions

Through the paradox of liberalism, the end – the goals established in the agreement, which have to be achieved within the existing status quo – is 'naturalized' – in other words, shown as self-evident, 'the way things really are'. Political, and even philosophical-anthropological, debates – reflecting on what humans are, what society is, what a 'good life' is, and so on – are sidelined. The focus turns into technical debates – how to achieve the end? How to measure the achievement? How to manage the resources? How to coordinate the actors?

'The state is seen as an impartial instrument for implementing plans and the government as a neutral, impartial and effective machine for providing services and engineering growth, while failures of bureaucracy are attributed to poor organisation and lack of training' (Protopsaltis, 2017, p. 11).

Thus, the political dimension of development issues is done away with, and poverty and exclusion are portrayed as a technical matter (Ziai, 2011, p. 31). The UN development agenda plainly represents a technical understanding of political issues: 'Politics operates supposedly on a neutral terrain and solutions are available that could satisfy everybody. Relations of power and their constitutive role in society are obliterated' (Mouffe, 2009, pp. 110–11).

Hence, the Millennium Declaration and the 230 Agenda promote policies without politics. That is, they propose courses of action without a political debate that might call into question the actual international power structures. Any political positions that rejects the status quo are systematically excluded.

Who is to blame?

It is generally accepted nowadays that a focus based on nation states impedes a proper understanding of contemporary complex and diverse global issues:

> Global value chains and supply chains crosscut sovereignty and intertwine different capitalisms and business models. Nation states are outdated as units of analysis in the era of global production networks and network societies .... Processes of nationalization and denationalization, 'bordering' and 'debordering' occur simultaneously.
>
> (Nederveen Pieterse, 2018, p. 182)

As explained above, the UN development agenda reproduces the country-focused logic that sharply divides internal and external development factors and power dynamics, and prioritizes the internal over the external. From this perspective, each country accounts for the political, social and economic dynamics within its borders, and as a result, it constitutes its identity – developed, developing, poor, underdeveloped and so on – in the international realm.

Dividing internal and external dynamics has important consequences in terms of power and responsibility. Focusing on each country's responsibility for its own development issues, the UN development agenda does away with the responsibility of third countries for the internal situation of any country. Thus, the UN agenda's rationale falls into an ambiguous and contradictory logic: the global dynamics that *crosscut any nation state's sovereignty* and generate social, economic and political problems, are to be tackled primarily *within each country*. Accordingly, the agenda implicitly defends that if any country is not developed, it is primarily because it did not do well in the past (internal conditions); developed (more powerful) countries will help in the future by generating the necessary international conditions for development.

This conclusion concurs with the results of Bexell and Jönsson's analysis of the ways responsibility is articulated in the UN agenda. The agenda raises 'global structural inequalities that cause contemporary problems without going into their origins or ascribing culpability to particular agents' (Bexell and Jönsson, 2017, p. 18).

> The documents do not explicitly assign blame in terms of agency or acknowledge contemporary implications or of historical causes of structural problems, such as debt, trade, environmental pollution and climate change. ... Root causes of the problems might not be appropriately acknowledged or understood. As a result, solutions risk addressing symptoms rather than causes.
>
> (Bexell and Jönsson, 2017, p. 20)

Responsibilities for current global problems are blurred. Moreover, this aspect complements the depoliticizing consequences of the technical approach to development issues. By ignoring their political character, the UN development agenda neglects the fact that development practices imply taking decisions that benefit some at the expense of others. Therefore, the responsibility for the effects of such decisions also disappears. The UN development agenda focuses on virtual future possibilities, not on the root causes of the problem.

There is no one to blame, only a universal 'we' that will transform the world.

Conclusion: the necessity of a new approach to development issues

This chapter looks at the Millennium Declaration and the 2030 Agenda through the antagonistic (not essentialist) lens proposed by Laclau and Mouffe, and concludes that the UN development agenda reinforces a single perspective on development issues – which accepts the status quo – and excludes alternative approaches; depoliticizes poverty, inequality and underdevelopment; and blurs the responsibility for the issues that the agenda aims to solve. In relation to the question posed in the Introduction of this chapter, we can conclude that rather than a global agreement that fully benefits all, the UN development agenda is a discursive formula that projects a concrete, partial proposal as universal, neutral and beneficial for everyone.

The analysis conducted above is not a mere theoretical, academic reflection with little to do with the complex reality of everyday global development problems. On the contrary, it is, firstly, a reflection about the most basic assumptions that condition our understanding of development issues, and accordingly *the way we tackle them in practice*. Secondly, it is an invitation to look for 'new points of departure for dealing with the global challenges of the twenty-first century as they expose colonial legacies' and an attempt to 'sensitize scholars to deeply rooted hierarchies and hegemonies in (inter-)actions' (Schöneberg, 2019, p. 98). Not reflecting on these assumptions and their effects could transform our well-intentioned efforts to find a solution into the causes of the problem.

The present world and its global challenges greatly differ from the international issues after the Second World War, when the principles and (especially) the purposes of the UN Charter were defined. After a long bipolar era (the Cold War), and a unipolar period (the 1990s and the 2000s), nowadays 'multipolarity is a given and is noncontroversial' (Nederveen Pieterse, 2018, p. 110). The essentialist approach corresponds to a unipolar or a bipolar understanding of the international realm, where one group aims to show its interests, motivations, principles and goals as universal. A non-essentialist approach, on the contrary, better reflects the complexity and diversity inherent to a plural multipolar world. By assuming the essentialist perspective described above, the UN development agenda watches the present world 'through the rear view mirror, through the lens of a stagnant and declining hegemony' (Nederveen Pieterse, 2018, p. xv).

In the search for new theoretical lenses that let us understand better the complexity of development issues, this chapter is an invitation to rethink global issues through relational and antagonistic lenses. Such a non-essentialist approach focuses on relations (not in essential traits), highlights the power dynamics that constitute the international realm, and enables a pluralist understanding of global issues, where different actors with different and legitimate interests, motivations, principles and objectives coexist. Such an approach would be, in my opinion, more suitable to properly tackle global issues in a multicentric world. Anyway, applying one approach or the other is a decision the observer has to take, and as explained above, every decision is political inasmuch as it benefits some at the expense of others.

Acknowledgement

The author thanks Gemma Craske and Judith Hardt for their assistance with this chapter.

References

Amin, S. 2006. The Millennium Development Goals: a critique from the South. *Monthly Review*, Vol. 57, No. 10, pp. 1–15. https://monthlyreview.org (Accessed 13 October 2017.)

Bexell, M. and Jönsson, K. 2017. Responsibility and the United Nations' Sustainable Development Goals. *Forum for Development Studies*, Vol. 44, No. 1, pp. 13–29.

Briant, J. 2017. Unheard voices: a critical discourse analysis of the Millennium Development Goals' evolution into the Sustainable Development Goals. *Third World Quarterly*, Vol. 38, No. 1, pp. 16–41.

Laclau, E. 2007. *Emancipation(s)*. London, Verso.

Laclau, E. and Mouffe, C. 2014. *Hegemony and Socialist Strategy: Towards a radical democratic politics*. London, Verso.

Mouffe, C. 2009. *The Democratic Paradox*. London, Verso.

———. 2013. *Agonistics: Thinking the world politically*. London, Verso.

Nederveen Pieterse, J. 2018. *Multipolar Globalization: Emerging economies and development*. Abingdon, UK, Routledge.

Pogge, T. and Sengupta, M. 2015. 'The Sustainable Development Goals: a plan for building a better world?' *Journal of Global Ethics*, Vol. 11, No. 1, pp. 56–64.

Protopsaltis, P. 2017. 'Deciphering UN development policies: from the modernisation paradigm to the human development approach?' *Third World Quarterly*, Vol. 38, No. 7, pp. 1–20.

Saith, A. 2006. From universal values to Millennium Development Goals: lost in translation. *Development and Change*, No. 37, pp. 1167–99.

Schöneberg, J. 2019. Imagining postcolonial-development studies: reflections on positionalities and research practices. I. Baud, E. Basile, T. Kontinen and S. von Itter (eds), *Building Development Studies for the New Millennium*. Cham, Switzerland, Palgrave Macmillan, pp. 97–119.

Stewart, F. 2015. The Sustainable Development Goals: a comment. *Journal of Global Ethics*, Vol. 11, No. 3, pp. 288–93.

Telleria, J. 2018. Can we 'Transform our World' without affecting international power relations? A political analysis of the United Nations development agenda. *Globalizations*, Vol. 15, No. 5.

United Nations. 1945. *Charter of the United Nations*. www.un.org/en/charter-united-nations/ (Accessed 11 March 2019.)

---. 2000. United Nations Millennium Declaration, Resolution 55/2 adopted by the General Assembly). www.un.org/millennium/declaration/ares552e.htm (Accessed 11 March 2019.)

---. 2015. *Transforming our World. The 2030 Agenda for Sustainable Development*, Resolution 70/1 adopted by the General Assembly. www.un.org/ga/search/view_doc.asp?symbol=A/RES/70/1&Lang=E (Accessed 11 March 2019.)

Ziai, A. 2011. The Millennium Development Goals: back to the future? *Third World Quarterly*, Vol. 32, No. 1, pp. 27–43.

---. 2016. *Development Discourse and Global History: From colonialism to the Sustainable Development Goals*. Abingdon, UK, Routledge.

Part II

The politics of social exclusion and policies for inclusion

Part II

Chapter 5

AN ALTERNATIVE READING OF THE CONCEPT OF 'INCLUSION': THE BOLIVIAN CONCEPT OF 'COMMUNITY WITH QUALITY OF LIFE'

Nelson Antequera Durán

Introduction

The Agenda 2030 for Sustainable Development is a global plan of action to take on the major current global social-economic concerns, such as poverty reduction, gender equity, sustainable economic growth, overcoming major inequities, peace and security, among others, all of which are transversal to environmental issues. The incorporation of the concept of social inclusion in the Sustainable Development Goals (SDGs) provides a new framework of development, focused on people and sustainability. Social and economic inclusion is seen as the guiding thread of the new global sustainable development agenda (UNDP, 2015, p. 29), seeking to transcend the economistic approach to development by using a dynamic analysis model. This model addresses processes that lead to the exclusion of communities from the benefits of development. From a social development perspective, it places human beings at the centre of development, alongside equality and human rights, and the need to give a political answer to the problems of integration. Social inclusion is a dynamic concept, still under construction, which aims to address the processes and social relations that lead to exclusion or inclusion. This perspective offers an opportunity to rethink the paradigms under which development models are elaborated at a global level, beyond locally produced knowledge and lived experiences.

The aim of this chapter is to debate the concept of social inclusion from a relational perspective. It is based on data collected during research carried out in the city of La Paz, Bolivia, regarding challenges to human development at the local level. We propose that the analysis of the processes of social exclusion in the local context should focus on the provision of care. Family and community are the units of analysis. On the one hand, it is in the family and community that social exclusion and its consequences are manifested. On the other hand, it is within the family and community that the conditions for processes of social inclusion are possible. The paradigm of '*Vivir bien*' ('live well' or 'good living'), also understood as 'community with quality of life', draws our attention to a different interpretation of reality, one that is based on relational analysis, and not merely on access to goods and services. From the relational perspective, we propose an analysis of human development at the local level, based on the concept of integral care, family and community, as privileged spaces for social integration.

It is a challenge for the social sciences to contribute to the discussion about development models and the social policies that arise from them. It is also an opportunity, for and from our disciplines, to take part in the construction of an inclusive and fair society, and also contribute to an improvement of people's quality of life. This reading enables a novel diagnosis and interpretation of social problems, and new social and sectoral policies can be derived that will not only overcome poverty or inequality in statistical terms, but ensure that national and local governments emphasize the creation of conditions that will work to strengthen communities. Thus, inclusive development must be understood as the construction of a 'community with quality of life' and conversely, community as a necessary condition for the quality of life. This refers to a relationship-centred approach: community is related to nature, and it is the relationship between people connected by a shared vision of the world.

Overarching concepts

In this section, we show the central approaches of the concept of social inclusion, human development, the basic needs approach and the relational approach. We discuss the continuities between these perspectives, and the possibility of building an alternative development paradigm that will allow us to face the social and global challenges addressed by the 2030 Agenda.

Human development

The notion of 'putting people at the centre of development' was first proposed by the International Labour Organization (ILO) in 1975 and coined the Basic Needs Approach (BNA). It mainly focuses on human well-being: 'Economic and societal development, says the BNA, is a matter of human well-being, which in turn is a function of meeting certain basic or human needs. We cannot really say that a society is developed unless it promotes a good life for all its citizens and affords them the freedom to choose it' (Crocker, 1992, p. 603). The BNA was the main precedent to the concept of human development, developed by prominent economic theorists, such as Amartya Sen. In 1990, the first UNDP *Human Development Report* incorporated Sen's main postulates:

> (*Development as Freedom*) is mainly an attempt to see development as a process of expanding the real freedoms that people enjoy. In this approach, expansion of freedom is viewed as both (1) the primary end and (2) the principal means of development. They can be called respectively the 'constitutive role' and the 'instrumental role' of freedom in development. The constitutive role of freedom relates to the importance of substantive freedom in enriching human life. The substantive freedoms include elementary capabilities like being able to avoid such deprivations as starvation, undernourishment, escapable morbidity and premature mortality, as well as the freedoms that are associated with being literate and numerate, enjoying political participation and uncensored speech and so on. In this constitutive perspective, development involves expansion of these and other basic freedoms. Development, in this view, is the process of expanding human freedoms, and the assessment of development has to be informed by this consideration.
>
> (Sen, 2000, p. 36)

According to Jolly and colleagues, the ILO's pioneering work on basic needs in the 1970s had helped lay the foundation for the human development approach (HDA):

> Both were – and still are – broad ranging and comprehensive strategies for economic and social development that provide a framework for analysis and guidelines for policy. In some respects, the basic needs approach has the edge in being more easily understandable and readily operational and the human development approach has the edge in having greater breadth of applications and more robust philosophical foundations.
>
> (Jolly et al., 2009, p. 3)

However, since its inception, the HDA has aimed to distance itself from the BNA. Sen himself was critical of the BNA:

> In fact, according to Sen, the BNA has often collapsed into a commodities approach and hence is subject to the criticisms of commodity fetishism. The human need for food has tended to be replaced by a focus on the food needed. Although the BNA recognized in principle that different amounts of the same commodity were needed by different individuals, it tended operationally to define 'basic needs' in terms of (certain amounts of) food, water, shelter, and hospital beds.
>
> (Crocker, 1992, p. 604)

In practice, however, the BNA has prevailed over the central proposals of the HDA. On the one hand, the HDA has been reduced to sectoral aspects such as health, education or nutrition, losing sight of the initial approach proposed by its promoters, which was much broader. On the other hand, although the HDA raises a greater number of indicators to measure human development, these indicators have become ends in themselves. 'In this regard, human development is similar to the basic needs approach of the 1970s' (Jolly et al., 2009, p. 5). Emmerij is more critical about this issue, stating that:

> The idea of basic needs lived on, but without the strategy and the macro-economic framework. What remained were specific items that should be attained, for example, achieving universal primary education by year X or eradicating a certain illness by year Y. This approach has been generalized by the UN in the Millennium Development Goals (MDGs) .... The idea of basic needs returned on the world scene in the 1990s in the disguise of the Human Development reports and approach.
> (Emmerij, 2010, p. 2)

Conversely, the Human Development Report 2016 states that:

> Human development is the development of the people through building human capabilities, by the people through active participation in the processes that shape their lives and for the people by improving their lives. It is broader than other approaches, such as the human resource approach, the basic needs approach and the human welfare approach.
> (UNDP, 2016, p. 2)

To what extent can the concept of inclusion effectively make the HDA transcend the BNA not only declaratively, but also effectively and in practice? Does the concept of inclusion qualitatively change the concept of development that underlies BNA and persists in the HDA? As an attempt to incorporate the efforts of nations to 'leave no one behind' into the SDGs and the sustainability perspective, social inclusion is a key element. Yet if the concept of inclusion is only understood as 'Human development for all' (UNDP, 2016), we will continue with a BNA that, as it has been argued so far, has been and is insufficient in the face of the great social, economic and sustainability challenges that present themselves today. However, we do believe that the concept of inclusion has the potential to become rich, suggestive and transformative by focusing on its relational perspective. It opens the possibility of a qualitatively different understanding of reality and of the processes of development, with regards to the quality of social relationships as a condition to achieve human development, 'focusing particularly on people's capability to choose the lives they have reasons to value' (Sen, 2000, p. 63).

Social inclusion and the relational perspective

Following the paradigm of human development, social inclusion places the human being at the centre of development. Thus, the debate is moving beyond the HDA by premising the social analysis on exclusion and poverty, assuming an analytical perspective centred on social relations. Social inclusion can be defined as:

> A systematic and permanent process of societies to enforce, respect and protect the human rights of all individuals in a society through the guarantee of conditions of equality, regardless of origin social of people. In other words, at the core of social inclusion is the possibility of access to social relations conducive to equality of the freedom of people to be what they want and value in life. This possibility of access to certain social relations is deeply mediated, first, by human rights and by the way in which they are respected and fulfilled by the State; secondly, by the options offered by the market and the legal (in) security that is behind the economic transactions; and thirdly, by ties and relations of collaboration or cooperation that are a basic source of cohesion and social capital of contemporary societies.
>
> (UNDP, 2015, pp. 48–9; translation by the author)

It is necessary to emphasize that this definition introduces the relational perspective as the *core* of social inclusion. From this perspective, social inclusion refers to a processual and dynamic reading of inequality, poverty and exclusion. Social inclusion, as a concept related to development, then requires an analysis of exclusion and poverty (UNDP, 2015, p. 49). Social exclusion refers to those processes by which individuals or social groups are marginalized from access to human rights, citizenship and the goods or services that enable them to have a plentiful life. Social exclusion, therefore, refers to the social relations of structural inequality. The understanding of social relationships and the processes that determine this exclusion is relevant (UNDP, 2015, pp. 51–2).

Sen stressed the importance of the relational perspective as the scope of human development: 'The expansion of freedoms that we have reasons to value not only enriches our lives and frees us from restrictions, but also allows us to be more complete social people, who exercise their own will and interact with – and influence in – the world in which they live' (2000, p. 31). The importance of community (even if defined only as groups) is also emphasized in recent UN publications as a new approach to human development:

> Human development is a matter of promoting not only the freedoms of individuals, but also the freedoms of groups or collectives. For the most marginalized and most deprived people collective agency can be much more powerful than individual agency. An individual is unlikely to achieve much alone, and power may be realized only through collective action.
> (UNDP, 2016, p. 8)

Social exclusion as a process has four characteristics. First, it is a dynamic process – exclusion or social inclusion can shift and vary throughout the lifetime of a person or the history of communities. Second, it is a relational process – it assumes that the relationship of groups or people with the rest of society creates unequal access to resources. Third, it is a multidimensional concept – dealing with different aspects of human development which are interdependent. Fourth, exclusion is a structural process – its causes are located in the structure of societies that generate unequal access to resources, as well as spaces of disintegration and expulsion or marginalization of certain sectors of the population with respect to others. Social inclusion as a common thread across the SDGs means reducing the poverty, inequality and vulnerability of certain social groups. Social inclusion considers not only vulnerable groups, but also the situations that affect society as a whole. In this way, it does not refer to the situation of certain (vulnerable) social groups, but to the relationships they have with respect to society (UNDP, 2015, pp. 33–8). The concept of social inclusion transcends the poverty focus as a stand-alone concept, by including multidimensional poverty and social vulnerability based on a fundamental element – relational analysis.

We believe that it is necessary to approach the analysis from a relational perspective, in order to overcome a notion of inclusion/exclusion understood as an autonomous structure that responds to a cultural or economic 'essence'. Relational models allow the understanding of the forms of social organization made by the transactions that then become social ties.[71] Eric Wolf (2001) proposes a concept of culture understood as part of the structure of

---

[71] Charles Tilly proposes to analyze social inequality from the 'relational models of social life that begin with transactions or interpersonal ties'. Relational analysis allows the treatment of categories of social inequalities as 'social inventions that solve problems and/or byproducts of social interaction' (Tilly, 2000, p. 34).

social relations. The concept of culture then allows us to gather, in a synoptic and synthetic way, material relations with the world, social organization and ideological configurations. The material relationship with the world refers to the capacity to act materially on it, to generate changes that (at the same time) will affect its capacity to act in the future. To act in the world and on the world, people create and use signs that guide their actions and relations with the world and with each other. Relational analysis allows us to understand the weight of culture in social life. By viewing culture as a set of shared notions and their representations, we can also make sense of how actors move within this framework of understanding built on previous interactions, and foresee their reciprocal responses within them. In this way, we can imagine culture no longer as an autonomous sphere, but as part of the structure of social relations (Tilly, 2000, p. 33). In this context, community is understood as the fundamental space for the production (and reproduction) of identity. It is also the space where social relations, interpersonal transactions and the material reproduction of the community take place. Participation in 'the community' implies participation in the economic life, the social organization and the symbolic space in which the representations about the world and society are transmitted and reproduced (Antequera and Coria, 2013).

Methodology

This chapter presents results from research in the project 'Diagnosis of Human Development in the Municipality of La Paz' commissioned by the Municipal Government of La Paz, and carried out between 2012 and 2014.[72] The study has three main parts. The first part analyzed the approach to social policies of the municipal government. Second, a quantitative and qualitative diagnosis was made about the population's situation and their concerns about

---

[72] The research 'Diagnóstico del Desarrollo Humano en el Municipio de La Paz' was carried out by a team of nine researchers, in addition to the research coordinator and author of this article. The research lasted two years (2012 and 2013). The researchers conducted 120 in-depth interviews in all the districts of La Paz. Group interviews were also carried out through focus groups. Other qualitative methods were applied: field observation, and attendance at meetings of neighbourhood organizations. As part of the research, the first two 'National forums for human development' were also held in La Paz. These events were attended by public and private institutions working on this issue, as well as civil society organizations. The results of the Forums and the research were published in thematic volumes under the series name 'Cuadernos para el desarrollo humano' [Papers for human development] (see GAMLP, 2016a, 2016b).

An alternative reading of the concept of 'inclusion' in Bolivia

human development. The third part is a conceptual proposal aimed to assist with a reorientation of the local government regarding its social policy. As part of the analysis to the approach to social policies, a document review was undertaken of the plans and programmes, budgets and reports of the municipality from 2005 to 2012 with respect to human development. Likewise, a diagnosis was made of all the social programmes of the municipality; this included interviews with different social actors for each of the areas of social policy: education, health, social protection, sports, advocacy and childhood services, among others. The people interviewed were local government officials, neighbourhood leaders, beneficiaries of social programmes, and representatives of institutions linked to the social issue. An analysis of the data was carried out according to population segments defined by age groups or vulnerable groups that are defined by the municipal programmes: childhood, youth, people with disabilities, older adults, women and victims of violence, among others. Finally, based on the results found, a conceptual proposal and social policy guidelines were presented as recommendations for policy-makers, synthesized within the 'community with quality of life' concept.

One of the main results of the extensive diagnosis is that a large part of the problems and concerns of the population related to the crisis in care, families and communities. We therefore focus on these issues, leaving aside other social policies, such as health services or educational services. The crisis of care and the crisis of the family brings us back to forms of 'social exclusion' whose expression is violent in all its forms. From these two areas, we base the proposal of 'community with quality of life' as an alternative approach to social policies based on the currently prevalent paradigm of economic development.

Social policy in the Municipality of La Paz

In this section, we briefly present the main characteristics of social policy in the context of the case study. The municipality of La Paz has around 700,000 inhabitants. According to the 2012 Census, basic needs are fulfilled for 55 per cent of the population, while 30 per cent are at the poverty line (although not considered poor) and 14 per cent are considered poor (basic needs not fulfilled).[73] In the national context, the municipality of La Paz has the largest population

---

73 According to the National Institute of Statistics, poverty is defined as the greater or lesser satisfaction of basic needs and not by income. The Basic Needs Satisfaction Index is defined by health, housing, education and basic services (INE, n.d.).

with basic needs fulfilled and the lowest percentage of people living under the poverty line in Bolivia. Social policy in La Paz, as in other local governments of Bolivia, is guided by a conception of development and human development assumed by the Bolivian state in the context of municipalization and popular participation introduced in the mid-1990s. From its beginnings, the concept of human development aimed to shift the emphasis from the economic aspect to the welfare of people as the ultimate goal of development. However, in practice, the human development policy was focused on materially fulfilling basic needs and poverty reduction. Furthermore, 'basic needs' are commonly understood as social infrastructure. As a consequence, social policy was mainly oriented to educational, sports and health infrastructure.

In 2009, the new Political Constitution of the State was approved. It was considered the begin of a new era, a time with great expectations from the majority of citizens who had voted for Evo Morales. The concept of *Vivir bien* ('live well' or 'good living') emerged as an alternative paradigm, based on the recognition of the limitations and failures of the previous models of development. There are at least two central concepts of the *Vivir bien* discourse or model. First, the pluralist nature of *Vivir bien* considers that there is not a single development model or goal to be reached. On the contrary, the goal is to construct certain social conditions that allow all social groups to live with a good quality of life, according to their own conceptions of what well-being means. The second point is the community nature of this paradigm. Learned from indigenous, native and peasant communities, 'community' is understood as an alternative to a centralist and pyramidal organization founded on the sum of individuals whose central reference of identity is the nation state.

However, the practical implementation of *Vivir bien* remains erratic and partial. It has been eroded and replaced by 'economic wealth' and the idea of development as infrastructure. The perception of civil society, as well of municipal administrators, is that more 'cement and brick' would result in the promotion of human development. Another feature of current national and municipal human development policies is their focus on vulnerable groups. In this way, both infrastructure works and social programmes focus narrowly on reducing poverty and serving marginalized populations.

Social exclusion from a relational perspective: the crisis of care and family in La Paz

The most relevant findings of the research are the problems and concerns identified by the interviewees. These are mainly citizen insecurity; intrafamily violence; femicide; human trafficking; violence of all kinds, especially against children; job insecurity; adolescent pregnancy; school violence; the increasing consumption of alcohol among adolescents; the crisis of the family; labour exploitation; the persistence of patriarchy; discrimination; the human costs of emigration, and the lack of opportunities for young people. The citizens' perception of growing 'insecurity' is related to poverty, inequality and labour instability; the crisis of care and the family; the inability of the community to protect its members; and the deterioration of social relations which eventually leads to violence and the feeling of a lack of protection. The crisis of care and family are manifestations of the limitations of the capitalist and liberal development paradigm as it affects quality of life.

The family is regarded as the institution that generates the material and subjective conditions for the survival of successive models of development, founded on capitalism. The reproductive role of the family has mobilized labour forces, particularly female, for the 'production of the producers' and for the reproduction of the same labour force through the bourgeois family model, in which the man fulfils the productive function while the woman is assigned the reproductive function, in particular that of care (Meillassoux, 1975, p. 202). The crisis of care is manifested in neglect by parents (with main pressure on mothers) of their sons and daughters; growing violence; and dysfunctional families – factors which have profoundly affected the family as the fundamental institution of society. This crisis is also one of the deep manifestations of the limitations of the developmentalist paradigm.

In our research, this situation became evident in a large group of families. The data shows that, apart from the 'basic needs met' index, care-givers feel the need to prioritize their role as providers at the expense of social/psychosocial neglect of their children. The people interviewed in the research stated that in order to meet family needs, the working hours of parents extended beyond 12 hours a day. In schools, teachers expressed their concern about the abandonment suffered by children, even though most of their material needs are covered. On this issue, we collected many testimonies, like the following:

> For example, nowadays a current problem is that parents have to spend most of their time at work. Children are left abandoned from 7–8 in the morning to 8, 9 or even 10 at night. The children are left to themselves and do not receive the attention they require.
>
> (Eva Riveros, coordinator of La Paz Foundation, 2012, in GAMLP, 2016a, p. 38)

Parents of different socio-economic status assume that the abandonment of their sons and daughters is inevitable in order to provide the material subsistence conditions for the family.

> I know of a pathetic case from my neighbour. I do not think that she is the only one going through something like this, many women do. This woman was abandoned by her first husband with a baby, then the second husband left her with another child. She kept both children. She holds a professional degree and had always worked before, yet she can no longer find a job and she pays high fees for the children to attend a private school. Can you imagine the pressure that she has, to raise her children and pay the school fees on her own? So, she is a mess. Working in any job she can get, earning what she can. But all that pressure is then taken on the children. When she arrives home, she beats the children and makes their life impossible. In the evenings, when the children should be sleeping, they are yelled at in order to get the homework done, until 2–3 in the morning. It is total chaos, it is happening in many houses, in many lives, to women as well as men, the family crisis is all over.
>
> (Yolanda Gutiérrez, community association, District 1, in GAMLP, 2016b, p. 18)

In the case of adolescents, this problem is similar. Most teenagers spend their time alone, because of nonexistent or deteriorated family relationships. In many cases, teenage girls must assume the roles of caregivers for younger children in the household. The violent relationships between parents, teenagers and young children result in deteriorating family bonds. In many cases, parents go to social services to ask for help since they can no longer deal with their children.

> When parents can no longer handle a relationship or the behaviour of their children, especially adolescents, they come to social services asking for the staff of the Children's Advocacy office to take charge of the situation. They come and say, 'I cannot deal with my son, here he is [my son], you solve the problem.'
>
> (Patricia Fuentes, social services coordinator, South Zone, 2012, in GAMLP, 2016b, p. 37)

Adolescents from an early age consume alcohol, which is an increasingly recurrent and widespread problem. The consumption of alcohol is complemented by the search for emotional referents through the formation of gangs, or early and conflictive courtships.

> Because parents are not present, teenagers go out to the streets, where problems with gangs are started. In many cases, since there is no control at home and because they participate in these neighbourhood groups, children and teenagers begin to consume alcohol at a very young age.
>
> (Eva Riveros, coordinator of La Paz Foundation, 2012, in GAMLP, 2016b, p. 37)

Adolescent pregnancy is one of the most visible expressions of abandonment and violence. It is evident that pregnancy, in a context of deteriorated social and family fabric, only aggravates and reproduces situations of violence, poverty and exclusion (GAMLP, 2016a). The incorporation of women into the labour market has changed gender relations, in many cases resulting in women assuming the productive (provider) and reproductive role at the same time. It is evident that the self-exploitation of women is aggravated by the fact that long working hours are added to the hours of domestic work, something with which men are not burdened (CEPAL, 2010).

In the case of the elderly, poverty is aggravated by abandonment and neglect. In many cases, elderly people go through situations of poverty not only because they cannot generate their own economic income, but because they are victims of mistreatment and dispossession of their material goods by their own family members (GAMLP, 2016a).

Of all these manifestations of violence, there is no doubt that violence against women is currently one of the most serious and urgent problems. In Bolivia, unfortunately, violence against women is almost considered as 'normal', and femicides are increasingly common. The state has only recently succeeded in attempting to legally sanction these cases; perpetrators are rarely held accountable.

In general terms, the research showed that the rupture of family ties does not only result in the abandonment of children, adolescents or the elderly, but also expresses itself in multiple forms of violence. Violence against children is widespread. The increase in cases of mistreatment and even of infanticide that are registered in the municipal social services is worrisome. Sexual violence against children is usually perpetrated by family members and thus often hidden.

> I'll give you an example of a case I had in El Alto. It was the father who raped his daughters. First, he raped his eldest daughter, who had a son, this girl died at 20, so the son was recognized by her mother and the rapist father. The second daughter was also raped, had a son and the same happened, the parents recognized him. The mother of the girls took care of the children. The third daughter was about to be abused, but she had the strength to speak up and the man was arrested. The rapist's wife came to shout at us saying: 'Now you have to provide me with food, what has he done? Yes, he is their father, if he were a stranger, we could complain, but he is their father, he has rights over them.'
> (public servant, temporary municipal shelter, 2013, in GAMLP, 2016b, p. 30)

The pressure experienced by parents to economically and materially support their families has resulted in an inability to provide care and protection. The economic and labour conditions give rise, cause, and at the same time are the cause of the current 'crisis of care'. Care is a fundamental need for the support of life and cannot be abandoned. Families, but especially women, have developed different strategies to cover this need, and our research diagnosed that the main strategy is the redistribution of care. The care of children has been delegated to grandmothers or older sons and daughters. Adolescents and young people are in charge of their own care, while young people are inserted into the labour market more and more quickly.

The predominance of the productive role of families that provides the material conditions for the reproduction of life results from the state's failure to take responsibility to generate these conditions, in addition to guaranteeing rights and basic services. It follows that the weakness of the state in generating conditions and guarantees is leading not only to a process of 'materialization' of family relationships, but also to a negation of the subject. It also makes an integral approach, with social participation of all actors, impossible. Therefore, the recognition of the condition of subject and rights must be understood from the relational and community perspective, and not from one of the individualism of modern citizenship.

All the problems and concerns listed above have been addressed by public policy only in a marginal way, and always from a poverty and social vulnerability approach. Social policy, at both the central and municipal level, has been characterized by its fragmented, sectoralized, focalized and assistentialist nature. These problematic characteristics are aggravated by insufficient resources and the precariousness of social programmes and services (GAMLP, 2016a). The current complex and unfavourable economic and labour conditions result in the progressive inability of the family to provide care and protection to its members. Without the family (in any of its current configurations) as the central and privileged space for the provision of care and protection, it is not possible to think of an alternative paradigm of development in terms of 'communities with quality of life', contextualizing relationality as the constituent element of the community. The community is not an abstract entity, but a significant space for affective, solidarity and identity bonds (GAMLP, 2016a, p. 60).

Community and quality of life

The analysis of the data has shown that the social problematic transcends the BNA. It shows us that the main social problems are not only related to infrastructure or public services. The current development model and economic policy have a deteriorating impact on the social fabric. Relational analysis allows us to understand the weight of culture in social life. By comprehending culture as a set of shared notions and their representations, we can recognize how actors move within this framework of understanding (built from previous interactions) and foresee their reciprocal responses within them. In this way, we can imagine culture no longer as an autonomous sphere, but as part of the structure of social relations (Tilly, 2000, p. 33).

The first dimension of relational analysis is the relationship with the world. It refers to those material resources that make it possible for children, in the present and in the future, to live a long and healthy life, have access to education, have a good standard of living, participate actively in their community and in the decisions that affect their lives, according to their own conceptions of a good life. From this perspective, health services, drinking water, appropriate housing conditions, protection or care services, among others, are necessary conditions in order to overcome situations of poverty and abandonment. However, from the capabilities approach, it is not enough to 'make these services available' to the impoverished population; it will be necessary to develop the community's capabilities in order to ensure that their needs and aspirations are met effectively.

The second aspect of the relationship with the world has to do with the relationship with nature. The quality of life approach implies the enjoyment of a healthy natural environment, direct contact with nature, access to clean water, clean air, and adequate and healthy food. From the relational perspective, we state that the quality of life, in the sense of human development, *Vivir bien*, social inclusion, and so on, must be understood, fundamentally, as the quality of social relationships. Community and community identity are built within social relationships, in the way that people participate within the social set. Economic development – access to goods – does not in itself lead to a better quality of social relations, although it is true that unequal economic development generates marginality, poverty, violence and social disintegration.

The increase in the rates of abandonment, insecurity, and violence in all its expressions and in all areas, is a symptom of a deterioration in the quality of social relations. In the diagnosis, we saw that the crisis of care is characterized by the deterioration of these relationships of affection, care and attention that are fundamental for the development of the human being. In a word, income poverty expresses itself as violence and neglect.

The third dimension of relational analysis has to do with culture in its broad sense; that is, with the explanatory framework that determines economic transactions and social interactions. Pluralism has great value in a society as diverse as that of Bolivia. This paradigm questions the hegemonic conception of development. The vision of development of any community will be determined by what that community decides it wants to develop into. In this way, the community is a space for freedom, of the possibility that its members live a life they have reason to value. Returning to the approach to freedoms, we can say that the development of capacities and expansion of opportunities should aim to be part of the relationship with the world, in social relations and in the construction of a common horizon of understanding the world (Antequera and Coria, 2013).

Social inclusion from a relational perspective: a proposal

As mentioned above, social inclusion is central to the SDGs as an attempt to incorporate the social perspective into the concept of sustainability. The concept of inclusion refers to the efforts of nations to 'leave no one behind'. It is a suggestive metaphor which alludes to a development model that generates an economy that provides basic services for everyone.

The research presented in this chapter argues that quality of life should be understood as the quality of relationships, and within communities as the conditions that ensure a good or better quality of life. We therefore propose a concept of inclusion that, in addition to its quantitative relevance, has a major qualitative attribute: the existence of community as a condition for inclusion. Community is understood as a social construction, which involves investment of time and resources. We have found in our study that the crisis of the family, care and community poses a complex problem, and is marginalized in public policies. Building – implicitly – on the BNA, the 'inclusive' character of economic, health or education policies is relegated to quantitative connotations. These policies are implemented aiming to reach those groups excluded from the benefits of development.

From a relational approach, the notion of inclusiveness can acquire a different connotation. Inclusive economic development, inclusive social policy, environmental sustainability and the construction of peace and security – dimensions of sustainable development proposed by the Agenda 2030 – aim at the universality of access to goods and services, but should also address the construction of social conditions that allow all social groups to live a life of quality according to their own conceptions of development and well-being.

Social inclusion is also linked to the human rights approach: 'Access to opportunities and capabilities that the human development perspective claims is directly linked to the possibilities of social inclusion from a human rights perspective' (UNDP, 2015, p. 43, translation by the author). Social conditions allow crucial interactions to take place in order to create interpersonal bonds that enable quality of social relations, the construction of a common and collective project, and a sustainable and harmonious relationship with the environment. Strong and healthy families and communities are preconditions for quality relationships and therefore for a good quality of life. However, from the relational perspective, family and community are historically contingent areas. The community (and family as a community) can either be strengthened, made cohesive, addressed as a political project, or on the contrary weakened and disintegrated. Therefore, relationships within the community need to be oriented to the construction of common values, and the strengthening of the capacities in order to collectively *make community* – in other words, to make the community a family (Antequera and Coria, 2013).

The family, as the smallest unit of the community, 'is considered, because of the few emotional bonds it preserves, as one of the last bastions of individual freedom, a very fragile one, however, because nothing predestines it to resist the corrosion of monetary relationships' (Meillassoux, 1975, p. 203). Faced with the destruction of the family, and all the affective and identity bonds that take place within it, we risk a sort of modern revival of slavery, where capitalism is the substitute for affective and identity bonds: 'for the savagery of absolute profitability, last form of the metamorphosis of human beings into capital, of their strength and intelligence into merchandise and of the "wild fruit of women" in investment' (Meillassoux, 1975, p. 203).

From this perspective, the family as the immediate affective and identity referent of its members will need to be the privileged and central environment from which a community can be built in which all its members are recognized, cared for and protected. Therefore, social inclusion should be understood from the relational and community perspective, and not from the individualism of modern citizenship. The state, and in our case study, local government, must assume the responsibility as a central actor in the construction of a society that protects and cares for its members, recognizing the importance of family and community. If the absence or deficiency of quality of life is a consequence of the deterioration of relationships and therefore of the community, it will be necessary that public policies and social programmes are ultimately oriented to strengthening the community at all levels.

Conclusions

The concept of social inclusion is central to the SDGs as an attempt to incorporate the social perspective into sustainable development. Social inclusion refers to the efforts of nations to 'leave no one behind'. It has been emphasized that quality of life should be understood as the quality of relationships and the community as the condition for a good (and better) quality life to be possible. We propose a concept of inclusion that, in addition to its quantitative attributes, has a qualitative approach: community as the condition for inclusion. We have shown that the crisis of family and care is a central problem for the construction of 'communities with quality of life' and yet this crisis is marginalized from public policies.

The paradigm of *Vivir bien* ('live well' or 'good living') leads us to a different reading of reality, based on a relational analysis – the role of community – beyond the material access to goods and services. From our interpretation of social problems, it is possible to outline new social and sectoral policies and recommendations for policy-makers: development must be understood as the construction of 'community quality of life'. A relationship-centred approach looks at the way people relate to each other with a shared vision of the world, and at the ways community is related to nature. This debate is not just an analytical, but a political challenge. In summary, we problematized the concepts of development, inclusion and exclusion based on a relational paradigm, allowing us to advance towards the SDGs through the 'the possibility of living better together'.

References

Antequera, N. and Coria, I. 2013. *Comunidad con calidad de vida. El desarrollo humano en el contexto municipal.* [Community with quality of life. Human development in the municipal context]. La Paz, Cuadernos para el Desarrollo Humano [Papers for human development], La Paz Municipal Government.

CEPAL (Comisión Económica para América Latina). 2010. *Tiempo total de trabajo (remunerado y no remunerado).* [*Total work time (paid and unpaid)*]. Santiago, CEPAL. https://oig.cepal.org/sites/default/files/tiempototaltrabajo.pdf (Accessed May 2018.)

Crocker, D. 1992. Functioning and capability: the foundations of Sen's and Nussbaum's development ethic. *Political Theory*, Vol. 20, No. 4, pp. 584–612.

Emmerij, L. 2010. The Basic Needs Development Strategy, background paper, World Economic and Social Survey. www.un.org/en/development/desa/policy/wess/wess_bg_papers/bp_wess2010_emmerij.pdf (Accessed March 2018.)

GAMLP (Gobierno Autónomo Municipal de La Paz, La Paz Municipal Government). 2016a. *El cuidado integral: la recreación de la vida en la comunidad* [Integral care: the recreation of life in the community], Cuadernos para el Desarrollo Humano [Papers for human development]. La Paz, GAMLP.

–––. 2016b. *Protección social comunitaria. Acciones y desafíos en el ámbito local* [Community social protection. Actions and challenges at the local level]. Cuadernos para el Desarrollo Humano [Papers for human development]. La Paz, GAMLP.

INE (National Institute of Statistics). n.d. webpage: www.ine.gob.bo/index.php/podreza-desarrollo/introduccion-3?highlight=WyJiXHUwMGUx-c2ljYXMiXQ== (Accessed 19 March 2019.)

Jolly, R., Emmerij, L. and Weiss, T. G. 2009. The UN and human development, UN Intellectual History Project, Briefing Note 8, July. www.unhistory.org/briefing/8HumDev.pdf (Accessed March 2018.)

Meillassoux, C. 1975. *Mujeres, graneros y capitales [Women, Granaries and Capitals].* Mexico, Ed. Siglo XXI.

Sen, A. 2000. *Development as Freedom.* New York, Alfred A. Knopf.

Tilly, C. 2000. *La desigualdad persistente* [Persistent Inequality]. Buenos Aires, Manantial.

UNDP. 2015. *Inclusión social: marco teórico y conceptual para la generación de indicadores asociados a los Objetivos de Desarrollo Sostenible*. Mexico, UNDP. https://evalsdgs.files.wordpress.com/2017/04/012-ods-final.pdf (Accessed May 2017.)

---. 2016. *Human Development Report 2016: Human Development for Everyone*. New York, UNDP. http://hdr.undp.org/sites/default/files/2016_human_development_report.pdf (Accessed May 2018.)

Wolf, E. 2001. *Figurar el poder: ideologías de dominación y crisis* [Envisioning Power. Ideologies of Dominance and Crisis]. Mexico D.F., CIESAS.

Chapter 6
SOCIAL GROWTH AND SOCIAL TRANSFORMATION: EXPERIENCES FROM THE CARIBBEAN

Aldrie Henry-Lee

Introduction

> If you fail to plan, you are planning to fail!
>
> Benjamin Franklin

As 2030 steadily approaches, developing countries have to redouble their efforts at fulfilling the Sustainable Development Goals (SDGs). Further, there is need to ensure that 'no one is left behind' and that social disparities are not widened. A concerted effort must be made to implement policies and programmes that can secure the best results. Given the specific vulnerabilities of small island developing states (SIDS), and their susceptibility to external shocks, only careful and thoughtful planning will ensure some measure of success in the fulfilment of the SDGs and a better rate of accomplishment than was achieved for the Millennium Development Goals (MDGs).

Strategic planning is essential to ensure the fulfilment of the SDGs. Strategic planning may be defined as 'A "big picture" approach that blends futuristic thinking, objective analysis, and subjective evaluation of values, goals, and priorities to chart a future direction and courses of action to ensure an organization's vitality, effectiveness, and ability to add public values' (Poister, 2010, p. 247).

This chapter examines social exclusion in two developing counties in the Caribbean, Jamaica and Haiti. The two countries were chosen for their varying Human Development Index (HDI) scores, cultural and social histories. Despite its higher HDI (0.719), Jamaica shares many of the same problems as Haiti, the poorest country in the Western hemisphere, with the lowest HDI (0.483) (UNDP, 2018c). Social transformation is urgently needed if these countries are to fulfil the 2030 Agenda. Unless there are radical changes at the macro, meso and micro levels, these nations and many of their citizens will remain on the peripheries of developmental change. For 'no one to be left behind' there must be a transformative shift of focus, from economic growth to social growth, and human rights and social needs must be placed at the centre of the policy process. Then and only then, will the SDGs have the slightest chance of being fulfilled before or even after 2030.

Using secondary data, the chapter seeks to answer the following questions:
- o Who are the socially excluded groups in Jamaica and Haiti?
- o What are the causes of their social exclusion?
- o How can they be 'socially included' in the development agenda in their countries?

A review of the literature

The debate continues about what constitutes social exclusion. While we do not engage in an in-depth theoretical debate of the dimensions of social exclusion, a brief review of the literature supports the definition of social exclusion used in this chapter.

There are several definitions of social exclusion. One states that 'social [exclusion] is exclusion based on the idea of denial of equal access to opportunities. Under any explanation for the causes of social exclusion or any of the mechanisms through which the effects of social exclusion are experienced, such denial of access results in geographic exclusion, economic exclusion, and denial of citizenship' (Funkhouser et al., 2002, p. 6). Others state that social exclusion is a form of discrimination which occurs when people are wholly or partly excluded from participating in the economic, social and political life of their community, based on their belonging to a certain social class, category or group (PACS, n.d.).

Some researchers grapple with the term 'social exclusion'. Farrington (2002), for example, outlines two categories of criticisms: definitional and socio-economic concerns. He cites Atkinson (1998), noting that social exclusion can mean 'all things to all people' (in Farrington, 2002, p. 8), especially since there are 'as many theories of social exclusion as there are writers on the subject' (Atkinson, 2000, cited in Farrington, 2002, p. 8).

The concern for Farrington (2001) is that the concept of social exclusion in itself may perpetuate theories and actualities of underclass. Citing Silver (1994, p. 545), he noted that this class hostility may breed 'a social boundary or a permanent division between the "ins" and "outs"'. He also notes of course the possibility that social exclusion discourse could 'ghettoize' the risk categories with new labels, and has the potential of publicizing the more spectacular of cumulative disadvantages, thus distracting the attention from the general rise in equality, unemployment and even family dissolution (Silver, 1994, p. 540, cited in Farrington, 2001).

Keller (2014), in analyzing the evolution of social exclusion, pointed to Touraine's (1992) understanding of the concept of social exclusion as a 'state' or condition. This understanding was challenged by Castel (1995, cited in Keller, 2014) as it did not examine the dynamics of social exclusion, or account for causal mechanisms. Castel further noted that it is misleading to label every situation of imbalance as social exclusion; exclusion by no means implies that 'people are located outside society, deprived of all their rights and absolutely separated from it' (Castel, 1995, cited in Keller, 2014, p. 26).

For our analysis, we posit that social exclusion is a denial of rights, and may be a deliberate or unintentional process of discrimination, or of limiting access to social goods and services considered valuable in the society. Social exclusion is both a process and an outcome. Data show that high levels of social exclusion exist in Jamaica and Haiti.

Social inclusion, the opposite of social exclusion, focuses on equality of outcomes for all. It also entails a deliberate implementation of strategies to provide opportunities for all in the social, economic and political processes in their societies.

The UN agendas: frames for social development

SIDS like Jamaica and Haiti first gained attention in 1992 at a global UN conference. The conference participants highlighted the vulnerability of some nations to global warming and sea level rises. In 1994, the UN Conference on the Sustainable Development of Small Island Developing States adopted a programme to deal with the needs of SIDS. The programme, called the Barbados Programme of Action (United Nations, 1994), outlined strategies to deal with climate change and sea-level rise, natural and environmental disasters, energy resources, tourism, biodiversity, marine resources, transport and communications, and science and technology. Specific actions were agreed to be taken at the national, regional and international levels in support of the SIDS.

When, two decades later, 2014 was declared the International Year of Small Island Developing States, these countries received special attention. There had been two other sessions on small states, in 2002 in Johannesburg and in 2005 in Mauritius. In 2010, the United Nations called for a review of the progress made in the implementation of the Mauritius Strategy, and in 2014, the international conference of small states held in Samoa reaffirmed efforts to achieve sustainable development. It was advocated that SIDS would need to promote sustained, inclusive and equitable economic growth, create greater opportunities for all, reduce inequalities, raise basic standards of living and foster equitable social development (United Nations, 2014). In the 2014 Samoa International Conference on SIDS, there was a reaffirmation of a commitment to the sustainable development of SIDS through a broad alliance of people, governments, civil society and the private sectors (United Nations, 2014). However, the proposed strategies are difficult to implement given the current social and economic challenges that confront SIDS.

Since the adoption of the Barbados Programme of Action (United Nations, 1994), and other international agreements, the vulnerability of SIDs such as Jamaica and Haiti has not decreased significantly. Given the very nature of SIDS, economic development with equitable social development has been elusive for them. Their characteristics impede their sustained development and the fulfilment of the SDGs. They continue to suffer from many problems, such as the increasing negative impacts of climate change on the islands, growing national debt and income inequality, and weakening competitiveness in the main economic sectors, tourism and financial services.

Before the SDGs, the world's attention was focused on the fulfilment of the MDGs by 2015. The MDGs however raised many questions and received much criticism, such as:

o Why had these particular goals and targets been chosen rather than others (Kanbur, 2004, cited in Khoo, 2005, p. 47)?
o How were the different goals and targets to be prioritized since difficult allocative decisions would have to be taken (Kanbur, 2004, cited in Khoo, 2005, p. 47)?
o Goal 8 on Global Partnership was seen not as an end, but as a means for achieving the other goals (Kanbur, 2004, cited in Khoo, 2005, p. 47).
o The MDGs, being donor-led, paid little attention to local contexts, effectively penalizing and stigmatizing the poorest countries where achieving the goals was a greater challenge (Easterly, 2009, in Melamed and Scott, 2011, p. 2).
o The MDGs missed out on critical dimensions of development such as climate change, the quality of education, human rights, economic growth, good governance and security (Vandemoortele and Delamonica, 2010, in Melamed and Scott, 2011, p. 2).

- o The MDGs neglected the poorest and most vulnerable since they were based on average progress at a national or global level (Holmes and Jones, 2010, in Melamed and Scott, 2011, p. 2).
- o The MDGs failed to take into account the initial conditions of the various regions and counties, that is, the difference in effort countries would need to make in order to make the same relative degree of progress (United Nations, 2012, p. 8).
- o The MDG agenda was not explicit about the perceived structural causes of poverty and social exclusion or in regard to strategies and policy actions necessary to address the structural causes to facilitate achievement (United Nations, 2012, p. 8).

However, the MDGs provided consensus on an international agenda. Moreover, some progress in their fulfilment was made (for instance in MDG 1, reduction in extreme poverty).

In September 2015, the United Nations committed to the SDGs to replace the MDGs. There are seventeen SDGs, which aim to end poverty, fight inequality and injustice, and tackle climate change by 2030. However, criticisms of the SDGs have also been expressed:

- o The goal on poverty requires further specification to address the provision of basic income and social protection to eliminate extreme poverty, as well as effective and equitable processes of wealth creation and distribution, employment and insurance in the present and the future (Deacon and St Claire, 2015, in International Council for Science, 2015, p. 18).
- o Additional dimensions should be considered for SDG 4 (Inclusive and Equitable Education) to address the problem that most educational policies and programmes do not yet reflect the purposes and goals of sustainable development (Sterling, 2015, in International Council for Science, 2015, p. 30). For example, lifelong learning is core to the UNESCO approach, but has not been emphasized in the SDGs.

Regardless of the criticisms of the SDGs, these current goals shape the way the world focuses on social development. While the increased policy attention is laudable, the historical analysis suggests that the shaping of the global developmental agenda begins in the developed countries. While the developing countries are members of the United Nations, they are not economic powers, and very few of these international commitments and conventions have been initiated in the developing world.

Whether the policy focus derives from the MDGs or the SDGs, the SIDS and other small developing countries have great difficulty meeting these goals. Further, neoliberalism has been detrimental for these countries. What is needed is a new global paradigm shift. Social growth and social transformation are key to sustainable development worldwide, and are needed to ensure that inclusive development for all, especially socially excluded groups, becomes a reality.

One approach that uses the term 'social growth' is the Friedrich-Ebert Foundation (FES) proposal for a progressive economic policy model. This model combines a concept of prosperity for all with sustainability and justice. While the approach is focused on Germany, the drafters position the model as a means to overcome economic and social crisis via social, and therefore fairly structured, growth. Its indirect aim is to alleviate environmental and political crises worldwide (Friedrich Ebert Stiftung, 2012). Social growth focuses on education, health care and climate protection, and would deliver the results that people expect from democratic politics, namely jobs and a share in the prosperity these jobs create (Friedrich Ebert Stiftung, 2012).

This is similar to the Nordic model. Some of the principal features of the Nordic model include:

> A comprehensive welfare state with an emphasis on transfers to households and publicly provided social services. The incentives and the balance between entitlements and obligations must support a high rate of labour force participation. Shared attributes of the Nordics include a large welfare state, a particular set of labour market institutions and a high rate of investment in human capital. A lot of public and/or private spending on investment in human capital, including child care and education as well as research and development (R&D); and a set of labour market institutions that include strong labour unions and employer associations, significant elements of wage coordination, relatively generous unemployment benefits and a prominent role for active labour market policies.
>
> (Andersen et al., 2007, pp. 13–14)

Social growth and emphasis on climate change

There are several definitions of social transformation, and it is both a process and an outcome which will result in social inclusion and social justice. For this chapter, we define social transformation as the necessary changes at the macro, meso (institutional) and micro levels to bring about social growth and equitable sustainable development. Social transformation and social justice are intricately linked: social transformation is key to the fulfilment of the SDGs.

'Justice is fairness or reasonableness, especially in the way people are treated or decisions are made. Our account of justice stresses the fair disbursement of common advantages and the sharing of common burdens' (Gostin and Powers, 2006, p. 2). Social justice can also be defined as justice in terms of the distribution of wealth, opportunities and privileges within a society (Oxford Living Dictionaries, n.d.). Social justice is the ultimate result of the attainment of equitable social growth and the fulfilment of the SDGs.

Methodological approach

In order to answer our research questions, we draw on secondary data. Research on Jamaica and Haiti is plagued by the paucity of relevant and recent data. The chapter offers data as available on the socio-economic and climate situation in both countries. It then provides examples of the disparities that exist among the poor and non-poor in both countries, and within the group of the economically poorest. The data used include national sources as well as studies and reports from international agencies.

Our review of the literature indicated that opportunities and challenges exist at the macro, meso and micro levels in developing countries. If equal opportunities and outcomes are to be obtained so that citizens in developing countries can enjoy social inclusion, then social transformation at all levels of the societies is imperative. The conceptual framework for this chapter was therefore developed based on the themes emerging from the literature review.

Acceleration of progress for all social groups in the society necessitates involvement of both external international and internal institutions. Through social transformation at the macro, meso and micro levels, social exclusion could be eradicated, and social growth, social inclusion and social justice could be attained for all *(Figure 6.1)*. The macro level refers to the international context and the economic and social global environments. The meso level is more localized, and includes the role of institutions in the development of social exclusion or inclusion; the economy, the social policy context and the legal and justice systems form part of the meso level. The micro level includes phenomena and processes in the communities and households in society.

Figure 6.1 Social transformation and social growth

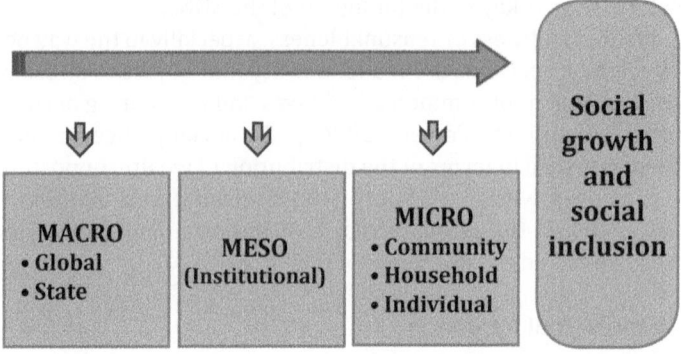

Social exclusion experiences: the cases of Jamaica and Haiti

Universal social inclusion is especially difficult to attain in countries such as Jamaica and Haiti. These countries, like many other SIDS, are characterized by significant susceptibility to economic and environmental shocks, small labour markets compounded by limited skilled labour and high unemployment, limited productive sectors and heavy reliance on imports; tourism as a driving force of the economy, an impending large increase in the size of the elderly population, and high levels of poverty and inequality (Williams et al., 2013, p. 9). These features hinder progress in the fulfilment of the SDGs.

SIDS and other small developing countries therefore need special global attention if they are to fulfil the UN 2030 Agenda. As SIDs, Jamaica and Haiti face enormous challenges as they attempt to reduce social exclusion among their citizens: social exclusion is a daily experience for thousands of Haitians and Jamaicans. The residents in rural and urban poor areas in Haiti and in 'garrison' communities in Jamaica are examples of socially excluded groups who are at risk that they will not see the SDGs achieved in their communities.

The challenging socio-economic background

Socio-economic conditions have generally improved in the last decades in Jamaica, while many advances were wiped out by the recurrent natural disasters and other challenges in Haiti. In both countries, nevertheless, large groups of persons remain who are not socially included and who do not benefit from whatever development process may be available.

Jamaica boasts a high HDI of 0.762; Haiti is in the group of countries recording a low HDI, at 0.493 (*Table 6.1*). [74] Nevertheless, the two countries share many vulnerabilities.

Levels of inequality are high, with Haiti recording an extremely high Gini coefficient of income inequality at 0.6079, and Jamaica a considerable level of 0.4546 (*Table 6.1*). Almost 60 per cent of the population in Haiti live on US$2 or less a day, and stark disparities persist, with the richest 20 per cent of households holding 64 per cent of total income in the country (World Bank, 2014). Poverty rates are higher in the rural areas (World Bank, 2014). Haiti also continues to be battered by high levels of violence in the urban poor areas and frequent natural disasters, jeopardizing sustainable growth (see *Box 6.1*). In Jamaica, poverty affects 21 per cent of the population (*Table 6.1*), despite its marginally less volatile environment.

Box 6.1 Facts about poverty in Haiti

1	Even before the earthquake of 2010 hit, 1.9 million people were in need of food assistance. Around 60 per cent of the population live on less than US$1.00 a day. As a result, malnutrition and anaemia run rampant. Haiti is the third hungriest country in the world.
2	Only 50 per cent of the people have access to an improved water source, such as a hand pump or a well. This means that most of the population depend on lakes, streams and rivers for their water, regardless of the cleanliness. Even if some people can get access to better water than others, a total of 80 per cent do not have adequate sanitation available. So, even if they run less risk of becoming ill from bad water, they are unable to clean themselves and are susceptible to disease and infection.
3	Only 50 per cent of children living in Haiti are able to go to school, while 30 per cent of those only progress to the fifth grade. As a result, half of Haitians are illiterate. Without a proper education, the people are unable to break free of the cycle of poverty.
4	Haiti is the poorest country in the world, with a poverty rate of 77 per cent, closely followed by Guinea with a 76.7 per cent poverty rate. The World Bank estimates that the earthquake caused about US$8 million in damage, or 120 per cent of the gross domestic product (GDP).

---

74 UNDP defines the HDI as 'a summary measure of average achievement in key dimensions of human development: a long and healthy life, being knowledgeable and have a decent standard of living. The HDI is the geometric mean of normalized indices for each of the three dimensions' (UNDP, 2018*b*).

| 5 | There is a large population of orphaned children in Haiti, many of whom are living on the streets. There were an estimated 380,000 prior to the earthquake and untold thousands were added to that number after it. There are also about 250,000 *restaveks*, or children working as servants and often treated as slaves. |

Source: Borgen Project (2015).

Table 6.1 Basic socio-economic data for selected countries and the region

Country	Population (000s)[1]	% children (under 15)[1]	Annual Growth rate (GDP) 2015[2]	Unemployment rate[3]	Gross public debt (% of total budget)	Gross public debt (% of total GDP)[4]	Poverty levels[5]	HDI[6]	Gini coefficient[8]	Corruption index and rank[1]
Jamaica	2,820	30.1	0.9	13.3	43.7[7] (interest & amortization)	131.5	21.2 (2015)	0.730	0.4546	-39/100 -83/176
Haiti	11,095	35.9	1.2	13.2	n/a	29.9	58.5 (2012)	0.493	0.6079	-20/100 -159/176
Latin America and the Caribbean	633,026		-0.1	8.1	n/a		28 (2014)	0.751		

Sources:
[1] 2018 data: Countrymeters (n.d.).
[2] World Bank (n.d.b).
[3] World Bank (n.d.c).
[4] Global Finance (n.d.)
[5] PIOJ and STATIN (2017), Jamaica Survey of Living Conditions (2015), World Bank (n.d.d).
[6] UNDP (2018a).
[7] PWC (2017).
[8] World Bank (n.d.e).

Children represent the future and have inalienable rights to social justice. However, **Box 6.1** illustrates the depth of child poverty in Haiti. Data for Jamaica show that approximately one in four children lives below the poverty line: a child poverty rate of 26.5 per cent was recorded in 2015 (PIOJ and STATIN, 2017). **Table 6.2** examines the disparities between poor and non-poor children in Jamaica using data from a national household survey. Mean household size is higher for the poor households. For poor children, their consumption and education expenditure are lower; school attendance is slightly less and they have less health insurance coverage. Although a larger proportion of poor households receive benefits from the country's social protection programme (PATH) than do their richer counterparts, as is to be expected, these findings highlight a vulnerability among the poor.

Table 6.2 Profile of poor and non-poor children in Jamaica

	Poor	Non-poor
Mean age (years)	9.26	8.93
Mean number of children in household	2.58	1.78
Mean household size	5.86	3.88
Mean annual consumption expenditure (JMD)	568,832.70	1,118,296.46
Mean days of school attendance (20-day period)	17.78	18.34
Mean education expenditure (JMD)	48,972.44	90,995.00
% with health insurance	3.3	15.0
% receiving assistance from PATH	81.8	61.8

Source: PIOJ (2014).

Sustained economic growth remains elusive in Haiti and Jamaica. **Figure 6.2** shows the insignificant growth rates over the 10 years to 2015. Economic growth in Latin America and the Caribbean has generally been on the decline. Jamaica has experienced less than 2 per cent average annual economic growth rates, while Haiti was exposed to extreme swings in growth rates, largely in reflection of the natural disasters.

Experiences from the Caribbean

Figure 6.2 Growth rates, Jamaica, Haiti, and Latin America and the Caribbean, 2005–15

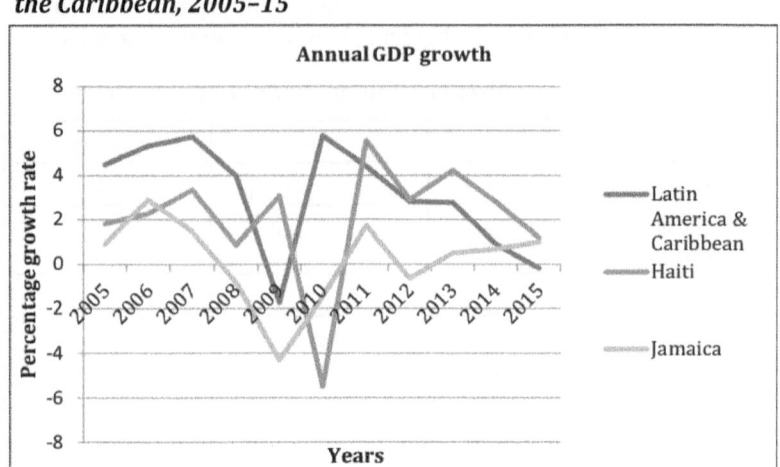

Source: World Bank (n.d.b).

An examination of other socio-economic data reveals other factors that may impede the fulfilment of the SDGs. Thus, as mentioned above, high levels of unemployment are characteristic of SIDS. Unemployment rates were recorded at 13 per cent for both Jamaica and Haiti, far exceeding the already high regional average.

Average life expectancy of males in Haiti and Jamaica was estimated to be 61 and 73 respectively, whereas for females it is projected to be slightly higher, at approximately 63 and 78 years respectively (World Bank, 2018). These outcomes are related to a range of factors: income levels, the availability and quality of social services, and gender dynamics.

Gender discrimination is a main driver of social exclusion. **Table 6.3** provides evidence of pervasive gender exclusion in Jamaica and Haiti. Unemployment rates are higher for females, with lower labour force participation rates. The proportion of seats held by women in the national parliament is higher in Jamaica than in Haiti, but far below the 30 per cent minimum observed in most countries. The proportion of women in ministerial positions in both countries stood at 20 per cent. As in many countries of the world, female-headed households face multiple disadvantages, from lower incomes to a poor recognition of their rights, in both Jamaica and Haiti.

Table 6.3 Gender participation indicators in Jamaica and Haiti

Indicator	Jamaica		Haiti	
	Male	Female	Male	Female
Labour force participation[1]	70.0 (2013)	56.25 (2013)	39.1 (2016)	33.1 (2016)
Unemployment[1]	9.2 (2016)	18.2 (2016)	11.4 (2016)	15.1 (2016)
Proportion of seats held by women in national parliament (%)[1]	17.5 (2016)		4.2 (2015)	
Proportion of women in ministerial-level positions (%)[1]	20 (2015)		20 (2015)	
Female headed household (%)[1]	45.4 (2015)[2]		40.6 (2012)	

Sources 1: World Bank gender statistics, various years; 2: PIOJ and STATIN (2017).

In terms of the macroeconomic situation, Jamaica has a high level of gross public debt which needs to be serviced, draining public resources from other government expenditure. It represents 131.5 per cent of total GDP, while the debt stands at only 30 per cent in Haiti (***Table 6.1***). A further factor impeding growth, social justice and implementation of the SDGs is the high levels of actual or perceived corruption. One of the local newspapers, the *Jamaica Gleaner*, reported that 'in a survey of 1,208 Jamaicans, the average person responded that 70 per cent of Jamaica's elected officials was corrupt, 80 per cent of the police force was corrupt and 50 per cent of government employees were corrupt' (Cunningham, 2014).

Transparency International has classified Jamaica as a country with serious corruption issues; the country's score is 39/100 (zero means highly corrupt, and a score of 100 represents the state of being very clean). The US State Department, in its March 2017 annual International Narcotics Control Strategy Report, described corruption in Jamaica as being 'entrenched and widespread'.

Last not least, the impacts of climate change pose enormous and increasing challenges to SIDs and retard their fulfilment of the SDGs. Climate change impact specifically also threatens any progress made in the reduction of social exclusion. The poor, those living in flood-prone areas, and women and children generally are among those most at risk. These countries, because of their geology, location and geography, are prone to several types of natural and human-caused hazards. The major threats include hurricanes, floods, landslides, droughts and earthquakes. Social disasters (civil unrest and disturbance) often follow the occurrence of natural disasters.

The *Caribbean Human Development Report 2016* (UNDP, 2016) revealed that between 1998 and 2012 there were thirty-nine natural hazards that affected the Caribbean region. Climate change poses a serious threat to these economies and societies. For example, the 2010 earthquake devastated Haiti, leaving 230,000 dead, and causing widespread destruction of infrastructure and water services (Conan, 2013). In the last decade, natural disasters cost Haiti US$8.36 billion. Hurricane Matthew, for example, severely damaged one of the most productive agricultural areas in Haiti. It followed a three-year drought which had already wiped out up to 80 per cent of crops and livestock. One-third of the population are currently food insecure, and up to 280,000 people are selling land and homes to survive (McCullough, 2017).

Table 6.4 gives a history of the high economic and human impacts of natural disasters in Jamaica. Storms alone have seen an impact as high as 3.4 per cent of GDP (2007) and billions of dollars.

Table 6.4 Economic and human impacts of selected storm events on Jamaica

Event	Year	Category	Cost (JMD)	Impact (% GDP)	Deaths
Hurricane Michelle	2001	4	2.52	0.8	5
May/June Flood rains	2002	–	2.47	0.7	n/a
Hurricane Charley	2004	4	0.44	0.02	1
Hurricane Ivan	2004	3	36.9	8.0	17
Hurricanes Dennis and Emily	2005	4	5.98	1.2	7
Hurricane Wilma	2005	5	3.6	0.7	1
Hurricane Dean	2007	4	23.8	3.4	6
Tropical Storm Gustav	2008	–	15.5	2.0	20
Tropical Storm Nicole	2010	–	20.6	1.9	16

Event	Year	Category	Cost (JMD)	Impact (% GDP)	Deaths
Hurricane Sandy	2012	1	9.7	0.8	1
March–June Rainfall[1]	2017	–	4	0.2	n/a

Source: ODPEM (2014), p. 64.

[1] PIOJ (2017.)

Table 6.5 examines the human and economic damages wreaked by natural disasters in Haiti. Death, injury and disruption in everyday activities are widespread during times of natural disaster. The frequency of these disasters does not facilitate quick economic or social recovery.

Table 6.5 Effects of natural disasters on Haiti

Natural disasters	Effects
23–24 May 2004 Torrential rains	Death toll 2,400, entire villages washed away. Extensive flooding.
September 2004 2 Hurricanes-Ivan and Jeanne	3,000 people killed and 30,000 displaced.
August–September 2008 Hurricanes Fly, Gustav, Hanna, Ike	800 killed, widespread damage, massive flooding, US$8 billion in property damage.
January 2010 Earthquake	300,000 killed and 30,000 commercial buildings damaged.
3–4 October 2016 Hurricane Mathew	600 killed and US$1.9 billion in damage

Source: University of Fondwa (2018).

Climate change, with its accompanying increase in natural disasters, has devastating effects on the economies of SIDS and retards their progress in the fulfilment of the SDGs. As is well known, when a natural disaster strikes, the poor, the socially excluded and the marginalized are the people most affected. They usually live in flood-prone and vulnerable areas, and are usually the slowest to recover when any disaster strikes.

With the recent disruption in the international agreement on the Paris Accord, international attention to the effects of climate change will be erratic. This has direct and urgent implications for policies, measures and actions to address social exclusion.

The socially excluded in Jamaica and Haiti

While the debate continues on the theoretical and definitional merits of the term 'social exclusion' (see the literature review above), we focus on the existence of groups in SIDS who are currently 'excluded' from benefiting from the development process. Consequently, this chapter seeks to answer the following questions:
o Who are the socially excluded groups in Jamaica and Haiti?
o What are the causes of their social exclusion?
o How can they be 'socially included' in the development agenda in their countries?

In answering the first of these questions, it is important to note that Jamaica and Haiti, as SIDS, suffer from social exclusion at the global level and have limited 'voice' on the international arena. Their vulnerabilities as SIDS also limit their international and local agency. Their economies are very vulnerable to external shocks. As developing countries, they do not have the same power leverage as the developed countries in multilateral organizations such the international financial institutions and the World Trade Organization. They are moreover susceptible to actions taken by developed countries in international markets. As argued above, insignificant economic growth, high poverty levels, inadequate access to decent work, and great levels of inequality have retarded progress in social inclusion in the development agenda in these countries. Further, high levels of debt and neoliberal policies have crippled their economies and diminished their influence. Corruption, too, is an issue. As nations, these two SIDS are at risk of being 'left behind' in the implementation of the UN2030 agenda.

Within these SIDS, there are certain groups and geographical areas that are socially excluded and at particular risk of not seeing the SDGs fulfilled. These include those persons who are living below the poverty line, and/or are disadvantaged because of gender or location. Poverty and social exclusion are intrinsically linked. Living below the poverty line, more often than not, is a cause as well as a consequence of social exclusion.

In Jamaica: poverty is higher in rural areas (CDB, 2016). Households with large sizes are more likely to be in poverty – an increase in the number of members in the household increases the probability that the household is poor (CDB, 2016). Female-headed households are also more likely to be poor (CDB, 2016). An increase in the elderly dependency ratio suggests increased likelihood of being poor (CDB, 2016). Additionally, an increase in the child dependency ratio leads to a significant increase in the probability of being poor (CDB, 2016). This means that female-headed households, children, the elderly and people in rural areas are most likely to be among those experiencing social exclusion. While poverty levels are higher in the rural areas, there is a significant group of people who are poor and socially excluded in the urban areas of Jamaica.

A particularly vulnerable group in Jamaica are residents in garrison communities. Garrisons are urban enclaves created to serve a political purpose and win elections. Stone (1986) first defined a garrison as 'a military stronghold based on political tradition, cultural values, beliefs, myths and socialization'. These garrisons consistently vote for the same political party by very large margins. There are at least fifteen garrison communities in Kingston, and their residents can be considered 'socially excluded'.

In these garrisons, poverty levels are high, they are violence-ridden, infrastructure is poor, and basic social services are inadequate. Social exclusion is high, as companies outside the community generally do not want to employ individuals living in the garrisons. Levy noted that:

> Employers refuse to consider applicants, even those with adequate education or those who have passed job requirement tests, once they hear their address. Some employers do not hesitate to say why they reject an application: 'You come from a bad area, where only robbers and gunmen and their families live.'
>
> (Levy, 1996)

Non-residents are usually afraid of the residents of the garrisons, and their social capital remains tied to their own communities. Shootings, murders and death form the landscape of garrison communities, and communities are sometimes locked down for days as the police try to restore order. The most recent violence exchange between the army, police and criminals involved the extradition of a notorious drug lord, 'Christopher Coke', in 2010. Dozens were killed in his garrison community (Schwartz, 2012). When violence flares up in these communities, children are traumatized, and schools are shut for days. Daily life is unstable and unpredictable.

Unemployment, poor parenting and lack of access to basic social services are the realities that face the residents in the urban poor communities (***Box 6.2***). These realities impede progress in the fulfilment of the SDGs.

Box 6.2 Some issues identified by residents in three urban poor communities

Community	Developmental challenges
Trench Town (SDC, 2011a, p. 7)	High levels of youth unemployment. High levels of adult unemployment. Limited or no opportunities for training and employment. High levels of high school dropout. Poor parenting.
Denham Town (SDC, 2011b, p. 51)	High levels of adult and youth unemployment. Low skills levels. High level of high school dropout. Low water pressure/no water supply. Negative perception/stigma of the community.
Ellerslie Gardens (SDC, 2016, p. 137)	High levels of adult unemployment. High levels of youth unemployment. Poor parenting. High levels of illiteracy innumeracy. Poor drainage facilities.

Source: Data from community profiles prepared by Social Development Commission (SDC), Ministry of Local Government and Community Development, Jamaica.

Crime and violence are predominant features in these urban poor communities. For example, in Denham Town, approximately 40 per cent of the households in the community claimed they were plagued by gangs and gang warfare, the latter being facilitated by the presence of derelict buildings and overgrown lots. The absence of street lights in underdeveloped/undeveloped areas also aggravated the situation (SDC, 2011b). Ellerslie Gardens is affected by violent acts stemming from internal gang and turf conflicts, and the area is a riot zone where any act of perceived injustice would result in the citizens blocking the main entrance into the capital town of Spanish Town (SDC, 2016).

In Haiti, too, poverty is highest in the rural areas. It is especially marked among landless people who depend exclusively on wage labour. Poverty is highest among the female-headed households too (IFAD, 2008). ***Box 6.1*** provided some basic information on poverty in Haiti. Data analysis reveals that 60 per cent of Haiti's population are socially excluded, and have limited access to the goods and services considered valuable in the society.

However, as in Jamaica, the impact of poverty and social exclusion is arguably even more intense in urban areas. ***Box 6.3*** provides a description of the quality of life in Cité Soleil, one of the largest slums in Haiti. Access to decent work, good-quality education and health care is elusive, and the residents remain 'socially excluded' from the benefits of sustained development.

Box 6.3 Features of social exclusion in Haiti

> 'Located on the perimeter of Port-au-Prince, Cité Soleil is one of the largest slums in Haiti. Living conditions for its estimated 300,000 residents are widely considered to be among the worst in the Americas. In stark contrast to its name (City of Sun), the area is generally regarded as one of the poorest and roughest areas in the Western hemisphere. Our survey results confirm this picture of dire living conditions, with 70% of households housing more than four members, and 81.4% of respondents claiming they do not earn enough money to feed everyone in the household. Only 6% claim to eat three meals a day, and a full 18% report they only eat every couple of days. 86% say they are unemployed, meaning they do not have a steady job with social benefits. Just over 49% claim to be self-employed, and 6.1% report having short-term "day jobs". Formal education is rare, with 56% having 8 years or less of schooling.'

Source: Willman and Marcelin (2010, p. 519).

This suggests that in both Jamaica and Haiti, slums and inner cities are places where citizens have limited access to the social goods and services considered valuable in the society. Here, SDGs 1, 10, 11 and 16 are at particular risk of not being fulfilled.

Identifying solutions: micro, meso and macro-level action

Our third question asks how the communities exposed to multiple layers of exclusion can be 'socially included' in the development agenda in their countries. Here, we argue that education is one key factor. The argument stems from observations on education outcomes, and well-established evidence on the potential contributions of education to securing an income, overcoming poverty, and serving as one of many factors towards addressing social exclusion.

Social exclusion from the education sector is evident in both countries. In Jamaica, mean years of schooling stood at 9.8 years, and 10 years for girls in 2017 (UNDP, 2018c), roughly corresponding to its HDI ranking, but too low to compete with OECD countries. In Haiti, the data show only 5.3 mean years of schooling, and even less for girls at 4.3 years (Haiti Partners, n.d.).

In Haiti, further analysis of education outcomes reveals that in 2013, 50 per cent of children in Haiti did not attend school, approximately 30 per cent of the children attending primary school were projected to not reach Grade 3, and 60 per cent were estimated to abandon school before Grade 6 (Haiti Partners, n.d.). Similarly, only 29 per cent of Haitians 25 years and above had attended secondary school, and the literacy rates for men and women are approximately 64 and 57 per cent respectively, well below the average for Latin America and the Caribbean, which is estimated at 92 per cent (Haiti Partners, n.d.).

Willman and Marcelin (2010) illustrate the challenges to education, describing an incident of massive physical violence experienced in school life in Cité de Soleil, Port-au-Prince (Box 6.4).[75]

Box 6.4 A teacher's account of school violence in Haiti

> 'I was in my classroom, teaching, when 10 thugs showed up and demanded I give them 1,000 gourdes. When I told them I didn't have it, they asked for 50 gourdes, which I gave them. Before departing, one of them raped another teacher. It was the teacher of the thug's very own child. These are examples of the violence lived in our area.'

Source: Willman and Marcelin (2010, p. 524).

Education can be a liberating force, and serve to increase social inclusion. Inclusive education, also impacting on outcomes, is seen as

---

75 Statistics concerning the frequency of such abject violence are not available; however, even if such scenes were to happen only once, they instil fear and a sense of impunity.

'a process of addressing and responding to the diversity of needs of all learners through increasing participation in learning, cultures and communities, and reducing exclusion from education and from within education' (UNESCO-IBE, n.d.).

At the micro-level, family and community-level efforts are vital. This is illustrated by the individual efforts of a mother to ensure that her children receive education, with the hope of breaking the cycle of inter-generational poverty (***Box 6.5***).

Box 6.5 Education as a liberating force from social exclusion in Jamaica

> Stephanie Williams (52 years old) who herself was born in poverty in a poor rural community in St Ann, made a promise to herself that if she had children, she would treat them better than she was treated. Fast forward to 2017, she is living up to her promises and her two daughters tell of the sacrifices she went through to ensure that they are well educated. She worked two jobs to ensure that they are taken care of, and in the process tries to further her own education. Williams, in describing her situation as 'abject poverty', speaks of her struggles to put food on the table at times.
>
> Two of her four children have since 'made her proud', the oldest who is a teacher and now helps the family, and another daughter who has had successful passes in her external examinations with exemplary grades. The children have managed to secure scholarships which have also aided in their successful education journey.
>
> Her financial constraints were her biggest stress factor: she believed that education was the way out of poverty and in the end always found a way out to ensure that education-wise they were taken care of. She threw partners, borrowed if she had to and even begged; but one way or another they had to have a good education as that was the way out of poverty for her.

Source: *Jamaica Gleaner (2017)*.

Micro-level efforts in isolation, however, do not suffice. Meso and macro-level interventions are necessary for social transformation.

Indeed, in Jamaica, the state has recognized the impact of poverty on its citizens and is committed to poverty alleviation. There have been several policies and programmes designed to reduce poverty in

Jamaica. The National Poverty Eradication Programme 1995 (NPEP) was enacted to reduce poverty in Jamaica through social, economic and infrastructural policies. Some of the programmes under this scheme were to bring electricity to rural areas, reduce health care costs, provide aid to homeless young people, and create investment opportunities in poor communities. There is a social protection programme – the Programme of Advancement through Health and Education, PATH (2001) – which is designed to improve the government's ability to provide social programmes to the public, and to promote good health and education. A draft National Poverty Reduction Policy is currently being reviewed by the government, opposition and people of Jamaica. There are also programmes implemented by international agencies. The World Bank for example has implemented projects which are centred on providing temporary employment for the poor, expanding access to secondary education, preventing and controlling the spread of HIV/AIDS, and providing access to basic social services for the poor (World Bank, n.d.). However, in spite of these policies and programmes, one-fifth of the population remains below the poverty line in Jamaica, as was indicated in *Table 6.1.*

Haiti, like Jamaica, has focused state attention on poverty. Examples include Haiti's *National Growth and Poverty Reduction Strategy Paper* (DSNCRP) 2008, which considers agriculture a pillar of pro-poor growth (IFAD, 2008), and the Country Strategic Opportunities Programme (COSOP) 2013–2018 (IFAD, 2013).

In spite of the various poverty reduction programmes and policies, levels of poverty, social exclusion and inequality remain high in both Jamaica and Haiti. Earlier, the impact of natural disasters was noted. The poor are hardest hit, and after a natural disaster, their access to basic social goods and services decreases significantly. In both countries, corruption, limited financial and human resources, poor services, and inadequate investment in basic social services are some of the main reasons that social exclusion remains high, and why the fulfilment of the SDGs for all remains elusive and challenging.

The underlying causes

As 2030 approaches, it is imperative that we examine the progress made to fulfil the SDGs, and propose strategies to ensure that all goals are met for all nations and social groups. We argue in this chapter that 'social exclusion' as a process and outcome impedes fulfilment of the SDGs for all.

Jamaica and Haiti were specially chosen for their varying HDIs, cultural and social histories. In the countries themselves, large proportions of the population are socially excluded from the developmental progress. Their choices are limited, and they are most likely trapped in a cycle of intergenerational exclusion. As small developing countries with island economies facing recurrent natural disasters, these countries have limited voice in shaping the global development agenda. Natural disasters have retarded progress in the fulfilment of the SDGs and may increase their social exclusion.

Within the countries, private social investment is limited, and socially excluded households and individuals need state support to break the cycle of social deprivation. This is so because the countries themselves are on the peripheries of the global development compass and are susceptible to external shocks: both countries experience 'social exclusion' on the global level, a process beyond the scope of this chapter.

SDGs 1, 10, 11 and 16 are at risk of non-fulfilment for both countries as a whole, for the socially excluded groups, and most urgently for members of the garrison communities in Jamaica and the urban slum residents in Haiti.

The causes of social exclusion are both external and internal. The fates of these socially excluded groups are connected to policy and interventions of the state and to the global environment. Within the countries, there are limited financial resources. High levels of corruption and the high repayment of debt impede social development and make it difficult to implement programmes to promote social inclusivity. In Jamaica, the poverty of the garrison communities can be seen to serve a political interest group – to ensure electoral victory for politicians –whereas in Haiti, there are just not sufficient human and financial resources to eradicate social exclusion. Social transformation is urgently needed to ensure that these socially excluded groups are not 'left behind' and that the SDGs are fulfilled for all.

A global and local political outlook: getting the 'excluded' included

To answer the final research question, reference is made to the conceptual framework presented in an earlier section. The eradication of social exclusion and marginalization would require radical transformation at the macro, meso and micro levels. At the macro level, the international development agenda must be one which emphasizes social growth that focuses on education, health care and climate protection; and delivers the results that people expect from democratic politics, namely jobs and a share in the prosperity these jobs create (Friedrich Ebert Stiftung, 2012). Also essential are some elements of the Nordic model with its emphasis on a set of labour market institutions that include strong labour unions and employer associations, significant elements of wage coordination, relatively generous unemployment benefits and a prominent role for active labour market policies (Andersen et al., 2007, pp. 13–14).

The international agenda must re-emphasize social protection, human development and climate change. While economic growth is important, it must be accepted that neoliberalism has not brought the equitable gains that were expected. There is an urgent global obligation to provide debt relief for these countries. Public debt has strangled any possibility for sustained economic and social growth. When a country owes 131 per cent of its GDP, and spends a large proportion of its budget on debt payment, as in the case of Jamaica, it becomes almost impossible to find the resources necessary for social development. In discussion with the International Monetary Fund (IMF), states must ensure that the livelihoods of the most vulnerable are not jeopardized by any stringent measures.

Haiti and Jamaica are members of the Caribbean region. Their regional body CARICOM has made several attempts at establishing a Caribbean single market and economy (CSME), but this have not been accomplished. Unless the Caribbean region negotiates as one single economic block, sustainable economic development will remain elusive. What would prove even more effective is a full integration of the Caribbean and Latin American region as one economic block. It would be more able to negotiate on the global economic level. Sustainable development is difficult to achieve without integration and partnership.

Also, at the macro level, within the countries, corruption has stifled the social gains made through the past decades. Governments must put in place all the necessary strategies to reduce all types of corruption. Governance structures should include effective and transparent opportunities for evaluation and accountability.

There is substantial research evidence to prove that investment in early childhood education is key. Governments in Jamaica and Haiti should increase their levels of investment in education. This remains a key to sustainable development.

At the meso (institutional) level, the poor deserve access to better services; the leakage of benefits to wealthier groups must be eliminated. Social protection services should be better targeted, timely and given more monetary value for the beneficiaries. While there are several non-governmental and advocacy groups which fight for and support the poor in Jamaica and Haiti, citizens have to take responsibility for their own actions and lives.

At the micro level, the citizens must demand more from their politicians and not withdraw from the process. Citizens' charters explaining their rights must be developed and disseminated. The SDGs must be localized for all communities in both countries, and the community members must democratically determine the priorities for their communities. They must be involved from the conceptualization to the evaluation of any programme, policy or project that affects them. Community members must be agents of change.

This radical social transformation cannot be accomplished overnight. Therefore, strategic policies must comprise short-term, medium-term and long-term plans with 'SMART' (Specific, Measurable, Agreed, Realizable and Time-based) objectives. Unless social transformations are pushed at the macro, meso and micro levels, the SDGs, and the SIDS agenda, are at risk of not being fulfilled and both social and economic growth is likely to remain unattainable.

References

Andersen, T. M., Holmström, B., Honkapohja, S., Korkman, S., Söderström, H. T. and Vartiainen, J. 2007. *The Nordic Model: Embracing globalization and sharing risks.* Helsinki, Research Institute of the Finnish Economy (ETLA)/Taloustieto Oy. https://economics.mit.edu/files/5726 (Accessed 7 August 2018.)

Atkinson, A.B. 1998. Social exclusion, poverty and unemployment.
A. B. Atkinson and J. Hills (eds), *Exclusion, Employment and Opportunity*, Centre for Analysis of Social Exclusion, London School of Economics, Case Paper 4.

Atkinson, R. 2000, 'Combating social exclusion in Europe: the new urban policy challenge. *Urban Studies*, vol. 37, pp. 1037–55.

Borgen Project. 2015. The top five facts about poverty in Haiti. https://borgenproject.org/top-five-facts-about-poverty-in-haiti/ (Accessed 11 March 2019.)

Caribbean Development Bank (CDB). 2016. The changing nature of poverty and inequality in the Caribbean: new issues, new solutions. St Michael, Barbados, CDB.

Castel, R. 1995. Les pièges de l'exclusion. *Lien social et politiques*, no. 34, pp. 13-21

Conan, R. 2013. Mexico: Cost of natural disasters hits US$20bn in last decade. BN Americas, 7 October. www.bnamericas.com/en/news/waterandwaste/mexico-cost-of-natural-disasters-hits-us20bn-in-last-decade/ (Accessed 11 March 2019.)

Countrymeters. 2018. Statistics, http://countrymeters.info/ (Accessed 10 January 2018.)

Cunningham, A. 2014. Highly corrupt: average Jamaican believes majority of public officials are shady. *The Gleaner*, 9 October. http://jamaica-gleaner.com/article/lead-stories/20141009/highly-corrupt-average-jamaican-believes-majority-public-officials-are (Accessed 11 March 2019.)

Easterly, W. 2009. How the Millennium Development Goals are unfair to Africa. World Development, Vol. 37, No. 1, pp. 26–35.

Farrington, F. 2002. Towards a useful definition: advantages and criticisms of social exclusion. www.researchgate.net/publication/242513425_TOWARDS_A_USEFUL_DEFINITION_ADVANTAGES_AND_CRITICISMS_OF_SOCIAL_EXCLUSION/download (Accessed 11 March 2019.)

Friedrich Ebert Stiftung. 2012. Social growth model of a progressive economic policy. International Policy Analysis. www.fes-china.org/en/publications/detail/social-growth-model-of-a-progressive-economic-policy-149.html (Accessed 29 March 2019.)

Funkhouser, E., Pérez Sáinz, J. P. and Sojo, C. 2002. Social exclusion of Nicaraguans in the urban metropolitan area of San Jose, Costa Rica, Working Paper No. 149, April. Washington DC, Inter-American Development Bank. https://ssrn.com/abstract=1814696 (Accessed 11 March 2019.)

Ginwright, S. and Cammarota, J. 2002. New terrain in youth development: the promise of a social justice approach. *Social Justice*, Vol. 29, No. 4, pp. 82–95.

Global Finance. n.d. Percentage of public debt to GDP around the world 2018. www.gfmag.com/global-data/economic-data/public-debt-percentage-gdp (Accessed 10 January 2018.)

Gostin, L. and Powers, M. 2006. What does social justice require for the public's health? *Public Health Ethics and Policy Imperatives*, Vol. 25, No. 4, pp. 1053–60.

Haiti Partners. n.d.. Haiti statistics: Haiti by the numbers. https://haitipartners.org/about-us/haiti-statistics/ (Accessed 11 March 2019.)

Holmes, R., Jones, N. and Espey, J. 2010. The MDGs and gender, Policy brief, June. London, Overseas Development Institute (ODI). https://www.odi.org/sites/odi.org.uk/files/odi-assets/publications-opinion-files/6006.pdf

International Council for Science. 2015. *Review of Targets for the Sustainable Development Goals. The science perspective.* https://council.science/cms/2017/05/SDG-Report.pdf (Accessed 11 April 2019.)

IFAD (International Fund for Agricultural Development). 2008. Enabling the rural poor to overcome poverty in Haiti. www.ifad.org/documents/10180/0b821a3f-c2bc-48a7-961d-91ef2eff14be (Accessed 11 March 2019.)

----. 2013. IFAD in Haiti. https://operations.ifad.org/web/ifad/operations/country/home/tags/haiti (Accessed 11 March 2019.)

Jamaica. 2011*a*. Community profile: Trench Town. Kingston, Social Development Commission, Ministry of Local Government and Community Development.

---. 2011*b*. Community profile: Denham Town. Kingston, Social Development Commission, Ministry of Local Government and Community Development.

---. 2016. Community profile: Ellerslie Gardens. Kingston, Social Development Commission, Ministry of Local Government and Community Development.

Jamaica Gleaner. 2017. Ultimate mom inspires her children: poverty no problem as love fills the void, 14 May. http://jamaica-gleaner.com/article/news/20170514/ultimate-mom-inspires-her-children-poverty-no-problem-love-fills-void (Accessed 11 March 2019.)

Kanbur, R. 2004. Growth, inequality and poverty: some hard questions, Working Papers 127133. Ithaca, N.Y., Cornell University. Department of Applied Economics and Management.

Keller, J. 2014. Exclusion as a social problem and a methodological issue. Ostrava, Czech Republic, University of Ostrava Faculty of Social Studies. http://projekty.osu.cz/vedtym/dok/publikace/keller_exkluze.pdf

Khoo, S.-M. 2005. The Millennium Development Goals: a critical discussion. www.researchgate.net/publication/242157552_The_Millennium_Development_Goals_A_Critical_Discussion (Accessed 11 April 2019.)

Levy, H. 1996. Urban violence and poverty in Jamaica. Centre for Population, Community and Social Change, University of the West Indies, Mona Campus, Jamaica.

McCullough, J. 2017. President Trump's misguided withdrawal from the Paris Climate Agreement. Huffington Post, 6 May. www.huffingtonpost.com/entry/president-trumps-misguided-withdrawal-from-the-paris_us_5935a8e0e4b0c670a3ce6743?ncid=engmodushpmg00000004&guccounter=1 (Accessed 11 March 2019.)

Melamed, C. and Scott, L. 2011. After 2015: progress and challenges for development. Background note, March. London, Overseas Development Institute. www.odi.org/sites/odi.org.uk/files/odi-assets/publications-opinion-files/7061.pdf (Accessed 11 March 2019.)
ODPEM (Office of Disaster Preparedness and Emergency Management). 2014. Jamaica Country Document on Disaster Risk Reduction. www.preventionweb.net/publications/view/46342 (Accessed 28 March 2019.)
Oxford Reference. https://www.oxfordreference.com/view/10.1093/oi/authority.20110803100515279 (Accessed 11 March 2019.)
PACS (Poorest Areas Civil Society programme). n.d. What is social exclusion? www.pacsindia.org/about_pacs/what-is-social-exclusion (Accessed 17 March 2017.)
PIOJ (Planning Institute of Jamaica). 2014. Jamaica Survey of Living Conditions, dataset. Kingston, PIOJ.
---. 2016. Economic and Social Survey Jamaica 2015. Kingston, PIOJ.
---. 2017. Macro Socio-Economic and Environmental Impact Assessment of the Damage and Loss caused by the March to June Rains 2017. https://www.pioj.gov.jm/Portals/0/Sustainable_Development/Macro%20Socio-economic%20and%20Environmental%20Impact%20Assessment%20of%20the%20Damage%20and%20Loss%20caused%20by%20the%20March%20to%20June%20201-7%20Rains.i.pdf (Accessed 17 March 2017.)
PIOJ and STATIN (Statistical Institute of Jamaica). 2017. *Jamaica Survey of Living Conditions 2015*. Kingston, Government of Jamaica.
Poister, T. H. 2010. The future of strategic planning in the public sector: linking strategic management and performance. *Public Administrative Review*, December, vol. 70, p. s246-s253. Georgia State University.
PWC. 2017. *Jamaica 2017/18 Budget*, 9 March. https://www.pwc.com/jm/en/research-publications/taxpublications/jamaica-2017-2018-budget.html (Accessed 20 March 2019.)
Schwartz, M. 2012. Jamaica's former p.m. opens up about coke arrest, extradition. *New Yorker*, 3 August. https://www.newyorker.com/news/news-desk/jamaicas-former-p-m-opens-up-about-coke-arrest-extradition. (Accessed 17 January 2019.)
Silver, H. 1994. Social exclusion and social solidarity: three paradigms. *International Labour Review*, Vol. 133, No. 5-6, pp. 531–78.
Stone, C. 1986. *Class, State and Democracy in Jamaica.* New York, Praeger.
Touraine, A. 1992. Inégalités de la société industrielle, exclusion du marché. In J. Affichard and J. B. de Foucault (eds), *Justice sociale et inégalités*. Paris, Editions Esprit.
UNDP. 2016. *Caribbean Human Development Report 2016: Multidimensional progress: human resilience beyond income.* New York, UNDP. http://hdr.undp.org/sites/default/files/undp_bb_chdr_2016.pdf
---. 2018a. Global Human Development Indicators. http://hdr.undp.org/en/countries

---. 2018b. Human development reports. http://hdr.undp.org/en/content/human-development-index-hdi (Accessed 4 July 2018.)

---. 2018c. Human Development data. http://hdr.undp.org/en/data

UNESCO-IBE (International Bureau of Education). n.d. Interview with Clementina Acedo, IBE director. http://internationaldiplomat.com/archives/528 (Accessed 11 March 2019.

United Nations. 1994. Barbados Program of Action (BOAP). https://sustainabledevelopment.un.org/conferences/bpoa1994 (Accessed 11 March 2019.)

---. 2012. Review of the contributions of the MDG Agenda to foster development: Lessons for the post-2015 UN development agenda. Discussion Note, March 2012. www.un.org/millenniumgoals/pdf/mdg_assessment_Aug.pdf (Accessed 12 December 2016.)

---. 2014. SIDS Accelerated Modalities of Action (SAMOA) Pathway. Resolution adopted by the General Assembly on 14 November 2014. United Nations. A/RES/69/15. http://www.2030caribbean.org/content/unct/caribbean/en/home/sustainable-development-goals/samoa-pathway.html (Accessed 11 March 2019.)

University of Fondwa. 2018. *The History of Natural Disasters in Haiti.* Fondwa, Haiti, University of Fondwa. https://ufondwa.org/history-natural-disasters-haiti/ (Accessed 24 August 2018.)

US Department of State. 2017. *International Narcotics Control Strategy Report.* www.state.gov/j/inl/rls/nrcrpt/2017/ (Accessed 28 March 2019.)

Vandemoortele, J. and Delamonica, E. 2010. Taking the MDGs beyond 2015: hasten slowly. *IDS Bulletin,* Vol. 41, No. 1, pp. 60–9.

Williams, A., Cheston, T., Coudouel A. and Subran, L. 2013. Tailoring social protection to small island developing states – lessons from the Caribbean, Social Protection and Labor Discussion Paper SP 1306. Washington DC, World Bank. http://documents.worldbank.org/curated/en/2013/08/18086868/tailoring-social-protection-small-island-developing-states-lessons-learned-caribbean (Accessed 26 May 2014.)

Willman, A. and Marcelin, L. H. 2010. 'If they could make us disappear, they would!' Youth and violence in Cité Soleil, Haiti. *Journal of Community Psychology,* Vol. 38, No. 4, pp. 515–31.

World Bank. 2014. Big cities fare better than rural areas, says first poverty analysis post-earthquake, press release, 11 December. Washington DC, World Bank. www.worldbank.org/en/news/press-release/2014/12/10/haiti-big-cities-fare-better-than-rural-areas-says-first-poverty-analysis-post-earthquake (Accessed 11 March 2019.)

---. 2018. Life expectancy at birth, selected countries and economies. Washington DC, World Bank. http://data.worldbank.org/indicator/SP.DYN.LE00.MA.IN?locations=HT-MX-JM (Accessed 11 March 2019.)

---. n.d.a. All projects: Jamaica. Washington DC, World Bank.

---. n.d.*b*. GDP growth (annual %), 1961–2017. Washington DC, World Bank. https://data.worldbank.org/indicator/NY.GDP.MKTP.KD.ZG?locations=HT-JM-ZJ (Accessed 11 March 2019.)

---. n.d.*c*. Unemployment, total (% of total labor force) (modeled ILO estimate), 1991–2018. Washington DC, World Bank. https://data.worldbank.org/indicator/SL.UEM.TOTL.ZS (Accessed 11 March 2019.)

---. n.d.*d*. Poverty headcount ratio at national poverty lines (% of population), 1985–2017. Washington DC, World Bank. https://data.worldbank.org/indicator/SI.POV.NAHC (Accessed 11 March 2019.)

---. n.d.*e*. Gini index (World Bank estimate), 1984–2016. Washington DC, World Bank. https://data.worldbank.org/indicator/SI.POV.GINI?locations=MX-JM-HT (Accessed 11 March 2019.)

CHAPTER 7
CRITICAL AND PROPOSITIONAL URBAN PLANNING: THE CO-PRODUCTION APPROACH IN KAMPALA

Gilbert Siame

A. Introduction

The world is becoming more urban every day. The global urban population is expected to increase to approximately 57 per cent of the world's population by 2050. Of the projected increase, 90 per cent will be in Africa and Asia. However, these two regions of the world remain very polarized and unequal. Watson (2014) argues that with the majority of urban populations living in deep poverty, and with minimal urban services, mainstream planning processes and outcomes may well increase the marginalization and inequalities that already beset these cities. The foreseeable urban future for many cities of the South is a polarized one, built on a long trajectory of urban exclusion based on evictions of urban poor residents from their urban land and denial of basic urban rights.

This has historically been masked in the professional use of legal processes to label large urban populations as 'illegal settlers', 'squatters' or 'informal', juxtaposed with policy positions such as 'urban beauty' and 'world-class city', among others, to deny millions of city residents their basic rights to the city. Thus, large swathes of urban poor populations in Southern cities have faced persistent and well-entrenched tactics to perpetuate social exclusion.

This chapter argues that the production of urban spaces in Africa needs to be reframed within the context of a weak and manipulative state, a highly unequal and divided society, and deep-seated conflicts within the state and society. The chapter makes an argument that mainstream planning approaches such as collaborative and communicative planning can no longer be relied upon to deal adequately with the politics of urban inclusion and lead to a new urban order that guarantees the rights of everyone to a decent and productive life. Therefore, new thinking needs to emerge to reframe past planning normativities into new approaches that deal with issues of urban exclusion, urban misgovernance and survivalist politics within the state and society. This chapter presents the concept of co-production as an alternative planning framework that can unseat entrenched manipulative practices of both the state and society, and consolidate progressive practices so as to produce inclusive planning processes and outcomes in African cities.

There are far-reaching literature on and critiques of the limitations of mainstream planning approaches in dealing with the challenges of contemporary urban development. The limitations are more pronounced in cities of the South and postcolonial urban conditions. How state and society engage on issues related to urban planning has been a prominent theme in planning theory for decades (Hillier and Healey, 2008; Albrechts, 2012).

Similarly, in the forty years since Habitat I, it has been proven difficult, if not impossible, to implement the explicit and implicit ambitions of the Vancouver Declaration (UN Conference on Human Settlements, 1976) within the scope of formal planning systems. Universally, the ambitions in the Vancouver Declaration were naively expected to be implemented within the mainstream urban development approaches. Thus, the call for alternative planning approaches based on emerging innovations in planning in the South has been unequivocal (Watson, 2014). Watson (2014) proposes that recent approaches and cases of planning taking place in global South[76] contexts offer a possibility of deepening the 'pot' from which to draw planning ideas and debates on urban social inclusion, and contribute to further internationalization of planning thought beyond mainstream planning experiences.

The focus of this chapter is on understanding state–society relations taking the form of co-production in many urban contexts of the global South. Co-production is a new way of settlement intervention, where the state engages and works with organized community groups to jointly produce knowledge, generate power dynamics and relations that empower the poor, and jointly produce urban services and spaces. In co-production, the mobilized groups of urban poor use tactics and methods to become hegemonic and pursue the ends of urban social inclusion. In the global South where existence of a united and democratic society (community and state) is far-fetched, as elsewhere globally, the chapter argues that striving

---

76 Global South means far more than a geographical South: 'It references an entire history of colonialism, neo-imperialism, and differential economic and social change through which large inequalities in living standards, life expectancy and access to resources are maintained; and opens new possibilities in politics and social science' (Dados and Connell, 2012, p. 13).

to achieve consensus on planning issues should not be the end goal of planning, but rather, engaging consciously and cautiously with power, diversity and conflict could reposition the core business of planning and simultaneously inspire a great degree of social inclusion.

The remainder of this chapter has five sections, beginning with a literature review on the limitations of mainstream planning theory, and on co-production as an alternative planning approach. The third section discusses materials and methods used in this chapter. Section D will present findings on co-production engagements in Kampala. In the fifth section, I 'talk back' to literature by comparing the findings and the literature debates before indicating final reflections on this study.

B. Planning in global Southern contexts

As stated by Dados and Connell (2012, p. 13) and de Stage and Watson (2018), the use of the terms Southern, Northern, global North, global South does not connote a geographical or intellectual binary, but rather refers to a level of development and to differences in governance characteristics. Debates on the relevance of mainstream planning theory have raged for decades now. Southern planning theorists argue that there are two major problems with mainstream planning theory. First, it is based on assumptions which are drawn from contexts such as strong and well-resourced states, and a strong civil society and increased role of cities. Second, these theories are generalized to all regions of the world, since it is rarely specified to which part of the world they actually apply.

These limitations are a basis for a clear discord between planning ideals and the urban realities of the global South. Mainstream planning ideas fail to engage with the postcolonial conditions of the South. Porter (2006) maintains that mainstream planning theories and approaches lack some important aspects: there is no analysis of the culture of the practice of planning and institutional set-ups in postcolonial contexts (Porter, 2016). Much of the planning in these Southern contexts fails to connect productively with questions of livelihoods, ways of life and governance arrangements. Unfamiliarity with these questions and conditions leads to the imponderability of routine urban exclusion practices (Pieterse, 2010). The ideas of the state, society and democracy are radically different from the realities obtaining in the cities of the South. However, there is growing literature in planning theory indicating a commitment to difference, to emerging ways of understanding and rethinking the urban and planning of the South (Watson and Odendaal, 2013; Odendaal, 2011; Porter, 2010; Albrechts, 2012). The next subsection discusses co-production as an alternative approach to planning.

Co-production: a review

Over the last three to four decades, a growing number of urban poor organizations have shifted from claim-making to co-production. This subsection examines the use of co-productive concepts and strategies by citizen groups and social movement organizations to enable individual members and their associations to secure 'effective relations with state institutions' that both address immediate basic needs and enable them to negotiate for greater benefits (Mitlin, 2008, p. 339; Boonyabancha and Mitlin, 2012). This form of co-production is radically different from that postulated by political economists and public administrators such as Ostrom, who consider co-production as 'the process through which inputs used to produce a good or service are contributed by individuals who are not in the same organisation' (1996, p. 1073). Ostrom's (1996) and Whitaker's (1980) ideas of co-production are fundamentally different from the way grassroots movements such as, for example, Slum/Shack Dwellers International (SDI) and the Asian Coalition for Housing Rights (ACHR) conceptualize and practise co-production in the cities of the global South. The latter focus on the politics of inclusion in cities of the South, and the idea of power, politics and partnership as central to the practices of grassroots co-production.

Co-production as an empowerment concept

There are many leading organizations working with urban poor populations in various cities in the global South. The Orangi Pilot Project (OPP) in Karachi, the Urban Community Development Office in Thailand, SDI and ACHR among others (Mitlin, 2014*b*, 2008; Archer, 2012) lead programmes to promote alternative settlement interventions in Asia, Africa and South America to advance the cause of the urban poor in city planning and development. In these citizen-led co-production engagements, the politics of social inclusion taking the form of conflicts are acknowledged, and multiple strategies can be adopted to promote outcomes that favour the urban poor. State-society relations are distinguished as they involve different kinds of strategies – conflict, cooperation and boycotts – all meant to push for a pro-poor urban agenda. As such, citizen-led co-production involves 'negotiating' with, or putting pressure on, the state so that local groups can be directly involved in the design, management and implementation of urban development programmes. Mitlin locates citizen-led co-production:

> within a broader struggle for choice, self-determination and meso-level political relations in which citizens both seek an engagement with the state and also are oriented towards self-management and local control over local provision in areas related to community development needs and aspirations. Mitlin defines coproduction as a political process that citizens engage with to secure changes in their relations with government and state agencies in addition to improvement of basic services.
>
> (Mitlin, 2008, p. 347)

Mitlin recognizes the role of power and conflict, state functionality and the structure of society in shaping the relationship between the state and society. She argues that 'the nature of groups arising from a grassroots co-production process offer particular benefits to the poor, extending political practice through drawing in new groups and persuading the state to respond positively' (2008, p. 353). Dubbing this citizen-led or grassroots co-production, Mitlin (2008) argues that co-production is different from standard 'participation' or 'partnership' arrangements. As opposed to Ostrom's position on co-production as a state-orchestrated cost-reduction project, Mitlin (2008) argues that the interpretation and practice of co-production strengthens citizen mobilization and so provides a platform for a wider civic and political engagement and reforms in the way state agencies function to advance social inclusion for the urban poor (Albrechts, 2012). This implies that co-production by grassroots movements is a social movement strategy that is designed to empower communities to achieve strategic gains for the majority of urban populations in the cities of the South.

Power as a capillary is a central theme of social inclusion discourses. While collaborative and communicative planning approaches do not give sufficient treatment to power (within state and communities, and in encounters between the two), co-production is about management of power and conflict to advance and protect the interests of citizens. Co-production challenges the dominant power of the state and seeks to shift power towards communities. Drawing on examples from civic movements and participation discourses of the urban poor in planning in Bolivia, Brazil and South Africa, Miraftab (2009, p. 34) argues that through persistent counter-hegemonic practices, the movements expose and upset the normalized relations of dominance ('war of positions'). The sites of power are multiple (Lindell, 2008) and shifting, as are the sites for counter-hegemonic movements. Analysis of squatter movements in the global South reveals that they breed counter-hegemonic and insurgent movements, mobilizing beyond the state's control and claiming their right to the city. Thus, co-production encourages both conflict and collaboration. Co-production can be related to the arguments by Holston (2008), as having capabilities that both produce stability in state–citizen relations and destabilize them.

The co-production approach to urban development is informed by certain ideals and principles, and these norms articulate certain values, notably social justice, equity, spatial integration, sustainability and accountability. These values may be appreciated differently from the perspectives of the state, the community and non-governmental organizations (NGOs). So stakeholders 'expect conflicts and clashes' between the different players (Albrechts, 2012, p. 53). As the values, interests and views of players are different, it is obvious to expect conflicts and clashes between traditionally closed systems (governments, private sector) and the open systems (communities, NGOs) linked to co-production. Thus, sometimes settlement intervention processes suffer from tensions between those partners embedded in the system (politicians and planners) and with access to the system, and those who function outside the system (NGO members and community residents) (Albrechts, 2012).

In the next subsections, I briefly explain the tools and practices used in co-production engagements.

Co-production tools and practices

All the organizations engaging in co-production share core principles, based on bilateral and multilateral engagements between actors (learning, cross-learning and unlearning). The NGO leads the process of introducing co-production approaches to city planning and production of the urban core form of organization. It convenes the mobilization of actors, for example via a savings scheme, a local group that draws together residents, mainly women, in low-income informal urban neighbourhoods to save, and to share their resources and strategies to address their collective needs (Mitlin et al., 2011). In all cases of co-production, there is encouragement for these groups to come together and form a critical mass at city level and nationally.

Another tool is knowledge and information-sharing through local and international exchange activities. This process helps to ensure that knowledge about cities and development ideas comes from the grassroots and is not imposed on them by professionals (Sheela et al., 2012). It is argued that learning, rooted at the 'lowest' level of society, consolidates individual and collective confidence (McFarlane, 2006). Writing about SDI activities in India, for example, McFarlane refers to these exchanges as 'trans-local urban learning assemblages' (2011, p. 69) of materials, practices, designs, knowledge, personal stories and local histories, and attitudes, which all shape what the city essentially becomes. The knowledge and information shared has to be generated, but this has to be done differently from conventional methods and approaches. To promote new ways of generating information and knowledge about cities, community residents, with the support of experts based in the NGOs and with support of the state (using a combination of tools and methods such as lobbying, protests and the state willingly working with the NGO) lead the implementation of comprehensive city-wide community surveys. This serves to create knowledge about cities and recommend programmes of intervention. Chatterjee and Mehta (2007) argue that the articulation of power and knowledge in practices of government is made manifest in the technologies of mapping and enumeration by which society makes itself visible to the state. The following section describes the methodology used in this chapter.

C. Methods and materials[77]

This study has sought to examine the 'everyday' practices in planning in Kampala. It used the case study approach, as recommended by Yiftachel and Huxley (2000, p. 911), who call upon planning theoreticians and practitioners to critically examine planning practices using case studies (Flyvbjerg, 2004). The study used the City of Kampala as a case and then chose three divisions – Kampala Central, Nakawa and Kawempe – to provide units of analysis. I selected Kinawataka and Mbuya settlement sites in the Nakawa division subcase, Kisenyi I, II and III settlement sites in the Kampala Central division subcase, and Bwaise (Kalimali and the surrounding areas) settlement sites in the Kawempe division subcase. The first point of contact during fieldwork was through email to the director

---

77 The interviewees have given their consent for verbatim quotations from their interviews. They all signed consent forms before being interviewed.

of ACTogether. ACTogether is a local NGO that works with the National Slum Dwellers Federation of Uganda (NSDFU) to promote and implement co-production activities in Uganda. The director assigned the following departmental heads for interviews: Water and sanitation; Profiling, Enumeration, Mapping; Savings and Livelihoods, Design (Engineer); and Administration and Documentation. After meeting the heads of departments, the group recommended that the head of the ACTogether Water and Sanitation Department act as the researcher's official research assistant in Kampala. Then, based on a review of documents process, I identified and listed all the relevant stakeholders and specific officers (positions) as participants in the interview process. The list of all organizations and officers I had identified was discussed with the research assistant, who later added other names, especially at community level, in the three subcases. The research assistant endorsed the list of community groups that I had independently proposed for interviews. In the following section, I present the findings.

D. Co-production activities and initiatives in Kampala

During the World Urban Forum (WUF) in May 2002 in Kenya, the minister responsible for housing and urban development in Uganda engaged with the international president of SDI and made a request for SDI to visit Uganda and help the government mobilize people living in informal settlements to facilitate joint interventions. Thus, the initial co-production processes in Kampala were initiated by the government of Uganda. Reports on the history of the partnership and urban planning in Uganda indicate that this was a period when the influence of opposition political parties in Kampala was rapidly rising, and the National Resistance Movement (NRM) and the president were exploring every avenue to control the capital city, Kampala. Thus, some research participants argued that the minister reached out to SDI to ensure improved relations between communities and the central government (interview, Silver Michael Owere, ACTogether official, 15 October 2015).

The state, through the Kampala City Council (KCC) and the Ministry of Lands and Housing, and the early National Slum Dwellers Foundation of Uganda (NSDFU) leaders implemented their first co-production projects through community-led profiling. In this case, they undertook enumeration in the form of a door-to-door, household-by-household community-driven census (counting, surveying and mapping) conducted to ascertain the actual living conditions of the urban poor. Enumerations are supported by technical organizations and seek to anchor partnerships between communities and local and national governments, and to bridge the knowledge gaps that perpetuate inequality. In the first joint project, KCC assigned the office of the community development officer (CDO) and community-based municipal staff, called parish administrators, to closely work with NSDFU during enumerations. Possibly because of the influence and pressure from central government, KCC linked Local Council One (LC One, a devolved community-based governance structure) leaders, introduced NSDFU to households, and explained the purpose of the enumerations. The ruling party and opposition political parties had to 'work together'. The LC One leaders assumed key leadership positions in NSDFU and have always played a key role in sustaining NSDFU activities in Kampala. These leaders know how to straddle state and community spaces and structures in order to advance the interests of NSDFU. During the enumeration exercise, state agencies considered the residents of Kisenyi area as a productive stakeholder group that could contribute positively to the way informal settlements were understood and managed. This was evidenced by the fact that the state at local level began to use the enumeration reports to guide interventions in the informal settlements.

> This enumeration was the first to specifically target on documentation of informal settlements and was useful for partners to understand the significance of community-led data collection in understanding informal settlements. The processes assisted government and stakeholders to appreciate the extent of development challenges affecting Kisenyi network in particular and other informal settlements communities in the City. Later, these reports served as guiding instruments for settlement recognition and interventions by both the state and Community residents.
> (interview, Mr Hassan Kiberu, national chair, NSDFU, 13 October 2015)

Later on, with ACTogether as a lead organization, the Partnership worked to introduce daily savings as a means to mobilize the community to grow NSDFU for more co-production engagements. During the formation of saving groups, while NSDFU was the major actor, KCC encouraged its decentralized structures at community level to support and to be active savers. The Kampala Partners demanded proof of community savings before they could approve infrastructure development projects and financing for every community. Savings were considered a clear expression of community interest in development projects. For example, community residents of Kisenyi mobilized themselves through savings, and contributed support to the projects in terms of labour and ongoing management of the infrastructure in the area. After the first project was constructed in 2004, residents and Federation members from surrounding communities demanded a replication of the project, but the state did not make available additional funds for land purchase and projects as demanded by the residents and NSDFU members.

> Despite having started saving in the Federation groups, many residents decided to quit the Federation when projects in housing, water and sanitation were no longer a real possibility for all. This led to some sort of decline in community enthusiasm regarding what the Partnership could deliver for people.
> (interview, Mr Waiswa Kakaile, engineer, ACTogether, 27 April 2016)

Additionally, in some cases KCC did not agree to endorse some settlements on land that the KCC considered was illegally occupied and belonged to private individuals and organizations. Up until now, land ownership and use rights-related conflicts between the city government and NSDFU have continued to create disputes between NSDFU and what is now the Kampala Capital City Authority (KCCA). KCCA has continued to evict residents and NSDFU members who trade or settle on private and state land. NSDFU has continued to oppose all manner of evictions using profiling, enumerations, mapping, and boycotts of selected Partnership meetings in Kampala.

The other activity that characterizes co-production relations and activities involves local and international exchange activities (ACTogether, n.d.). The partnership has since 2003 used exchange programmes to shift minds and change values and perceptions on how a pro-poor urban development agenda can be maintained through sustained partnerships with organized community residents in the informal settlements. NSDFU used exchange programmes to build rapport and solidify relationships with state officials including top politicians. For example, in 2004, leaders from NSDFU, a structural engineer from ACTogether and a structural engineer and planner from KCC and the Ministry for Works went to Kenya and Tanzania to specifically learn about the use of alternative building technologies in order to apply such knowledge in the construction of the inaugural water and sanitation project in Kisenyi.

> After an exchange on alternative building materials, the Ministry for Works became one of the negotiators and advocates for KCC to allow the use of alternative building materials to construct water and sanitation facilities in Kampala. As such ACTogether and the Federation used the exchange creatively to convince state technical staff to allow the use of construction technologies and materials produced by the Federation.
>
> (interview, Mr Waiswa Kakaile, engineer, ACTogether, 8 February 2016)

The research participants from NSDFU argue that the principal aim of exchange activities is to empower people who have not gone to school to understand and implement what they desire to achieve for their households and communities. The various exchange activities that were undertaken in Kampala served as an 'alternative classroom', a second opportunity to learn by doing. Based on NSDFU exchange visit reports (SDI, 2015), it is evident that through exchange programmes, people participate in activities to ensure cross-breeding of ideas, cross-learning and innovation on all themes in which the Partnership has been engaging.

The Nakawa division subcase

Early co-production engagements in the Nakawa division were introduced in 2007. The Kinawataka and Mbuya settlements in the Nakawa division were chosen for market upgrading and construction of a communal water and sanitation facility. Kinawataka and Mbuya shared a trading space for hundreds of informal traders from many nearby areas, but the place lacked public water and sanitation infrastructure, and people resorted to the use of plastic bags for disposing of human waste. Furthermore, traders lacked physical infrastructure to support their trading activities.

The first community-led area upgrade initiatives started with mobilization for savings and enumerations, and led to the formation of the first four saving groups in the Banda, Mbuya, Bukotu and Chambogo areas of Nakawa division. After enumerating the area in 2010–11, partners initially agreed to construct a communal water and sanitation project in Mbuya and upgrade a market in the Kinawataka area. Since then, however, the market project has been affected by major tensions and factions resulting from different interests in the area and beyond. Various groups in the area demanded compensation for providing land for the project, while NSDFU insisted on zero compensation, arguing the project was for the community. The state took a seemingly neutral stance but opted to push for the project actualization through fronts and disguised agents. This was designed to avoid complications and challenging political gymnastics.

> The land where the water and sanitation facility were to be developed belonged to KCCA under Nakawa Division. However, the land was settled on for over a period of 20 years by the local people who did not have chapters to claim legal ownership and use rights. When plans to upgrade the market were presented to the members of the community, many challenges emerged. We have not yet reached an agreement at community level to enable the market redevelopment to start.
> (interview, Mr Stephen Byangaba, LC One chairman, Kinawataka market, 12 February 2016)

Initially, NSDFU approached the Nakawa Division Council to allow the partnership to improve infrastructure for the traders and settlers. However, NSDFU was advised to engage with the vendors first before engaging with the council over the land. The council stayed out of the project and land negotiations because it was expected that the processes would cause conflict since the community was not ready to agree easily to the proposals. During interviews with Mr Waiswa Kakaile (ACTogether engineer, 8 February 2016), it was established that KCCA put NSDFU in front to deal with the challenges and secure community support for the projects. Fearing rejection and not sure which vendors to engage with, NSDFU ignored the advice by KCCA to engage with the traders first, but instead went on to engage with local leaders. Later, NSDFU approached LC One chairperson Mr Stephen Byangaba, and presented the proposals on the redevelopment in the area. At this stage, the meetings between NSDFU and the LC One chairperson were not backed by popular support from the traders and local land owners. Later, the LC One chairperson talked to the KCCA regional council and engaged with traders and property owners in the area regarding the proposed projects. After several meetings, land for the community water and sanitation project was secured. Construction lasted from early 2012 to mid-2013.

Later in 2013, without consolidating community support, especially from the traders, the Partnership endorsed NSDFU's proposal to upgrade the Kinawataka market to serve as a launch pad for the joint urban renewal programme. While the initial construction of water and sanitation projects was not delayed, the market redevelopment plans suffered from setbacks. It had emerged that land ownership at Kinawataka market was controlled by relatively wealthy individuals and groups, and that KCCA was constrained by institutional and political limitations in their attempt to control and manage what happened in the area.

> We found that the area had about 1,000 people who operated in the market and these were categorized into tenants, sub-tenants, landlords, structure owners, political party representatives, Local Council One Chairmen, more women, and fewer young people. The majority were tenants, seconded by sub-tenants and the minority were the landlords. We presented the report during the MDF [municipal development forum][78] at KCCA in 2015. The LC 1 [chairperson] is like the area president, and we cannot work in there without his endorsement.
> (interview, Sumayiya, national youth leader/saver, Nakawa, NSDFU, 12 February 2016)

The group with the highest influence on what happens in the Kinawataka market area included the LC One chairperson who owned the largest number of stores and shops, and the landlords. Tenants constitute the largest proportion but have less influence on what happens on the land. However, they also demanded assurances from the partnership about shop and house ownership after redevelopment. This fragmentation in land ownership and control of use in Kinawataka compelled some sections of society to demand full compensation before works on the market redevelopment could start. The landlords, tenants and structure owners refused to cooperate with the Partnership to allow the area to be redeveloped. They would not allow temporary relocation for construction to commence.

> The past has shown that the poor, especially tenants, are usually displaced permanently, regardless of promises. We upgraded a market in Wandegeya in 2014 in Kampala Central near Makerere University, and most of the initial occupants/owners/traders were displaced contrary to the promises. We cannot risk again!
> (interview, representative from Nakawa Federation, 4 February 2016)

The landlords and the LC One leaders are among the most powerful group of people, and nobody can succeed at working in Kinawataka without their support. The LC One leaders are connected to senior politicians and have the ability to influence what happens in the area. The chairman of the landlords' committee also occupies the position of LC One chairperson, has many positions and a large network. However, the chairperson cannot make decisions unilaterally,

---

[78] See ACTogether (2015).

as there is a ten-member 'local cabinet' that draws representation from many segments. Thus, to upgrade Kinawataka, the Partnership needed to go beyond the members of NSDFU, and the office of the LC One chairperson. While landlords and local leaders were the most powerful, the tenants formed an influential potential voting bloc for the politicians, especially the governing National Resistance Movement (NRM).

While the community is divided and split along various fault lines, the state too is not a monolithic entity. The 2010 KCCA Act empowers Nakawa Division Authority with an absolute mandate to govern the division and to provide services for all residents. The Ministry of Lands, Housing and Urban Development (MLHUD) has some degree of mandate, as the Physical Planning Act of 2010 gives it the mandate to oversee land use planning and housing functions in Uganda. It should be noted that local government institutions and legislation equally share some degree of mandate on governing Kampala. It was observed that there is fragmentation, contradiction and undermining of each other in the way the state agencies respond to the issues in the informal settlements (interview, Mark Bwambale, acting deputy director, Directorate of Physical Planning, KCCA, 13 October 2015). Just as society is shaped by diverse community segments, the state in Kampala is also fragmented and responds differently to community issues. Narratives from MLHUD officials indicate that staff from MLHUD feel KCCA has absolute authority on issues affecting Kampala. Indeed, KCCA has its own funding and is empowered to make decisions without necessarily engaging with ministry officials. This means KCCA can wilfully ignore the Decentralization Policy, and the legal mandates of MLHUD.

> This institutional and community fragmentations have created considerable conflicts and contradictions during the interventions. We are negotiating with the land owners, with planners and with the informal settlement dwellers so that we do land sharing in Nakawa. To avoid creating a physical clash of government institutions and ideas, negotiations are strategically facilitated by ACTogether. Without ACTogether, many state agencies would not work together to deliver service for people in the informal settlements.
> (interview, Mr Pade Joseph, commissioner, Urban Development, MLHUD, 15 October 2015)

During a personal interview with Mr Stephen Bogere (senior sociologist, MLHUD, 20 October 2015), revelations were made regarding the differences within governmental institutions. The differences were clearly manifest in Nakawa, as each institution pursued its own mandate and responded to co-production initiatives proposed by SDI differently. Institutions equally had various ways and channels of engaging with different community structures and leadership.

The Kawempe division subcase

After the Kampala Central division, this division was the second to implement co-production activities in 2005. The three initial savings groups in Kawempe suffered setbacks caused by poor leadership and abuse of group funds in the period from 2008 to 2010, leading to the subsequent dissolution of the groups in the period 2010 to 2012. The funds were reportedly misappropriated by the group leaders (interview, Ronald Kasalu, chairman, NSDFU Kawempe division, 3 February 2016). Respondents from NSDFU and ACTogether argued that abuses of the funds created an opportunity for valuable lessons and led to a reorganization of the NSDFU movement in the division. Much of the radical transformation in Kawempe started happening in later years.

> In Kawempe, we now have 2,802 members of different saving groups and networks. We have 33 saving groups which are structured by eight committees that have specific mandates in the Federation activities. We have always worked very closely with the Kawempe Municipal Division in addressing water challenges, promoting livelihoods, reducing evictions and promoting dialogue. Initial challenges provided an important learning opportunity for us and our partners.
> (interview, secretary for NSDFU Kawempe division, 15 October 2015)

Despite initial leadership failures in Kawempe, NSDFU members were committed to the SDI-established process of choosing leaders based on commitment and loyalty to NSDFU practices. The established processes and methodology include inbuilt conflict-resolution and peace-building mechanisms. NSDFU in Kampala prides itself on the fact that its leadership is based on the notion of sacrifice, self-determination and commitment to making society more socio-economically inclusive. During a personal interview, the executive director of ACTogether (Lutwama Muhammed, 23 October 2016) stated that NSDFU and ACTogether do not agree with government's push for use of elections as a means of choosing leaders for the

Federation. The fear among NSDFU members is that if state-like elections are introduced in NSDFU, the entire process of choosing leaders will be monetized. NSDFU fears that elections might turn NSDFU into a middle-class money-spinning political club.

> I am the father of the Federation in Uganda. I will continue being chair and it's only death and God who will take me away, I love what I do, and nobody pays me. I initiated the Federation activities in 2002. There is no need to vote, not everybody who has money and who can talk well can make a good community leader. Federation is about sacrifice and commitment to the public good.
> (interview, Mr Hassan Chiberu, national chairman, NSDFU, 12 February 2016)

However, research participants from MLHUD contend that the Partnership faces several challenges, including assertions by government officials that ACTogether 'appointed' some leaders for life to certain positions in NSDFU. The country team leader of the Cities Alliance, Mr Samuel Mapala, who happens to be the former commissioner for urban development and whose office is based in the MLHUD building, echoed the views of MLHUD on issues of transparency in the NSDFU leadership.

> There has been no democracy in the Federation and this is one of the landmark failures of the ACTogether. When the Federation uses undemocratic processes, and when some people overstay in their positions, they become dictatorial and stop to listen and respect to the members. For example, some people in Kawempe abused group funds and the NEC did not take any action to protect the savers, they lost their savings. Leadership problems are common at both regional and national levels. We blame the NGO for this unfortunate situation in the Federation.
> (interview, Mr Samuel Mapala, country team leader, Cities Alliance, 14 October 2015)

The relationship between NSDFU and ACTogether is largely shaped by the role of professionals in implementing co-production engagements. ACTogether does not implement but helps NSDFU to lead in the implementation of many co-production initiatives. Incidents of contestation between NSDFU and the NGO technical staff clearly exist. Many NSDFU representatives and NGO staff argued that when NGO technical staff start working against the ideals of NSDFU, the movement uses its tools of savings, enumerations and exchange activities to build solidarity which works to eject the technocrats.

> The technocrats have many plans and we stop their dirty deals midway through what we call plan B. We have the networks and we know what is happening in the NGO and in the entire Federation and in the City. We want to maintain a transparent and open Federation processes and its key role in the co-production processes.
>
> (interview, Ms Katana Goleti, national treasurer, NSDFU, 8 February 2016)

Narratives from both the community and ACTogether show that some members of NSDFU feel that they are sufficiently empowered and need to take charge of all activities. Some members of ACTogether (the NGO), however, argue that there is no such thing as 'empowered enough'. Some NSDFU respondents maintained that NSDFU acts like a watchdog for NGO staff. NSDFU members shout and force the NGO staff to respect the roles and regulations of NSDFU. It was observed that the NGO and state officials at MLHUD know NSDFU is strong and can challenge the actions of the technocrats.

> The Federation should start making independent decisions on how they should be governed. When the Federation starts shouting to technocrats working for the NGO, then that should be seen as progress on the empowerment front. The Federation must be empowered to halt wrongdoing by technocrats from all institutions (NGO and state). In an event that a leader is not delivering, the decision that a failing leader should step down should come from the bottom. It should be people from respective groups, or the region who should tell the person to step down.
>
> (interview, Skye Dobson, former executive director, ACTogether, 5 December 2015)

> I want to tell you that we have the mechanism to speak to power and we are respected, listened to and our issues are taken seriously. What is key for the Federation movement in Uganda is to ensure that groups and community members have begun to question their leaders at group, network and regional levels and in government. We do not fight government, in fact they are our core partner, but we have resisted their control of the Federation.
>
> (interview, Mr Hassan Chiberu, chairman, NSDFU, 12 February 2016)

Having presented the findings, I use the following section to present an integrated analysis of co-production activities in the development processes of the City of Kampala.

D. Conceptualizing co-production urban development

This section integrates empirical and theoretical materials to achieve a conceptually backed interpretation of co-production engagements and relations in the development of Kampala. The research findings establish the basis for interpretation of how co-production engagements in the City of Kampala provide empirical support for an enhanced theoretical framework in planning and urban development, which contributes to ideas of state–society engagement in the cities of the South. Thus, I use both normative and positive analyzes to make sense of the findings and discuss these findings for intellectual significance for alternative urban development approaches that embody normative efforts for social inclusion.

This section is divided into two main subsections, understanding the conceptual significance of co-production processes and the nature of the state and society in the global South, and understanding how a weak state is made to be accountable to and engage with the urban poor through a co-production approach. The following subsection provides an interpretation of the use of co-production tools to show how these tools organize power and channel state–society relations to achieve social inclusion gains for the urban poor groups and individuals.

How the state interacts with society in the process of co-production

This subsection analyzes how communities and the state relate during the co-production process. Co-production engagements and relations such as a continued push by the state for evictions, reluctance to accept new design and planning standards as established by NSDFU, and the use of surveys and reports, all show that it is not possible to assume that co-production interactions are always collaborative (as communicative and collaborative planning theory has suggested) and that at times co-production can also involve conflict and resistance. This study has showed that low-level conflicts were necessary to destabilize manipulative tactics of the state and communities to engender an inclusive urban decision-making processes. The evidence from Kampala shows co-production as an alternative planning approach which repositions planning as both a collaborative and a conflicted process, depending on strategies adopted by communities and the state as well as the issues of interest to actors. Co-production challenges major assumptions on the idea of the state and society to allow for parties in urban development to engage with and not avoid the nasty politics of inclusive urban development in Southern cities. The process of co-production seems to be a fitting model because the relationship between 'the citizen' and 'the state' in many global South cities seldom resembles the kind of deliberative democratic models of citizen participation promoted by normative discourses on state–society relations in the mainstream planning literature.

Actual urban governance in the South involves various layers of relations between the state and civil groups as well as relations within and between civil groups (Lindell, 2008). Many regions of the South are characterized by weak institutions, lack of adequate information, and high levels of poverty and inequality, which in turn act as barriers to discursive decision-making processes (Robins et al., 2008). Corbridge and colleagues (2005) call for a nuanced analysis and understanding of various ways people encounter the state as 'a citizen, client and/or subject' in postcolonial cities. 'Theorising the entangled geographies of state and society in postcolonial society' (Corbridge et al., 2005, p. 19) opens up analysis to narratives and spaces for manoeuvre, agency and negotiation in postcolonial urban contexts (Das and Poole, 2004). These aspects – such as clientelism, group formation, knowledge generation and reaching out through exchanges – which facilitate manoeuvres by community residents are clearly factored into the co-production tools and are used carefully to aid the social inclusion of the urban population.

The structure and agency of co-production is governed through the co-production tools of savings, information generation and knowledge exchange. In Kampala, these tools helped the communities and the state to assume and act from multiple sites where practices of governance were exercised and contested (Lindell, 2008), displaying a variety of players, various layers of relations and a broad range of practices of governance with various modes of power at different scales. Clientelism and patronage are very much part of sociopolitical cultures in the South, as citizens straddle 'civil society' and 'state' spaces to become visible and be 'heard'. Straddling multiple spaces and sites of governance is recognized and appreciated in co-production This could be seen in the conflicted negotiations in the Mbuya and Kinawataka areas of Kampala.

In the cities of the South, strategies of survival and well-being depend on the ability to establish multiple strategic relationships and become accessible to multiple powerful players. Co-production relations in Kampala do not dispel but rather engage with clientelistic relations, conflicted and opposing power dynamics, and recognize that both the state and society are deeply divided and can take on multiple identities to secure their interests (Watson, 2003; Mitlin, 2014*a*; Yiftachel, 2009), along fault lines of livelihoods, political affiliations, mandates, gender and social class. As differences continue among the partners in Kampala, it is evident that the tools of co-production do not seek to gloss over, bridge or avoid these social issues and the ideas of social diversity and social inclusion, but rather, the tools recognize and work with deep difference (Watson, 2003, 2014) to achieve social and material gains for the urban poor. Vanessa Watson argues that mainstream planning ideas are 'problematic' in the global South, which is 'characterized by deepening social and economic differences and inequalities and by the aggressive promotion of neoliberal values by dominant nation-states' (2003, p. 31). This argument by Watson has increasingly become a global phenomenon since the post-2008 global economic recession.

Watson maintains 'there is not yet sufficient recognition of just how deep difference can be, and how planners can frequently find themselves in situations characterized by conflicting rationalities' (2003, p. 395). As evidenced in Mbuya, Kinawataka, Kawempe and Kisenyi, co-production processes showed that planners in the NGO and the state can take the time to listen to community voices, pay attention to dissenting views and recognize the multiplicity of actors both in the community and within the state system. In the face of the multiplication of players and conflicting rationalities, state-centric perspectives of governance that focus exclusively on the workings of the formal institutions of the state are considered insufficient for grasping the complex webs of power at work in many cities in the global South. Co-production recognizes this fact and works to deepen engagements with informality, in line with the postulations of Chatterjee (2004). Co-production engages with the call by Robins and colleagues for 'more attention to contextual understandings of the politics of everyday life, and to locating state, NGO and donor rhetorics and programs promoting "active citizenship" and "participatory governance" in the conditions' (2008, p. 1069) of the urban South. The savings, mapping and surveys as well as knowledge exchange in co-production processes in Kampala did point actors to the 'everyday' of Kampala life. While recognizing difference and diversity, federating brought the community 'together', enumerations highlighted development gaps, and the exchange of knowledge transformed minds and actions for all involved in the Kampala Partnership.

> After an exchange on alternative building materials, the Ministry for Works became one of the negotiators and advocates for KCC to allow the use of alternative building materials to construct water and sanitation facilities in Kampala.
>
> (interview, Mr Waiswa Kakaile, engineer, ACTogether, 8 February 2016)

The process of promoting a different way of managing cities and regions through co-production is not always smooth. Positions and knowledge epistemologies are contested. The resistance using multiple methods and for varied reasons by some groups in Nakawa division to allow for an upgrade of the Kinawataka market (see the findings section) points to the relevance of Robins and colleagues' (2008) argument: it is more realistic in postcolonial contexts to build on existing practices and strategies, including social protest, all of which people regularly use to secure resources. Ploger (2004, p. 73) emphasizes the 'importance of respecting the role of strife and antagonism in real-world planning practice'.

I argue that without use of co-production tools, the experiences of both the state and society might have been markedly different. Co-production lowered the degree of battles among professionals and with the community. Co-generation of survey results in Kisenyi meant that the state could not vociferously object to the relevance of data and information. The tools allowed for respect of diversity of views and perspectives, and promoted different ways of knowing and learning. When the state cannot object to alternative settlement ideals, when lack of knowledge of the depth of settlement realities is countered with community-verified data and information, and when the alternative becomes the community driven option, the state gets twisted somehow to act in line with community demands. This was clear in Kampala.

Quiet insurgency in the co-production process

Bradlow (2013, p. 128) argues that partnerships between organized 'community residents and state systems provide space for conflict between grassroots players and institutions of the state'. The conflicts force each party to search for and articulate the values that they bring to co-production processes seeking to deliver services. Conflict in the co-production process in Kampala has occurred but has not taken the form of violence and 'insurgency' (the term used by James Holston (1998) to describe civic resistance in urban Brazil).

Conflicts and community resistance to manipulative state policies and actions during co-production in Kampala take subtle and covert forms.

Study findings show that communities in Uganda are generally less inclined to open and violent protest on the issue of service provision when their demands are not met, and are more inclined to covert resistance. Community action on service provision and recognition of informal settlements appears to take a form that is closer to the ideas of Asef Bayat in the context of the Middle East (Bayat, 2010; see also Perera, 2016). Bayat argues that instead of waiting for an uncertain revolution, many people in this region are more likely to support a non-violent approach to reform, based on strongly organized social movements. Those urban citizens who lack the institutional power of disruption are more likely to assert their demands through the use of public space, selling goods on the street or building shacks on land even where it is illegal. Bayat calls this the 'quiet encroachment of the ordinary'. NSDFU also follows a strategy of SDI, which is anti-violence (Abahlali baseMjondolo, n.d.). The majority of the members are women,[79] and therefore there is a need to protect the rights of women to participate. Where protests turn violent, they argue, women are excluded. The resistance shown in Nakawa on the market upgrade, and the refusal by NSDFU and ACTogether to yield to state demands on elections as a way of choosing leaders of NSDFU, point to the successful use of what may be referred to 'quiet insurgency' among NSDFU members and the NGO. In contexts where the state can be brutal against citizens, protesting quietly may yield better gains than radical insurgency. Thus, this chapter advances a positive analysis that quiet insurgency is a useful approach for securing the socio-economic interests of the urban poor.

The state and society as fractured entities

The state is not a homogenous entity. It is conceptualized as a dynamic ensemble of relations and syntheses that at the same time produces the institutional structure and knowledge of the state. Lindell, reflecting on market governance in Maputo, Mozambique, establishes that 'there are multiple sites and layers' (2008, p. 1879) where the state in Africa practises a broad and often contradictory range of practices of governance. Issa and David argue that theorizing the state in the South should involve analyzes of the relationship

---

[79] Uganda is politically divided, and when there are political divisions in Kampala, these can erupt in violent conflict.

between state agencies and political parties, as well as "clientelism and corruption, intra-state contradictions, frequent policy reversals, and the existence of weak state institutions"(2012, p. 141). Hence the actions of the state are fragmented between both formal and informal processes (Roy, 2009). The multiple lines of engagements between state institutions and community groups in Nakawa indicates that the state never had a shared position on how to work with the various community entities. The practices of co-production in all the three subcases in Kampala show that divisions exist between and within central and local levels of the state. In many parts of the global South, the state remains highly centralized, with actual decentralization, local democratization and shared governance having uneven or conflicted processes (Watson, 2009, 2006). Limited capacity, resources and data at the local level have further hindered decentralization processes and the implementation of cooperative governance. Generally, traditional urban planning and management systems have encountered challenges because they have relied on assumptions (Devas, 2001) regarding the existence of stable, coherent, effective government at both national and local level, as well as a strong civil society (Watson, 2009).

Co-production recognizes this fact and seeks to engage fractured and weak state systems to achieve urban sustainability ideals of social justice and equity. This chapter argues that planning must engage with policy made on a field of power struggles between different state agencies and interests, where knowledge and truth are contested, and the rationality of planning is exposed as a focus of low-level conflict within the state. This is what Flyvbjerg has called 'real-life rationality' (1996, p. 383), where the focus shifts from what should be done to what is actually done. While Foucault saw discourse as a medium which 'transmits and produces power', he points out that it is also 'a hindrance, a stumbling-block, a point of resistance and a starting point for an opposing strategy' (1990, p. 101). Understandings of planning as a spatial practice that is related to the state and the production of space should acknowledge power relationships that are shaped by national and local histories and cultures (Huxley, 2000). The success of co-production rests with recognition and engagements of the low-level conflicts and diversity of urban discourses experienced within and between actors in the state and society.

E. Conclusions and further reflections

The key findings are that co-production processes and tools were useful for building initiatives for improved state–society relations in Kampala. The co-production methodologies in Kampala were essential in building both individual and collective capabilities to engage with the state to challenge the conventional ways of doing planning and to begin to initiate new ways of producing the urban. While divides and divisions were a permanent mark of communities, the communities used their new capabilities to devise various tactics to engage with a divided and conflicted state to resist imposition of settlement interventions. The research discovered that intra-state alignment is rare, and the state in Kampala did not act in unison and often held different positions on various development and planning issues during co-production. The research notes that co-production is about both conflict and collaboration. Where both state and community had a common interest, collaboration was used. On the other hand, overt conflict was initiated by community groups whenever their interests were threatened. Co-production in Kampala shows that it is possible to be critical and propositional in the field of planning in the global South.

I argue that co-production in Kampala managed to 'deepen the theoretical pot' in planning, and supported attempts to contribute to internationalization efforts in planning theory and on debates on urban social inclusion. The case study advanced theoretical ideas on the limitations of mainstream planning theories to guide planning in those parts of the world where the state and society are affected by poverty, inequality, institutional weakness and conflict. The chapter extends the debates on how the state and society are typically understood in the field of planning.

On a normative basis, I argue that both the state and society in the South are characterized by divisions and divides which weaken their capabilities to assert and protect 'public' 'community' interest. With competing interests within the state and within society, the interface between state and society is conflicted and contested. The chapter further asserts that to assume in planning that both the state and communities in the global South are naturally willing to participate in inclusive community development processes for the good of society is erroneous and misleading. The Kampala case establishes that use of co-production strategies has the capacity to mobilize, align and consolidate 'community' action to engage with the state and begin to shift state–society interface power dynamics towards the 'community', thereby making the state more responsive to the social needs of urban poor communities.

With the idea of 'leaving no one behind' in the SDGs, especially SDG 11, and the call for participatory planning processes to achieve the New Urban Agenda (UN Habitat, 2017), the concept of co-production seems to have the potential to configure new ways of producing cities in highly uncertain urban environments in the global South. With large swathes of urban populations living and working informally, co-production could lead to a rethink of how planning envisages and structures public participation to ensure inclusivity in city development processes and outcomes to contribute towards attainment of global development agreements. More studies on social inclusion and alternative urban visions and processes could benefit from advanced studies on planning as a governance tool, and power as the elephant in the room.

References

Abahlali baseMjondolo. n.d. Slum Dwellers International statement on the attacks on Kennedy Road Settlement, Durban, South Africa. http://abahlali.org/taxonomy/term/slum_dwellers_international/slum_dwellers_international/ (Accessed 18 January 2019/)

ACTogether. 2015. Nakawa Municipal Development Forum meeting, 15 July. www.actogetherug.org/nakawa-municipal-development-forum-meeting/ (Accessed 18 January 2019.)

---. n.d. Exchange. http://ACTogetherug.org/index.php/features/exchange (Accessed 10 May 2016.)

Albrechts, L. 2012. Reframing strategic spatial planning by using a co-production perspective. Planning Theory, Vol. 12, No. 1, pp. 46–63.

Archer, D. 2012. Baan Mankong participatory slum upgrading in Bangkok, Thailand: community perceptions of outcomes and security of tenure. Habitat International, Vol. 36, No. 1, pp. 178–84.

Bayat, A. 2010. Life as Politics. Amsterdam, Amsterdam University Press.

Boonyabancha, S. and Mitlin, D. 2012. Urban poverty reduction: learning by doing in Asia. Environment and Urbanization, Vol. 24, No. 2, pp. 403–21.

Bradlow, B. 2013. City learning from below: urban poor federations and knowledge generation through transnational, horizontal exchange. International Development Planning Review, Vol. 37, No. 2, pp. 129–42.

Chatterjee, p. 2004. The Politics of the Governed: Reflections on popular politics. New York, Columbia University Press.

Chatterjee, R. and Mehta, D. 2007. *Living with Violence: An anthropology of events and everyday life.* New Delhi and Abingdon, UK, Routledge.

Corbridge, S., Williams, G., Shrivastava, M. and Veron, R. 2005. *Seeing the State: Governance and governmentality in India.* Cambridge, Cambridge University Press.

Dados, N. and Connell, R. 2012. The global South. *Contexts,* Vol. 11, No. 1, pp. 12–13.

Das, V. and Poole, p. 2004. *Anthropology in the Margins of the State.* Santa Fe, N.M., School of Advanced Research Press.

De Satgé, R. and Watson, V. 2018. *Urban Planning in the Global South: Conflicting rationalities in contested urban space.* New York, Springer.

Devas, N. 2001. Does city governance matter for the urban poor? *International Planning Studies,* Vol. 6, No. 4, pp. 393–408.

Flyvbjerg, B. 1996. The dark side of planning: rationality and 'Realrationalität'. S. J. Mandelbaum , L. Mazza and R. W. Burchell (eds), *Explorations in Planning Theory.* New Brunswick, N.J., Center for Urban Policy Research Press, pp. 383–94.

———. 2004. Phronetic planning research: theoretical and methodological reflections. *Planning Theory and Practice,* Vol. 5, No. 3, pp. 283–306.

———. 2006. Five misunderstandings about case-study research. *Qualitative Inquiry,* Vol. 12, No. 2, pp. 219–45.

Foucault, M. 1990. *The History of Sexuality: An introduction, vol. I,* trans. R. Hurley. New York, Vintage.

Hillier, J. and Healey, p. 2008. *Contemporary Movements in Planning Theory: Critical essays in planning theory, Vol. 3.* Aldershot, Ashgate.

Holston, J. 2008. *Insurgent Citizenship: Disjunctions of democracy and modernity in Brazil.* Princeton, N.J., Princeton University Press.

Huxley, M. 2000. The limits to communicative planning. *Journal of Planning Education and Research,* Vol. 19, No. 4, pp. 369–77.

Issa, A. S. and David, A. K. 2012. The challenges of leadership and governance in Africa . *International Journal of Academic Research in Business and Social Sciences; Bahawalpur,* Vol. 2, No. 9, pp. 141–57.

Lindell, I. 2008. The multiple sites of urban governance: insights from an African city. *Urban Studies,* Vol. 45, No. 9, pp. 1879–901.

McFarlane, C. 2006. Transnational development networks: bringing development and postcolonial approaches into dialogue. *Geographical Journal,* Vol. 172, No. 1, pp. 35–49.

———. 2011. *Learning the City: Knowledge and translocal assemblage.* West Sussex, UK, Wiley-Blackwell.

Miraftab, F. 2009. Insurgent planning: situating radical planning in the global South. *Planning Theory,* Vol. 8, No. 1, pp. 32–50.

Mitlin, D. 2008. With and beyond the state: co-production as a route to political influence, power and transformation for grassroots organisations. *Environment and Urbanisation,* Vol. 20, No. 2, pp. 339–60.

Mitlin, D., Satterthwaite, D. and Bartlett, S. 2011. Capital, capacities and collaboration: the multiple roles of community savings in addressing urban poverty, IIED Poverty Reduction in Urban Areas, Working Paper No. 34. London, International Institute for Environment.

---. 2014a. Politics, informality and clientelism: exploring a pro-poor urban politics, Working Chapter No. 34. Manchester, Effective States and Inclusive Development (ESID). www.effective-states.org (Accessed 13 March 2019.)

---. 2014b. Towards an inclusive urban planning and practice. H. Moksnes and M. Melin (eds), *Claiming the City: Civil society mobilisation by the urban poor*. Uppsala, Sweden, Uppsala Centre for Sustainable Development, pp. 15–31.

Odendaal, N. 2011. Reality check: planning education in the African urban century. *Cities*, Vol. 29, No. 3, pp. 174–82.

Ostrom, E. 1996. Crossing the great divide: coproduction, synergy, and development. *World Development*, Vol. 24, pp. 1073–87.

Perera, N. 2016. *People's Spaces: Coping, familiarizing, creating*. New York and London, Routledge.

Pieterse, E. 2010. Cityness and African urban development. *Urban Forum*, Vol. 21, No. 3, pp. 205–19.

Ploger, J. 2004. Strife: urban planning and agonism. *Planning Theory*, Vol. 3, No. 1, pp. 71–92.

Porter, L. 2006. Rights or containment. The politics of Aboriginal cultural heritage in Victoria. *Australian Geographer*, Vol. 37, No. 3, pp. 355–74.

---. 2010. *Unlearning the Colonial Cultures of Planning*. Surrey, UK, Ashgate.

---. 2016. *Unlearning the Colonial Cultures of Planning*, rev. edn. London, Routledge.

Robins, S., Cornwall, A. and von Lieres, B. 2008. Rethinking 'citizenship' in the postcolony. *Third World Quarterly*, Vol. 29, No. 6, pp. 1069–86.

Roy, A. 2009. Why India cannot plan its cities: informality, insurgence and the idiom of urbanisation. *Planning Theory*, Vol. 8, No. 1, pp. 76–87.

SDI (Slum/Shack Dwellers International). 2015. *Annual Report 2014–2015*. https://knowyourcity.info/wp-content/uploads/2015/07/SDI002_Annual_Report_Spreads_v2-1.pdf (Accessed 18 January 2019).

Sheela, P., Baptiste, C. and d'Cruz, C. 2012. Knowledge is power – informal communities assert their right to the city through SDI and community-led enumerations. *Environment and Urbanisation*, Vol. 24, No. 1, pp. 13–26.

United Nations. 1976. *The Vancouver Declaration on Human Settlements*, A/CONF.70/15. Vancouver, B.C., United Nations Conference on Human Settlement. www.un-documents.net/van-dec.htm (Accessed 17 January 2019.)

UN Habitat. 2017. *New Urban Agenda*. New York, UN Habitat-III Secretariat. http://habitat3.org/wp-content/uploads/NUA-English.pdf (Accessed 11 April 2019.)

Watson, V. 2003. Conflicting rationalities: implications for planning theory and ethics. *Planning Theory and Practice*, Vol. 4, No. 4, pp. 395–407.

---. 2006. Deep difference: diversity, planning and ethics. *Planning Theory*, Vol. 5, No. 1, pp. 31–50.

---. 2009. Seeing from the South: refocusing urban planning on the globe's central urban issues. *Urban Studies*, Vol. 46, No. 11, pp. 2259–75.
---. 2014. Co-production and collaboration: the difference. *Planning Theory and Practice*, Vol. 15, No. 1, pp. 62–76.
Watson, V. and Odendaal, O. 2013. Changing planning education in Africa: the role of the Association of African Planning Schools. *Journal of Planning Education and Research*, Vol. 20, No. 20, pp. 1–12.
Whitaker, G. 1980. Coproduction: citizen participation in service delivery. *Public Administration Review*, Vol. 40, No. 3, pp. 240–6.
Yiftachel, O. 2009. Critical theory and 'gray space': mobilisation of the colonized. *City*, Vol. 13, No. 2, pp. 246–63.
Yiftachel, O. and Huxley, M. 2000. Debating dominance and relevance: notes on the 'communicative turn' in planning. *International Journal of Urban and Regional Research*, Vol. 24, No. 4, pp. 907–13.

CHAPTER 8
BETWEEN CONTROL AND COMPASSION: THE POLITICS OF NEIGHBOURHOOD COMMUNITY SERVICES IN URBAN CHINA

Judith Audin

Introduction: social work and the transformation of urban residents' committees in post-socialist China

In today's China, the general transformation of the urban landscape goes with the invention of new lifestyles. At the end of the 1990s, the end of the work unit (*danwei*) system characterized a new organization of space based on the separation of the workplace from the residence. In the context of the 'neighbourhood community building' (*shequ jianshe*) reform, the residents' committee (*jumin weiyuanhui*) – an organization under the lowest level of the urban administration – is transforming and inventing new forms of local governance after the end of the *danwei* system. Hired and supervised by the local level of administration (the street office – *jiedao banshichu*), the residents' committees are in charge of implementing public policies (the household registry system, family planning, birth control policies, welfare programmes), but also organizing sociocultural activities and mediating local conflicts. The president of the People's Republic of China from 2002 to 2012, Hu Jintao, introduced in 2004 the concept of a 'harmonious society' (*hexie shehui*). This concept suggested a 'top leadership concern to ameliorate social conflicts and balance the interests between different social groups in society' (Wong, 2013, p. 128). In the following years, a field of social work started to grow in public administrations, especially in the Ministry of Civil Affairs. Scholars conceive social work in China as an emerging discipline and profession, different from philanthropy and governmental social services in terms of theoretical framework, practice and values. However, the development of social work as a profession in China remains a government-led project, and this undermines the complete and formal social work training of a social worker (Li et al., 2017).

Urban neighbourhoods in China are not simply residential spaces. They were sites of political and social control during the Maoist era (Whyte and Parish, 1984). Throughout the economic reforms, neighbourhoods became para-administrative units. Experiments in social service provision have been promoted in urban China through neighbourhood-based social work in order to build 'harmonious neighbourhood communities' (*hexie shequ*) and develop a 'people-centred' approach (*yi ren wei ben*). A category of 'weak and vulnerable social groups' of residents became the target population of service provision, shaping a new format of social work. The paradigm of 'harmony' in the governance of urban neighbourhoods echoes the objective of the central government to ensure 'social stability' (*shehui wending*).

The development of social work in Chinese urban neighbourhoods thus appears more focused on the prevention of social tensions than on the inclusiveness in the living environment, as stated in UN Agenda 2030, especially Article 11, aiming at developing 'sustainable cities and communities': 'make cities and human settlements inclusive, safe, resilient, and sustainable'. Yet the shift in Chinese approaches to social work can help us understand the way policies and practices shape a hybrid discourse, between socialist and neoliberal notions (Anagnost, 2008). The hybrid configuration combining the socialist legacy and a new neoliberal vocabulary forms a complex mixture in the case of neighbourhood community reform:

> the discourse of 'community' that has appeared in recent years turns upon a similar logic in seeking to develop more localized and economic forms of governance, where citizens are mobilized and trained to govern themselves. At the same time, this discourse embodies a substantial ethical element, where good 'community' governance is seen as being dependent on raising the moral 'quality' of urban citizens.
>
> (Bray, 2006, p. 533)

The neighbourhood – under the concepts of 'community' and 'harmony' promoted by the Chinese state – refers to a territory of policy rather than a grassroots initiative by residents. The new forms of social work produced at the local level show a new frame of definition of 'society', from 'masses' to 'social groups', and humanistic paradigms such as the 'people-centred' approach. In theory and in practice, local social work in neighbourhoods constitutes a technology of government (Leung et al., 2012), through both quantitative policy-making and qualitative forms of service provision. Since the Hu-Wen administration, social work has been a tool of control against the social infractions of both welfare recipients and local social workers themselves, which does not seem to promote inclusive and sustainable neighbourhoods following the Agenda 2030 recommendations.

Western European and Chinese academic research in the social sciences has published a great amount of analysis about Chinese local organizations since the beginning of the Maoist regime (Whyte and Parish, 1984). Associated with surveillance, propaganda and social control, the function of residents' committees has evolved alongside the reforms of the market economy (Read, 2000). Read (2012) carried out an in-depth investigation on residents' committees in Beijing, highlighting the political implications of this form of organization, situated between state and society. Other scholars studied the models of 'community governance' using many variables, including social capital, attachment theory and measures of participation, but without clarifying the day-to day interactions between frontline social workers and residents (Xu and Chow, 2006). Most of the scholarly literature studies the residents' committee from a political perspective, as objects of new 'governmentality' (Bray, 2005; Leung et al., 2012), or as tools of political participation (Heberer and Göbel, 2011). Chinese research about residents' committees tends to build a theoretical and technical framework of 'good' community governance, focusing on the way grassroots organizations can foster the emergence of a Chinese civil society (Li, 2008).

In urban China, residents' committee workers are now instructed to provide a range of local services to the local residents. What are the power forces that shape and redefine social work? Social work in neighbourhoods is produced by both policy documents and actual infrastructure, as well as the face-to-face interactions between the inhabitants and the 'community residents' committee staff' (*shequ jumin weiyuanhui gongzuozhe*). As a link between the inhabitants and the administration, the residents' committee can be seen as an incomplete street-level bureaucracy (Lipsky, 2010): the workers are not public servants.[80]

Located according to a geographical area of intervention, this para-administration is marginal to the life of wealthier residents in high-standard neighbourhoods. Many of them do not know where their residents' committee office is located. The new residential compounds are built around narratives of modern, civilized citizens living in an international metropolis, and by the residents' yearning for comfort, order and privacy. The urban neighbourhood has thus become more and more conformant to the social image of the 'good life' (Pow, 2009). Interestingly enough, even in these luxury compounds,

---

80 The street-level bureaucrat is defined as a civil servant directly in contact with the citizens and in charge of implementing public policy (Lipsky, 2010).

there is an office of the residents' committee, providing services to the vulnerable residents in need (older people for example).

Following a Foucauldian approach inspired by Nikolas Rose's concept of 'government through community', David Bray suggests that the new *shequ* policy of social welfare provision is based on

> a new generation of 'red experts', trained to re-establish social order, collective responsibility, and moral civilization within a fractured urban community. They are the other face of the 'socialist market economy,' and they force us to realise that transition in China is far more complex than we had ever imagined.
>
> (Bray, 2005, p. 190)

This chapter studies, through an ethnographic lens, the way social work in urban residential communities developed in the context of the economic reforms, turning from the work unit to the residential neighbourhood. A local mass organization, the residents' committee, gradually took over missions of social assistance, becoming an 'welfarist' street-level bureaucracy. Since the 2000s, social work in urban neighbourhoods has been carried out through an intertwined dynamic of 'control of' and 'services to' designated vulnerable urban groups, while other social groups in need remain mostly excluded from these channels of 'integration', based on the stability of urban residency.

My research on the daily work of residents' committees in Beijing and Chongqing is based on an ethnographic methodology: fieldwork consisted not only of in-depth interviews with residents' committee workers and local inhabitants, but also in direct and participatory observation (by becoming a 'volunteer' for one residents' committee). I selected different social contexts in two provincial-level cities, Beijing and Chongqing. In each city, I compared contrasting neighbourhood types: the historical city centre, where residents' committees have existed since the 1950s; work-unit housing (*danwei xiaoqu*), developed by the public sector from the 1960s to the 1990s; and commodity residential compounds (*shangpinfang xiaoqu*), developed in the 2000s by real-estate developers (*kaifa gongsi*). The ethnographic fieldwork focuses on the relationships between the community workers and the ordinary residents in order to shed light on the practice of social work 'from below'.

Parallel to long-term ethnographic fieldwork, I studied the internal norms produced at the national level, at the city administration level, and at the neighbourhood community level in the many publications on neighbourhood communities and residents' committees issued by the Ministry of Civil Affairs. This literature review illustrates the way official and internal norms of policy-making are established in the residents' committees' work.

First of all, this chapter shows how, in the context of economic reforms towards the market economy in China, urban neighbourhoods became a new field of experimentation for social work and service provision at the local level. Second, it focuses on the way social work takes place through the everyday governance of neighbourhoods by community workers, oscillating between control and compassion. Finally, it discusses the limitations of this territorialized community social work in urban China in the light of urban socio-spatial segregation, as well as by highlighting the forms of vulnerability and discrimination of the community workers themselves.

The urban neighbourhood and the residents' committee at the core of the redefinition of social service provision in post-Mao urban China

The redefinition of social work in urban China has its roots in the complex historical evolution of residents' committees during Maoist and post-Maoist China. During Maoist China, urban society was structured according to a tight network of surveillance. Introduced in the 1950s, the household registration system aimed to control population flows from the countryside to the cities. In addition, the work-unit system, which provided employees with housing and social services (food tickets, education for children, medical care), contributed to the building of a 'cellular' society (Lü and Perry, 1997, p. 11). Residence and workplaces were closely connected as a way to limit the mobility of the population.

From political surveillance to social work: the historical trajectory of residents' committees

Introduced in the 1950s to monitor the people who were not employed in a work-unit, the residents' committees were a marginal organization in cities (see the Regulations adopted by the First National People's Congress, 1954). The members of each committee were 'activists' recruited among the residents who were loyal to the Communist Party, and who were asked to keep the neighbourhood in order. Compared with the sphere of intervention of work-units, which was based on employment, the territory of the residents' committees was located in the city centre to manage older residential areas. There, the residents were more heterogeneous and harder to discipline. The local activists of the residents' committee were called 'small-feet patrols' (*xiaojiao zhenji dui*) because they were mostly composed of older women with bound feet,[81] retired or unable to work, recruited by the street office[82] among the inactive yet politically reliable residents. According to my interviews with the sons and daughters of early members, their income was very low: a member could not earn more than a monthly compensation of CNY 15. They had political functions (mobilizing the masses, delivering official messages, education), security and sanitary missions (assisting the police, checking household registration, watching the levels of hygiene in buildings) but also paid special attention to people in need (the sick, old, disabled, children) and were responsible for conflict mediation (Frolic, 1981, ch. 11).

After the Cultural Revolution, the Chinese central government gradually introduced economic reforms and launched the campaign for 'spiritual civilization' during which it started to revitalize the residents' committees. These new missions were connected to the new measures of flexibility of the household registration system, allowing more mobility to the cities. Their action targeted more precisely the new problematic population in cities, especially the urban poor. Despite a project of institutionalizing 'community services' (*shequ fuwu*) in urban residents' committees, the monthly salary of residents' committee agents remained very low. The committees were composed of low-skilled workers. After the Tian'an men repression of 1989, important social and spatial change occurred.

Housing in China was considered as a part of the social welfare provided by the state, and allocated through the work-unit. In the 1980s, the reforms undertaken in the cities progressively introduced a real-estate market. Housing was commodified over the next decade: families who rented apartments in the public system and work-unit system were able to buy their apartments for a preferential price, while apartments in the newly built residential compounds were sold at market prices. In 1998, the decision to stop work-units from allocating housing contributed to the fast transformation of the spatial and administrative structure of the Chinese city. In a parallel movement, the economic reforms, especially under the expression

---

81 Interviews with residents, confirmed in Feng Rui's report (1998, p. 108).
82 The street office (*jiedao banshichu*) is the local government unit in Chinese cities.

'socialist market economy' introduced in 1992, affected the public system of work-units as well as the former system of employment and social protection. Originally characterized by a secure form of employment and social benefits under the expression 'iron rice bowl' (*tie fan wan*), labour politics became more unstable. Sociologist Ching-Kwan Lee (1999) describes this period as 'disorganized despotism', explaining that factory managers gained power, given their capacity to dismiss workers without being limited by counter-powers from the Party or the labour unions. The number of 'laid-offs from the public system' (*xiagang*) led to the emergence of various social groups falling 'out-of-the-frame' of the *danwei*. The economic reforms led to the emergence of 'social cleavages' (Sun, 2003) in Chinese society (urban unemployment, poverty) and new social issues such as the ageing population as a consequence of the one-child policy, introduced in 1979. There was a need for 'off-*danwei*' social services.

In parallel, as a consequence of the housing reform, the urban landscape started to disconnect from the workplace. The public authorities had to deal with this new situation, while continuing to maintain public order. The new law of residents' committees, promulgated in December 1989, institutionalized the residents' committees as assisting bodies for the administration. In 1992, a special regulation reinforced their security missions, and they were considered as 'the eyes and ears of the state' (Wong and Poon, 2005, p. 414). Therefore, the urban neighbourhood became more and more important to the management of social affairs (Bray, 2005, pp. 166–72), with experimentation in terms of social service provision, defined by the Ministry of Civil Affairs. New guidelines were introduced in order to turn residents' committees into 'community service providers' (*shequ fuwu*) in 1993. This official document identified urban issues: an ageing population, growing unemployment, decline of the work-units, an increasing marginalization process, rising risks of social tensions, and increasing numbers of migrant workers in the cities (Xu, 2008, p. 28). Many urban workers laid off from the industrial *danwei* of Beijing became residents' committee workers. Luigi Tomba (2014, pp. 62–87) confirms this for Shenyang.

However, the financial structure of this new generation of neighbourhood leaders was unclear. The residents' committees were supposed to become social service agencies, specialized in re-employment support, and various forms of charity work. They also supervised local-level services such as bicycle repair shops, house-cleaning services and hairdressers. However, without a decent salary, the members actually provided paid social services, which was seen as unfair by the population in need (Yan and Gao, 2007, p. 234; Yeung et al., 1999). At the end of the 1990s, after a decade of local experimentation in managing the urban poor, the Ministry of Civil Affairs introduced a programme of social assistance, the urban minimum livelihood income (*zui di shenghuo baozhang*). In parallel, the salary of residents' committee members increased (Cho, 2010). Experiments in neighbourhood management were made with various 'governance models' in Shanghai, Shenyang and Wuhan (Bray, 2005).

In the 2000s, housing mainly became a commodity managed through the real-estate market. In this context, the notion of 'neighbourhood community' (*shequ*) emerged as a new way of managing the population: the territorializing of public action reaches down to the most local unit, the 'neighbourhood community' (*shequ*). The new policy published by the Ministry of Civil Affairs officially introduced 'neighbourhood community building' (*shequ jianshe*) as the new guideline of local management of urban society nationwide. According to the Ministry of Civil Affairs, the '*shequ*' is defined as 'a social collective formed by individuals who live in a fixed area'.[83] Each *shequ* manages 1,500 to 5,000 families, on a larger area than in the past. The missions of the *shequ* residents' committee focus on protecting the environment, providing education, and being in charge of local politics, 'grassroots democracy' and Party building (Bray, 2005, p. 535). In other words, the new focus on 'community' in urban neighbourhoods:

> is a result in part of the central government's apparent inability to provide the basic human services and meet welfare needs for its citizens. Consequently, the concept of community in China has changed in order to fill the services gap created when the central government moved to a market economy, and in so doing decentralised its responsibilities.
> (Xu and Chow, 2006, p. 206)

The urban neighbourhood reconfigured the field of social inclusion from the *danwei* system towards a residency-based system.

The complex legitimacy of the residents' committee agents in urban neighbourhoods

The new generation of residents' committees faces a complex legitimacy. Even if the status and missions were gradually codified by the 'neighbourhood community building' policy in 2000, the official

---

[83] Official documents published by the Beijing City Government, 2001.

status of this organization is still defined by the 1989 Organizational Law. The unclear legacy between past and present norms reinforces the ambiguity of this organization. Located in each neighbourhood, the residents' committee carries the paradoxical status of 'autonomous grassroots organization for the masses' (*qunzhong jiceng zizhi zuzhi*) supervised by the local administration: the street office recruits the workers. According to the 8th article of the Organizational Law, the local residents elect the workers every three years, but in practice, local elections are not often competitive (with seven candidates for six positions, for instance), and not always based on direct votes.[84] More importantly, elections are organized after the previous recruitment of workers by the local administration at the level of the street office. The street office confirms the elected members after the election. Most residents are not really interested in these local elections.

The 'community building' reform initiated the diversification of the employees' tasks as well as the professionalization of the structure. According to my interviews in Beijing, residents' committee employees had an average monthly wage between CNY 1,200 and 1,800 in 2007.[85] It increased to CNY 3,000 in 2012 and to CNY 5,000 in 2018. Their salary varies according to their status and to various processes of recruitment: some of them are part-time staff members, retired from their previous jobs; others went through a more selective recruitment and became 'neighbourhood community workers' (*shequ gongzuozhe*). Older volunteers or unemployed older women (*lao da ma*) no longer characterize the residents' committee. The staff are mostly recruited according to their skills. Today's residents' committee employees are younger (although committees are still partly composed of middle-aged women), and more qualified. Their current missions include executing official policies such as birth control, but also entertaining the neighbourhood, offering services and mediating local conflicts. The boundary of assignments between the residents' committee and the local Chinese Communist Party (CCP) branch is difficult to identify.

---

84   According to my fieldwork on elections in Beijing in 2009 and 2015, the voting system mainly followed indirect modes, through residents' representatives *(jumin daibiao)* or household representatives *(hu daibiao)*.

85   The average annual income for urban areas in 2007 was CNY 46,507, or CNY 3,876 per month, according to the National Bureau of Statistics (n.d.). In 2016, the average income reached CNY 105,161, or CNY 8,763 per month, according to the Beijing Statistical Yearbook 2017 (National Bureau of Statistics, 2017). The salary of the staff is low, but it is still a multiple of the minimum income for vulnerable groups *(dibao)* in Beijing.

Despite the more competitive recruitment, the workers' non-recognized affiliation with the administration justifies a low-income, low-status and ambiguous job description, sitting between a 'bureaucracy' and an NGO. The official definition as 'autonomous organization for the masses' implies that the staff works not only for the street office but also for the residents. They focus on specific social groups: the 'weak and vulnerable groups' (*ruoshi qunti*), listed as recipients of specific care, and more closely watched. Following the 'neighbourhood community' (*shequ*) reform, the residents' committees have taken on more and more social missions. They play a more important part in the official objective of 'social stability' (*shehui wending*). The urban neighbourhood thus represents a place of reduction of potential social tensions as a result of the professionalization of this local-level organization. The residents' committee staff members have not entirely become street-level bureaucrats or qualified social workers, nor have they become NGO workers.

Between control and compassion: the politics of 'neighbourhood community services' *(shequ fuwu)*

The slogan of the neighbourhood community reform, 'serving the residents'[86] (*wei jumin fuwu*), suggests the importance of service provision to *shequ* residents. The territorialized form of services and the way they are allocated through the residents' committees shows that social work constitutes a tool for alleviating social tensions and pacifying society in urban China. The concrete practices of social work develop under two dimensions: bureaucratic forms of control and surveillance, and more qualitative forms of neighbourhood animation.

The politics of quantity: numbers, surveillance, and monitoring the urban poor

In today's China, the governing of the population within one geographically defined area appears under many strategies. First of all, the local administration delegates a series of tasks carried out by the residents' committees at the local level. It is the case of 'numbers' (Wang, 2013), used for census, for the birth records or for reports to the upper-level administration. The workers are also required to relay

---

86 This is an intentional echo of the famous 'Serving the people' (wei renmin fuwu) slogan of Mao Zedong.

the voice of the public authorities during sensitive political events. Indeed, during important political events in China (the CCP Congress, the Olympic Games and so on), residents' committee workers mostly carry out administrative and security missions in the neighbourhood. When the period ends, they focus on sociocultural activities. More importantly, the residents' committee is the front-line organization in charge of controlling, following and watching disadvantaged residents. In China, the evolution of social work leads to a conception of society from 'masses' to 'social groups', but also to the development of surveillance to prevent social infractions (Dubois, 2003, p. 18).

This culture of distrust (Dubois, 2003, p. 54) appears quite clearly in the procedure of allocation of minimum urban welfare called *dibao*.[87] The application process goes through a mechanism of surveillance and in-depth investigation by residents' committee agents and community workers, who select the eligible candidates:

> There are many criteria to meet. ... Now, the *dibao* amounts to 330 yuan per month. The city does not provide it to migrant workers.
> (residents' committee agent, Beijing, 2 November 2007)

> The *dibao* is only for the people aged over 40.
> (director of a residents' committee, Chongqing older neighbourhood, 13 July 2015)

> I have received the *dibao* for two years: 330 *yuan* per month.[88] It's not easy to get it. You have to go yourself to the residents' committee, or else no one will take care of you .... You have to be from Beijing; if you aren't, then you aren't eligible. ... I'm unemployed and I'm sick, I'm diabetic ... I have to go to the hospital twice a month, and the residents' committee checks that I'm still sick.
> (*dibao* recipient, Beijing, 20 April 2008)

> One must correspond to the criteria (*fuhe tiaojian*). For instance, if you were in your 20s, it would never work. It is about the ability to work. One needs to actively look for a job (*jiji*). We can't give the *dibao* to everybody. ...

---

87 For more details about this safety net in urban China, see *Cho* (2010).
88 In 2018 in Beijing, the basic amount was CNY 1,100 per month (with variations depending on the situation of the recipient).

> We cannot give the state money to young people who never tried to work. We need time to prove one cannot work.
> (director of a residents' committee, Beijing, 21 May 2008)

> I was a factory worker. I quit because the job made me sick. But because I quit before retirement age [55 to 60 years old], I did not have any income. I have been a *dibao* recipient for many years.
> (*dibao* recipient, Beijing, 4 June 2008)

Residents' committee agents inspect the entire life of welfare recipients; they look for any material infraction (a pet, a mobile phone and the like) but also to any moral infraction (political opposition). In neighbourhoods, solidarity and surveillance tend to mix, with a climate of suspicion surrounding the allocation of welfare. The participation of residents in the surveillance confirms the ambivalent attitudes towards urban poverty (Rocca, 2006, pp. 117–35). Even if the social policies have developed, economic inclusion is not universal. According to our fieldwork, the only way to become a *dibao* recipient is to show incapacity to work. In addition, the *dibao* allocation is territorialized and unequally located, depending on local needs. There are far more applicants than welfare recipients.

This context leads to a form of competition between applicants, and there are precise criteria to evaluate the social needs based on the material environment and the lifestyle of each family. Neighbours participate in the investigation regarding each *dibao* applicant. Public notifications are put on the wall of the neighbourhood to inform people of a family's application. This type of public notification stays on the wall for one week, during which the residents are invited to control the official declaration. This control procedure is used for any welfare programme application, from *dibao* to social housing. This surveillance by 'the masses' (*qunzhong*) – as it is officially called – is accepted by residents, community workers and even *dibao* recipients, who are encouraged to show loyalty to the programme in order to keep receiving their allowance (Solinger, 2008). For all of them, this procedure is a way to discipline welfare recipients and to make them more responsible:

> *Dibao* induces laziness. If the state gives a person money, they will never look for a job.
> (long-term resident, Beijing historical city centre, 29 April 2007)

> The surveillance by neighbours is normal. This welfare programme is only given to the poorest population. A *dibao* allocation to one person means than another person cannot benefit from it so the must be a lot of attention to who can get it.
>
> (*dibao* recipient, Beijing historical city centre, 28 April 2007)

> People who receive the *dibao*, it's because they can't find work, so because they are sick. To get it, you have to go and see the residents' committee, fill out the forms and provide the documents, for example medical prescriptions. Generally you have to be over 35 years old. The committee sends these documents to the Office of Civil Affairs. After a few months you receive the payments. The committee puts up a notice informing the residents and they are asked for their opinion about the recipient .... I haven't had any problems but for other people, payments have been suspended because other residents reported them.
>
> (*dibao* recipient, Beijing, 28 April 2007)

In return, the *dibao* recipients play their part as victims in this game of submission, and the programme has two perverse effects. First of all, because of the local bureaucratic selection of applicants, the recipients are not always those most in need (Solinger, 2008, pp. 44–5). Second, the system is also characterized by embezzlement by employees or by recipients themselves, a form of 'marginalization via subversion of state design' (Solinger, 2008, p. 45). Moreover, sometimes violence in the words or actions of welfare applicants can help them get the allowance. Community workers fear these violent outbursts, because violence goes against the principles of a 'harmonious society' and 'social stability' (*shehui wending*) and the workers could lose their jobs. If a person starts screaming, the workers try to calm them down and find a solution, which means they might agree to open a welfare application:

> Residents' committee agents only help the residents who like them. Or the ones they fear could bring them trouble. The *dibao* recipients get this welfare not because they need it but because they go to the office every day and complain. That is why they validate their application. They are afraid that these people might get angry.
>
> (resident, Beijing, 29 April 2007)

Many interviews show that 'the louder one screams, the more chances one gets that the public system will find them a solution'. The pressure of social protest can be efficient to become a social service recipient. The quantitative politics of the *dibao* is a tool in order to preserve social stability in a defined territory rather than a general system of welfare. In recent years, following Xi Jinping's access to power, and the national goal of fighting against corruption, the *dibao* programme has evolved 'in sniffing out corruption among both local leaders and recipients' (Solinger, 2017, p. 57).

The politics of 'quality': local animation and moral education

The second dimension of the territorialized form of social work by residents' committees also has a more qualitative dimension, under the effort to 'reach out to' the residents. Residents' committee workers spend a lot of time in the office fabricating 'numbers', but they also spend a lot of time out of the office, in the neighbourhood, 'down to the homes' (*xia hu*). There is an effort to understand the vulnerable residents, to know their problems and to anticipate their expectations. This effort to reach out can be seen in the way the workers do not wear suits but ordinary clothes, and speak the local dialect rather than Mandarin when they are with the residents. They emphasize the importance of listening, of therapeutic dialogue, which is connected to a psychologizing ethos of social work: people with social problems tend to be seen as mentally unbalanced.

> It is about showing them a more positive attitude, to take care of their own problems. We try to change their mentality (*sixiang*).
> (community worker, Chongqing historical neighbourhood, 15 July 2015)

There are a growing number of training programmes in psychology for residents' committee employees, which suggests a neoliberal orientation of social work where the disadvantaged groups are considered as too 'passive', and are encouraged to become more proactive in the management of their problems. This corresponds to the findings of other researchers:

> As threats to social harmony were attributed to personal failings, the 'self' emerged as pivotal target of change in government programmes, and psychological intervention was endorsed as an important tactic for achieving the desired individual changes.
> (Leung et al., 2012, p. 10)

As a second element of neoliberal social work, according to Rose's approach to 'government through community' (Rose, 1999), state institutions reshape the field of social welfare, by leaving sectors of welfare provision to charity-like and community organizations. In the Chinese context, the residents' committees clearly have experienced a 'welfarist incorporation' (Howell, 2015) since the 2000s. The residents' committee staff members have become 'social workers' developing 'closer care' in urban neighbourhoods, but with few resources and qualifications in this field. In other words, local work takes its roots in a neoliberal rationality of social work, but it still remains under the leadership of the Party-state.

In the Chinese context, the provision of social services is framed by strict political principles: in their roles as providers of social services and mediators of social relations, social workers were simultaneously conceived as significant promoters of the party's rule and allies of the state in social management (Leung et al., 2012). As a consequence, local animation in the neighbourhoods constitutes a tool of social control. Social and cultural services are framed by the official political norms of the Chinese state. According to our fieldwork in Beijing, the residents' committee workers intervene as information and service centres for their residents, explaining to them how to fill out forms and getting all the documents ready for official procedures. However, they also serve as official informers, since they know precise details about their population. One agent in charge of 'security' cooperates with the local police station in order to maintain the public order. As for the social activities organized for the residents, leisure is often a component of support campaigns for government policies.

New techniques of communication (using WeChat, a popular mobile phone app) to inform the residents go together with more traditional forms of popular mobilization, for instance by keeping active a network of residents-volunteers to watch the streets (Audin, 2017). The local animation takes several forms: singing or dancing groups, calligraphy or computer classes. Public presentations in the neighbourhood are organized on a regular basis. Through these activities, the residents' committees introduce norms of 'good behaviour' in the local animation. All cultural events are framed into a civic and moral education of the population (patriotic songs are sung at local choirs, the projection of films is approved by the local administration, and so on). The recurrence of the term 'civilized behaviours' (*wenming xingwei*) as a key principle (especially important before the Olympic Games in Beijing) illustrates this idea. The social events organized by the residents' committee often deal with learning the principles of hygiene in the public space, or the benefits of healthy eating and exercising. Each activity is systematically photographed, filmed or reported, and is later published on the neighbourhood walls.

The narrative of the 'harmonious community' is thus materialized through real-life examples of local residents displaying happy faces during these socializing events.

Facing social challenges in contemporary urban China, the public authorities reappropriate several social fields which used to fall under the responsibility of work-units in the past decades. 'The state is gradually placing itself at the service of society' (Rocca, 2004, p. 171). In other words, local social work takes the form of community work and local services, producing new forms of 'care' for the 'weaker', more 'vulnerable' categories of the urban population. The interactions between frontline workers and residents are more intense with politicized residents (local 'activists') and with poor or disabled residents, who have free time and more motivation to participate in the low-cost community events. The growing acknowledgement of the needs of these residents is part of the state strategy to avoid social tensions at the local level.

The 'neighbourhood community' and neoliberal politics of local services: fostering selective and incomplete social inclusion

The *shequ* policy produces a series of attempts to care for and follow the integration of vulnerable social groups, but social inclusion remains selective and incomplete because the field of social work in China developed as a geographical conception of social welfare, and not as a universal ethos of social rights. Indeed, the scope of the 'vulnerable groups' targets specific social groups and people among urban residents while excluding other disadvantaged groups. Moreover, the efforts towards social inclusion stay at the level of the neighbourhood and thus do not challenge the main factor of social segregation in the city: the unequal system of housing provision, construction and demolition. Finally, the front-line agents who are responsible for the provision of services in order to foster social inclusion in the neighbourhood also face vulnerability and discrimination themselves.

The complex network of micro-local NGOs and socio-spatial segregation

The evolution of both housing policies and social policies in urban China reinforces the incomplete and even inadequate allocation of services by the grid system of neighbourhood community residents' committees. Social inclusion in neighbourhoods remains selective and limited, which explains the development of a sublevel of social work by a great variety of 'social organizations' (*shehui tuanti*), also called NGOs. These organizations revolve around residents' committees because they need their support in order to be officially registered at the local administration (Chan, 2013, p. 190). They complete the incomplete field of social work of government-sponsored frontline agents of the residents' committees, especially in the case of the most vulnerable social groups, who live in invisible forms of housing such as the underground tunnels[89] in Beijing (Huang and Yi, 2015) or in precarious housing such as workers' dormitories located directly on the production sites. In general, migrant workers (*nongmingong*) are excluded from the provision of social housing (Wissink et al., 2013; Huang and Tao, 2015).

Facing systematic discrimination and exclusion over the first decades of their presence in cities, migrant workers' residential location in neighbourhoods depends mainly on budgetary constraints (Wissink et al., 2013). According to our fieldwork, lower-income migrants tended to look for cheaper rents, in 'urban villages' (*chengzhongcun*) in the periurban areas and in the dilapidated one-storey houses (*pingfang*) in the traditional alleyways of the city centre (*hutong* in Beijing). Better-off migrants could live in commodity housing and in work-unit apartment blocks in periurban areas. There were almost no interactions between residents' committee staff and migrant workers: residents' committees could supervise the foundation of NGOs in favour of migrants' rights, but in most cases, these NGOs worked with networks that were independent from the residents' committees (Chan, 2013, p. 190).

Also, the urban poor and the migrant workers did not share the same living standards or lifestyles, and they did not build common local networks. In the urban neighbourhoods of Chongqing and Beijing, migrant workers were on average younger than local residents. In spite of being more economically active, they had lower living standards than local residents. Most of them were tenants and not homeowners. Their length of residence was shorter than for locals. Most importantly, migrant workers in Beijing are excluded from the social activities and welfare programmes of residents' committees in the neighbourhood: 'they are not long-term residents, they belong to

---

89   In a context of unequal access to housing, disadvantaged groups have turned to apparently unfit spaces for housing. Among those informal housing forms are the *basements and civil air defence shelters in Beijing.*

the floating population (*liudong renkou*) so we are not in charge' was the justification given by residents' committee workers.

In Chongqing, where the municipality received a significant arrival of rural migrants in the context of the building of the Three Gorges Dam, community workers had more consideration for these migrants, but there was still a sense of discomfort: 'the floating population are among the most difficult people to manage in this job'.[90] Excluded from community welfare programmes, migrant workers develop other social networks, and in some cases they are still able to create ties in their neighbourhood (Wu and Logan, 2016). The sublevel of local NGOs ensures the provision of services to excluded social groups such as migrant workers, but they depend on personal energies and relationships with the government in order to exist. They are not present everywhere. This is why the territorialized system of neighbourhood solidarity based on the residents' committee contributes to the emergence of an 'underclass' of vulnerable people, falling below the safety net provided to the urban poor and weak urban social groups (Thornton, 2017).

Moreover, the orientation of the 'territorialized' form of social work does not address the inequalities created in the national territory, as well as at the level of cities. For example, neighbourhood community resources in Chongqing were lower than in Beijing, and community workers said they needed to organize more activities and assistance programmes but with fewer resources:

> We are ten years late in terms of community work compared with Beijing and Shanghai. Yet our social issues are ten times heavier than in those rich cities!
> (community worker, Chongqing newly built compound, 23 July 2015)

Moreover, in Beijing, neighbourhoods with different needs all get the same resources in terms of staff and financial help. As a consequence, the workers based in difficult neighbourhoods would prefer a more adequate distribution of resources depending on the level of priority of social problems. As we saw in the previous section, the residents' committee workers offer counsel to their residents rather than real solutions to serious problems. Their means of action are too limited: 'We know their problems but we have no power' was a recurrent explanation. The objective of political stability also leads to an attempt to offer mediation in locality-based conflicts and find

---

90 Community worker, Chongqing, newly built compound, 22 July 2015.

solutions for unsatisfactory situations. However, the complexity of most situations and the different interests at stake make compromises all the more difficult to find. First of all, the structure of residents' committees is the same in all the neighbourhoods of the city, whether the social issues are serious or not:

> We are located in a historical district of Chongqing. In this community, we have a lot of people over 80 years old to look after. We also have more *dibao* recipients than in the newly built residential compounds. There is more social work here!
> (community worker, Chongqing older district, 9 July 2015)

The territorialized form of social work cannot address the main problems caused by the housing policy (see Hsing, 2010). Territorial inequalities introduced new forms of social conflict and conflict management: these social tensions caused by the urban politics of demolition-relocation or issues of commodity housing management are important at the local level. Housing conflicts illustrate many unbalanced power relationships: interest coalitions between developers and city officials, leading to the phenomenon of forced housing evictions. Caught in this unbalanced power relationship between the residents and the demolition teams, the residents' committee agents must carry out the eviction policies by trying to convince the residents to move out as quickly as possible.

> In this case, we cannot do anything else. Because the local government pays our salary and they ask us to help the demolition teams, we have to execute the task. ... And anyway, we also get evicted in the process because our office also gets destroyed during demolitions and evictions and we get transferred to another place. There is nothing we can do.
> (director of a residents' committee, Beijing historical city centre, 25 April 2015)

Indeed, the neighbourhood is a place for limited social inclusion in a context of socio-spatial segregation.

The vulnerability of residents' committee agents: facing low recognition, inventing new forms of local legitimacy

Despite their missions as social service providers, the residents' committee agents also show signs of vulnerability and exclusion. First of all, their work is faced with low recognition both from the residents and from the administration. According to interviews with residents, the residents' committee 'deals with the residents' problems' (*guan jumin de shiqing*). The way residents understand the job is always very vague. Most inhabitants show indifference or ignorance towards this organization. My ethnographic fieldwork revealed that the majority of residents are not even aware of the residents' committee's existence. Residents who have a 'normal' job rarely spend time in the neighbourhood during office hours, so they never interact with the social workers. Many residents I interviewed were not clear about their missions, randomly quoting 'political propaganda', 'helping the poor' or 'taking care of the old'.

Most of them criticize their lack of autonomy towards the administration. Many believe that their committees 'don't represent' (*bu daibiao*) them. Because of the hierarchical position in relation to the street office, the residents' committees are hardly seen as trustworthy by the residents. This is why the many efforts by some agents to commit and to show their hard work also bring sympathy and encouragement from the residents.

Moreover, the residents often complain about their committees not knowing (*bu liaojie*) the neighbourhood as deeply as they should, especially in newly developed urban areas.

> Can you believe that? Our residents' committee is composed of people who are all sent from outside the neighbourhood! This organization was supposed to represent our interests .... This is not possible, they don't live here, and they don't know this place. In these conditions, how can they pretend to protect my interests?
>
> (resident in a recent residential compound, Beijing, 28 December 2007)

This problem is owing to the professionalization of residents' committees. The employees do not necessarily live in the neighbourhoods where they work. In addition, because of their low salary, very few of them can afford to live in high-standard residential compounds, which reinforces the social and geographical distance from the local inhabitants.

In most cases, the residents consider the residents' committee as an 'inefficient' structure, pointing out a limited capacity of action: 'they have no power' (*mei you quanli*); 'they cannot solve the problem' (*jiejue bu liao*). Moreover, in luxury housing compounds, an important proportion of homeowners have strong social prejudice against the frontline workers: 'their education level is too low' (*suzhi tai di*).[91]

---

[91] The Chinese notion of '*suzhi*' expresses a form of social judgement based on education, good manners and so on.

Finally, the residents' committee workers often face personal criticism because they are the closest 'administrative' unit. The residents often accuse the workers of being responsible for their frustration, dissatisfaction or anger against the public authorities, or the inaction of another branch of the government. Yet in spite of criticism and mockery, the general existence of this local organization is rarely put to question. Although they complain about the workers for being 'useless', a majority of residents do not think the residents' committee should disappear. For example, long-time Beijingers, especially if they lived in the *hutong* or if they come from other major cities, have heard of this organization. Some mention their memory of the socialist period. More generally, people usually think of the residents' committee as a potential source of help. They regard it as 'useful, in case we get into some trouble'. However, because of the limited autonomy of action, the residents' committee can only help for small problems and report more serious issues to the upper levels of the Chinese administration. The paradox is that many residents go to the office to complain on a daily basis, but at the same time, most consider this organization as the only available unit where people would hear them if they needed to be heard.

As for the residents' committee workers, they all mention the difficulty to 'adapt' both to the residents and to the public administration. They must be 'flexible' and loyal to two different 'leaders' at the same time. Taking care of the administrative tasks is a priority, but all the residents' committee workers I met during my fieldwork in Beijing and Chongqing also worked hard to be acknowledged by (at least some of) their residents. Some agents mobilized informal relationships; others used their talents (singing, playing a music instrument) to reach out to the residents. Residents' committee agents play changing roles depending on the situation.

Sociologist Vincent Dubois analyzed the double attitudes of front-line public agents (police officers, social workers, teachers and so on) during their daily work in France (Dubois, 2003, pp. 73–136). Dubois shows that local agents switch attitudes when they face welfare recipients, striving at being legitimate to them as much as to their hierarchy. This 'double face' strategy of frontline workers is also present in China. In one case, residents' committee workers might choose to show the face of the 'public servant', referring to official policies, and in another, they might show their own personality to a resident. Also, the workplace of the residents' committee is not limited to the office. Workers often seek informal contact with the residents in order to foster more trust. For example, when they first address an inhabitant, the norm is to 'avoid politics' (Eliasoph, 1998) and use small talk.

> Even if we cannot get in touch with everybody directly, we find ways to know their situation. I'm not saying the residents must inform us about everybody's business, but eventually, we end up knowing it. For example, when I chat with one person randomly met outside, I keep alert about all the small details. By showing interest for her family, her neighbours, it seems that I'm just chitchatting, but in fact, I learn who just got married, who just got pregnant, it's part of the job.
> (community worker, Beijing workers' housing compound, 28 April 2007)

In Beijing, the staff in many residents' committees had to develop personalized face-to-face contact with at least several residents. Their influence on the local area could grow thanks to an important personal investment in the local life of residents and to a solid network of loyal supporters. The agents relied on their ambiguous identity, and used not only official ways (official announcements in newspapers and on the walls), but also informal tactics to obtain their cooperation (little gifts provided by the street office, face-to-face friendly interactions, personal networks).

> The residents' committee organized a distribution of small gifts for the Spring Festival: one big bottle of cooking oil, one big bag of flour and one big bag of rice. 'It is a special attention for our *dibao* recipients, who often cannot afford those daily commodities.'
> (observation, Beijing commodity-housing compound, 2 February 2015)

These examples help bring new perspectives on the way 'incomplete civil servants' (Massicard, 2015) work in urban China: the difficult working conditions of residents' committee employees lead them to rely mainly on their own personal 'talents' instead of their 'bureaucratic identity'. The efficiency of neighbourhood governance depends on personal energy as much as on institutional incentives: the agents thus produce a fragile balance, mixing public interest (official agenda) with private ones (friendship, mutual favours and so on), without leading to a crisis in local governance and without leading to a full integration of the *shequ* into the public administration. At this level of government, the ambiguity of the residents' committee leads to the emergence of a specific, in-between professional ethic.

The staff work under high pressure, for a low salary. Residents' committee agents express feelings of both satisfaction for getting a job in the public sector, and frustration because of the high pressure and limited income. Far from the idea of a monolithic bureaucracy, fieldwork reveals that working in a residents' committee office conveys contradictory, changing subjectivities, between enthusiasm and disenchantment.

In general, the agents face high levels of expectation but are still equipped with few means of action and get modest wages. The lack of professional management techniques constitutes a handicap for everyone, especially for the oldest staff members. The limited infrastructure and the important amount of problems to deal with contribute to their judging the job 'difficult', 'hard' and 'tiring'. Elements such as overtime work, low wages, daily mediation of conflicts and litigation, criticism and claims from everywhere increase their feeling of being poorly considered.

> I hope that advantages will get better for community workers. ...
> I mean, we are important, we are the people who work for social stability!
> (director of a community residents' committee,
> Chongqing older neighbourhood, 9 July 2015)

Being employed in a residents' committee may mean being part of the urban administration, but it is not a way to get promoted and reach higher levels in the administrative hierarchy.

The employees come from very different social backgrounds, but most of them have been through previous professional difficulties. Being part of the residents' committee guarantees three-year professional stability and offers minimum social protection: it is 'better than nothing'.

> Before working in the residents' committee, I had a lot of small jobs.
> ... Yes, you can say I was recruited here as a 'person of multiple talents' *(laughter)*!
> (community worker, Chongqing older district, 15 July 2015)

A growing number of university graduates turn to this work sector because of the high competition on the labour market; it is a way for them to get an urban resident's permit (*hukou*) after graduation. After a few years, if they find better work opportunities, they usually resign.

The development of social work as a field of specialization of the residents' committees also offers employees new perspectives, in spite of the low salary. Some of them 'like helping others'. A few symbolic objects such as the official stamp or the official sign at the entrance of the office can convey feelings of recognition. The workers strive at being recognized, legitimized and accepted by their residents. Many statements, such as 'this job is all about trust', illustrate this attitude. Although they are often considered as extensions of the administration, they spend much time cultivating personal interactions with their residents.

> I am very good at keeping good relationships with the residents. You know, I live in the area too, this is a good way to be integrated into the neighbourhood.
> (community worker, Chonqging older district, 15 July 2015)

Finally, the missions of the residents' committee consist of a difficult task: executing official decisions from above, even if these are unrealistic, unfair or not welcome by the residents.

> You know, our most difficult problem is the autonomy. We should be totally independent from the official administration and really put ourselves at the service of the residents. But we cannot do it, because concretely, the administration uses us to execute tasks for them.
> (director of a residents' committee, Beijing historical city centre, 1 October 2015)

It is a way for the political institutions to avoid direct contact with the population: the residents must first report to their residents' committee before getting appointments with upper levels of the administration.

> I want to do well. But I feel as if I am not specialized enough. I am not qualified enough for such heavy social missions. I study a lot but I need to continue. I really spend a lot of time trying to work well. But the salary is so low!
> (community worker, Chongqing, older neighbourhood, 14 July 2015)

The residents' committee employees, who execute public policy in direct contact with the inhabitants, appear as a particular type of 'street-level bureaucrats'. This is a precarious, low-wage, overtime line of work. Even if they tend to be younger and more educated than before, the residents' committee workers have low qualifications, little self-esteem and no hope of better professional opportunity. During my fieldwork, I identified a majority of women, aged 22 to 57.

The status of this organization is complex because the agents are caught in two different networks: the city administration and the local neighbourhood. This explains why the staff members are not always committed to their social missions.[92] The shift in formats of social work from work units (*danwei*) to community (*shequ*) contributed to institutionalize residents' committees as the structurally disadvantaged workers of the Chinese urban administration.

Conclusion

In conclusion, the transition from *danwei* to urban communities has produced new territorialized practices of social work in an ambiguous system of governance, between bureaucratic policy-making and local innovation, in twenty-first-century urban China. Under the policy of 'community building' (*shequ jianshe*), urban neighbourhoods have become spaces of experimentation on front-line social work and local social control. The gradual professionalization of residents' committees has developed new forms of services at the local level aiming at stabilizing and pacifying Chinese society at the most local level, under strict Party-state leadership: application of poverty programmes, politicized forms of education and social animation. The daily work of the residents' committee staff, between administrators and social workers, is an attempt to keep up with the acceleration of social change and to prevent the emergence of social issues. In this context, social work in urban China functions as 'work on society'. However, the low recognition and low-paid job, the heavy work both in the office and outside, the blurred frontiers between administrative work and community work, and the exclusion of the most vulnerable populations and the growing social and spatial segregation in cities constitute real limits to the sustainability of urban neighbourhoods in urban China. The politicized and territorialized implementation of social work in neighbourhood takes place in a fragile equilibrium, relying mostly on the personal energies of the residents' committees' staff members.

---

92   See also Fang (2017).

References

Anagnost, A. 2008. From 'class' to 'social strata': grasping the social totality in reform-era China. *Third World Quarterly*. Vol. 29, No. 3, pp. 497–519.

Audin, J. 2017. Civic duty, moral responsibility, and reciprocity: an ethnographic study on resident-volunteers in the neighbourhoods of Beijing. *China Perspectives*, No. 3, pp. 47–56.

Bray, D. 2005. *Social Space and Governance in Urban China. The danwei system from origins to reform*. Stanford, Calif., Stanford University Press.

---. 2006. 'Building 'community': new strategies of governance in urban China. *Economy and Society*, Vol. 35, No. 4, p. 530-549.

Chan, K.-M. 2013. The rise of civil society in China. É. Florence and p. Defraigne (eds), *Towards a New Development Paradigm in Twenty-First Century China: Economy, society and politics*, Abingdon, UK, Routledge, pp. 179–202.

Cho, M. Y. 2010. On the edge between 'the people' and 'the population': ethnographic research on the minimum livelihood guarantee. *China Quarterly*, No. 201, pp. 20–37.

Dubois, V. 2003. *La vie au guichet: relation administrative et traitement de la misère*. Paris, Economica.

Eliasoph, N. 1998. *Avoiding Politics. How Americans Produce Apathy in Everyday Life*. Cambridge, Cambridge University Press.

Fang, Y. 2017. Why China's welfare warriors have had enough of front-line work. *Sixth Tone*, 12 June. www.sixthtone.com/news/1000318/why-chinas-welfare-warriors-have-had-enough-of-front-line-work (Accessed 15 June 2017.)

Feng, R. 1998. Mass-line policing: Weikeng Public Security Committee, Beijing. M. Dutton (ed.), *Streetlife China*, Cambridge, Cambridge University Press, pp. 107–11.

First National People's Congress. 1954. Regulations on the Organization of Urban Neighborhood Office (*chengshi jiedao banshichu zuzhi tiaoli*), adopted at the Fourth Meeting of the Standing Committee of the First National People's Congress on December 31, 1954.

Foucault, M. 2000. *Essential Works of Michel Foucault: Vol. 3. Power*, ed. J. D. Faubion. New York, New Press.

Frolic, M. 1981. *Mao's People: Sixteen Portraits of Life in Revolutionary China*. Cambridge, Mass., Harvard University Press.

Heberer, T. and Goebel, C. 2011. *The Politics of Community Building in Urban China*. London, Routledge.

Howell, J. 2015. Shall We Dance? Welfarist Incorporation and the Politics of State-Labour NGO Relations. *The China Quarterly*, No. 223, pp. 702–23.

Hsing, Y.-T. 2010. *The Great Urban Transformation: Politics of land and property in China*. New York, Oxford University Press.

Huang, Y. and Tao, R. 2015. Housing migrants in Chinese cities: current status and policy design. *Environment and Planning C: Government and Policy*, Vol. 33, pp. 640–60.

Huang, Y. and Yi, C. 2015. Invisible migrant enclaves in Chinese cities: underground living in Beijing, China. *Urban Studies*, Vol. 52, No. 15, pp. 2948–73.

Lee, C.-K. 1999. From disorganized dependence to disorganized despotism: changing labour regimes in Chinese factories. *China Quarterly*, No. 157, pp. 44–71.

Leung, T. T. F., Yip, N. M., Huang, R. and Wu, Y. 2012. Governmentality and the politicisation of social work in China. *British Journal of Social Work*, pp. 1–21.

Li, Y. 2008. Community governance: the micro basis of civil society. *Social Sciences in China*, No. 1, pp. 132–41.

Lipsky, M. 2010. *Street-Level Bureaucracy: Dilemmas of the individual in public services.* New York, Russell Sage Foundation.

Lü, X. and Perry, E. (eds). 1997. *Danwei. The changing Chinese workplace in historical and comparative perspective.* New York, Armonk.

Massicard, E. 2015. The incomplete civil servant. The figure of the neighborhood headman (muhtar). M. Aymes, B. Gourisse and E. Massicard (eds), *Order and Compromise: Government practices in Turkey from the Late Ottoman Empire to the early 21st century,* Leiden, Netherlands, Brill, pp. 256–90.

National Bureau of Statistics. 2017. *Beijing Statistical Yearbook 2017.* http://tjj.beijing.gov.cn/nj/main/2017-tjnj/zk/indexeh.htm (Accessed 23 July 2018).

---. n.d. Statistics. www.bjstats.gov.cn/nj/main/2009-en/content/mV48_0317.htm (Accessed 12 June 2018).

Pow, Choon-Piew. 2009. *Gated Communities in China: Class, Privilege and the Moral Politics of the Good Life.* London, Routledge

Read, B. L. 2000. Revitalizing the state's urban 'nerve tips'. *China Quarterly*, Vol. 163, pp. 806–20.

---. 2012. *Roots of the State: Neighborhood organization and social networks in Beijing and Taipei.* Stanford, Calif., Stanford University Press.

Rocca, J.-L. 2004. Is China becoming an ordinary state? B. Hibou (ed.), *Privatizing the State.* London, Hurst, pp. 169–82.

---. 2006. *La condition chinoise.* Paris, Karthala.

Rose, N. 1999. *Powers of Freedom: Reframing political thought.* Cambridge, Cambridge University Press.

Solinger, D. J. 2008. The dibao recipients: mollified anti-emblem of urban modernization. *China Perspectives*, No. 4, pp. 36–46.

---. 2017. Manipulating China's 'minimum livelihood guarantee': political shifts in a program for the poor in the period of Xi Jinping. *China Perspectives,* No. 2, pp. 47–57.

Sun, L. 2003. *Duanlie* [Cleavage]. Beijing, Shehui kexue wenxian chubanshe.

Thornton, p. M. 2017. A new urban underclass? Making and managing 'vulnerable groups' in contemporary China. V. Shue and p. M. Thornton (eds), *To Govern China: Evolving practices of power.* Cambridge, Cambridge University Press.

Tomba, L. 2014. *The Government Next Door: Neighborhood politics in urban China*. Ithaca, N.Y., Cornell University Press.

Wang, D. 2013. Operating norms and practices of residents' committees: the consequences and limits of management by numbers. *China Perspectives*, No. 1.

Whyte, M. K. and Parish, W. L. 1984. *Urban Life in Contemporary China*. Chicago, Ill., University of Chicago Press.

Wissink, B., Hazelzet, H. and Breitung, W. 2013. Migrant integration in China: evidence from Guangzhou. F. Wu, F. Zhang and C. Webster (eds), *Rural Migrants in Urban China: Enclaves and transient urbanism*. London, Routledge, pp. 99–120.

Wong, L. 2013. Improving the Chinese welfare state in the new millennium. É. Florence and p. Defraigne (eds), *Towards a New Development Paradigm in Twenty-First Century China: Economy, society and politics*, Abingdon, Routledge,, pp. 127–43.

Wong, L. and Poon, B. 2005. From serving neighbors to recontrolling urban society: the transformation of China's community policy. *China Information*, Vol. 19, No. 3, pp. 413–42.

Wu, F. and Logan, J. R. 2016. Do rural migrants 'float' in urban China? Neighboring and neighborhood sentiment in Beijing. *Urban Studies*, Vol. 53, No. 14, pp. 2973–90.

Xiao, L., Xiao, Y., Zeng, S. and He, X. 2017. Degree or examination: what is the foundation of the social work workforce in China? *International Social Work*, Vol. 62, No. 1, pp. 1–14.

Xu, F. 2008. New modes of governance: building community/shequ in post-danwei China. A. Laliberté and M. Lanteigne (eds). *The Chinese Party-State in the 21st Century: Adaptation and the reinvention of legitimacy*, London, Routledge, pp. 22–38.

Xu, Q. and Chow, J. C. 2006. Urban community in China: service, participation, and development. *International Journal of Social Welfare*, Vol. 15, No. 3, pp. 198–208.

Yan, M. C. and Gao, J. G. 2007. Social engineering of community building: examination of policy process and characteristics of community construction in urban China. *Community Development Journal*, Vol. 42, No. 2, pp. 222–36.

Yeung, A., Fung, K. K. and Lee, K. M. 1999. Implementation problems in the development of urban community services in the People's Republic of China: the case of Beijing. *Journal of Sociology and Social Welfare*, Vol. 26, No. 3, pp. 159–61.

CHAPTER 9

THE RIGHT TO CENTRALITY AND DISCURSIVE ARTICULATIONS: A CASE OF CITY PLANNING POLICIES IN DELHI

Ashok Kumar

A. Introduction

When policy intentions and outcomes on the ground are completely at variance from each other, it is time to analyze and critically explain cities with new theories. Urban policy in India, for example, is increasingly aimed at promoting an inclusive city involving all citizens in the process of producing space, and benefiting from economic activities including technology-led efficiency dividends. More recently pronounced city planning policies have made inclusivity one of their central planks. For instance, the policy document of the Smart City Mission clearly advocates 'sustainable and inclusive development' (Ministry of Urban Development, 2015, p. 6). At the same time, the policy also emphasizes the idea of the city as an arena of economic growth leading to a better quality of life. Keeping a balance between inclusivity, sustainability and economic growth appears to be difficult, and the idea of the city as a vehicle for economic growth appears to be winning over equally important ideas of inclusivity and sustainability. So in order to unearth real policy intent, new theories deserve consideration.

The chief claim of this chapter is that even seemingly inclusionary planning policies could end up in multiple exclusions, leading to multiple deprivations through discursive articulations adversely affecting the right to centrality of the urban poor. The right to centrality is not about locating the poor in central parts of a city. The right to centrality refers to the participation of citizens – including the poor – in decision-making processes underpinning the production of spaces. The right to centrality is the right to urbanity. Forced displacement and gentrification are not part of the right to centrality. Therefore, centrality does not necessarily imply location near or in the city centre; it refers to accessibility to well-paid work, affordable mobility, decent housing and basic services such as water, sanitation, health care and education.

City planning policies in Delhi

A housing policy introduced in 2009, *Rajiv Awas Yojana*,[93] was intended to provide shelter to the urban poor by commoditizing their properties, but shows exclusionary consequences. It led to gentrification of the spaces inhabited by the poor, such as slums, when these depleted environments are converted into modern built environments for the rich and middle classes. Redevelopment of slums through public–private partnerships in the cities of Delhi and Mumbai is another instance of exclusionary planning. I regard spatial exclusions not only as the displacement of citizens from one place to another, but also exclusion from work, particularly for poor women, or the extinction of their traditional occupations even when they are resettled in the same place, but in a different form of built environment. Both these exclusions along with isolation from the city could be explained and challenged through Henri Lefebvre's 'right to centrality' (1996). Although the subject of social exclusion through public policy is a well-established area in the field of urban studies, planning scholars in India have not yet paid adequate attention to the idea of 'spatial inclusions as exclusions' in Indian cities. This chapter fills this gap by examining the processes of planning, redevelopment, rehabilitation and resettlement in two slums of Delhi.

In this chapter, spatial injustices against the urban poor are viewed as violations of the 'right to centrality' as postulated by Henri Lefebvre. Prominent Indian urban policies and two case studies of slums located in Delhi are used as illustrations of discursive articulations reflective of redevelopment-led planning practice. Discursive articulations are purposive and dynamically strategic. I use Henri Lefebvre's conceptual formulation of the right to centrality to comprehend spatial exclusions, which are theorized as the expansion of the urban frontier by forcefully ousting the urban poor from their homes and workplaces, and disrupting their everyday lives in order to make way for the middle classes in Indian cities. Spatial inclusion in this paper means struggles to secure the urban, the right to centrality.

Second, it is argued that incidents of spatial injustice in slums could easily be reconstructed afresh as menace and danger to the city's elite and middle classes. Once a new meaning is given and a new object is reconstructed through what Mustafa Dikeç calls 'discursive articulations', 'a perceptive field' is reconfigured (Dikeç, 2004, p. 192). Once public perceptions of dominant classes and decision-makers are reconstructed, places such as slums appear as reconstituted objects of policy interventions, which represent new solutions to newly

---

93   The housing policy was named after Rajiv Gandhi, former prime minister of India.

reconfigured problems. Exclusionary processes causing displacement could then easily be carried out, perpetuating violations of the right to centrality, the right to urban.

Theoretical underpinnings of the right to centrality and discursive articulations are explored in the second part of this chapter. Links of the right to centrality with the 2030 Agenda for Sustainable Development are then briefly discussed. The third and fourth parts of the chapter use discursive articulations as an instrument to analyze current economic policies and planning policy regimes. Through the lens of discursive articulations, the cases of Kathputli and Bhalswa Jahangir Puri in Delhi are examined to show how the right to centrality is violated. The chapter ends with some concluding insights.

B. Theoretical considerations and methodology

Theorizing the Indian city is a complex task, because Indian society is complex and uncertain. Social divisions based on class fold into divisions based on caste, religion, region, language and food habits, just to name a few factors. This makes the Indian city difficult to comprehend. In this paper, the right to centrality is used as a framing device for understanding the Indian city.

The right to centrality

Displacements and evictions of low-income families are the visible spatial manifestations of rising levels of urbanization in India. Over-riding reasons for displacements and evictions in Indian cities are clashes and conflicts between the needs of the urban poor and the aspirational classes. It could be a conflict about the legitimate use of a planned park as an open space by middle-class communities in their neighbourhood, and the same park being used for open defecation by a poor boy who has no access to sanitation facilities (Baviskar, 2003, 2006; also see Dupont, 2008). It could be that spaces are presently held by marginal groups for living, but are desired by the rich and powerful for building a promenade (Bhan, 2009). It could also be the rounding-up by the state of persons who are asking passers-by for money from the streets, in order to protect 'national pride' during a mega sporting event (Cook and Laing, 2011). Any of these situations could lead to displacements and evictions of marginal groups from the city.

Another significant part of this scholarship views harshness of urbanization as a consequence of the 'expansion of the urban frontier, a making way and making space for the new Indian middle class, through the smashing of the homes and livelihoods of the urban poor' (Roy, 2011*a*, p. 259; also see Watson, 2009). Spaces occupied by marginal groups that are today objects of 'expanding urban frontiers' were historically located on the edges of the cities. Being located on the margins, the occupation of these lands did not invite immediate state action against the urban poor and they were allowed to stay on these lands. Over a period of time, these settlements have grown and expanded like other settlements. Today when cities and towns are fast expanding, these spaces are fast becoming part of the city, and decision-makers are beginning to realize the value of these lands, paving the way for action against the poor, who are termed 'illegal occupiers'. However, forced removal is not restricted to Indian cities. As data on global evictions and displacements from urban areas clearly demonstrate, displacements and evictions are a global phenomenon (see Speak and Kumar, 2016).

On the other hand, the SDG targets 11.1 and 11.2 of the 2030 Agenda for Sustainable Development (United Nations, 2015) clearly seek to 'upgrade slums', and provide 'affordable housing' and transportation that poor people can use. This is further reinforced by the Universal Declaration of Human Rights, particularly Article 1. I. *The Challenge of Slums: Global report on human settlements 2003*, an argument is presented for '"an inclusive city" approach by local authorities who are increasingly responsive and accountable to their citizens, seeking to benefit all constituents and embracing principles of good governance' (UN-Habitat, 2003, p. 165). The UN-Habitat inclusive city concept implies the inclusion of slum populations in the general population, by providing integrated infrastructure, secure land tenure, enhanced livelihood opportunities, mobilization of urban finance, public–private partnerships and good governance. The Constitution of India is also steadfast about inclusivity, and article 21 about the Right to Life is a classic example of this. Further, we can draw on a number of important articles from the Constitution of India (Articles 30, 340, 341 and 342) that deal with the eradication of poverty and inclusivity.

However, in less than two and half decades, the development agenda in India has moved from welfare-oriented policy regimes to market-led policies. Generally speaking, urban planning policies have followed economic policies: cities have become one of the central sites for the implementation of market-led policies. The Government of India is directly involved in framing urban planning and development policies. If the urban poor come in the way of implementation of these policies, they are to be set aside. The building of flagship projects like the Delhi Metro (underground public transport) and the 2010 Commonwealth Games held at Delhi are two notable examples of making way for 'development'. Redevelopment of slum lands is another illustration of restructuring and modernizing the city. The chief point is that development displaces; development led by the private sector or a public–private partnership displaces even more, apart from being inequitable and unjust.

It is in this context that the rhetoric of inclusive city policies is folded into economic growth policies, and is used as a device to paper over the real consequences of these policies for the urban poor. Current urban policies, if anything, have perpetuated displacements and evictions, and consequently continued to push the poor towards the physical and societal periphery. Urban poor are evicted from the urban, from the centrality – including physical as well as political and economic centrality. Evictions of squatters from the city to its margins could be treated as the domination of urban space by the elite, when evicted spaces are rendered out of reach of the urban poor, owing to new land uses such as malls and entertainment plazas. Geographical distance from major places offering employment marginalizes the poor by making access to these places potentially expensive. Here exploitation in the form of loss of livelihoods and domination in the form of evictions from the city to the margins are not only socially and spatially manifested, but also socially and spatially produced and reproduced. Speak (2012) has showed that women evicted from the urban area cannot return to the inner city because of mobility and cost constraints. The distance between the urban area and its periphery is prohibiting enough for them to stay away from centrality, the urban of Lefebvre.

At this stage, the appropriate question is: What is the right to centrality? The right to centrality refers to primarily two aspects. First, the right to centrality means that citizens have the right to play a prominent role in decision-making processes concerning the production of space. Second, citizens have the right to stay put and physically shape the central parts of a city. Therefore, upholding the right to the city means that voices of *citadins* majorly influence the urban lived space – *habiter*. In other words, the right to participation and the right to appropriation are two pivotal components of the right to centrality. Removal of the working classes from central Paris provided the context to Henri Lefebvre's formulation of the idea of the right to the city (Purcell, 2003, p. 578).

Lefebvre (1996) views the urban as a 'sociospatial form of centrality', which mediates between 'large social order ... (the state and state-bound knowledge, the capitalist world economy), on one hand, and the contradictory level of everyday life' (Kipfer et al., 2012, p. 119) on the other hand. Struggles to secure the inclusive city mean struggles for the urban, for centrality. It is argued that not everyone is completely evicted. Reconfigured physical spaces vacated by the urban poor after evictions do accommodate the male urban poor at the lowest rungs as porters, security guards and so on. I would like to identify this situation as *peripheral centrality*: being outside even when located inside. These are generally contracted jobs with private companies, and workers are paid extremely low wages. Women and children are relocated from the city centre to resettlement colonies, which are generally located several miles away from city centres, compelling men to live separately from their families while women alone have to look after the children and take on other household responsibilities (see Speak, 2012; Chant, 2013).

Henri Lefebvre's (1996) notion of the urban reconstructs the meaning of the city by focusing on the urban as the centrality operative between everyday life, and the state or the global:

> Practices of centrality are sometimes linked to physical forms in reasonably stable ways. This is the case, for example, when economic power is concentrated in downtown financial districts or airport complexes. Sometimes, centrality remains momentary, however. General strikes or semi-autonomous popular festivals can create 'dense' forms of subaltern life or counter-power which leave few physical traces.
> (Kipfer et al., 2012, p. 119)

The concept of centrality is identified as fluidity, which does not have to be located in the centre of the city, and does not have to be a physical entity, as can be seen in the case of counter-power, expressed by temporary social movements, emerging and dissipating depending on several processes enveloping such movements. It is in this context that the right to the city 'legitimates the refusal to allow oneself to be removed from urban reality by a discriminatory and segregative organization' (Lefebvre, 1996, p. 195).

Explanations embodied in the right to centrality enable a move towards the concept of an inclusive city, free of conflict among classes over territory. In this journey, one crucial way to address the problem of marginalization of the urban poor is to take the 'urban' seriously. Even before Lefebvre, two meanings were associated with the city: the Roman *civitas* meaning human relationships, and *urbs* meaning built forms. This implies that 'the city is built form as well as a human relationship – a material place that visibly and tangibly expresses human needs and aspirations, supporting or hindering their fulfilment' (Tuan, 1988, p. 316). This historical definition identifies the city as a given site where communities succeed or fail in forging meaningful human relationships. This way of imagining the city treats it as a physical entity where humans could playfully cultivate relationships.

Read in another way, the idea of low-income housing provision at a sub-zonal level in the *Master Plan for Delhi, 1981* (DDA, 1962) has clear resonance with the right to centrality. The idea was simple: low-income housing would be provided at the area level in all parts of the city. This meant that the urban poor would not be ghettoized in one corner of the city. However, the Delhi Development Authority (DDA) did not implement this inclusive policy. When it was contested in the Delhi High Court, one judge gave a favourable verdict for the people. However, in June 2014 the case was dismissed in favour of the DDA. An attempt to secure the right to centrality was once again thwarted.

Discursive articulations

Arjun Appadurai argues that 'dissensus, alterity and otherness are the discursive conditions for the circulation and recognition of a politicized subject and a public "truth"' (1994, p. 23). Discursive articulations have also been taking place at a global scale where cities of the West are marked as dominant economic nodes, while cities in low-income countries are represented as chaotic sites of underdevelopment, a patchwork of informal development and slums:

> While global cities, mainly in the First World, are seen as command and control nodes of the global economy, the cities of the global South are scripted as megacities, big but powerless. Off the map, they are usually assembled under the sign of underdevelopment.
>
> (Roy, 2011*b*, p. 308)

In this chapter, I am interested in understanding the implications of discursive manoeuvrings and articulations at the city level. For city-level analysis, recent scholarship produced by Mustafa Dikeç is most promising. Drawing on Jacques Ranciere, Dikeç shows that 'space is produced through practices of articulation'. Production of space is undertaken through systems of representation, urban policies being one of these systems of representation to create a certain kind of spatial order through 'various practices of articulation' such as 'spatial designations, namings, categorizations, mappings, statistics and so on' (Dikeç, 2007, p. 172).

According to the framework of discursive articulations, in the first instance, incidents of spatial injustices are converted into violent incidents occurring in places which are constructed afresh as places of menace and danger to the very existence of a country. Once a new meaning is given and a new object is constructed through what Dikeç calls 'discursive articulations', 'a perceptive field' is reconfigured (Dikeç, 2004, p. 192). Once this is done, places such as slums appear as reconstituted objects of policy interventions, which represent new solutions to newly reconfigured problems. Dikeç discusses five instances of reconfiguration of a perceptive field. These are new institutional structures (such as resident welfare associations and public–private partnerships in Delhi); new anti-ghetto laws (such as the recently written Section 133 of the Code of Criminal Procedure, 1973 of India related to nuisance, and Bombay Prevention of Begging Act 1959 made applicable to Delhi in 1960, making begging, hawking and peddling in public places offences punishable by imprisonment or fine); profiling and objectification (collection of information about urban poor seeking jobs, particularly as drivers and housekeepers in middle-class households); collaboration with other ministries to prevent delinquency; and the creation of a new department within a ministry dealing with internal security (see Dikeç, 2004, pp. 198–9). The ground is thus prepared for the criminalization of slum dwellers or any other such group.

In India, the recent history of environmental law cases in higher courts reveals quite similar trends of discursive articulation. It has turned discourse about slums from places of inadequate infrastructure and places of residence for persons who need shelter and cannot afford anything better because of their income poverty, to slums as a 'nuisance', which is defined under Section 133 of the Code of Criminal Procedure, 1973 of India as 'obstruction to a public place or way, trades or activities hazardous to the surrounding community, flammable substances, objects that could fall or cause injury, unfenced excavations or wells, or unconfined and dangerous animals' (Ghertner, 2011*a*, p. 26; also see Ghertner, 2011*b*). The inclusion of activities hazardous to the surrounding community in the definition of nuisance clearly has unjust consequences for the urban, and particularly for people living in slums, as shown by Baviskar (2003), where violence leads to the death of a slum resident caught up in a clash with middle-class residents.

Policies like the world city narrative in India are the most visible attempt to achieve cities of appropriate behaviour, human behaviour which is of course suited to economic growth, at the price of increasing human suffering, routinely seen in violent demolitions, evictions and displacements (Baviskar, 2006). Ignoring the social and economic aspirations of more than half of their inhabitants, city and state governments are attempting to remake Mumbai in the image of Shanghai and Delhi in the image of London (Dupont, 2011). These are cities hosting world-class commercial, residential, recreational and circulation (transportation) spaces meant for high and middle-income professionals working in high-end knowledge industries. The poor remain at the receiving end when attempts are made by governments to make space for the world-class cities and purportedly their rightful inhabitants.

Urban policies aimed at normalizing oppressive urban planning practices have to be exposed and new inclusive policies have to be rewritten instead, which would not fall prey to normalizing processes and discourses. To see the actually existing inclusive cities, policy-makers must be alerted about co-optation through discursive articulations. As pointed out earlier, the practices of discursive articulations include 'spatial designations, namings, categorizations, mappings, statistics, and so on' (Dikeç, 2007, p. 172). Now I move on to examining discursive articulations in selected policy regimes in the next section.

C. Economic policy regimes as discursive articulations

Rohan Kalyan (2014, p. 57) explores the paradox of urbanization in post-independence India. Staggering economic growth in urban concentrations acts as magnets for movement of rural populations to the city, en masse, in hopes of deriving their share of benefits. Yet it is this oversupply of labour to the cities that makes them highly competitive and unexpectedly deprives migrant populations of opportunities for improvement, making the economic and spatial growth of urban India hardly inclusionary. The invisibility of this paradox propels waves of emigrants, who crash against the shores of impenetrable urban environments, obliterated into rudimentary 'tenements of survival'.

Represented as a paradox, economic growth and urbanization have an intrinsic positive relationship. The urban sector has contributed over 60 per cent to the national GDP (Kundu and Samanta, 2011, p. 55); the McKinsey Global Institute estimated that transitional areas, semi-urban areas and urban areas have contributed as much as 82 per cent to India's GDP in 2012 (2014, p. 15). These views were also echoed by the erstwhile Planning Commission of India (PCI) in its eleventh and twelfth five-year plans. The National Institution for Transforming India (NITI Ayog) – the organization that replaced the Indian Planning Commission – has similar views on cities, as is clear from its support for the current government policies on urban development (Bhattacharya and Rathi, 2015).

While cities are creators of national wealth, they are also sites of inequalities of enormous magnitudes between the various economic and social classes. However, these inequalities could be bridged by creating a certain minimum level of housing and access to critical services such as water, power, education, health care, and reducing income inequalities, among other policies. This approach known as 'distributive justice'. came to prominence due to John Rawls's path-breaking work on 'a theory of justice' (Fleischacker, 2004), and most liberal democratic governments globally, including the Government of India, follow policies of distributive justice to a lesser or greater degree.

City planners who believe in the ethics of distributive justice contend that economic growth is important to move forward for any form of inclusive city planning because investments are required for any kind of welfare-centred planning efforts. They believe that decent and adequate housing for the urban poor, for example, could be provided only if the economy is growing at a faster rate. In other words, there is no welfare without economic growth. One of the key concerns in this chapter is that even if faster economic growth is important for the country to be able to invest in its poor in cities, it is even more important to debate the nature of such economic growth, if an inclusive city and city planning are to secure the right to centrality. In other words, the problem of oppositional duality between economic growth and social welfare needs to be addressed in the case of urban planning. This duality will not melt away simply because the economy begins to grow faster.

Inclusive economic growth

Inclusive economic growth is an assertion of the strong economic base of the city economy. This may include, but is not limited to, high economic growth (high annual GDP growth and high per capita GDP growth), high per capita income, high levels of urban GDP, high levels of conspicuous consumption, high inward investment, and highly educated and trained residents or a world-class migratory workforce. Governing institutions of the state act as enablers for building a strong economic base for the city economy. Economic growth in such cities is clearly spearheaded by the private sector, with the state actively promoting growth avenues. Primarily focused on economic growth through the unfettered free market, a report titled 'India's urban awakening: building inclusive cities, sustaining economic growth' shows its firm belief in inclusive and sustainable economic growth (Sankhe et al., 2010). Similar arguments are presented more forcefully in another report titled 'Urban world: mapping the economic power of cities'. It is estimated that cities 'totalling around 2,000, are projected to contribute 75 per cent of global growth by 2025' (Dobbs et al., 2011, p. 7).

In its approach paper to the *Eleventh Five Year Plan 2007–2012* (PCI, 2008), the PCI unambiguously expressed its economic strategy:

> Rapid growth is an essential part of our strategy for two reasons. Firstly, it is only in a rapidly growing economy that we can expect to sufficiently raise the incomes of the masses of our population to bring about a general improvement in living conditions. Secondly, rapid growth is necessary to generate the resources needed to provide basic services to all.
>
> (PCI, 2006, p. 2)

Two years later, the *Eleventh Five Year Plan* carried forward its message of inclusive economic growth by making it the most important goal (PCI, 2008). The *Eleventh Five Year Plan* builds a case for inclusive growth by identifying a number of important issues:
- o First, the economy of the country has been experiencing a high economic growth rate, which it never experienced before. This is a good condition for inclusive growth.
- o Second, most of the wealth is created by the private sector, and the role of the state is considered to be that of a facilitator for the private sector do its job efficiently.

o Third, generally, high and middle-income groups have benefited from this sustained high economic growth, while other groups have not.
o Fourth, the government also expects that this trajectory of high economic growth, in all probability, will continue in the future. Therefore, the government believes that identified social and economic groups should also benefit from India's economic success.

Apart from the current government policies, the sixth chapter of the *Eleventh Five Year Plan* on 'Social justice' states: 'Inclusive growth demands that all social groups have equal access to the services provided by the State and equal opportunity for upward economic and social mobility' (PCI, 2008, p. 101).

These egalitarian longings aside, the *Eleventh Five Year Plan* does not provide any concrete mechanism for obtaining 'the right to centrality', particularly in relation to the city, although it is emphasized that freedom of enterprise will help eradicate inequalities and bring about sustainable development. There is no doubt that the share of people living below the poverty line has decreased since the 1991 economic reforms. However, as the *Twelfth Five Year Plan (2012–2017)* notes, the total number of people living below the poverty line is still as high as 350 million people or 29.8 per cent of the total population (PCI, 2013a, p. 5). Since the poverty line, in whatever way it is defined, constitutes a bare minimum existence, every third person is merely surviving, and not living a decent human life. However, the Plan insists, 'The objective of the Twelfth Plan is faster, more inclusive and more sustainable growth' (PCI, 2013b, p. 320).

Further, the PCI states that the:

> broad vision of the Eleventh Plan includes several inter-related components: rapid growth that reduces poverty and creates employment opportunities, access to essential services in health and education especially for the poor, equality of opportunity, empowerment through education and skill development ... recognition of women's agency and good governance.
> (PCI, 2008, p. 2)

The emphasis, however, remained on 'inclusive growth at 9 per cent per year' (PCI, 2008, p. 11). The critical question is what will happen to inclusive growth, if the high trajectory of economic growth is not sustained, as was the case from 2010 onwards? Will the poor in Indian cities go hungry, unclothed and without shelter? What will happen to those strategic measures for the urban poor? A staggering number of the poor living below the poverty line does not spell hope; it only creates critical doubts about the Plan intentions.

The PCI continued to focus on inclusive growth in the *Twelfth Five Year Plan*. This time, however, various dimensions of inclusiveness are more clearly identified. Six dimensions of inclusiveness are poverty reduction, group equality, regional balance, reduction in income inequality, empowerment through participatory democracy, and an increase in employment opportunities (PCI, 2013*a*, pp. 5–8). Out of the six parameters, three (poverty reduction, reduction in income inequality and the creation of employment opportunities) clearly have an economic focus, while the others focus on identity, participation and spatiality. Both economic and non-economic dimensions of inclusiveness are important for securing the right to centrality in a city. However, the Plan tries to resolve all issues with a focus on enhanced productivity, income, employment and participation. Growing the economy is important, but other important values such as fairness and justice also deserve a place of prominence. On this account, the Plan provides little innovation. The text of the five-year plans clearly articulates market individualism that dominates over the collective public interest of citizens.

As far as the city is concerned, high economic growth manifests itself in high-end built environments, including enclave housing for the elite and high-income white-collar workers and businesses, a large number of malls serving the exclusive needs of high earners, fully functional transport networks serving middle-income workers' mobility, and other facilities to provide for their education, leisure and other needs.

D. Planning policy regimes as discursive articulations

With multiple objectives to achieve, the Government of India has formulated an array of policies for the urban sector (see ***Table 9.1***). Apart from the stated goal of benefiting the urban poor, these policies appear framed in economic growth. Whatever their actual intent, these urban policies aimed at inclusive economic growth have hardly been able to create inclusive cities in India, particularly since 1991, when structural policy initiatives about liberal economic thinking came to the fore. Let us take a look at the following illustrations to clarify the point.

Jawaharlal Nehru National Urban Renewal Mission, 2005

Covering sixty-five cities with INR 120,536 crores funding allocated over a period of 7 years, the Jawaharlal Nehru National Urban Renewal Mission (JNNURM) was launched by the prime minister of India in 2005 as a reform-based city modernizing project. The Mission contained several mandatory and optional reforms to be actuated by the states, urban local bodies and parastatal organizations. Most of the economic reforms were implemented, while governance and community engagement reforms were not implemented.

The neoliberal mandatory reforms agenda comprised:
o   Property tax reforms successfully carried out in 30 cities.
o   The Urban Land (Ceiling and Regulation) Act, 1976 (ULCRA) was repealed in several states, but there is no evidence of opening-up of land markets as a result of the repeal.
o   Rationalization of stamp duty for transfer of property was largely successful.

Other mandatory reforms that were partially implemented or not implemented were:
o   Adoption of the 74th Constitutional Amendment Act, but half-heartedly implemented.
o   Community Participation Law not framed.
o   Public Disclosure Law not framed.

Thus, the focus of JNNURM was firmly placed on efficiency in urban governance, with the ultimate objective of making cities levers of economic growth. This is like 'reform urbanism' 'where urban infrastructure projects serve as the conduit for the liberalization of the economy' (Roy, 2014, p. 134). Although inclusion of urban poor was mentioned in the Mission document (Ministry of Urban Development, 2005), it was assumed that once cities begin to grow economically at higher rates by attracting national and global investments, growth will have a positive effect on the urban poor.

A review of the JNNURM in 2010 revealed that the Mission did not even succeed on its own terms. Most of the reforms, for example, could not be carried out, and only few projects were implemented. Over 84.5 per cent of funds were spent on transportation and physical infrastructure, including water, sewerage, stormwater drainage, bridges and roads. Delhi spent its share of funds, INR 5,243 crore, on the redevelopment of Connaught Place, purchase of low-floor buses, and construction of 9,000 houses for the urban poor (Sivaramakrishnan, 2011, pp. 40–1). The Ministry of Housing and Urban Poverty

Alleviation (MHUPA)'s own report points out that the Mission has suffered from a number of 'shortcomings' and 'constraints'. By March 2012, the actual release of funds just exceeded 39 per cent of the total approved project costs, and 'only 10 per cent or less of the projects had been completed' (MHUPA, 2014, p. 15).

As far as the right to centrality is concerned, three points deserve a mention. First, whatever number of houses for the urban poor has been constructed under JNNURM, in several cities including Delhi, the houses have not been handed over to the legitimate owners even years after their completion. Second, housing for the urban poor is located at the margins of the cities, for example in Delhi and Chandigarh. Third, the size of dwelling units (approximately 350 sq. ft.) is too small for a family of five or six persons. From these markers, one can conclude that this sort of policy includes less and excludes more because far-flung housing hardly helps the low-income families largely working in the informal sector in locations in and around city centres.

Rajiv Awas Yojana, 2013

Rajiv Awas Yojana (RAY), a policy launched by the United Progressive Alliance (UPA) government, was to be implemented from 2013 to 2022. The policy has a laudable mission: 'Rajiv Awas Yojana (RAY) envisages a "Slum Free India" with inclusive and equitable cities in which every citizen has access to basic civic infrastructure, social amenities and decent shelter' (MHUPA, 2013, p. 5). However, the real intent of the policy appears to be to integrate slums with the rest of the city by integrating city infrastructure with that of the slums, and also by commoditizing slum properties and making them available in the free market for sale and purchase with the ultimate goal of creating a slum-free India (MHUPA, 2013).

Commoditization and monetization of the properties of slum dwellers is very similar to a much-hyped proposal made by the world-famous Peruvian economist Hernando De Soto (2000). This policy, even if successfully implemented, could not create an inclusive city because it does not make any attempt at creating economic, political and social opportunities for slum dwellers to obtain the right to centrality. Slum dwellers remain at the lowest step of the economic ladder because of the lack of decent training facilities for them, and decent educational facilities for their children. This will make sure that their children continue to serve the rich and middle classes for the foreseeable future, making them politically subservient. Lack of decent livelihood opportunities only exacerbates this crisis of exclusion.

After the government changed at the centre, a new policy titled 'Pradhan Mantri Awas Yojna' or Prime Minister's Housing Scheme (now renamed Housing for All) was launched in 2016, which subsumes the RAY. Pradhan Mantri Awas Yojna intends to achieve the goal of 'affordable housing for all by 2022' (MHUPA, 2016, p. 11). We find similarities between several elements of RAY and the inclusive city in outlined by UN-Habitat in 'The Challenges of Slums. *The Challenge of Slums: Global Report on Human Settlements 2003'*. However, slum rehabilitation through the private sector, which views land as a resource, does not ensure affordable housing for the urban poor. Considering land as a resource and public–private partnerships as an institutional mechanism prioritizes the profit motive over the right to centrality.

National Urban Housing and Habitat Policy, 2007

In the National Urban Housing and Habitat Policy, 2007, the Government of India intended to urgently meet the housing needs of the economically weaker sections and lower income groups (MHUPA, 2007). However, the idea that housing needs of the urban poor could be fulfilled through private sector provision appears to be a non-starter. For example, since 2007, the formal urban housing market has been flooded with middle-income and high-end housing. In the formal sector, so-called affordable housing is entirely unaffordable to the urban poor; a dwelling unit price starts at INR 1,500,000 when the total annual income of a person from lower income groups would not exceed more than INR 250,000 per year. Non-availability of low-income housing in the formal housing market along with commodification of the existing housing stock spells doom for an inclusive city. The urban poor are left with no alternative but to resort to occupying spaces that are deemed illegal by the state as well as by middle and high-income groups.

A selective review of government policies does not instil a lot of confidence for building the inclusive city where the right to centrality could be upheld. Arguments by policy-makers, whether economists or city planners, point in the direction of exclusivity rather than inclusivity. According to this neoliberal planning rationality, cities as engines of economic growth contribute large shares to national GDP through economies of scale and economies of agglomeration, a large consuming middle class, industrial diversity, world-class labour power and infrastructure (Yusuf, 2012).

However, urban planning policies, like any other policy, are made in a politically charged strategic environment. Global and national attempts intermix to produce these policies. For example, discursive manoeuvres started much earlier to promote the inclusive city that could be built on the principles of the neoliberal belief of private sector-led high economic growth where the state would play an important role of enabler activist and facilitate the efficient and smooth working of the capitalist system.

Table 9.1 Urban sector policies in India

S. no.	Name of the policy	Objectives of the policy	Ministry of Government of India
1.	National Urban Livelihoods Mission (NULM), 2013	To focus on organizing urban poor in their strong grassroots-level institutions, creating opportunities for skill development leading to market-based employment and helping them to set up self-employment ventures by ensuring easy access to credit.	MHUPA
2.	The Right to Fair Compensation and Transparency in Land Acquisition, Rehabilitation and Resettlement Act, 2013	To modernize the process of land acquisition for current development needs of the country including urban expansion.	Ministry of Rural Development
3.	Rajiv Awas Yojana (RAY), 2012; Now subsumed under Housing for All.	To make a 'Slum-free India' with inclusive and equitable cities in which every citizen has access to basic civic infrastructure and social amenities and decent shelter.	MHUPA
4.	Shyama Prasad Mukherji Rurban Mission, 2016	To deliver integrated project-based infrastructure in the rural areas, which will also include development of economic activities and skill development?	Ministry of Rural Development

City planning policies in Delhi

S. no.	Name of the policy	Objectives of the policy	Ministry of Government of India
5.	Real Estate (Regulation and Development) Act, 2016	To regulate the real estate market, protect home buyers, induce investment, and provide conflict resolution mechanisms.	MHUPA
6.	Model State Affordable Housing Policy, 2015	To create an enabling environment for providing 'affordable housing for all' with special emphasis on Economically Weaker Sections (EWS) and Low Income Groups (LIG), and other vulnerable sections of society ... and to ensure that no individual is left shelter less.	MHUPA
7.	National Urban Housing and Habitat Policy, 2007	To incorporate various policy subcomponents as different chapters to reflect the current direction of the Government of India. These may include shelter, skill development, rental and social housing, and affordable housing.	MHUPA

Source: compiled by the author.

E. The right to centrality in Kathputli and Bhalswa Jahangir Puri

The critical point is that several discursive moves are made globally and nationally. Slums are presented as problem areas and the inclusive city as a strategic solution to a discursively reconfigured and reconstructed problem designed for intervention by the state and the private sector. Now I move to a discussion on two case studies.

Kathputli Colony: a movement towards slum-free Delhi

Kathputli Colony is located on 5.2-hectares of land owned by DDA, with an estimated population of 15,000 persons (DDA, 2017, p. 15). In accordance with the 2013 policy of 'slum-free cities' under RAY, Kathputli Colony was earmarked for in-situ rehabilitation and redevelopment by DDA following the provisions of the Master Plan for

Delhi 2021 (DDA, 2007). The redevelopment scheme is said to adhere to the guidelines underlined by the UN Committee on Economic, Social and Cultural Rights on the Right to Adequate Housing, identifying a transparent, participatory approach as a mandate for any such projects (UN Habitat, 2014, p. 3).

However, there exists a startling gap between the modernist intentions of postcolonial governments drenched in public–private initiatives, and the influential forces operating in the production and dislocation of slums in India. It can be seen as the beginning of an assault of the right on the centrality of the poor, encouraged and facilitated by discursive articulations. In the government lexicon, it is a slum with an unhealthy environment: dark, narrow lanes lined with solid waste and sewage, cramped semi-permanent houses with little ventilation, insufficient sanitation infrastructure and services.

Kathputli Colony is a forty-year-old informal settlement in the western part of Delhi, near Shadipur Bus Depot abutting Kirti Nagar Delhi Metro station. It has a vibrant social fabric comprising families of puppeteers, magicians, acrobats, craftsmen, painters, dancers, acrobats, jugglers and storytellers from Rajasthan, and folk artists from Uttar Pradesh, Andhra Pradesh and Haryana. Most of these workers skilled in traditional crafts need large open spaces to practise and perform. Others include unskilled labour mostly from Uttar Pradesh, Bihar, Maharashtra and Gujarat. This space comprises residential use interspersed with local convenience shops, workshops for specialized crafts, and small establishments for raising pigs, poultry and goats, and for street performers and folk artists. The voices of these vibrant communities are represented by their *pradhans* or local leaders. A civil society organization formed in 1978 along with two NGOs represents the interests of the artists living in this colony. Kathputli Colony remained a vibrant community till the residents were finally evicted in early 2018 with a promise that they would be rehabilitated and resettled in situ after the area is fully developed.

Figure 9.1 Kathputli Colony as a vibrant community, 2014

Source: author (23 February 2014).

The redevelopment project is being implemented through a public–private partnership arrangement. The project involves the building of 14-storey housing complexes for 2,800 families, with two-room apartment for each family with a total built space of 25 sq. m. To complete this work, a development contract was awarded in 2009 to a private construction company, Raheja Developers, on the condition that they would utilize 60 per cent of the land area to construct and deliver new residential blocks free of cost to the slum dwellers, and use the remaining 40 per cent for commercial and other purposes. The developers have ambitions to create the Raheja Phoenix – a 54-storey sophisticated integrated residential and commercial complex – inspired by the Burj Khalifa building complex in Dubai (Dupont et al., 2014, p. 41; also see **Figure 9.2** for the developer's plan).

Figure 9.2 Kathputli Redevelopment Plan

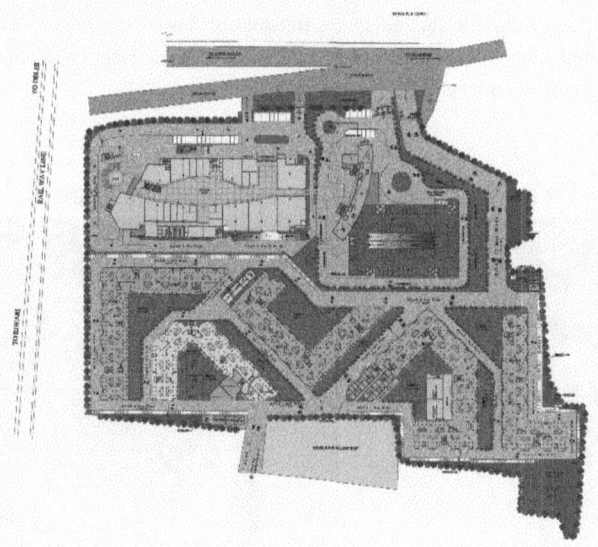

Source: Raheja Developers (2018).

From the perspective of residents of the area, the redevelopment project as it is conceived by the Raheja Builders has a number of inconsistencies and contradictions. First, slum dwellers clearly cannot practise and perform their traditional crafts, like puppetry, from tiny apartments. As one Pradhan told us in 2017, 'Houses [flats] being given are too small for our families. Even if they were double in size, how can we work from flats?' Second, slum dwellers have been temporarily relocated to different places in the city. About 2,800 families are relocated to a nearby transit camp 'at Anand Parbat and will be brought back to the redeveloped Kathputli Colony within two years' (DDA, 2017, p. 16). Another group of 492 families were offered flats in Narela, located approximately 32 km from Kathputli Colony on the outskirts of Delhi. Several families told us that finding work in this area is going to be too difficult. The transit camp at Anand Parbat resembles a ghetto; it is intimidating, unsafe, and has a dark atmosphere, haunting the residents. This accommodation becomes too hot in the summer because of the construction material used for the roofs. Third, given the proposed commercial and residential development on the remaining 40 per cent of the land, it is highly likely that the process of gentrification will result in the displacement of original Kathputli Colony residents (see *Figure 9.3*). That is why:

Kathputli residents are opposed to this development, objecting to being forced into high-rise apartments with little space. Their livelihood activities require outside space, freedom of movement, reciprocity and stimulation, which is developed within the organic form of an informal settlement built on shared interest and activities.

(Speak and Kumar, 2016)

Figure 9.3 Redevelopment of the Kathputli Colony, 2018

Source: author (8 May 2018).

Fourth, although DDA promises to hand over flats to Kathputli residents within two years, the previous interventions by the development authority do not instil confidence. For example, since 2016 a series of unsuccessful interventions were made by the DDA under the subtle misnomer of 'community participation'. Consultations were substituted with the provision of incomplete information. Conflicts between the NGOs advocating holistic representation of the diverse communities soon ended their role as communicators between the residents and the DDA. The *pradhans* hailed as the principal interlocutors between the authorities and the people are sceptical regarding the DDA's efforts in addressing the genuine grievances of the evicted residents. The DDA could not produce evidence other than the minutes of correspondence between the community and the developer, which was in turn responsible for informing the DDA. The list of surveyed households, their property rights and precise eligibility criteria for entitlement to a flat in the rehousing scheme remained undisclosed to the residents till 2014, despite relentless right to information (RTI) applications. The rehabilitation procedure is just another way to drive people out of the city. The DDA has been exemplary in this regard, with 2018 witnessing the final stage for the removal of slum dwellers. In 2016, the DDA adopted an intimidating *'parchi katao transit camp jao'* ('get yourself a slip and move to the transit camp') (Basu, 2016). These attempts were met with protests about forced expulsions. Evictions have made headlines and have also received strong dissent from professionals in the fields of planning and urban development, questioning the justice of the DDA's policy, and the premise for denial of choice (Banda et al., 2013).

Fifth, decades of existence had meant growing families and vertical expansion of houses. Yet while counting households, these upper floors were not treated as separate units and their residents were not entitled to a dwelling unit in the upcoming project. Even the cut-off date for eligibility for resettlement underwent several changes, exposing the indecisiveness of the authorities. The prospect of consent organized by the developer argued for a lack of prior involvement of the residents in the drafting stage of the agreement. The absence of direct confrontation between the authority and affected people culminated in tension and distrust, connecting unheard voices, undone attempts and unexploited opportunities. DDA's calculating without numbers approach has created discrepancies regarding about 350 residents eligible for rehousing (Dupont et al., 2014, p. 43). The residents negotiated their involvement in the process of redevelopment through a committee consisting of twelve *pradhans*, evolving relationships with influential politicians and conversing with ministers. The former member of the Legislative Assembly's inability to protect the interests of the slum dwellers led to his defeat in the 2014 elections.

The Kathputli Colony experience so far shows that residents have been left with reduced work opportunities to practise their traditional crafts, even if they are able to secure flats from the DDA within two years. Speculatively, this relief is likely to be temporary because the process of gentrification is expected to drive these people out of this area over time. Even if they are not driven out by economic forces, finding alternative work would be very difficult. To uphold the right to centrality – even when located in the centre of the city – appears to be full of uncertainties. Location in or near the centre of the city is no guarantee for upholding the right to centrality.

Bhalswa Jahangir Puri: a resettlement colony in north-west Delhi

The next case shows how the right of the people to centrality has been compromised in Bhalswa Jahangir Puri, by shifting them to the periphery. A Delhi High Court ruling in 2006 banned the use of handcarts and cycle rickshaws in the Chandni Chowk area of Old Delhi. 'The ruling was presented as a move to ease traffic congestion and begin the implementation of an alternative mass transport system ... Discourse on sustainability and environmental pollution was used to justify the action' (Speak and Kumar, 2016). Drawing from a report prepared by the Lok Shakti Manch, I examine how the right to the centrality of people living in the resettlement colony of Bhalswa Jahangir Puri has been compromised.

Bhalswa resettlement colony houses 3,521 families, according to a response to an RTI application made to the Delhi Urban Shelter Improvement Board. It is located approximately 25 km from the city centre. Residents of Bhalswa started living here from November 2000; some arrived in the resettlement colony in 2002.

A majority of the residents of Bhalswa came to Delhi from the states of Uttar Pradesh, Bihar, West Bengal and Rajasthan during the 1970s and 1980s. They were shifted to Bhalswa between 2000 and 2002 from eleven settlements located in several places in Delhi, including Preet Vihar, Seelampur, Teenmurti, Ashok Vihar, Jahangirpuri, Gautampuri (Yamunapushta), Garhi, Dakshinpuri and Nizamuddin. Before the resettlement process was completed, a majority of the people worked in the city as labourers in factories, domestic help, hawkers and vendors, service deliverers like drivers, electricians, plumbers and so on. Out of all workers, one-third were employed as permanent workers in the city (Lok Shakti Manch, 2014, pp. 4–5).

After resettlement in Bhalswa, however, over 40 per cent lost their jobs. Those who kept their jobs have to travel distances exceeding 20 km to reach their workplaces. Most women lost their jobs because they could not manage the long-distance travel to workplaces. Women got the additional responsibility of looking after children alone as men stayed in the city for work, returning occasionally (Speak, 2012). Children were forced to work as domestic servants, rag pickers or looking after small shops with their parents and in other's shops as helpers. A study carried out by Lok Shakti Manch (2014), a prominent NGO in the area, found that 54 per cent of the workers were able to retain their jobs notwithstanding commuting and financial difficulties. Today a large proportion of families are involved in the informal sector, with household enterprises such as making brooms, *papads*, small utensils, *bindis*, festive decorative items or decorative items for garments. In terms of movement from various parts of the city, and also in terms of loss of livelihoods, the right to centrality suffered a huge setback; in some cases, families could not even get together for weeks as male workers have to stay in the city in order to continue with their jobs. Bus services are unreliable and Delhi Metro does not come close to Bhalswa.

Residents have very little access to physical infrastructure. Residents said[94] that before resettlement, they had easy access to good-quality water and no expenditure was incurred for obtaining water. However, after resettlement over 64 per cent of respondents are unable to get proper access to water. Some have even had to dig bore wells and use hand pumps to access groundwater. Nearly 94 per cent depend on multiple sources of water and tankers by Delhi Jal Board (Lok Shakti Manch, 2014). Some have to buy drinking water, while other get it from their workplaces located as far away as Rohini and Jahangirpuri. Being located near the Bhalswa landfill site, residents get contaminated groundwater.

Before resettlement, over 70 per cent of the residents used public toilets at no charge for women, and a small charge of INR 1 for men on a daily basis. A small percentage of households had personal toilets and bathrooms. After resettlement, however, sanitation has become one of the biggest problems for the residents of Bhalswa. Only six out of ten public toilets are working. People are heavily dependent on public toilets as no space for constructing private toilets was provided (Lok Shakti Manch, 2014, pp. 16–17). Doors of the working toilet blocks are broken, and the toilets are unpleasant and dirty. Although sanitation facilities are nominally free, actually people are asked to pay by rent seekers. There is no clarity on day-to-day maintenance.

The condition of power is no better. Before resettlement, over 77 per cent of households got electricity through hookups and with the help of local leaders. Nearly 14 per cent of pukka houses had expensive electrical fittings. After resettlement, things have worsened. There is no provision for regular electricity supply. Power is provided for a few hours and because of privatization, electricity charges have

---

94 Every year a group of planning students accompanied by faculty from the School of Architecture and Planning (SPA) Delhi and Newcastle University, UK conduct a scoping study. This information is taken from a study conducted in 2018.

increased, making power unaffordable for the residents. Currently, there is no electricity supply in most of the houses in the area because of non-payment of bills (Lok Shakti Manch, 2014, p. 17).

Because of the problems pertaining to water, sanitation and access to electricity, health issues have taken hold. Before resettlement, residents lived in a comparatively healthy environment. Nearly all had access to proper health facilities. After resettlement, the health condition of the residents has gradually deteriorated. Most residents are affected by water-borne diseases. While the proportion suffering from coughs, colds and fevers increased from 82.5 per cent to 96.6 per cent, the major increase has been seen in gastrointestinal disorders (such as diarrhoea), stomach pain, body pain, joint pain, skin problems and typhoid. These ailments have resulted from lack of proper drinking water facilities, drainage water outflows, lack of sanitation facilities and accumulation of stagnant water. According to 96.2 per cent of the respondents, no health facilities are located in Bhalswa (Lok Shakti Manch, 2014). Most of the government hospitals and dispensaries are located in the centre of the city, while most of the resettlement colonies are located on the periphery. Even when health facilities are available, there is no accessibility to registered medical practitioners and dispensaries. Since there is no government hospital available in Bhalswa, people have to go to Jahangirpuri for medical check-ups. A major part of the income of Bhalswa residents is spent on health care.

Urban poor are assisted by the government via the Public Distribution System (PDS). Even before resettlement, a majority of women did not want cash transfers or smart cards to access subsidies on food grains; instead, they wanted a better functioning PDS that could be run by self-help groups or cooperatives. Before resettlement, from 1965 till 1997, everybody had universal ration cards. In 2002, the ration system was classified into three categories (above poverty line (APL), below poverty line (BPL) and Antyodaya Anna Yojna (AAY), introduced in 2004). AAY is the scheme to provide highly subsidized food to millions of the poorest families. The launching of these schemes has resulted in a duplication of cards. In 2009, people started to make new cards, but then 170,000 BPL cards were cancelled without any explanation; again in August 2010 ration cards were cancelled in the name of providing new biometric cards, which also did not happen. In this way, slum dwellers and rehabilitated people were pushed out towards the periphery of the system. While everyone eligible was entitled to a ration card, difficulties in applying for ration cards arose because of irregularities, incorrect information entered, and the process is tedious. Even those residents who have ration cards have to use public transport in order to get their rations. People have to spend around Rs 20–30 travelling to ration shops located 1–3 km from their houses.

Although women had to perform additional household tasks, they also assumed agency in the absence of their husbands, as Roshanara recounted:

> At Nizamuddin, my husband purchased groceries and rations. I rarely ventured out. Here, he went looking for work and I was forced to buy rations. That is how I came out. Upon realising that shop-owners were denying us our rightful provisions, we started organising ourselves. Soon we started taking up other causes too. Then the RTI Act came and we realised that if armed with information, we can take any Government authority to task.
>
> (Quoted in Kattakayam, 2012)

Poor access to physical infrastructure, fewer work opportunities for women, men working in the city because of the lack of employment opportunities, peripheral location, nearness to a large dump site causing air and water pollution, and consequently the deteriorating health of residents in Bhalswa, suggest that the right to centrality is not being upheld. Like the in-situ redevelopment affecting the majority of households in Kathputli, Bhalswa also appears to sideline the right to centrality. Resettlement and rehabilitation under a government scheme do not work any better.

F. Conclusions

This chapter shows that the right to centrality cannot be upheld under the present nature of the government's redevelopment, resettlement and rehabilitation policies. Both cases amply demonstrate that the residents are disadvantaged after relocation. People at the receiving end are not only slum dwellers generally and slum women particularly, who get excluded through development dominated by masculine norms and thought processes. Government policies do mention inclusivity as one of the cornerstones, but only rhetorically. Policy implementation results in multiple deprivations, making it very difficult to uphold the right to centrality. However, SDG 11 and various provisions of the Constitution of India show that their implementation could act as alternative frameworks for achieving the right to centrality for the poor.

References

Appadurai, A. 1998. Dead certainty: ethnic violence in the era of globalization. *Public Culture,* Vol. 10, No. 2, pp. 225–47.

Banda, S., Vaidya, Y. and Adler, D. 2013. The case of Kathputli Colony: mapping Delhi's first in-situ slum rehabilitation project, Working Paper 3. New Delhi, Centre for Policy Research.

Basu, S. 2016. Delhi's Kathputli Colony demolition: residents protest the loss of homes, and a way of life. www.firstpost.com/living/delhis-kathputli-colony-demolition-residents-protest-the-loss-of-homes-and-a-way-of-life-3172406.html (Accessed 14 March 2019.)

Baviskar, A. 2003. Between violence and desire: space, power and identity in the making of metropolitan Delhi. *International Social Science Journal,* Vol. 175, pp. 89–98.

———. 2006. Demolishing Delhi: world class city in the making. *Mute,* Vol. 2, No. 3, pp. 88–95.

Bhan, G. 2009. 'This is no longer the city I once knew': evictions, the urban poor and the right to the city in millennial Delhi. *Environment and Urbanization,* Vol. 21, pp. 127–42.

Bhan, G. and Shivanand, S. 2013. (Un)settling the city: analysing displacement in Delhi from 1990–2007. *Economic and Political Weekly,* Vol. 48, No. 3, pp. 54–61.

Bhattacharya, S. and Rathi, S. 2015. *Reconceptualising Smart Cities: A reference framework for India.* New Delhi, Center for Study of Science, Technology and Policy.

Chant, S. 2013. Cities through a 'gender lens': a golden 'urban age' for women in the global South? *Environment and Urbanization,* Vol. 25, No. 1, pp. 9–29.

Cook, I. and Laing, M. 2011. Visibility and the policing of public space. *Geography Compass,* Vol. 5, No. 8, pp. 610–22.

DDA (Delhi Development Authority). 1962. *Master Plan of Delhi 1981.* New Delhi, Ministry of Urban Development.

———. 2007. *Master Plan of Delhi 2021.* New Delhi, Ministry of Urban Development.

———. 2010. Zonal Development Plan: Planning zone 'K-II' (Dwarka). www.rgplan.org/Zonal%20plan/ZonalPlansReports2010/Zone%20K-II%20(Dwarka)%20Reports.pdf (Accessed 14 March 2019.)

———. 2017. Rehabilitation of Kathputli Colony. *Delhi Vikas Patra,* Vol. 16, No. 4, pp. 15–17.

———. n.d. Urban extension projects – Dwarka. https://dda.org.in/planning/dwarka_popu_area.htm (Accessed 14 March 2019.)

De Soto, H. 2000. *The Mystery of Capital.* London, Basic Books.

Dikeç, M. 2004. Voices into noises: ideological determination of unarticulated justice movements. *Space and Polity,* Vol. 8, No. 2, pp. 191–208.

———. 2007. *Badlands of the Republic: Space, politics and urban policy.*, London, Wiley-Blackwell.

Dupont, V. 2008. Slum demolitions in Delhi since the 1990s: an appraisal. *Economic and Political Weekly*, Vol. 43, No. 28, pp. 79–87.
---. 2011. The dream of Delhi as a global city. *International Journal of Urban and Regional Research*, Vol. 35, No. 3, pp. 533–54.
---. 2013. Which place for the homeless? Scrutiny of a mobilisation campaign in the 2010 Commonwealth Games context. *South Asia Multidisciplinary Academic Journal*, Vol. 8, pp. 1–21.
Dupont, V., Banda, S., Vaidya, Y. and Shankare Gowda, M. 2014. Unpacking participation in Kathputli Colony: Delhi's first slum redevelopment project act 1. *Economic and Political Weekly*, Vol. 49, No. 24, pp. 39–47.
Fleischacker, S. 2004. *A Short History of Distributive Justice*. Cambridge, Mass., Harvard University Press.
Ghertner, D. A. 2011*a*. The nuisance of slums: environmental law and the production of slum illegality in India. J. S. Anjaria and C. McFarlane (eds), *Urban Navigations, Politics, Space and the City in South Asia*. London, Routledge.
---. 2011*b*. Rules by aesthetics: world class city making in Delhi. A. Roy and A. Ong (eds), *Worlding Cities, Asian Experiments and the Art of being Global*. Oxford, Wiley-Blackwell.
Kalyan, R. 2014. The magician's ghetto: moving slums and everyday life in a postcolonial city. *Theory, Culture and Society*, Vol. 31, No. 1, pp. 49–73.
Kattakayam, J. 2012. Bhalswa resettlement colony makes headway on woman power. *The Hindu*, New Delhi, 17 September.
Kipfer, S. Saberi, P. and Wieditz, T. 2012. Henri Lefebvre: debates and controversies. *Progress in Human Geography*, Vol. 37, No. 1, pp. 115–34.
Kundu, D. and Samanta, D. 2011. Redefining the inclusive urban agenda in India. *Economic and Political Weekly*, Vol. 46, No. 5, pp. 55–63.
Lefebvre, H. 1996. *Writings on Cities*, trans. E. Kofman and E. Lebas. Oxford, Blackwell.
Lok Shakti Manch. 2014. *The Inventory for a City's Development – A report on resettlement*. New Delhi, Lok Shakti Manch.
McKinsey Global Institute. 2014. *India's economic geography in 2025: states, clusters and cities: Identifying the high potential markets of tomorrow*. Mumbai, McKinsey Global Institute.
MHUPA (Ministry of Housing and Urban Poverty Alleviation). 2007. *National Urban Housing and Habitat Policy 2007.* New Delhi, MHUPA, Government of India. http://dtcp.ap.gov.in/webdtcp/pdf/HousingPolicy2007.pdf (Accessed 14 March 2019.)
---. 2013. *Rajiv Awas Yojana: Guidelines for slum-free city planning*. New Delhi, MHUPA, Government of India.
---. 2014. *Inclusive Urban Planning, State of the Urban Poor Report 2013*. New Delhi, Oxford University Press.
---. 2016. *Pradhan Mantri Awas Yojana*, New Delhi, MHUPA, Government of India.

Ministry of Urban Development. 2005. *Jawaharlal Nehru Urban Renewal Mission.* New Delhi, Ministry of Urban Development, Government of India.
---. 2015. *Smart Cities Mission.* New Delhi, Ministry of Urban Development, Government of India.
PCI (Planning Commission of India). 2006. *Towards Faster and More Inclusive Growth: An approach paper to the 11th Five Year Plan.* New Delhi, Oxford University Press.
---. 2008. *Eleventh Five Year Plan 2007–2012, Inclusive Growth, Vol. I.* New Delhi, Oxford University Press.
---. 2013a. *Twelfth Five Year Plan (2012–2017), Vol. 1: Faster, more inclusive and sustainable growth.* New Delhi, Oxford University Press.
---. 2013b. *Twelfth Five Year Plan (2012–2017), Vol. II: Economic sectors.* New Delhi, Oxford University Press.
Purcell, M. 2003. Citizenship and the right to the global city: reimagining the capitalist global world order. *International Journal of Urban and Regional Research*, Vol. 27, No. 3, pp. 564–90.
Roy, A. 2011a. The blockade of the world class city: dialectical images of Indian urbanism. A. Roy and A. Ong (eds), *Worlding Cities, Asian Experiments and the Art of Being Global.* Oxford, Wiley-Blackwell.
---. 2011b. Conclusion: postcolonial urbanism: speed, hysteria, mass dreams. A. Roy and A. Ong (eds), *Worlding Cities, Asian Experiments and the Art of Being Global.* Oxford, Wiley-Blackwell.
---. 2014. The inclusive city: a new paradigm for urban planning in India. MHUPA (ed.), *Inclusive Urban Planning: State of the urban poor report 2013.* New Delhi, Oxford University Press.
Roy, A. and Ong, A. (eds). 2011. *Worlding Cities, Asian Experiments and the Art of being Global.* Oxford, Wiley-Blackwell.
Sivaramakrishnan, K.C. (2011) *Re-visioning Indian Cities. The Urban Renewal Mission*, Delhi, Sage.
Speak, S. 2012. Planning for the needs of urban poor in the global South: the value of a feminist approach. *Planning Theory*, Vol. 11, No. 4, pp. 343–60.
Speak, S. and Kumar, A. 2016. Fit and miss-fit: the global spread of urban spatial injustice. S. Davoudi and D. Bell (eds), *Justice and Fairness in the City: A multidisciplinary approach to 'ordinary' cities.* London, Policy Press.
Time. 2014. The world's largest community of street performers is about to be torn apart, 4 March. http://time.com/12073/india-kathputli-colony-of-street-artists-to-be-demolished/
(Accessed 14 March 2019.)
Tuan, Y. F. 1988. The city as a moral universe. *Geographical Review*, Vol. 78, No. 3, pp. 316–24.
UN Habitat. 2003. *The Challenge of Slums: Global report on human settlements 2003.* London, Earthscan for United Nations Human Settlements Programme.

---. 2014. The right to adequate housing, fact sheet no. 21/rev.1. Geneva, United Nations.
United Nations. 2015. *Transforming Our World. The 2030 Agenda for Sustainable Development* (Resolution 70/1 adopted by the General Assembly). New York, United Nations.
Watson, V. 2003. Conflicting rationalities: implications for planning theory and ethics. *Planning Theory and Practice,* Vol. 4, No. 4, pp. 395–407.
---. 2009. The planned city sweeps the poor away ... urban planning and 21st century urbanisation. *Progress in Planning*, Vol. 72, pp. 151–93.
Yusuf, S. 2012. *Catalyzing 21st century growth: the role of innovative cities, presentation.* Washington DC, World Bank Institute.

Chapter 10
UNDERMINING THE SDGS: INFORMALITY, PATRONAGE AND THE POLITICS OF INCLUSION IN MUMBAI

Joop de Wit

Introduction

When the so-called low-caste household of Mrs Shanti migrated from a poor Indian state to a Mumbai slum in 1993 she managed to obtain a small plot in an illegal slum, part of an encroached formal no-development zone. Through a relative who settled there earlier, she met an agent linked to a political party to whom she had to pay a sizable lump sum, plus INR 80 monthly as rent or protection money. She was directed to another 'agent' who offered to informally get her a ration card for INR 4,000, a process that would otherwise take many months with the submission of all sort of proofs she did not have. She now had access to cheaper foodstuffs in subsidized food shops, but more importantly, it meant proof of being a Mumbai resident, which enabled her to obtain a voter identity card. She understood that the agent had his own interest in her helping him when he said that he now expected her and her husband to vote for his party.

Shanti believed she had done well and that she had some security of tenure, and in due time informal arrangements for access to drinking water and toilets were made. Yet, in processes not clear to her, the Mumbai Municipal Corporation decided to act upon the formally illegal status of the area and announced an eviction: 5,000 houses, thirty-six toilets, two temples, clinics and other amenities were turned to rubble. People returned, and perhaps amazingly, were allowed to stay. However, things had changed. More wealthy and powerful residents such as shop keepers and cattle shed owners had captured larger pieces of land towards the drier, higher ground and the main road. The poor were left with low-lying plots and huts to the back near a dirty creek, but Shanti and many inhabitants are still there today, even while services – toilets, drinking water, sanitation – are poor and problematic, keeping the slum people dependent on brokers and fixers to help them out.

Ironically, the very same political parties which allowed (and benefited from) squatters to settle there, are currently being contacted by powerful developers and contractors with a view to putting pressure on them to change the Mumbai city master plan. If their joint efforts succeed, this would allow very lucrative housing construction on what is and remains an illegal site. Such informal processes have worked in other city areas, yielding rich returns (case study from de Wit, 2017, pp. 1–2).

This chapter is about people like Shanti and many others who, over time, migrated to Mumbai, facing similar or even more hurdles to get access to somewhat secure shelter and basic services such as water and sanitation, and also access to schools and hospitals. She is only one of the many people who survive at great odds at the bottom of the city's hierarchy of power and money, in a metropolis home to an estimated 2,5 million people who are chronically poor (MGGM, 2009). The case brings out a puzzling coincidence of formal (no-development zone) rules and informal dynamics where people settle in an illegal slum after which water mains are illegally tapped to extend water to slums. It also underlines the importance of 'being connected' – in my terminology as a 'client' to have some support from a 'patron' or a broker (network). Informal, personal relations are critical.

This chapter argues that 'informality' has a much deeper impact, as much of the context of poor people is indeed 'informal'. For example, the informal sector accounts for 68 per cent of total employment in Mumbai, employing the bulk of the urban poor. Poor people may first visit an informal quack in case of health issues; they borrow from money lenders at exorbitant interest rates, especially when needs are high; they may enrol their children in informal, poorly regarded evening classes to patch up low-quality formal education (de Wit, 2017, pp. 141ff). I will argue that the (formal) local state seems quite remote for poor people who largely fend for themselves, with a lot of 'self-help' or local-level improvisation plus neighbour/caste-level support.

Mumbai's local state – the municipality, housing and planning agencies, politicians, the police – is also marked by high levels of informality. This appears to undermine regular policy-making in Mumbai, in conditions which have been described as 'endemic corruption' (Pethe et al., 2012). Administrative corruption is rife especially in the housing and real estate sectors, and politics is perceived to be quite dirty, with indications of 'vote buying' (Bjorkman, 2013). Politicians have poor reputations, if only as they are seen to accept money from business sectors in very opaque transactions to finance their election campaigns (PRAJA, 2011).

One factor that seems to fuel informal strategies is the assumption – or reality – that existing 'formal' systems of administration only work up to a certain level of efficiency, and that therefore, resorting to informal systems can be a logical, almost unavoidable step (see the work of Pethe et al., 2012). Observers agree that Mumbai is marked by weak governance, problematic planning and democracy: it is not in control of major policy areas such as infrastructure, housing and poverty programmes (Clark and Moonen, 2014). While Shanti's case serves as an example that combining informal strategies with coincidental contacts with the formal local state can yield benefits, there are neither clear rules nor guarantees. Also other, or poorer, people easily fail when using the same tactic. They are at risk of being neglected in both the formal and informal systems, if they are not part of effective networks, and/or are unable to pay basic bribes. Such disadvantaged groups are mostly found in poor slum pockets: members of the Dalit caste, and minorities such as recent migrants and Muslims. Girls and (single) women are invariably poorer in all such groups, with quite precarious livelihoods.

This chapter has three interrelated objectives. It first argues that what is called 'informality' is not an incidental and unfortunate deviation from accepted norms and benchmarks of ('good') governance or democracy. Rather, in Mumbai, it is an integral, if not dominant, trait of power-driven politics and governance (de Wit, 2017, p. 7). I argue that poor people in the city largely live in an 'informal world', and that the most effective coping strategies or 'demand-side dynamics' are informal. Cleverly managing their meagre resources, they exert agency by linking to useful networks and by voting strategically. They are certainly not simply victims, or actors unable to adjust to changing circumstances. Evidence shows that 'the informal' can offer opportunities and openings not allowed by formal laws, provisions and policy (Benjamin, 2008). Yet on the other hand it is imperative to understand how poor people are overwhelmed by the conditions and predicaments they face. They have little choice, in order to survive, but to deal with socio-administrative and political structures which tend to be adverse or even hostile, especially for those already most excluded (or adversely incorporated) in terms of labour, health, education and safety (de Wit, 2010). This realm of informality needs to receive much more attention in academic research, and even more so by official, NGO, national or international agencies engaging with poverty reduction policies, or pursuing the agenda of the Sustainable Development Goals (SDGs) and beyond (Mohmand, 2016).

Second, I suggest, on the basis of evidence from Mumbai, that poor people are negatively affected by the impacts and implications of the neoliberal policies that the city has embraced relatively enthusiastically from the early 1990s (Banerjee-Guha, 2009). New governance modalities – contracting out, public–private partnerships, allowing for-profit firms to deliver hitherto publicly provided services in health and education – have negatively impacted on the poor who always relied on public clinics, hospitals and schools (MCGM, 2009). Such developments are framed here in discourses of 'multi-stakeholder governance'. It is not the government alone that 'governs'; governance becomes a process of actors/actor groups now named 'stakeholders' with a stake in a policy or project, who are assumed to 'cooperate to solve collective (local) problems' (Hyden et al., 2004).

This global paradigm shift entailed a reduction in the role of the local state, which by and large had enjoyed a monopoly in public services delivery. Residents who used to rely on these services now reappear as stakeholders expected to participate as 'clients' in policy arenas, and actively pursue their interests. Impacts have naturally been different for different actors, and more powerful stakeholders, such as the Indian middle classes and business firms, have tended to benefit. Other, weaker stakeholders face negative impacts in terms of accountability, democratic control, and especially the scope for voice and impact in such arenas (Swyngedouw, 2005). I argue that Mumbai's neoliberal governance plays out badly for the city's poor people, as they are being squeezed between reduced public delivery of quality services such as education and health, and the need to pay (high) fees in better (good) private ones. Inequality, already considerable and persistent in terms of hierarchical caste and gender relations, is on the rise in a city where half the population lives in slums but which also has India's highest number of billionaires.[95]

Whereas the 'stakeholder discourse' has agreeable associations of pluralism and participation, such promises do not work out for Mumbai's poor, given their weak power position, fragmentation and heterogeneity. It would help if they could organize as weak individual stakeholders into more powerful and united organizations to claim or fight for uniform and fair entitlements. In contrast, this chapter

---

95 World Inequality Lab: 'India's richest 1% earned about 7% of national income in 1980; that figure rocketed to 22% by 2014. Over the same period, the share held by the bottom 50% plunged from 23% to just 15%' (2018, pp. 125-7). A clear relationship is established between the advent of neoliberal reforms and rapidly increasing inequality.

starts from the assumption that, rather than organizing horizontally and acting as a collective, poor/slum people prefer cultivating vertical contacts in the form of patrons or brokers who do have access to arenas (de Wit and Berner, 2009). This can be seen as a pragmatic strategy: they react to everyday service delivery dynamics and the propensity of officials and politicians to rely on informal relations though 'vertical governance' (Kumar and Landy, 2009).

By and large, current governance shifts seem to have undermined the position of Mumbai's poor, who now appear as (alarmingly) weak stakeholders who have trouble articulating their voices (particularly as a class or group). In stark contrast, India's private sector, which was quite small and weak before the advent of neoliberalism, has grown enormously, with indications that its powers in terms of political influence are becoming very problematic. One indication is evidence of crony capitalism (*Economist*, 2014; *Frontline*, 2014), but this chapter focuses only on the role of private-sector firms in financing and hence partly controlling the campaigns of Mumbai's politicians (de Wit, 2017).

This chapter finally argues that the above is critically important with a view to the lofty ideals and high expectations framed in the SDGs. It engages especially with SDG 16: 'Promote peaceful and inclusive societies for sustainable development, provide access to justice for all and build effective, accountable and inclusive institutions at all levels' (United Nations, 2016). Basic but urgent matters – governance, inclusion, participation, rights and security – take centre stage here. Where this chapter focuses on participatory democracy and governance, it particularly targets two sub goals under SDG 16: develop effective, accountable and transparent institutions at all levels, and ensure responsive, inclusive, participatory and representative decision-making at all levels. SDG 16 is both an end in itself, and a crucial part of delivering/institutionalizing sustainable development in all countries. Here I agree with the Foundation for Democracy and Sustainable Development (2018) that this SDG 'has in fact been seen by many commentators as being *the* transformational goal and key to ensuring that the agenda can be accomplished', as it addresses the very basics of public administration and, hopefully, inclusive democracies.

Chapter outline

After a brief introduction of concepts and perspectives such as 'multi-stakeholder local governance', 'informality' and 'patronage democracy', I picture conditions for approximately 6 million people in the sprawling Mumbai slums – and then delineate and target those most poor and vulnerable at the bottom of the city's hierarchy of classes, castes and gender. I argue that they largely live in an informal world, and consider 'demand-side dynamics': how do poor people get access to basic services and protection. The focus then shifts to 'supply-side dynamics' as regards key agencies such as the Mumbai municipality, housing agencies and the police – all of which are critically influenced by informal dynamics such as bribery and what is called 'vote bank politics' in the city. Implications of local governance shifts for poor people are assessed, where the poor are pictured as weak stakeholders in Mumbai's starkly neoliberal policy context, and where they now compete with growing middle classes and private-sector businesses and firms which have increasingly strong voices in the corridors of power. Poor people are seen to get sidelined in politics also. Their votes may help bring to power politicians who are more interested in repaying their (financial) obligations to rich firms which sponsor their election campaigns. Once elected, they are less interested in formulating and implementing long-term policy and reforms to support those poor and vulnerable. Their support is by and large fragmented and individualized, and mediated with a view for them and their parties to come to or remain in power – far beyond considerations of social justice.

SDG 16 and the importance of informality

I consider SDG 16 with its broad aim to promote peaceful and inclusive societies, provide access to justice and build effective, accountable and inclusive institutions as central to chances to book progress in all other, more sectoral or thematic fields. It is about 'effective and inclusive public institutions that can deliver quality education and healthcare, fair economic policies and inclusive environmental protection' (United Nations, 2016). This seems the more operational SDG, targeting implementation dynamics with a view to ('good') governance and effective policy-making. Sachs agrees here, arguing that 'good governance' is an essential condition to make progress 'at all levels, local, national, regional, and global' (2012, p. 2208). While this chapter targets the local governance level, that level obviously cannot be separated from regional and national governance – even in such cases where decentralization has resulted in more administrative and fiscal autonomy in a municipality or district office.

Transparency International stresses 'the importance of tracking SDG 16', while correctly realizing the importance of 'bad governance': there will be 'no sustainable development without tackling corruption' (Transparency International, 2017). As is argued below, fiscal and political dynamics remain critical, as does the nature and quality of public institutions – which are considered critical to SDG 16.

But what precisely are these institutions, and why are they critical to governance, and by implication, to implementing policies supporting the SDGs? How do they link to governance or 'good governance'? Governance is defined as:

> the formation and stewardship of the formal and informal rules that regulate the public realm, the arena in which state as well as economic and societal actors interact to make decisions .... It is a multi-stakeholder process with weaker and stronger actors who need to cooperate to solve collective (local) problems.
>
> (Hyden et al., 2004, p. 16)

This useful definition first underlines that, since the advent and consolidation of neoliberalism, there have been fundamental governance shifts (Baud and de Wit, 2008) where it is no longer the government alone that 'governs' but (groups of) actors who are 'co-governing' in what can be seen as complex multi-actor governance arenas. For example, in Mumbai, up until the 1990s, public services for middle and low-income groups were by and large exclusively provided directly by public agencies, notably the Municipality: public schools, public clinics and hospitals, water and (maintaining) infrastructure. Contractors were employed in the fields of housing, sanitation and infrastructure for specific public services. When India – and with it Mumbai – opened up its economy and embraced neoliberal reforms from around 1991, new arrangements became dominant, including large-scale privatization of service delivery and new models of policy/project implementation through public–private partnerships (Banerjee-Guha, 2009). When considering the livelihoods of the poorest in Mumbai, we will find such dynamics to be one important factor undermining their position – contributing to patterns of exclusion through new hurdles in services delivery.

As noted, this 'multi-stakeholder governance model' holds promises of pluralism, increased participation and accountability, but by and large it does not seem to work well for poor, illiterate and/or poorly informed citizens with (very) little power. In reality, it turns the poor into 'weak stakeholders' who cannot easily compete with other, more powerful actors active in local governance arenas (Swyngedouw, 2005). The above governance definition next makes a useful distinction between 'the rules of the game' or the 'institutional context' with its formal, and importantly informal, rules, and the more dynamic, political arena where we can observe 'who gets what, when and how'. This chapter understands institutions as *'the rules of the game* in society which direct and constrain human (inter-) action'. This is about norms, values, customs and traditions in society, as in fashion or allowed dress codes, how society considers poor people, gender relations or culturally determined traditions that persist over time. On the other hand, such rules need to be enforced: the definition of institutions then also refers to specific *organizations* ('the players') empowered by the state or other powers to monitor and enforce such rules (Mohmand, 2016, p. 9). For example, the Central Bank is the (formal) institution enforcing monetary rules; (formal) courts enforce (formal) rules as regards justice.

How to then define the informal as separate from the 'formal'? I agree with Helmke and Levitsky (2004) that the defining issue is whether or not the rules are defined, written up as well as enforced by the state and its institutions (like the state empowers the Central Bank or Supreme Court). They define informal institutions as 'the socially shared rules, usually unwritten, that are created, communicated, and enforced outside of officially sanctioned channels'. Such institutions include norms and values underlying India's caste system and gender relations, but also 'institutionalized' informal rules governing systems of corruption and nepotism. That could be the 'normal' or accepted rates to extort a bribe from a hawker, or additional payments to obtain a licence, birth certificate or pension. Informal practices and relationships, for example in patronage relations or bribery, have become 'institutionalized'. Caste councils in India are informal institutions, enforcing caste rules, and may stop a Muslim boy marrying a Hindu girl, and punish them (Mohmand, 2016, pp. 14, 19).

These may be legitimized by power centres or ideologies outside the formal state, where the concept of multi-centric local governance is useful. It refers to different foci of governance to include the formal municipality itself, but also a very powerful politician or businessperson/firm, a traditional chief or court, or a local mafia outfit – even if the latter remain in the background. Mohmand finds that informal local institutions are critical to determine how citizens engage with the state in several arenas and activities:

> they organise vote banks within communities for parties, candidates and municipal governments, thereby affecting participation in elections; they mediate disputes and dispense justice as substitutes to formal legal mechanisms; they regulate citizens' access to services (schools, health centres), and they mediate interactions with local governments, thereby affecting access to information, and participation in deliberative forums.
>
> (Mohmand, 2016, p. 18)

All this is very relevant to the position and contexts of many poor people worldwide who feel totally let down by the state, if only where interactions with officials and the police 'are marred by rudeness, humiliation and harassment' (Nayaran, 2000, p. 8). Partly for such reasons, they find their options for justice, access to services and even to vote in elections not with the 'formal local state', but rather in informal local governance institutions (ILGIs) and relations. So, while Transparency International (2017) and Sachs (2012) rightly advocate promoting good governance to book SDG progress, things are rather more complex, if only as they neglect the importance, often dominance, of informality (and among other things, also of power and politics/politicization) in relation to poverty and policy. Informality is (as yet) poorly understood, and more often than not neglected in designing and implementing policy:

> informal local governance institutions are inherently problematic targets for public policy intervention. They are diverse, poorly understood, barely mapped and strongly rooted in local history and local socioeconomic structures. This makes our current task of conceptualising and defining ILGIs both more difficult and more important because policy interventions to either support or constrain such local institutions are necessarily linked to a better understanding of the conceptual distinctions that exist across them.
>
> (Mohmand, 2016, p. 7)

To make matters even more complex, informality is not limited to state–society interactions: it includes a wide range of undocumented, (semi-) illegal, secretive, 'corrupt', and mostly personalist/ particularistic actions and relations, starting from, but undermining and transforming, formal (state) institutions and relations:

> Key here is that corruption is directed by a variety of rules. Corruption has a social element to it, as transfers are not only financial, but have wider social and cultural implications. This is broadly referred to as 'social

corruption'. Clientelism and nepotism are examples of this, as corruption is widely seen as a form of social exchange .... Patron–client relations, in their most basic form, are guided by a social and political exchange. The patron grants favours in return for goods, loyalty, political allegiance and other services from his dependent clients.

(Titica and Edmond, 2018, pp. 10–11)

All this goes to show that it is important to examine the role of *both* formal and informal institutions in local governance in relation to current (SDG) approaches to address chronic poverty and increasing inequality.

This chapter especially maps the informal domain. Yet all is not well with formal governance institutions either. One area of concern, as noted by Sachs (2012), is the capacities and the political will at all levels of administration. Even if there is commitment from national/central governments, there is no guarantee that policies, even if framed and budgeted, will be very effective. An important dimension is whether central governments can effectively motivate or even force lower levels of administration to implement specific poverty-reduction policies and programmes.

In India as a federation and with a history of intra-state decentralization, states are governed by their own elected state-level parliamentarians. These have or claim considerable power and discretion to neglect or dilute central dictates and to cream off budgets, if not formally, then informally. Second, the actual implementation of any existing or new (pro-poor) policy is ultimately the domain of local governments or urban municipalities – the level where people meet the local state. The argument here is that, if there is no sustainable development at this local level, there will be none at all (Boex, 2013). Unfortunately, across the developing world, many local governments already find it very hard to deal with the day-to-day challenges of basic service delivery, infrastructure or law and order. Weak formal institutions, limited capacities, undue politicization and restricted budgets transfers are some factors (for India, see Dhar Chakrabarti, 2001).

To complete this analytical framing aimed to help understand how (inclusive) governance and policy-making – needed for effective (SDG) policy – can be invaded/transformed/manipulated through informal dynamics and so undermine such efforts, two final points need to be made. Underlying the SDG approach are common notions of 'universality' and 'inclusion', for example that *all* poor people in a slum do obtain the uniform policy benefits they are entitled to, such as subsidized food, drinking water or toilets. However, as will be explained in more detail below, services may only reach beneficiaries on a personal, individualistic basis – and not as uniform policy. As argued convincingly by Berenschot (2010), who advanced the notion of 'the mediated state', state services are often provided on an individualized basis with allocation mediated by officials and politicians. In such cases, the latter have a personal (not public welfare) interest in terms of money/bribes and/or votes, in a way 'selling state services' (Blundo, 2006).

Second, there is a need to unbundle this feel-good term of *'inclusion'*. It may be assumed that it is generally good to be included, with prospects for 'voice' as in democracy, or for proper wages if people are included in the labour market. My definition of inclusion (in the field of education) stresses *involvement* (which can be seen as participation) and *empowerment,* where the inherent worth, dignity and rights of all people are recognized. An inclusive school promotes and sustains a uniform sense of belonging, and practises respect for the talents, beliefs, backgrounds and ways of living of its members.

All this raises questions which will be checked with the case for Mumbai's poor – invariably from so-called low castes and disadvantaged classes. Can they participate; is there any respect or appreciation for their very limiting, largely informal contexts? And finally, the very framing of the concept of 'inclusion' for poor and marginal(ized) people needs to be questioned, as this could also mean 'adverse incorporation' (Hickey and du Toit, 2007; Wood, 2003). They may be part of employment and political structures not fundamentally helpful (or in fact forming constraints) to reduce their poverty or misery. Existing informal support systems can help reduce survival risks, but inhibit chances to mobilize wealth at the same time. Impartially probing such possible micro-level scenarios is critical for any chance at sustainable development, not least in terms of political inclusion.

Mumbai's poor people largely live in an informal context

I started this chapter with the case of Shanti: the example of a migrant woman who managed to obtain a foothold in the city fully through informal means – even if the slum where she lives remained illegal and eviction chances high. We might guess that she would have gone nowhere far, if she had had to rely on the red-tape and corruption-prone 'formal local state', or indeed if it had resolutely banned people from the site all along. A couple of things worked in her favour: she had an already established and helpful relative in the slum, some savings to activate informal processes (while poorer people's problems start right here) and she was not from the (formerly 'outcaste') Dalit caste – for whom access and networking are normally most precarious. Without realizing it, she – and her fellow illegal squatters occupying the same slum area – had the same interests as nearby powerful private-sector developers and contractors. The very politicians allowing (and earning from) the illegal encroachment by squatters over many years, were eventually being contacted and rewarded by the latter to support changes in the Mumbai Development Plan. Such strategies had worked in other slum areas, leading to good profits in real estate (de Wit, 2017, p. 25). The context of their informal lobbying is neoliberal Mumbai: if Shanti's slum were to be legalized for formal housing, this would be done under the Slum Redevelopment Scheme (SRS). This is a vehicle for public–private–community partnerships, where contractors negotiate with the SRS Authority and 'communities' about sharing slum lands. Typically, one part is allocated for lucrative private development and another smaller part with basic units for eligible slum inhabitants. A case study of one such SRS project very clearly brings out the most vulnerable groups:

> Although the SRS policy does not differentiate between owners and tenants, in reality, the tenant households, lacking any legal status, had no claim to a formal tenement unit in the new scheme. They would be evicted from their hutments once the scheme commenced. They had neither representation in the Community Based Organisations nor support from the leaders, the builder or the municipal Ward Office. This group, the most vulnerable, was invisible in the scheme. The second most adversely affected category were older residents without valid official proof of their residency. Despite residing in the slum before 1995, they neither possessed any valid documents nor did they have the financial stability to acquire the same via fraudulent means. This group typically consisted of the poorest of the poor – single women, households with very old members, those with a woman main earning member and alcoholic husbands, daily wage earners or those having intermittent, unsteady work. The latter group also did not have a close connection with the slum leadership and therefore no clout for negotiating their status in the scheme. These households were not eligible in either of the lists drawn by the two competing builders.
>
> (Desai and de Wit, 2007, p. 18)

These then, are the people who survive at great odds at the bottom of the city's hierarchy of power and money: an estimated 2.5 million chronically poor inhabitants (MGGM, 2009) who foremost deserve our concern and care. The quote already brings out the importance of 'being connected' – in my terminology as a 'client' to have some support from a 'patron' or a broker (network). However, where patronage is ultimately a reciprocal relation, very poor people with little to offer – money for bribes, assets, useful contacts – are at risk of being sidelined. True, they have that one critical asset in the form of a vote, but, as we shall see, the election process is not quite clean and many politicians are not helpful or reliable (Vaishnav, 2017). This means that informal, personal relations are critical. I would even argue that informality has a much deeper impact, given that much of the context of poor people is 'informal'. One source mentions that the informal sector accounts for 68 per cent of total employment in Mumbai (Revi, 2012), and this sector employs the bulk of the urban poor.

In addition, the local state seems quite remote for poor people who largely fend for themselves. As noted before, there is plenty of 'self-help' or local-level improvisation plus neighbour caste-level support (de Wit, 2017, pp. 141ff). It is unfortunate, but a fact that confirms a wider, cruel logic, that the Mumbai police precisely target those most vulnerable – and most unlikely to have money or powerful friends – for extremely rough and sometimes fatal treatment. One indication is that victims of custodial deaths in Maharashtra are mostly from minorities such as Dalits and Muslims – rarely so-called higher-caste Hindus or richer/more powerful people (Sequeira, 2014). This already hints at one dynamic of exclusion where the state protects its wealthier, connected, majority, elite communities more than those forced to live on the margins of Mumbai society.

A key matter for all poor people is *health*, where it is commonly known that 'out of pocket' payment for health services is a major cause for households falling into poverty (starting with indebtedness), or deepening the misery of existing poverty. Slum health conditions compare very unfavourably with non-slum urban areas. Health agencies only reach 30 per cent of the urban poor; only about 62 per cent of mothers living in slums receive postnatal care. Today, less than 25 per cent of Mumbai's people use *public* dispensaries and hospitals; all others use *private* facilities, which now by far outnumber public health facilities. Experts worry about the 'commodification' of health care, where medical care has become a for-profit industry which is being targeted by business houses.

A similar tale can be told about *education*, where formerly well-performing public schools are closed (and their lucrative premises sold), while there is a mushrooming of private schools, private tuition and evening classes, sometimes managed by politicians as a profit industry (Boo, 2012). In the past five years, the number of Mumbai private schools increased by 32 per cent, while the number of municipal schools only rose by 1 per cent. The MCGM (2009, p. 88) report notes a wide and growing gap between public and private schools, which together accentuate rather than balance class differences.

The share of formal sector *employment* is falling along with an increase in casual work and a significant feminization of the work force. Nearly half the people working in the informal sector are migrants (MCGM, 2009, p. 52). Labour mobility is limited, partly as cash is demanded for probably all attractive (that is, formal) jobs. Most slum households have lower or higher (and high-interest) levels of debt, sometimes burdening them for many years.

Slum or *low-income housing policies* are lacking, apart from the rather ill-fated and very expensive SRS efforts (Nainan, 2012; for a comprehensive overview see de Wit, 2017, pp. 145–50). As indicated by Manecksha (2011), the poor (from relocated slums/so-called project-affected persons) are being pushed to Mumbai's periphery, where already most recent migrants have settled. New SRS units are mostly constructed here, in what observers see as massive, poorly planned and constructed 'ghettoes'.

Thus, while the supply of the basics of 'social protection' is already under severe pressure, the funds here are often skimmed off by ruthless, rent-seeking officials, politicians often plus fees for touts and intermediaries. The bribes extracted from poor people – bribes to the police, weekly illegal collections from hawkers and shops on the streets, or simply to obtain a birth certificate – can be seen as extra taxes limiting their options further. This happens against a background of reported reductions in central funding for important poverty programmes such as the Integrated Child Welfare Program, or policies to support mothers and women, or for urban housing policies. In terms of food security, the failing Public Distribution System of ration shops with cheap foodstuff mostly fails those most in need, as it too is rife with corruption (de Wit, 2017, pp. 140–1; Kumar and Landy, 2009).

By and large, Mumbai's poor and slum people are facing huge odds to reverse strong trends which increasingly seem to undermine their position as a group (in slums), and as a disadvantaged class, in social, economic and political respects. I need to emphasize that all this occurs in a gendered context where men and women play markedly different roles, starting with the division of labour at the household level. As part of India's strongly patriarchal society, (poor, low-income, disadvantaged-caste) women and girls get saddled with almost all reproductive tasks – while also often working for wages and managing street-level communities. Most of the diverse failures of the local state to provide reliable support in health, toilets, drinking water as well as personal safety end up on their plate. If the SDGs are about targeting those most deserving and in greatest need, much if not all attention is needed for massive numbers of Indian women and girls facing miserable conditions.

Limited claim-making powers and defensive collective action

Poor people face additional challenges in their 'demand or claim-making capacity' regarding may be called 'social handicaps'. They are often (semi-) illiterate – hence lacking relevant knowledge; poor (with fluctuating, informal sector wages); of so-called low caste, such as the Dalits who are over-represented in the slums; newcomers to the city (hence lacking useful contacts and networks); members of a minority, or women. I believe that, more broadly, many poor city people live in a largely 'informal world', where they are engaged in informal sector work, live in informal, often unrecognized/illegal settlements, and depend on informal and exploitative money lenders. Together, these facts lead to fundamental vulnerability and exclusion risks, where people basically have to fend for themselves under conditions where nothing is easy.

Trust – outside the relative safety of household and family – is often in short supply, and the poor and less poor (fiercely) compete among themselves for scarce opportunities (well illustrated for a poor slum by Boo, 2012). They operate in an environment characterized by unreliable institutions, negligent or even predatory government agents, and multiple but volatile sources of household income – in Wood's (2003, p. 468) term, by 'destructive uncertainty'.

Being exposed to rough and often murky stakeholder arenas, it is critical for the poor as a group or class – all facing very similar urgent challenges of city livelihoods – to unite, organize and claim both better services and deeper, structural improvements in their position. Unfortunately, this seems to happen rather rarely. One reason is the fact that all slums harbour heterogeneous populations, making it difficult to define a 'community' or find a viable unit for collective action. Mumbai slums are generally quite peaceful, with people from diverse backgrounds living together in relative harmony. However, divisions or even factions do exist, based on income, but also, perhaps increasingly, linked to *identity* factors including caste, religion, ethnicity and gender. Tenants have other interests than 'house or hut owners'. These differences may not generally play a role, but may hinder collective action, or play up due to internal or external factors.

One such factor is the coexistence of various highly competitive political parties, which can accentuate slum divisions during election campaigns. As explained in more detail elsewhere (de Wit and Berner, 2009), relations between the poor and city agencies are marked by (and cannot escape) a pervasive patronage logic, which ultimately affects all efforts aimed at 'empowering' the poor or at engaging them in 'participation', be it by a foreign donor, a municipality or a local NGO. Rather than being vehicles of empowerment and progressive change, slum community-based organizations (CBOs) and their leadership often block progress, controlling or capturing benefits aimed at the poor and misusing them for private (political) interests (see the case study in de Wit, 2010).

I start from the assumption that, rather than organizing horizontally and acting as a collective – more likely in a defensive reaction, such as resisting an eviction, rather than in a proactive, 'claim-making' action – poor/slum people prefer cultivating vertical contacts in the form of relationships with patrons or brokers – which itself may be part of engrained Indian customs. Such mediators do have access to arenas of influence and power in a context where the formal state is rather remote. We may term them 'patron–client or patronage relations', when there is some stability over time between a poor person and another one with more resources and/or contacts, and where some degree of reciprocity and trust exists. So, while such relations may offer some relief, they also serve to sustain poverty, especially when a patron is exploitative. This may present what Wood (2003, p. 468) has termed a 'Faustian bargain', discounting a possible better future in favour of survival in the present which contributes to chronic poverty:

> The dangers of not being a client, of not being protected, of losing 'membership' of the local commander led community are immense. Better to be with the devil you know.
>
> (Wood, 2003, p. 468)

This, again can be framed as 'adverse incorporation' – now a poor person is being protected by a patron, but on very unfavourable, poverty-sustaining terms. Yet such more 'traditional' patrons and mediators – perhaps marked by authority, respect and non-political forms of prestige – have made way in Indian cities for 'new leaders' or 'brokers' with a proven, much more instrumental capacity to get things done, but now always at a price in terms of money. Increased inter-party competition has led to a proliferation of such mediators/brokers/fixers linked to several parties, so that people may choose those most effective. As noted, Berenschot (2010) in this respect refers to 'the *mediated local state*', where politicians (acting like 'street level politicians' through their local-level agents) and officials are primarily seen as mediators channelling state and policy benefits to selected (particularistic, not all/uniformly/universally) beneficiaries and slum pockets (which, in Mumbai are seen to constitute 'vote banks', as explained later).

This is one form of rent-seeking where they benefit as individuals by 'selling' state benefits (Blundo, 2006). The latter aptly calls this the 'informal privatisation of street level bureaucracy'. Officials as 'bribe takers' earn informal monies; politicians and their slum-level party agents promise or provide services against (the promise of) a vote. It appears as if the propensity of the local state – or better its individual officials and politicians – to deliver (collective or individual) benefits on a personalized patronage or 'vote bank' basis is met with slum people who adjust to such an informal policy logic.

Mumbai megacity and its tainted public administration

Mediators are critical to offer 'life chances' to poor, vulnerable people and those confronted with an urgent crisis who turn to the local state for support. Mumbai exemplifies such trends, which I shall now elaborate as in the changing *supply* of essential services for the poor. Mumbai scores poorly on many indicators in the ranks of global cities, not least owing to very poor governance. Approximately half of its population live in numerous slums, where facilities and services – drinking water, shelter, toilets and cleanliness – are always substandard, and appalling in more recent, poorer, more marginal slums (slum pockets) – in spite of Mumbai being India's richest municipality. More or less in concert with such other state and parastatal agencies, it is the Mumbai Municipal Corporation BMC that provides the services most important for poor people: services such as water, urban transport, public schools and hospitals, as well as solid waste management. Yet both administrative and financial capacities have been and are under stress, and it is actually remarkable that the city is as liveable as it is considering the multifaceted challenges it faced over the years (MCGM, 2009; de Wit, 2017, pp. 177ff).

With a view to contextualizing city poverty and politics, I now reflect on the nature of Mumbai's governance, where we necessarily need to delve beyond the 'formal façade' of governance agencies and institutions. Not all is well here: informality seems the dominant governance domain:

> The BMC, which supposedly runs the city, although there is scant evidence of that, has an annual budget of $4 Billion and is a byword for graft. Corruption is pervasive in many departments, offices and official transactions in an informal, shadow market economy of governance. With a massive annual budget (larger than that of several Indian states), and without debts, it is an attractive place to govern.
>
> (*Economist*, 2012)

This fact was emphasized in media reports relating to the 2012 municipal elections, with a discourse picturing Mumbai as a 'very important prize to win', implying great riches for victorious politicians. Hence, it appears that the main reason to get elected to be a municipal councillor – with the encouraging Marathi name '*Nagar Sevak*' or 'city servant' – is the almost unlimited access to all sort of informal earnings. Councillors are the key patrons of constituencies – heading a pyramid of informal patronage relations from ward to neighbourhood on to street level. As shown below, an average councillor gets cuts by allowing for (illegal) water connections, slum hut extensions, or helping to release accused people from the police. City planning is weak, and strongly influenced by the powerful, such as construction/developer firms and large business houses (see Nainan, 2012). Budgets are misused, and coordination between the agencies governing the metropolis is very problematic – partly owing to inter-agency rivalry fuelled by political party competition (Pethe et al., 2012; de Wit, 2017, pp. 89ff).

Informality in a 'patronage democracy': adverse incorporation in local democracy?

India is considered by many as the world's largest democracy, and this is indicated by basics such as the presence of multiple parties both at national and state level, with new parties arising and others fading. Multi-party elections are supervised by a well-respected Election Commission, while media are quite open and critical. India could almost be seen as another 'liberal democracy'. However, if we look closer, not all is well. Taking critical account of more informal dimensions yields other, in my view more truthful, perspectives, for example this assessment by Varshney:

> However, for all its achievements, India's democracy has considerable flaws. If electoral competitiveness were the only yardstick to judge a democracy, India today would qualify as a great success. Over the past two decades, the incumbents have repeatedly lost elections. Since incumbents can control the state machinery that conducts elections, it is clear that elections are genuinely competitive, and that popular will, barring individual exceptions, is clearly expressed. What happens between two elections, however, is very different. India's democracy has become Janus-faced. Political power is used at the time of elections to please citizens. During the years between the elections, it is often used to accumulate wealth, treat citizens in an unfeeling manner, and humiliate adversaries crudely. Following their bosses, the permanent bureaucrats – administrators and policemen – act as accomplices in this project. Empowered at the time of elections, the citizen often feels powerless until the next elections arrive. Entry into schools and treatment in hospitals often depends on whether a politician or bureaucrat can call on your behalf, or whether you have a bribe to pay. Corruption also marks the issuance of driving licenses, property registration, enrolment in the employment guarantee scheme and payment of wages. The list can go on.
>
> (Varshney, 2011)

Chandra (2004, p. 1) is quite gloomy where she refers to a 'malign' democracy in India, which 'has malfunctioned in a serious way for India's most vulnerable citizens' (2004, pp. 4–5). This however, is about the *form* of India's democracy, perhaps more accurately the *outcome/impact*, and not the *nature* of India's democracy. Where it actually works quite well is in the (formal) organization of elections, voting, counting and delivering a verdict which is respected by all parties (italics following de Wit). She characterizes India as a 'patronage democracy' and, as will be discussed below, its elections as 'auctions':

> India's is a 'patronage-democracy' in which elections have become auctions for the sale of government services. The most minimal goods that a government should provide – security of life and property, access to education, provision of public health facilities, a minimum standard of living – have become, for large numbers of people, market goods rather than entitlements. This is a violation of modern norms of governance. Worse, this violation affects citizens unequally. And worst of all, this violation has become routinized in everyday imagination, so that it is now no longer perceived as illegitimate. Just as democracy in India has become business as usual, so has the politics of patronage.
>
> (Chandra, 2004, p. 5)

However, as noted, we need to highlight another very problematic or insidious dimension here, which is the financing (with black money) of the increasingly costly election campaigns, where private-sector business firms play a critical role. In Mumbai, two dynamics operate. First, candidates standing for elections need lots of cash to finance their increasingly expensive election campaigns. Some is needed for propaganda materials, for street meetings and to pay a large number of party cadres and paid volunteers to act as local and street-level agents. Yet probably the main expenses include the 'goodies' ('freebies' or 'political machine inducements') that are offered or promised to the voters. Such pre-election goodies include a range of incentives such as small alcohol bottles, clothes, cooking utensils, but also outright cash in return for the promise to vote for that candidate:

> We talked to a young party worker of the dominant local party Shiv Sena who had been very active before and during the 2012 local elections, as party agent and also to convince people to vote for his party (he did not attend school for two months). He told us that the allocation of money in elections depended from case to case. In case of a hotly contested battle between two opposing candidates for a councillor seat, money would flow easily, and people would benefit happily. When there is a general anticipation that one dominant candidate is likely to win in a constituency anyway, rather less or no money may be allocated. He mentioned that amounts of Rs. 5,000 for all votes in a household were not uncommon, with Rs. 500 for an individual vote (and not 1,500 or Rs. 5,000 as per rumours).

> He said that he and his neighbourhood friends had a pretty good idea as to who was voting on whom.
>
> (de Wit, 2017, p. 238)[96]

Such dynamics confirm the Chandra thesis of a market for votes – showing how far Mumbai's vernacular local democracy has drifted away from liberal democracy: 'With the help of money, elections are turned into a great spectacle and the electoral arena converted into a big market space where money mediates between the candidates and the electorate' (Prabash, 2010, p. 88). The well-respected chief election commissioner (CEC) refers to a dynamic where economic inequality leads to political inequality – with the poor 'adversely incorporated' in a system that does not seem to work for them. Two quotes from him in an Indian newspaper on this matter of 'big' or 'black' money illustrate this:

> CEC Mr. Brahma said, in view of the high cost of election campaigning in terms of media advertisements and public rallies, that the use of 'big money' in politics is a major concern today. 'If wealthy individuals and the corporates pay to the political party or the candidate in order to make him listen to them, this undermines the core principles of democracy and *transfers the economic inequality to political inequality.*
>
> (Indian Express, 2015a, italics by author)

> Following the consultation, the CEC gave a statement 'that the use of black money during elections had to be checked as it created imbalance in a democratic system' .... 'Black money impinges democracy. Black money and muscle power disturb level playing field. Though money cannot guarantee votes, the one who can spend more has an upper hand.'
>
> (Indian Express, 2015b)

On the basis of extensive research in Mumbai, initial indications (de Wit, 2017, pp. 246ff) are that its poor people pragmatically play along with the game, hoping to claim at least one sure benefit in terms of 'goodies' from local democracy – apart from omnipresent pre-election promises. Many voters accept cash or other freebies – which may or may not translate into voting for the dispensing party, dependent on how safe they feel not to do so. Some even take cash from several candidates. Yet a majority seem to first scan for the

---

96 For much more detail see de Wit (2017, ch. 5), 'Politics or Poli-tricks? Local democracy and slum voting in the 2012 Mumbai elections.'

candidate's identity in terms of religion, caste and ethnicity (language, state origin) as an initial preference.

Another main consideration – consistent with the premises underlying the 'patronage democracy' and 'mediated state' – is that the poor may subsequently – or already from the start – look for a person with a proven record as a stable and reliable broker, with solid moneyed networks to pull many strings (Bjorkman, 2013). Candidates with a reputation of being generally helpful and able to 'pull funds into our slum' may be most popular. It may be considered yet one more sign of the pragmatism of candidates and political parties – but also the voters – to condone or use informality and corruption as long as it serves their short-term interests, given the way vernacular democracy has come to be institutionalized.

Conclusions: informal power and money dynamics determine beneficial inclusion

This chapter considered key constraints in the field of local governance, service delivery and local democracy, seen as critical to the prospects to achieve the SDGs, but which have not earned the attention they deserve. Based on a study of everyday dynamics in the megacity of Mumbai, it highlighted the importance of 'informality' in relation to conditions of large numbers of its poor(est) and marginalized slum people. The focus was on informality in terms of administrative and political corruption, electoral malfeasance and a reliance on personalist relations of patronage and brokerage. I specifically engaged with SDG 16, considered as most directly relevant for 'promoting peaceful and inclusive societies, provide access to justice and build effective, accountable and inclusive institutions' (United Nations, 2016). This is the more operational SDG, targeting implementation dynamics, where I agree with others such as Sachs (2012: 2208) that a degree of '"good governance" is an absolutely essential condition to make progress in all SDGs 'at all levels, local, national, regional, and global'. Transparency International (2017) argues that 'there will be no sustainable development without tackling corruption'.

I have framed this chapter's analysis in debates on the divide between 'formal and informal institutions', notably in terms of informal local governance institutions and how these do or do not mediate access to much needed basic services (Mohmand, 2016). Other perspectives relate to particularistic relations of patronage and brokerage which underlie the concept of the 'patronage democracy'. Using the image of 'elections as auctions', Chandra (2004) argues that governments do not uniformly provide the most essential goods and services according to legal and policy entitlements, but rather in return to votes and/or bribes, where the key line is 'Vote for me and I will get your work done' (Chandra, 2004, p. 3). Such a democracy malfunctions especially for India's most vulnerable citizens, who are the focus of this chapter.

In addition, I traced the advent of neoliberal reforms for Mumbai – privatization, public–private partnerships, deregulation – with concomitant dynamics of commodification. While poor and lower-income people could always rely on more or less free public services – health care, education, sanitation – they are now often forced to rely on privately provided services. In terms of 'multi-stakeholder local governance' (Swyngedouw, 2005), they now appear as rather weak stakeholders where other classes and castes evolved to grow powerful and resourceful. Notably, these include Mumbai's growing middle classes and the unfettered and increasingly powerful private business sector, with indications of far too close ties between business actors/firms and politicians, which contribute to crony capitalism in the metropolis.

Even while poor people cleverly manage their meagre resources, exerting agency by pragmatically acting on opportunities, by and large they are overwhelmed by the above rapid changes in the economic and political context which they cannot control and often do not understand. Unavoidably, managing livelihoods is most problematic for Mumbai's group of chronically poor – perhaps 2.5 million people. Elderly people, tenants in illegal slums, members of the so-called lowest castes, especially Dalits, and minorities such as Muslims and recent migrants were identified as most vulnerable and in need of support – of governments and hopefully now in the context of implementing the SDG agenda. Yet in all these groups, it is women and girls who are most at risk of exclusion, discrimination and outright exploitation – leading to untold daily misery, even while they are always expected to run households in the context of India's patriarchal society.

This chapter yields three major conclusions, which double as recommendations with a view to enhancing the chances that the institutional and financial expenses of the SDG machinery will actually translate into tangible improvements. First, I argue that 'informality' is not an incidental and unfortunate deviation from what are accepted norms and benchmarks of ('good') governance or democracy.

Rather, in Mumbai, it is an integral, if not dominant trait of power-driven politics and governance (de Wit, 2017, p. 7). It was shown that poor slum people in Mumbai largely live in an 'informal world' and that the most effective coping strategies are in the domain of the informal. Evidence shows that 'the informal' can offer opportunities and openings not allowed by formal laws, provisions and policy (see Benjamin, 2008). They survive in socio-administrative and political structures which tend to be adverse or even hostile, especially for those most excluded (or adversely incorporated) in terms of labour, health care, education and safety. This realm of informality needs be given much more attention both in academic research and by agencies engaging with poverty-reduction policy.

In addition, I conclude that poor people are negatively affected by the impacts and implications of the neoliberal policies that Mumbai city has eagerly embraced from the early 1990s (Banerjee-Guha, 2009). Impacts have naturally been different for different actors, where more powerful stakeholders such as the Indian middle classes and business firms are seen to have benefited. In contrast, such governance shifts and reforms have negatively impacted on the city's poor people, as they are being squeezed between reduced public delivery of quality services such as education and health care – and the increasing need to pay (high) fees for better (good) private ones. Inequality, already considerable and persistent in terms of hierarchical caste and gender relations, is on the rise in a city where half the population lives in slums – but which also has India's highest number of billionaires. While the more powerful middle classes do manage to organize, for example in resident welfare associations, joint collective action or sustained claim-making efforts on the part of poor people are rare. One reason concerns the extremely heterogeneous population of the slums in terms of different castes and income groups, 'owners' versus tenants, Hindus versus people of other faiths, men versus women, ruling versus opposition party supporters. Another complication is that people can be simultaneously included, excluded and adversely incorporated in systems of employment, service delivery and local democracy, which undermines their power and bargaining positions.

This chapter identifies the omnipresence of informality and related vertical patronage/dependency relations as the key impediment. Rather than organizing horizontally and acting as a collective, poor/slum people resort to cultivating vertical contacts in the form of patrons or brokers who do have access to decision-making arenas (de Wit and Berner, 2009). By 'positioning for patronage', they are seen to react to everyday service delivery dynamics and the propensity of officials and politicians to rely on informal relations through 'vertical governance' (Kumar and Landy, 2009).

All this leads to my conviction that the above is critically important with a view to the lofty ideals and high expectations framed in the SDGs. In targeting what I consider the more 'operational' SDG 16 and its correct emphasis on 'building inclusive institutions', I perceive risks, if institutions and conditions 'beyond the façade of the formal local state' are neglected. Concrete progress at the level of poor households can only materialize if not only formal institutions such as the municipality, the police, a ministry or the local council, but also informal institutions are concretely taken into account.

Beyond this case study of Mumbai, I therefore suggest there is an urgent need to engage with critical, even if opaque and admittedly hard to study, informal processes. This will yield rich, alternative insights into actual, 'everyday' realities and processes that determine entrenched poverty and social exclusion. I therefore agree with Transparency International (2017) that the SDG machinery, international donor agencies and NGOs need to engage with the opaque realm of informality. They often rely on concepts and theorization that fit poorly with poor people's everyday realities, or rely on technical approaches or fixes without considering wider everyday administrative and political conditions. This naturally carries the risk of building on or supporting doubtful or deceitful government agents/agencies/policies. Including analyzes of and acting upon systems of informality would at least make it clearer as to how governance systems – and ultimately the SDGs – work and for whom precisely: elites, rich or (very) poor.

References

Baud, I. and de Wit, J. W. (eds). 2008. *New Forms of Governance in India: Shifts, models, networks and contestations*. New Delhi, Sage.

Banerjee-Guha, S. 2009. Neo-liberalising the 'urban': new geographies of power and injustice in Indian cities. *Economic and Political Weekly*, Vol. 44, No. 22, pp. 95–107.

Benjamin, S. 2008. Occupancy urbanism: radicalizing politics and economy beyond policy and programs. *International Journal of Urban and Regional Research*, Vol. 32, No. 3, pp. 719–29.

Berenschot, W. 2010. Everyday mediation: the politics of public service delivery in Gujarat, India. *Development and Change*, Vol. 41, No. 5, pp. 883–905.

Bjorkman, L. 2013. 'You can't buy a vote': cash and community in a Mumbai election, MMG Working Paper 13–01. Göttingen, Germany, Max Planck Institute. www.mmg.mpg.de/fileadmin/user_upload/documents/wp/WP_13-01_Bjorkman_Cant-buy-a-vote.pdf (Accessed 9 November 2016.)

Blundo, G. 2006. Dealing with the local state: the informal privatization of street-level bureaucracies in Senegal. *Development and Change*, Vol. 37, No. 4, pp. 799–821.

Boex, J. 2013. The world we want? Promoting the notion that all development is local. blog.metrotrends.org/author/jboex. (Accessed 29 April 2017.)

Boo, K. 2012. *Behind the Beautiful Forevers; Life, death and hope in a Mumbai undercity.* New Delhi and New York, Hamish Hamilton.

Chandra, K. 2004. Elections as auctions. *Seminar*, No. 539, pp. 1–7. www.india-seminar.com/2004/539/539%20kanchan%20chandra.htm (Accessed 19 September 2013.)

Clark, G. and Moonen, T. 2014. *Mumbai: India's Global City. A case study of the Global Cities Initiative, a joint project of Brookings and JPMorgan Chase.* Washington DC, Global Cities Initiative.

De Wit, J. 2010. Decentralized management of solid waste in Mumbai slums: informal privatization through patronage. *International Journal of Public Administration*, Vol. 33 (Nos 12 and 13), pp. 767–77.

———. 2017. *Urban Poverty, Local Governance and Everyday Politics in Mumbai.* London, New York and New Delhi, Routledge.

De Wit, J. and Berner, E. 2009. Progressive patronage? Municipalities, NGOs, community-based organizations, and the limits to slum dwellers' empowerment. *Development and Change*, Vol. 40, No. 5, pp. 927–47.

Desai, P. and de Wit, J. 2007. The slum redevelopment scheme in Malad, Mumbai: evidence from the field. Mumbai, unpublished research report.

Dhar Chakrabarti, P. G. 2001. Urban crisis in India: new initiatives for sustainable cities. *Development in Practice*, Vol. 11 (Nos 2 and 3), pp. 260–72.

Dobbs, R., Smit, S., Remes, J., Manyika, J., Roxburgh, C. ,and Restrepo, A. 2011. Urban world: mapping the economic power of cities. McKinsey Global Institute. www.mckinsey.com/featured-insights/urbanization/urban-world-mapping-the-economic-power-of-cities (Accessed 23 March 2019.)

Foundation for Democracy and Sustainable Development. n.d. UN Sustainable Development Goal (SDG) 16 – importance of participatory institutions & policymaking. http://www.fdsd.org/ideas/sustainable-development-goal-sdg-16-democratic-institutions/ (Accessed 8 July 2018.)

Frontline. 2014. Reliance factor, 21 March. https://frontline.thehindu.com/cover-story/reliance-factor/article5746172.ece (Accessed 20 April 2016.)

Helmke, G. and Levitsky, S. 2004. Informal institutions and comparative politics: a research agenda. *Perspectives on Politics*, Vol. 2, No. 4, pp. 725–40.

Hickey, S. and du Toit, A. 2007. Adverse incorporation, social exclusion and chronic poverty, Working Paper 81. Manchester, UK, Chronic Poverty Research Centre.

Hyden, G., Court, J. A. and Mease, K. 2004. *Making Sense of Governance: Empirical evidence from sixteen developing countries*. London, Lynne Rienner.

Indian Express. 2015a. No state poll funding sans radical reforms, 24 March.

---. 2015b. Poll panel for stringent law to deal with political funding, 31 March.

Kumar, G. and Landy, F. 2009. Vertical governance: brokerage, patronage and corruption in Indian metropolise. J. Ruet and S. Tawa Lama-Rewal (eds), *Governing India's Metropolises*, London and New Delhi, Routledge, pp. 105–34.

Manecksha, F. 2011. Pushing the poor to the periphery in Mumbai. *Economic and Political Weekly*, Vol. 46, No. 51, pp. 26–8.

MCGM (Municipal Corporation of Greater Mumbai). 2009. *Human Development Report: Mumbai 2009*. Prepared by All India Institute of Local Self Government with support by UNDP and Ministry of Housing and Urban Poverty Alleviation. Mumbai, MCGM.

Mohmand, S. K. 2016. Informal local governance institutions: what they do and why they matter, Working Paper 468, Sussex, UK, Institute of Development Studies (IDS).

Nainan, N. K.B. 2012. *Lakshmi Raj; Shaping Spaces in Post Industrial Mumbai: Urban regimes, planning instruments and splintering communities*. Amsterdam, University of Amsterdam Ph.D. thesis.

Narayan, D. 2000. *Voices of the Poor: Can anyone hear us?* New York, World Bank and Oxford University Press.

Our crony capitalism index. Planet plutocrat. The countries where politically connected businessmen are most likely to prosper. 15 March 2014. *The Economist:* https://www.economist.com/international/2014/03/15/planet-plutocrat

Pethe, A., Tandel, V. and Gandhi, S. 2012. Unravelling the anatomy of legal corruption in India: focusing on the 'honest graft' by the politician. *Economic and Political Weekly*, Vol. 47, No. 21, pp. 55–62. https://mpra.ub.uni-muenchen.de/39306/ (Accessed 12 November 2015.)

Prabash, J. 2010. India: mounting influence of money power in elections and the crisis of representation. *Asia-Pacific Journal of Social Sciences*, Vol. 1, pp. 85–95.

PRAJA. 2011. Mumbai Report Card, Municipal Councillors. www.praja.org/.../concillors-report-card-november (Accessed 14 January 2012.)

Revi, A. 2012. Expansion of cities remain unaffected by India's worsening economy. *India Today*, 30 November. www.indiatoday.in/magazine/business/story/20121105-india-economy-worsening-but-cities-expanding-760325-1999-11-30. (Accessed 20 December 2018.)

Sachs, J. 2012. From Millennium Development Goals to Sustainable Development Goals. The Lancet, Vol. 379 (9 June).

Sankhe, S., Vittal, I., Dobbs, R., Mohan, A., Gulati, A., Ablett, J., Gupta, S., Kim, S., Paul, S., Sanghvi, A. and Sethy, G. 2010. India's urban awakening: building inclusive cities, sustaining economic growth. McKinsey Global Institute. www.mckinsey.com/featured-insights/urbanization/urban-awakening-in-india (Accessed 23 March 2019.)

Sequeira, R. 2014. Why victims of custodial deaths in Maharashtra only from minorities, Bombay High Court asks, Times of India, 1 August. https://timesofindia.indiatimes.com/india/Why-victims-of-custodial-deaths-in-Maharashtra-only-from-minorities-Bombay-HC-asks/articleshow/39378139.cms (Accessed 19 January 2019.)

Swyngedouw, E. 2005. Governance innovation and the citizen: the Janus-face of governance beyond the state. *Urban Studies*, Vol. 42, No. 11, pp. 1991–2006.

Titica, K., and Edmond, P. 2018. Chicken now, not eggs later: short-termism, underdevelopment and regime stabilisation in the DRC's oil governance, Discussion paper 2018/01. Antwerp, Belgium, University of Antwerp Institute of Development Policy (IOB).

Transparency International. 2017. No sustainable development without tackling corruption: the importance of tracking SDG 16. www.transparency.org/news/feature/no_sustainable_development_without_tackling_corruption_SDG 16 (Accessed 28 December 2017.)

United Nations. 2016. Final list of proposed Sustainable Development Goal indicators. https://sustainabledevelopment.un.org/content/documents/11803Official-List-of-Proposed-SDG-Indicators (Accessed 20 December 2017.)

Vaishnav, M. 2017. *When Crime Pays: Money and Muscle in Indian Politics*. New Haven, Conn., Yale University Press.

Varshney, A. 2011. India's battle for democracy has just begun; the urban middle class is now the base of the anti-corruption movement and has the resources to last. *Financial Times*, 29 August. www.ft.com/content/7158efa8-cf41-11e0-b6d4-00144feabdc0 (Accessed 18 February 2014.)

Wood, G. 2003. Staying secure, staying poor: the 'Faustian bargain'. *World Development*, Vol. 31, No. 3, pp. 455–71.

World Inequality Lab. 2018. *World Inequality Report*. https://wir2018.wid.world (Accessed 23 August 2018.)

Chapter 11
POLITICS OF CASTE-BASED EXCLUSION: POVERTY ALLEVIATION SCHEMES IN RURAL INDIA

Rachel Kurian and Deepak Singh

Government-sponsored schemes, such as poverty alleviation, employment generation and welfare programmes, as well as affirmative policies to promote the representation of marginalized groups, are key measures used to promote social inclusion in developing countries. These programmes, while well-intentioned, are however not always effective in contexts where prevailing power relations oppose initiatives challenging their structural position in society. This paper deals with caste-based exclusion and the associated structural violence experienced by the so-called 'low-castes' or Schedule Castes (SC) in rural India, where dominant caste-based power relations uphold ideological biases and cultural practices that legitimize and enforce the exclusion of the so-called 'low-caste' groups. In spite of affirmative action on the part of the government, these groups continue to remain economically disadvantaged (Nandwani, 2016).

Caste-based discrimination contradicts the principles of Sustainable Development Goal (SDG) 16, which focuses on peace, justice and inclusion for all. This chapter argues that effective inclusion of the SCs, or the Dalits – the name they have assumed themselves – would require new conceptual and policy frameworks that identify the different power relations, as well as the interlocking and cumulative nature of exclusionary practices that inform their daily lives, and restrict them from accessing the full benefits of government intervention. The chapter shows that multiple forms of violence and discrimination threaten the human development, human rights and human security of Dalits, and especially Dalit women, because of inter-relational aspects between class, caste and patriarchy. It also exposes the limitations of targeted interventions that do not acknowledge these power relations and outcomes, as well as the necessity of multidimensional action, including strategic alliances and collective mobilization with committed groups, to reduce exclusion and to promote, in line with SDG 16, a just and sustainable inclusion of Dalits in society.

Important legislation and inclusionary policies supporting the Dalits have been implemented in India since it gained its Independence in 1947. The Government of India adopted a new constitution in 1949 that included Articles 15 and 17, under Fundamental Rights, prohibiting discrimination and untouchability.[97] Subsequently, laws such as the Anti-Untouchability Act of 1955, which became the Protection of Civil Rights Act in 1979, and the Prevention of Schedule Caste and Schedule Tribes Atrocities Act (1989) were passed, penalizing violence and discrimination against Dalits.[98] The government also introduced reservations for SCs and Scheduled Tribes (STs) in the public services, including for civil service jobs in administration and education and other public services. In view of their poor economic status, Dalits living in rural areas were also eligible for government-sponsored poverty alleviation programmes.

The law, complemented by favourable policies and programmes, is in line with promoting the social inclusion of the Dalits. The provisions are also in line with the objectives of SDG 16, and its targets including the removal of all forms of violence (16.1), promotion of the rule of law (16.3), reduction of corruption and bribery (16.5), the development of effective, accountable and transparent institutions (16.6), ensuring responsive, inclusive, participatory and representative decision-making at all levels (16.7), and the promotion of and enforcement non-discriminatory laws and policies (16b). The Government of India has also promoted the political representation of women by passing the 73rd Amendment to the Constitution in 1992, mandating that at least 33 per cent of the seats in local government (*panchayat*) and one-third of chairpersons of *panchayats* be reserved for women. In many ways, the content of laws and policies since Indian independence has favoured social inclusion of Dalits and of women. Yet in spite of such measures, as will be outlined in the subsequent sections, Dalits and Dalit women in particular continue to face different types of exclusion which limit the potentially positive outcomes of legislation and special schemes. There is therefore a need to analyze the nature and implications of the entrenched forms of social exclusion, and to develop appropriate strategies so that Dalits enjoy sustainable forms of social inclusion.

The chapter is developed along the following lines. Using Johan Galtung's concept of different forms of violence, and using available

---

97 One of the main authors of the Indian constitution, Bhimrao Ramji Ambedkar, belonged to the SCs and took up this issue as the first minister of law in postcolonial India. Under his influence, protective and preventive measures with regard to SCs were included in the Indian Constitution (adopted in 1949).

98 These included the Anti-Untouchability Act of 1955 (subsequently the Protection of Civil Rights Act, 1979) and the Prevention of Schedule Caste and Schedule Tribes Atrocities Act (1989).

secondary research, the chapter shows how the combination of physical, structural and cultural violence has led to long-term deficits in the human rights, human development and human security of the Dalits. The piece complements this macro data by using micro-level analysis in two villages to expose the local-level dynamics of caste-based power relations in the daily lives of the Dalits, demonstrating how the interlocking and cumulative nature of exclusions and exploitation prevented them, and particularly the Dalit women, from accessing their legal entitlements. It shows how these forms of violence combined to shape the politics of Dalit social exclusion and inclusion – the latter often reflecting a form of perverse incorporation where caste-based norms and practices were retained. The final sections pull out the implications for their rights, development and security, and the promotion of their sustainable social inclusion.

About our methodology

There are two important methodological considerations that frame the analysis. The first has to do with the focus on local interactions. The paper is guided by Sally Moore's notion of 'semi-autonomous social fields', which have 'internally generated rules': the more 'immediate forces that dictate the mode of compliance or noncompliance to state-made legal rules' (1973, p. 721). She has argued that the failure of legislation to bring about social change is often because 'new laws are thrust upon going social arrangements in which there are complexes of binding obligations already in existence', with these obligations being more effective than the laws (1973, p. 723), resulting in 'piecemeal' legislation that 'only partially invades the on-going arrangements' (1973, p. 743). This chapter shows how caste-based exclusion and patriarchal norms function in semi-autonomous fields with power relations that enforce compliance along lines of inequality and discrimination. These controls can often be stronger than the law, and manifest in the daily interactions of people.

The second is the focus on the interactions during the year 2009. This choice of 2009 is based on the understanding that it an important moment to assess the effectiveness of favourable government intervention to remove caste-based exclusion. The pro-SC Bahujan Samaj Party (BSP) had risen to power, and a Dalit, Mayawati Prabhu Das, had become the chief minister of Uttar Pradesh in 1995, and served four other terms in office. This political progress

Politics of caste-based exclusion in rural India

was accompanied by extra attention by the government to countering caste-based atrocities, as well as the appointment of more SC officers in the government administrative services, with special officers to monitor progress and implement schemes. The pro-Dalit BSP, which was ruling the province during 2009, lost the provincial elections in 2012 to the Samajwadi Party (SP), leading to the disbanding of many of the privileges, schemes and monitoring system started by the BSP in Ambedkar villages. In March 2017, the Bhartiya Janata Party (BJP), a 'right-wing Hindu' party of the 'upper castes', defeated SP with a huge majority in the province. [99]While field work has also been done after 2009, the interactions of that year reflect how class and caste relations in society operate to promote exclusion and exploitation even when the political climate and government interventions are meant to promote inclusion.

Characteristics of Dalit exclusion

According to Galtung, '(w)ith the violent structure institutionalized and the violent culture internalized, direct violence also tends to become institutionalized, repetitive, ritualistic, like a vendetta' (1990, p. 202). In his lecture 'Religions, hard and soft' (1994) Galtung noted that religious sanctions associated with the caste system under Hinduism could be seen as a form of structural violence manifested in both economic exploitation and political repression of those at the bottom of the caste pyramid. His earlier work viewed patriarchy, together with racism and class ideologies,

---

99   BJP, currently ruling at the centre too, works from an ideology to transform India into a Hindu theocratic state based on the principles of the book called 'Manusmriti'. 'Manusmriti' advocates a society based on four social hierarchies in which Dalits belong to the lowest ladder of the society without any human rights and dignity. The BJP chief minister of Uttar Pradesh, Yogi Adityanath, was/is the head priest of the Gorakhnath shrine in Gorakhpur district. He is a supporter of the Rashtriya Swaim Sevak Sangh (an extremist Hindu group) and founder of Hindu Yuva Vahini (a militant youth wing). Under his leadership, Dalits and minorities are under tremendous fear and stress for their safety and development. There has been open violence, exercised by right-wing Hindu cow vigilante groups against Muslim minorities, and the killing of Dalits and burning of houses by 'higher castes' in Saharanpur. In 2005, Adityanath led a 'purification drive' which involved the conversion of Christians to Hinduism. In one such instance, 1,800 Christians were reportedly converted to Hinduism in the town of Etah in Uttar Pradesh. He said, 'I will not stop till I turn UP and India into a *Hindu Rashtra* (Hindu state)' (www.synergiafoundation.in/news-analysis/yogi-adityanath-cm). Thus, the recent political changes and the rise to power of the BJP government at the national level are unlikely to remove caste-based exclusion and the exposure of Dalits to structural, cultural and personal violence.

as part of structural violence, leaving women with low status, which exposed them to 'cultural violence' whenever religious ideology was used to 'justify or legitimise direct and structural violence' against them (Galtung, 1990, p. 291). However, he later argued that patriarchy combined 'direct, structural and cultural violence in a vicious triangle', with rape, repression and intimidation being part of the triangle along with structural violence and cultural violence. The result was that patriarchy institutionalized violence by ideologically internalizing dominant and subordinate relationships, along gender, caste and identity lines, with low-status women being the ultimate victims (Galtung, 1996, p. 40).

In Galtung's typology of violence, structural violence can be said to exist whenever 'human beings are being influenced so that their actual somatic and mental realizations are below their potential realizations' (1969, p. 168). His distinction is between physical violence (direct violence on the body), structural violence (which harms and kills without physical contact) and cultural violence (which legitimizes the other two forms of violence). This threefold typology of violence is especially suited to understanding long-term and enduring processes of caste-based power relations and discrimination in rural India. The notion of violence can be captured by the use of cultural violence to legitimize or obscure how unequal power relations result in both unequal life chances, and in direct physical violence, often with impunity. The next few paragraphs review research highlighting how different forms of violence operated to produce long-term disadvantages and deficits in relation to Dalits' human development, human rights and human security.

Arguably, caste is one of oldest and most pervasive forms of social stratification, and results in injustices based on ascribed role differentiation. Caste stratification, traditionally associated with the Hindu religion, is sustained by an ideology that legitimizes inequality according to the status of birth. Interactions between castes are restricted, and differential privileges and burdens are accorded, according to people's position in the caste hierarchy. The so-called 'higher castes', and more particularly the Brahmans, have over time developed rules that helped ensured superior status for themselves in the overall social hierarchy; the British colonizers helped entrench this system (Thapar, 1979, p. 27; Srinivas, 1966, p. 5). Historically, caste controls have been most violently enforced on those at the lowest rungs of the caste ladder, the so-called SC, or Dalits.[100] Through daily practices of humiliation and coercion, the ideology of Dalits as 'untouchables', and hence as the 'others' and 'outsiders' to the caste system, persisted. They were viewed as regressive, barbaric and irrational, in contrast to those within the caste system.

Caste discrimination in India, based on 'ascriptive' characteristics, has led to the long-term deprivation of the Dalits through limiting their access to education, employment and income, leading also to 'passive discrimination' where the lower castes themselves are discouraged and lack the self-confidence and encouragement to challenge the historical social and economic barriers against them (Thorat and Newman, 2007, pp. 4121–2). As a result, the living standards of the Dalits are associated with lower physical and human capital, and their returns on these assets (particularly schooling) are noticeably lower than those for the non-SC individuals (Kijima, 2006). Caste continues to operate in the labour markets by assigning Dalits to relatively low-paid jobs, and even those with high educational qualifications face discrimination at different levels (Banerjee and Knight, 1985; Thorat and Attewell, 2007).

The caste system also governs relations between individuals and groups through practices of humiliation (Guru, 2000). These can be seen from the following examples, demonstrating the insecurities of the Dalits in many spaces. While government policies and programmes promoted the education of children from the SCs, Dalit children often experience prejudice, punishment and rejection in the school system, by the other children, teachers and even the parents of the children, resulting in a relatively high degree of dropping-out and poor performance in exams, which in turn affect their future life chances (Sedwal and Kamat, 2008). In a similar manner, the government-sponsored midday meal scheme and the public distribution systems continue to experience problems of caste discrimination and restricted access to the Dalits (Thorat and Lee, 2003). Discriminative practices include Dalits not being allowed to enter non-Dalit households or even eat together (70 per cent of the villages), restrictions to entry of religious places (64 per cent of the villages), denying or restricting

---

100   While the official categorizations still use the specific subcastes under the category of SC, the term 'Dalit' has increasingly been used as a preferred term by the groups themselves. Literally meaning 'down-trodden' or 'oppressed' or 'broken pieces', the term 'Dalit' was taken up initially by the Dalit Panthers, a protest organization founded in 1972 in Maharashtra. By the 1970s and the 1980s, different and wider themes were taken up by Dalit politics, challenging Hindu Brahmanical hegemony and including the plight of the 'backward castes', peasants, women and tribal groups (Omvedt, 2006, p. 6).

access to irrigation and water facilities (32 per cent of the villages), public and private services, purchase and use of private and public land, including housing, and entry into village shops, restaurants and police stations (Shah et al., 2006).

These exclusions are often maintained through coercion, threats and physical violence, reflecting the deficits the Dalits suffer with regard to their human security. The latter involves protection against individual violence as well as 'human rights, good governance, access to education and health care and ensuring that each individual has opportunities and choices to fulfil his or her potential' (Annan, 2000, quoted in Commission on Human Security, 2003, p. 8) and the importance of dealing with, among others, insecurities that threaten human survival or the safety of daily life, or imperil the natural dignity of men and women (Sen, in Commission on Human Security, 2003, p. 8).

The human security 'discourse' also highlights 'interconnections between conventionally separated spheres, which helps it to link diverse organizational worlds; and a motivating focus on human vulnerability and the human rights that flow for every human being from basic human needs' (Gasper, 2005, p. 242). It recognizes that the social relations and the forms of governance that form part of the daily existences of people mediate the effectiveness of such interventions. As Truong and colleagues have argued, 'the referent of security is not just the individual with rights and entitlements, but also the social relations that mediate human life in ways that ensure its quality and flourishing' (Truong et al., 2006, p. xii). In these ways, the notion of human security allows for understanding interconnections and their cumulative impact on the daily lives of individuals. It also underscores the significance of the local and local agents in promoting exclusion and inclusion, and the need for a comprehensive framework of strategies and interventions to counter these problems and enable effective inclusion.

These processes have been institutionalized and practised over centuries, exposing the Dalits to a rigid and pervasive form of structural violence and social injustice. They have resulted in major deficits with regard to their human rights and human development (Thorat, 2009; Thorat, 2007, pp. 5–8). As a result, these groups have been historically disadvantaged with regard to their social and economic entitlements, and even today continue to face discrimination in economic, social, political and cultural social relations, resulting the majority living in deprivation and poverty (Thorat, 2009, p. 9). Religious beliefs, societal practices and laws have also often exposed women to 'multiple and overlapping patriarchies', requiring the law to take into account the rights of women in the specific patriarchal arrangements (Sangari, 1995).

The combined effects of violence and deficits to the human rights, human development and human security of the Dalits imply their sustained social exclusion. The term 'social exclusion' is most often used in the European context, for example, to refer to socio-economic exclusion, such as long-term unemployment, or systematic exclusion of certain groups from integration and citizenship rights (Silver, 1995). It is important to recognize that social exclusion is a dynamic and ongoing process, reflecting 'the dynamic processes of being shut out, partially or fully, from any or all of several systems which influence the economic and social integration of people into their society' (Commins, 2004, p. 68). Applying the concept to the problem of caste in India allows for better insights into how various forms of disadvantage overlap and reinforce one another (Rodgers et al., 1995).

Social exclusion goes beyond income poverty to allow for the multidimensional nature of social deprivation of specific groups, like castes and women (de Haan, 1998).[101] Sukadeo Thorat was the first to pioneer the use of the concept of social exclusion to analyze dynamics of caste-based discrimination and their impact on SCs. Developing Ambedkar's claim that the primary unit in a Hindu society is caste, Thorat argued that caste functions to ostracize and deny basic human rights to the perceived lowest castes, through a host of caste-based exclusionary practices. According to him, the caste system works as a 'regulatory mechanism to enforce the social and economic organization through the instruments of social ostracism (or social and economic penalties) which has been reinforced with the justification and support from the philosophical elements in the Hindu religion' (Thorat, 2007, p. 3). This 'forced exclusion' resulted in restrictions experienced by different groups in accessing and using land, labour, credit and other resources. The outcome is occupational

---

101 Studies, initially undertaken on behalf of the ILO's International Institute of Labour to explore the value of this approach in different contexts and countries, showed that while there were differing ways of defining and understanding the excluded, they did show links between poverty, inequality and lack of productive employment. The UNDESA report (2010) used the social exclusion approach to understand poverty by taking into account identity, social relations, as well as non-material dimensions of deprivation (p. 3). Social exclusion has also been extended to include among others, lack of security, lack of justice, lack of participation and representation (Bedi and Kurian, 2004).

immobility, with those belonging to so-called higher castes assuming rights and privileges of control. Inequality, a lack of freedom and the denial of basic human rights thus frame and influence the quality of life, indeed life itself, for those assigned to the lowest castes.[102]

Accordingly, Thorat proposed a dual solution for promoting social inclusion of Dalits: a set of policies for economic empowerment (remedies to improve their access to land, capital, quality employment and education, for example), and equal opportunity legislation to provide safeguards against caste discrimination, through caste reservation policies and other, similarly targeted policies. He also emphasized the importance of participation of discriminated groups themselves in different forms of governance if more 'inclusive' policies are to be devised (Thorat, 2008). Many of these ideas have been taken on board by the government in its policies. The next section demonstrates why, in spite of these provisions, laws and programmes do not produce the intended outcomes.

Case study of Dalit exclusion

The section complements the available macro-level data by focusing on micro-level analysis in two villages, selected to expose local-level dynamics of caste-based power relations in Dalits' daily lives. Since caste-based discrimination is more visible and pervasive in villages, and since three-quarters of SCs, who make up 16 per cent of the Indian population,[103] are located in the rural areas, the authors decided to select two rural case studies. The aim is not to generalize from these two cases, but to demonstrate 'up close' how interlocking and cumulative forms of violent exclusions prevent Dalits, and especially Dalit women, from accessing their official legal entitlements. As noted previously, the focus on local interactions allows for a deeper understanding of how laws and policies, which may be well designed, still have to be struggled for, as the Dalits' lives are embedded in semi-autonomous social fields where caste-based power relations enforce compliance along lines of inequality and discrimination in the daily interactions among people of different castes and across gender lines.

---

[102] Thorat (2007) has shown that caste-based exclusion occurs in the economic sphere (denial of employment, capital, land, etc.), and in access to social services (provided by government or private agencies). Finally, exclusion is practised in certain jobs because of notions of purity and pollution. All these factors have resulted in denial of equal opportunities to the excluded groups.

[103] This figure would be higher if all Muslim and Christian Dalits were included.

Politics of caste-based exclusion in rural India

Exclusions at the local level

The micro-level interactions are based on surveys and interviews undertaken in 2009 in two neighbouring villages, Barai Kalyanpur and Nagla Bhakti, located in the Awagarh subdivision of Etah District in Uttar Pradesh, the largest state in India. As noted earlier, analysing local-level interactions is a useful methodology for understanding how caste-based discrimination and patriarchal norms can limit the impact of laws and policies on the lives of people (Moore, 1973, p. 721).

Both of the selected villages had a substantial Dalit or SC population, eligible for a range of poverty-alleviation and other special support programmes. This suggested a relatively favourable environment for economic and social inclusion of the Dalits, since SCs constituted 87 per cent of the village population in Barai Kalyanpur and 66 per cent in Nagla Bhakti. Most of the families who owned less than 1 hectare of land were Dalits; thus, most of the Dalits were eligible for the poverty-alleviation and welfare schemes. The important programmes that promote inclusion included the Mahatma Gandhi National Rural Employment Guarantee Scheme (MGNREGS), entitling poor households to 100 days of waged employment during one financial year; housing schemes – Mahamaya Awas Yojna, Indira Awas Yojna and Mahamaya Sarvajan Awas Yojna – which provided financial assistance for building a 'pucca' (good) shelter; pension schemes for widows, the disabled and the aged; and public ration distribution schemes (PDS) to supply grain and essential commodities to the poor on a regular basis at subsidized prices in through a network of fair price shops. There were also scholarships and other facilities that they could take advantage of. In addition, one of the villages, Barai Kalyanpur, referred to as an 'Ambedkar' village,[104] received a package of eleven welfare schemes, monitored by an 'Ambedkar Cell' headed by the principal secretary to the provincial government/chief minister. Special instructions for scheme implementation in the 'Ambedkar' village were given to the district officers and downward units at the block and villages.

Our village-level surveys showed that Dalits did not fully benefit from these programmes. While they were entitled to 100 days of

---

104 The use of the term 'Ambedkar' village is linked to the Dalit leader, Dr Bhim Rao Ambedkar, and his championship for the cause of the Dalits as reflected in the Constitution, which among other statements, explicitly prohibited discrimination on the grounds of 'religion, race, caste, sex or place of birth' (Article 15)(Human Rights Watch, 1999, app. A).

waged employment under the Rural Employment Guarantee Scheme, the survey showed that poor Dalit families received some 13 days of employment (and payment) and 10–12 days of employment over a period of two years in Barai Kayanpur and Nagla Bhakti respectively. Furthermore, just 0.5 per cent of the Dalits in both villages were able to access the finance under the housing schemes, while only 20 per cent of the Dalits accessed pensions which should have been available to widows, the elderly and the disabled. Dalits did fare better in accessing the public distribution scheme: 70 per cent of the Dalits in Baraia Kalyanpur benefited from government-subsidized food and essential commodities, the equivalent figure in Nagla Bhakti being 60 per cent.

There was however little or no knowledge of scholarships and other possibilities to support the studies for children of SCs. Thus, in spite of government efforts spanning decades, the majority of the Dalits continued to remain poor and excluded from the benefits of most government supportive schemes. In addition, there were no significant differences in the situation of the Dalits in both villages, although those living in the 'Ambedkar' village were relatively well off in some aspects. The following sections highlight the local-level dynamics of exclusions and inclusions in the daily lives of the Dalits.

Exclusions in governance

In line with the official national requirements, there was information placed on the notice boards of the block development offices on relevant legislation such as the Untouchability Offences Act 1955, the Protection of Civil Rights Act (PCRA) 1976, and the SC & ST (Prevention of Atrocities) Act, 1989 to protect the Dalit community. Information was also given on some eighteen different welfare schemes, including the Mahatma Gandhi National Rural Employment Guarantee Act (MGNREGA), old age and widow's pensions, pensions for persons with disabilities, Ambedkar village development scheme, Indira Awas Yojna, the below-poverty-line (BPL) ration, Antodaya, clean toilet scheme, free tube-well boring scheme, loans for self-employment, as well as schemes for the empowerment and support of poor girls such the *Savitri Bai Phule Balika Madad Yojna*[105] and the

---

[105] *Savitri Bai Phule Balika Madad Yojna* (Savitri Bai Phule Girl Child Support Scheme) was named after Savitri Bai Phule, wife of a great Dalit social reformer, Jyotiba Phule, who dedicated her life to teaching children from Dalit communities.

Mahamaya Garib Balika Ashirvad Yojna.[106] Such notices suggested that the national government and bureaucracy complied with the requirements that the details of support schemes be placed on public notice.

However, field surveys showed that insufficient efforts were made to disseminate this information to the targeted underprivileged. Most of the low-income Dalits who also had low levels of education were unaware they were eligible for these schemes and thus did not apply. It was clear, therefore, that the government had to take extra efforts to communicate effectively and encourage the excluded to avail themselves of schemes in their favour.

Village development was managed by an elected local government, which functioned as a form of self-governance (*panchayati* raj institutions – executive committee of the village republic). While the supportive schemes were based on national and state polices, it was the local government in the village, or the *panchayat*, led by the *sarpanch*,[107] that was influential in the implementation of the schemes. The role of caste was clearly visible in local governance and in the distribution of the benefits of programmes. The *sarpanches* of both villages belonged to the 'higher' Verma/Thakur castes who generally support the right-wing Hindu nationalist party, BJP.[108] The Dalits, who formed the majority of the population, voted for BSP, although there were several instances when they were intimidated and forced to vote for BJP.

The *sarpanch* continued to wield power in the *panchayat*, with members from the 'lower' castes accepting this situation. While some Dalits were elected, their attendance at meetings remained negligible, as the office bearers of these *panchayats* were mostly from the dominant caste, with Dalits not being informed about the meetings and their voices suppressed during the meetings.

---

106 The *Mahamaya Garib Balika Ashirvad Yojna*, which literally means the 'Mahamaya poor girl child blessing scheme', was named after Chief Minister Mayawati, who led the government in Uttar Pradesh (1995, 1997, 2002–2003 and 2007–2012) and who supported many projects for the upliftment of the Bahujans, or the Scheduled Castes and Scheduled Tribes. This scheme entitled all girls in families below the poverty line to a government fixed deposit (FD) of INR 22,000 in the form of a National Savings Certificate (NSC), which would be in the name of each girl born on or after 15 January in a family living below the poverty line.

107 A sarpanch is the elected head of the village panchayat.

108 That the two sarpanches were supporters of BJP was confirmed during the research and focused group discussions, as well as from other local sources and the local sources and Diocesan Board of Social Service (NGO) workers.

At the same time, the village-level *gram sabha* (general body of the village republic) meetings were critical spaces for the selection of the beneficiaries under various welfare programmes. Among the issues reviewed were proposals for roads, drainage, street lighting, sanitation and jobs, the monitoring of schools, and health and child development centres. The development plan for the villages, including the approval of quarterly expenditures and the *panchayat* budget, were all undertaken in these *gram sabha* meetings. The exclusion Dalits experienced in these discussions meant that their voices and hence their access to benefits were limited.

The norms and practices of patriarchy also pervaded local government, countering the value of progressive legislation promoting female representation as heads of local government. The village of Nagla Bakhti was part of Misakala *panchayat*, which was a reserved constituency for a woman *sarpanch*. The caste hierarchy was firmly established through the formally elected head of the *panchayat* being a woman from the Thakur (higher) caste. However, the dominance of patriarchal norms meant that her husband and father-in-law functioned as *de facto* heads of the *panchayat*, with many referring to one or the other as the *sarpanch* in the area. Barai-Kalyanpur – the Ambedkar village – was also a *panchayat* reserved for a female *sarpanch*. It too was headed by a woman from the Verma (upper caste), although her husband, who was the former *sarpanch*, was referred to as the *sarpanch*. Thus, enforcing quotas for women, government legislation with the intention of promoting women's political empowerment, was not effective, as caste and patriarchal power relations at the local level prevailed.

Politics of caste-based exclusion in rural India

Box 11.1 Dulare

> Dulare, a man from the 'untouchable' Balmiki caste, narrated the pain and humiliation he felt when a Muslim family beat him up just for standing on a gully with a big sack of straw on his head, so that he could not see an elderly Muslim women coming from the back. The lady abused Dulare for his act of insensitivity, and words were exchanged. As a result, men of the Muslim family came and thrashed him severely. Further, they approached Dulare's neighbour who used to take loans from this Muslim family. Dulare's neighbour was also from the Balmiki community, and there was a government water hand pump on his land. Under the influence of the Muslim family Dulare was not allowed to take water from that hand pump. After lots of harassment, Dulare filed a complained against both families in the police station under the SC/ST Atrocities Act 1989 section 3(1)10. It punishes a person for a term of not less than 6 months which may extend to five years who 'intentionally insults or intimidates with intent to humiliate a member of a Scheduled Caste or a Scheduled Tribe in any place within public view'. When the villagers supported Dulare's family, the administration was forced to take action and both families apologized to Dulare.

Caste-based atrocities

One of the pervasive characteristics of caste discrimination in many Indian villages is the prevalence of physical violence and coercion by the upper castes towards the Dalits. The Atrocities Act was specifically passed to deal severely with these forms of aggression. However, in both villages, there were several instances where the 'lower' castes were subject to threats and brutality. At the same time, it was not uncommon for Dalits who challenged caste-based violence on the basis of the Atrocities Act to face further exclusion, physical violence and intimidation on the part of the 'upper' castes. The following examples show how the upper castes were able to intimidate the community, the police and even the justice department. At the same time, these cases also show how Dalits have responded, using both collective action and the law to protect themselves and gain privileges.

In spite of laws that have prohibited untouchability, such practices remained common in both villages. For example, lower-caste people were not allowed to sit at the same level as those belonging to the higher castes, even after political changes had introduced a change in power. Even the *sarpanch* of nearby Punhera *panchayat*, Ashok Balmiki, was not allowed to sit on the same cot as the 'higher' caste *panchayat* members in the same village. In Isa-Nagri (Esoli Panchayat), Balmiki families were not allowed to touch the government water hand pump, which is used by the whole village. These families were expected to wait for someone to come and pour water from the hand pump into their bucket.

These cases illustrate the systematic use of physical and personal violence in enforcing caste discrimination in spite of legal penalties associated with such practices, and in many cases, with the tacit or real consent of the state machinery. Even in Ambedkar village (***Box 11.1***), the police were hesitant to challenge the status quo, and it was only through mobilization on the part of the villagers from the 'lower' castes that attention was given to this problem.

Government land distribution scheme and implementation

Ownership and use of land in villages is of vital importance as a source of income and survival, and government land-distribution schemes could be viewed as key to countering poverty and social exclusion. Given the skewed distribution of land in the region and the poor status of Dalit communities, the government initiated schemes to distribute land to Dalits with the intention to provide a means of survival and upward mobility. The field research showed that such distribution was severely opposed by those in power if they felt that it encroached on their own perceived rights. As most of the land was held by the 'upper' castes, this meant even if Dalits were entitled to and received land through the government schemes, they faced opposition, threats and violence when actually using the property for productive purposes (***Box 11.2***).

Box 11.2 Suresh

> Suresh belongs to the Jatav (Scheduled) caste and lives in Nagla Bakthi – the non-Ambedkar village. While he was working on his agricultural field, five people from the Thakur community passed through it, harming his crop. When he requested them not to pass through his crop as it was getting harmed, the Thakurs claimed that he had insulted them. They abused Suresh and insulted him using derogatory remarks. The Thakurs decided to teach Suresh and family 'a lesson', and came armed and attacked them. Suresh then filed a case under SC/ST Atrocities Act, but all the witnesses were pressurized by the upper castes not to support him. The opposition advocate, at the Etah session court, was also a close relative of the Thakur community, and no other advocate dared to go against him. Suresh changed advocates six times, but continued to face the same problem again and again from his advocate. Suresh has been fighting case for the past eight years. He is mentally tired and his income is also drying up, but he says, 'I am fighting this case to protect my family because as long as case is in the court, Thakurs can not attack us ... if I compromise .... and the case goes in their favour, then they will attack me again.'

Their complaints were also not filed or taken higher, as the local police, who were required to do the required first information report (FIR), were aware of the local power relations and did not wish to oppose those in power, resulting in 'upper' castes often being allowed to commit atrocities and deny Dalits their rights to the land. Thus, while land was redistributed, its use and potential were dependent on the decisions of the upper castes. This was the case with Dalits from the Ambedkar as well as the non-Ambedkar villages. Some of these dynamics are reflected in the two examples given below (***Boxes 11.3*** and ***11.4***).

In Nagla Bhakti for instance, nine families from the SCs received land under the state distribution scheme. However, the Etah district session court declared their ownership to be illegal. The court in its judgement said that the papers, which are presented in the court by the people who owned this land, were forged documents. It was found that the *patwari* (the land accountant, who was subsequently suspended) had written the number as 148 acres of land for distribution in the *Tehsil* document instead of 48 acres, and had distributed the extra land to many people from nearby villages. The nine families from the

SCs, who developed this land and went through a tedious process with their small savings to pay for this piece of land, were deprived in the land distribution scheme.

Box 11.3 Ramnaresh

> Ramnaresh, from the Kori (weaver) caste, had purchased some land from the government, and laid the foundation for his house, but his neighbour, Mahesh Pal (from the *Thakur* higher caste), objected saying that it did not leave him sufficient space to move his tractor. Ramnaresh showed Mahesh Pal all the legal documents establishing his ownership of the land, indicating the necessary space for the tractor to pass by. Mahesh Pal, with his friends, spoke to the head of the village panchayat and overnight built a brick road encroaching on Ramnaresh's land, removing the foundation for the house. With the support of some villagers, Ramnaresh took up this issue with the government. As a result, the land revenue officer measured the land and decided in favour of Ramnaresh. However, the Thakurs refused to accept this outcome. When Ramnaresh tried to file a petition against the Thakurs, the local police, including the superintendent in charge, refused to accept it. This forced Ramnaresh to go to the police headquarters in Etah district. During his visit to Etah, the Thakurs set fire to Ramnaresh's house, resulting in injury to the livestock, as well as destruction to grain and clothes. Under pressure from the poorer groups in the village, the police finally came to the place and wrote a report in favour of Ramnaresh. The Thakurs in the meantime denied their involvement in the fire. The issue was taken up at the *panchayat* and a compromise was reached by which Ramnaresh was allowed to use the 'controversial' land as long as he allowed the Thakur's vehicle to pass along it. The Thakur was penalized INR 2,000 (US$35) for the loss of Ramnaresh's household goods. The result was that Ramnaresh could not park his vehicle or graze or tie his cattle on the controversial land, as Thakur Mahesh Pal frequently moves his tractor on this land.

Another example (***Box 11.4***) shows how lack of finances stemming from feudal modes of payment (including debt bondage) and labour control also play a part in preventing access to land.

Box 11.4 Nahid

> Nahid s/o Nattu, aged 45, from the Muslim Sakka (waterman) caste, received some 1/10 acre of land from the *panchayat*, but he did not have money to pay to the *patwari* in order to measure and allot that land to him. His whole family – three sons and three daughters – worked on the land of Thakur Shyampal along with him. His family were not paid in wages but instead received 50 per cent of the crop they harvested. Nahid's family remained dependent on the landlord as his family needed his share of the grain for their basic subsistence needs. This resulted in Nahid having to borrow extra grain and money from the landlord for any extra or unexpected expenditure (such as ill-health) which he then had to repay from his share of the crop. Thus perpetual debt bondage, based on caste and class power relations, meant that he was unable to access the government land distribution schemes.

What comes out clearly from these examples is that a combination of mechanisms, including class and caste power relations, as well as physical and structural violence, are used to control the Dalit groups, often perpetuating their exclusions in different domains such as at work, within the community, and over their labour. Thus, including them in government schemes means countering these controls and exclusions in those interlocking domains, and going beyond a single or targeted government intervention.

The functioning of the MGNREGA – Nagla Bakhti

The Mahatma Gandhi National Rural Employment Guarantee Act (MGNREGA) (2005) is meant to provide 100 days of employment for unskilled manual workers each year, and an entitlement to an unemployment allowance should the work not be provided. At a meeting organized by a member of a supportive NGO, it was found that the majority of those enrolled under the MGNREGA in Nagla Bhakti were from SCs and Backward castes. However, they received only between five and twenty days of work over a two-year period (2007–09), even though the money allocated for the scheme had been spent.

The meeting served as an important platform to air the grievances of the so-called lower castes. The Dalits spoke in anger about the close ties that existed between the *sarpanch* and the supervisor of the programme – who had to report regularly to the *sarpanch* – and the fact that they belonged to the same Thakur caste. They also spoke about their frustration at the malfunctioning of the MGNREGA, including directly challenging the role of the *sarpanch* in the way the scheme was implemented. Given the increasingly political nature of the agitation, the *sarpanch* was forced to address the workers.

As mentioned previously, while Prabha Kumari is the legal *sarpanch* of Misa Kala Panchayat, her husband and father-in-law took all the decisions, executed projects and even represented her at meetings – and were also often referred to and called *sarpanch*. In this instance, the husband addressed the group as the *sarpanch*, and indicated that he had given the contract for the scheme to a man who paid the workers. He was of the opinion that this was perfectly appropriate even though it was work registered under the MGNREGA. On hearing this, the workers got angry and submitted all their job cards to the *sarpanch*, made the news public in the newspaper, and submitted a memorandum to the district magistrate. This led to further confrontations between the *sarpanch* and the workers. When workers went to the *sarpanch* for employment, he told them, 'Go and ask work from the media and district magistrate, I don't have work for you.' However, seeing the increasing hostility of the workers and their threats to take further action, he agreed that he would return the job cards and requested the workers to apply for work in writing, so that he could understand how much work is required; and if work was not available, he could apply for their unemployment allowance.

When asked why not even a single job card was issued to women under MGNREGA, the '*sarpanch*' responded that he understood that women do not like to work in construction, as it is against their tradition and not considered good work for them in the village. Women's groups too accepted this argument and requested that if any 'suitable' work such as working in plant nurseries or tree planting should become available, or if some other work which can be done from the home were created, then they would involve themselves in the MGNREGA.

This case is important on several scores. It highlights the close relationship between castes and class factors: the *sarpanch* and the contractor benefited on both these scores. These links resulted in a distortion of supportive government schemes and programmes. It also shows that such patronage relations can exist without impunity, with laws controlled by upper castes and classes. The case also illustrates the patriarchal ideology, which assumed that it was not good for women to work in construction, although this was the only work available. At the same time, lower castes are clearly ignorant of their rights, or unable to get the rightful income (in lieu of days of work) they are entitled to under the scheme. However, the case also shows how collective action and struggle – including using the power of the media – can challenge some hierarchies.

Housing scheme – Indira Awas Yojna

There are several welfare schemes available for the Dalits and the poor. One of the most important was the Indira Awas Yojna (IAY, Indira Housing Scheme) which provided housing grants for those officially categorized as 'below the poverty line'. Most of the Dalits are eligible for this support. However, the 'custom' was that all eligible persons applying for such a grant had to pay the *sarpanch* Rs 5000 if they wished to avail of the support. This payment was rationalized by the *sarpanch* on the grounds that he has to pay the block development officer in order that the grant be sanctioned. Under these circumstances, the poor who applied for these schemes were forced to take out loans to pay the required amount. These loans were provided by the Thakurs, who were also the local moneylenders and demanded a very high interest rate (36–72 per cent per annum).

'We paid Rs 5000 each to get a house under IAY,' say women in Barai Kalyanpur. Every family took loans either from their relatives or from the moneylender to pay the bribe, and they were still repaying it back on high interest rates of up to 3 per cent per month (36 per cent per year). Many families like Mehru Nisha, extremely poor and a widow (for 12 years) took a loan to pay the bribe. She and her children worked on a daily wage basis. Every family was granted INR 35,000, but some of the families only received INR 25,000, and were awaiting the remaining amount. From this budget, families were only able to raise the walls of a single room, and they lived under a polythene sheet.

There were people in the village who were given loans for self-employment schemes. However, all of them paid bribes to *'suvidha data'* – meaning service providers. According to the loan officer, Rakesh Gupta from Khadi Gram,[109] 'it is [a] prepaid channel …. pay

---

109 A Gandhian movement to promote khadi (cotton) and home-made handicrafts for self-reliance.

money and get benefit'. However, 'even if [a] loan application passes through Rakesh Gupta, there is no guaranteed that concerned bank will grant it,' says Reverend Luther, the local priest in Jalesar Church who works with rural Dalit in the area.

In spite of strong support from the then chief minister herself, there had not been, during the last six months of 2009, a single registration under Mahamaya Garib Balika Ashirvad Yojna in this 'Ambedkar' village. The same is the case with Savitri Bai Phule Baliaka Siksha Madad Yojna (Singh, 2009, p. 32), though the government officers of the Secondary Education Department stated that INR 94.46 crore (INR 940 million) had been deposited in the accounts of 62,975 eligible girl students, for their encouragement, and as many as 52,082 bicycles had also been distributed.[110] However, when asked in the village meetings in Barai Kalyanpur, no one, except the NGO workers, knew about the scheme.

Caste prejudice and collaboration were also part of the implementation issues. For example, the *panchayat* documents (*Panchayat Barai Kalyanpur,* 2003–04), indicated that in the selection process of beneficiaries for IAY, a list was prepared by the *sarpanch,* and an affidavit declared 'The undersigned (both *sarpanch* and *panchayat* secretary) have visited above listed families and investigated personally their socio-economic status, that there is no one in the village poorer than the listed names. Therefore, the families are found genuinely eligible for the mentioned scheme.' In reality, it was Ram Sahay (Brahmin/Thakur) and Ram Charan (Brahmin) who received the housing benefits, even though they already owned houses as well as fertile agricultural land.

Violence in the daily lives of the Dalits

The issues raised above are related to the ways in which caste and class have influenced the implementation of specific schemes. While those in power often hijacked the schemes, the cases also involved the use of physical violence, humiliation and other means of coercion in order to maintain the status quo. In addition, many of the schemes were fragmented interventions, and did not take on board the range of vulnerabilities, struggles and contestations that shape the lives of Dalits, making it even more difficult for them to access special programmes and benefits. The story of Somvati Devi, from Ambedkar

---

110 Information provided by the Chief Minister's Office in 2009 during field work.

village, illustrates the nature of the oppressions that form part of the lives of the Dalits, underscoring the need for an integrated framework of interventions (***Box 11.5***).

Poverty and insecurity – based on both caste and class criteria – framed her existence. She and her family did not have any means of production, except her own labour at the age of 60. She continued to wash the clothes of upper-caste families. In return, she received 10 kg wheat every six months from each family. The remuneration was fixed per family and was not dependent on the number of clothes she washed. If the family had two sons and they were not married, the family would give only 10 kg rice. If the two sons got married, the amount would increase to 20 kg extra wheat per family. On the other hand, there was no increase of benefits if the family had (married or unmarried) daughters.

Somvati's story is illustrative of the myriad exclusions and human insecurities that form part of her daily existence, and which do not allow her to access either her human rights or special programmes which are meant to be for her empowerment. Her life demonstrates the ways in which progressive legislation and programmes were either hindered or actively usurped by the upper castes and classes for their own benefit. Caste, class and gender power relations intersected to maintain the status quo.

Box 11.5 Somvati

> Somvati Devi, a Dalit woman in the village of Barai Kalyanpur (the Ambedkar village which has been targeted for special schemes) was around 60 years of age and from the *Dhobi'* (washerman) caste, and in addition fell under the category of the 'poorest of the poor'. She was eligible for financial support as well as land under a scheme initiated by the Uttar Pradesh government. However, being illiterate, she paid for the services of an intermediary who promised to register land under her name. He cheated her and asked her to work on some free land owned by government. Unaware of the deception, she continued farming this land, until it was acquired by Mazhar Khan, one of the powerful men of Barai Kalyanpur village, who bribed the authorities and registered a substantial amount of land in his wife's and son's name under the same scheme.

> The land that Somvati had been farming on for the last six years was technically registered as part of Mazhar Khan's land. The Khan family asked Somvati to leave the land. Somvati and her family resisted him. The next day relatives, especially women of the Khan family, thrashed Somvati on the field. The landlord registered a case against Somvati under section 98A pertaining to the illegal occupation of land, while the police arrested her son Rameshwar and kept him in the police station for three days without charging him with any offence, pressuring him to sign a paper indicating that his family occupied disputed land so that they could charge him under section 98A. Rameshwar refused to sign the paper. In the meantime, his relatives and villagers along with the *patwari* contacted the superintendent of police of Etah and some other higher authorities, demanding that police should either issue a 'challan' (penalty order) or release Rameshwar. Rameshwar was released as there was no evidence against him.
>
> In spite of her situation, Somvati did not have an MGNREGA job card, although her son did have one, but he was ill with tuberculosis and unable to work. In fact, out of the 200 job cards in the Panchayat area, not a single MGNREGA job card was issued to women. With insufficient income, Somvati could not take her son to the hospital for treatment. The *sarpanch* stated that there were no funds sanctioned from the government for this purpose. Somvati also applied for the old age pension but the panchayat head did not support this action. Reports indicated that influential people were against her receiving it. Somvati had applied for housing facilities under IAY long ago, but was again denied by the *sarpanch*, who claimed there was no quota available at present. However, richer persons in the village who were also of a 'higher', Brahmin caste, such as Ram Sahay and Ram Charan, were provided with a house under the scheme.

From violent exclusions to human insecurity and exploitation

As the case study evidence has shown, the combination of structural, cultural and personal violence, stemming from caste discrimination, continued to limit the value of legislation and government programmes promoting the social inclusion of Dalits. Humiliation and coercion were used to denigrate the Dalits and control them in the villages. As Galtung suggests, psychological violence can damage 'the soul' (1969, p. 169), and destroys feelings of dignity and self-worth. Less overt forms of violence as well as physical and structural violence reinforce patterns of social injustice and social exclusion over time. In addition, caste-based discrimination is closely linked with economic exploitation, as reflected in the examples of housing, land, employment generation and other welfare schemes. Protection against individual violence and ensuring access to the basic aspects of human security were far from being achieved in practice. The element of 'freedom from fear' embedded in the notion of human security was rarely met in practice for Dalit women, in particular, since their multiple exclusions were often maintained through coercion, threats and direct physical violence, including sexual violence. This means that implementing the law in specific localities requires taking into account the violations of women's rights in the local patriarchal arrangements.

The analysis showed that prevailing power relations undermine government policies, when people's status as dominant groups is threatened. In this case, those higher up the caste hierarchy actively resisted progressive measures and regulations, using a variety of controls which included ideological/religious exclusionary practices as well as physical coercion and political influence. As noted by Galtung, '(w)hen the structure is threatened, those who benefit from structural violence, above all those who are at the top, will try to preserve the status quo so well geared to protect their interests' (1969, p. 179). Furthermore, inclusive policies are often developed and implemented by people who have historical, cultural and psychological biases that influence the terms of inclusion and exclusion.[111]

In the context of caste-based discrimination, historical biases associated with discriminatory practices of exclusion still prevail in rural village society, influencing the people and institutions who implement anti-discrimination programmes locally. As a result, inclusionary policies and programmes may be implemented while patterns of exclusion remain or even intensify. The 'model' of social relations may not be structurally altered. For example, greater

---

111   In critically reviewing the social inclusion policies of the European Union, O'Brien and Penna (2009) observed that social inclusion policies there were embedded in a particular 'integrative' model of Europe, and it was necessary to 'unpack' this model and its assumptions, to understand why the policies countering social exclusion were not so effective. They found that the policies reflected 'traditional social profiles' and stereotyping of groups, and put an emphasis on dealing with the consequences rather than the causes of discrimination and inequality. Inclusionary policies would need to focus on a particular political programme of integration based on specific norms, values and institutions.

participation by Dalits in government programmes provided them with some chances of short-term employment, some income and some food, but they retained their prior low-caste-based social status. This in turn ensured they were incorporated, but adversely incorporated, into programmes meant for their benefit, at the lowest levels only, and sometimes they were even excluded as the benefits were diverted to others with higher status and more control.

Based on the multiple forms of exclusions embedded in different fields of power relations, strategies of change for Dalits will need to be developed at different levels, and political alliances will need to be established across caste and identity groups, to effectively promote the sustainable social inclusion of Dalits in future. The need becomes even more urgent as many government programmes were removed in the subsequent period with the changing political climate.

Concluding remarks: politics of exclusion and inclusion

It was clear that despite being the electoral majority in both villages, Dalits were confronted with class, caste-based and patriarchal power relations that enforced multiple exclusions and physical coercions, hindering their access to government-sponsored poverty-alleviation and other welfare programmes. These practices were acquiesced to by the local police, lower bureaucracy and judiciary, who were aware of the power of the dominant castes, and in some cases had strong social relations with them. The government programmes remained compartmentalized, with the result that Dalits were faced with inadequate information, bureaucratic hindrances, and could not benefit fully from these schemes.

These government interventions also did not deal with the interlocking and cumulative nature of the problems that Dalits face in their day-to-day lives. In the process, Dalits continued to experience social subordination, multiple exclusions, and deficits with regard to human rights, human development and human security, in both the Ambedkar and non-Ambedkar villages. In addition, patriarchy intersected all of society, reinforcing male authority at all levels, with Dalit women usually belonging to the lowest ranks of the social hierarchy, and most vulnerable to violence, insecurity and problems of accessing welfare and other schemes.

The government policies and programmes meant to support inclusion contained implicit or explicit norms of inclusion which often imply that the 'excluded' groups are expected to fit into and accept a particular model of society, which has historically been linked to the more powerful groups in society. In spite of political changes and positive intervention on the part of the government, caste-based boundaries remained. These norms and practices of the dominant upper castes also influenced the politics of inclusion, resulting in manipulating the implementation of the schemes, while promoting an adverse incorporation of the Dalits through limiting and shaping their involvement. In these ways, the structural, cultural and personal/physical violence against Dalits, and particularly Dalit women, is so embedded in society that breaking the mould involves challenging the status quo, confronting the values and practices of the more powerful castes, and the patriarchal structures that have dominated the Indian system historically and to this day.

Under these circumstances, it is important to recognize that a single strategy or intervention cannot counter the interlocking and cumulative nature of exclusions. Multiple strategies taken at different levels and with different stakeholders need to be developed to help governments to promote, in line with SDG 16, a more equitable, just and inclusive society. The success of collective organization and struggles, however limited, has however demonstrated the value and significance of supporting and involving the Dalits themselves in challenging the status quo. They are the people who know the lived experiences of exclusion and are vital to bring about change.

In a positive contrast, activities of the Andhra Pradesh Vyvasaya Vruthidarula Union (APVVU), a federation of 428 trade unions of rural informal workers organized at the subnational administrative unit, demonstrate the potential of such multiple-level strategies, networks and struggles to effectively work for the empowerment of the Dalits, workers in the informal economy and poor women.[112] At the same time legislation, favourable government schemes and supportive NGOs need to use a more comprehensive framework of

---

112 One of the authors of this article, Deepak Singh, worked with APVUU from 2011 till 2015. He there personally witnessed the empowerment of many Dalits in the region, who mobilized to struggle for their rights with the support of concerned and committed groups including human rights civil society organizations, national and international trade unions, and progressive civil servants. Over a 30-year period, most Dalits, who had worked as bonded labour on the land of the so-called upper castes, exposed to humiliation and physical abuse, were able to own land, get regular work under the government rural employment schemes, have access to the benefits of government welfare programmes and even gain respectable positions in local government. Most importantly they were able to confront and counter legal, social or other rights violations by the dominant castes (see www.apvvu.org/index.php/about-apvvu).

intervention, recognizing and challenging the cumulative effect of the different forms of exclusions and violence at the local level and in the daily lives of the excluded. What the experiences of the Dalits in this article have shown is that promoting sustainable inclusion for the excluded involves developing appropriate conceptual tools as well as the policy frameworks that acknowledge and counter the multiple and cumulative exclusions they experience, and it entails recognizing the need for multiple alliances and multiple strategies that promote, in line with SDG 16, a more equitable, just and inclusive society.

References

Annan, K. 2000. Secretary-general salutes international workshop on human security in Mongolia. Two-day session in Ulaanbaatar, 8–10 May 2000, press release SG/SM/7382. www.un.org/press/en/2000/20000508.sgsm7382.doc.html (Accessed 15 March 2019.)

Banerjee, A., Datta, B. M. and Mullainathan, S. 2009. Labor market discrimination in Delhi: evidence from a field experiment. *Journal of Comparative Economics*, Vol. 37, Issue 1, pp. 14–27.

Banerjee, B. and Knight, J. B. 1985. Caste discrimination in the Indian urban labour market. *Journal of Development Economics*, Vol. 17, Issue 3, pp. 277–307.

Bedi, A. and Kurian, R. 2004. *Poverty, Gender and Social Exclusion in Mauritius.* Report prepared for the African Development Bank.

Commins, P. 2004. Poverty and social exclusion in rural areas: characteristics, processes and research issue' *SociologiaRuralis,* No. 44, pp. 61–74.

Commission on Human Security. 2003. *Human Security Now.* New York, Commission on Human Security. https://reliefweb.int/sites/reliefweb.int/files/resources/91BAEEDBA50C6907C1256D19006A9353-chs-security-may03.pdf (Accessed 15 March 2019.)

De Haan, A. 1998. Social exclusion: an alternative concept for the study of deprivation?' *IDS Bulletin*, Vol. 29, No. 1, pp. 10–18.

———. 2007. *Reclaiming Social Policy: Globalisation, social exclusion and new poverty reduction strategies.* New York, Palgrave.

Galtung, J. 1969. Violence, peace, and peace research. *Journal of Peace Research*, Vol. 6, No. 3, pp. 167–91.

———. 1990. Cultural violence. *Journal of Peace Research*, Vol. 27, No. 3, pp 291–305.

———. 1994. Religions, hard and soft. *Cross Currents*, Vol. 47, Issue 4. www.crosscurrents.org/galtung.htm (Accessed 11 April 2019.)

———. 1996. *Peace by peaceful means: peace and conflict, development and civilization.* Oslo, Norway: International Peace Research Institute Oslo; Thousand Oaks, CA, US: Sage Publications, Inc.

Gasper, D. 2005. Securing humanity: situating 'human security' as concept and discourse. *Journal of Human Development and Capabilities*, Vol. 6, No. 2, pp. 221–45.

Geyer, R. 1999, Can EU social policy save the Social Exclusion Unit and vice versa? *Politics*, Vol. 19, No. 3, pp. 159–64.

Government of India. 2002. *Tenth Five-Year Plan*. New Delhi, Government of India. www.planningcommission.nic.in/plans/planrel/fiveyr/10th/10defaultchap.htm (Accessed 15 March 2019.)

Govinda, R. 2008. Re-inventing Dalit women's identity? Dynamics of social activism and electoral politics in rural north India. *Contemporary South Asia*, Vol. 16, No. 4, pp. 427–40.

Guru, G. 2000. *Dalit*: reflections on the search for inclusion. Peter R. de Souza (ed.), *Contemporary India: Transitions*, New Delhi, Sage, p. 59.

Human Rights Watch. 1999. *Broken People: Caste violence against India's 'Untouchables'*. New York, Washington, London and Brussels, Human Rights Watch. www.hrw.org/reports/1999/india/ (Accessed 15 March 2019.)

Kijima, Y. 2006. Caste and tribe inequality: evidence from India, 1983–1999. *Economic Development and Cultural Change*, Vol. 54, No. 1, pp. 369–404.

Moore, S. F. 1973. Law and social change: the semi-autonomous social field as an appropriate subject of study. *Law and Society Review*, Vol. 4, No. 4, pp. 719–46.

O'Brien, M. and Penna, S. 2009. *Theorising Welfare: Enlightenment and modern society*. New York, Sage.

Nandwani, B. 2016. Caste and class. *Review of Market Integration*, Vol. 8, No. 3, pp. 135–51.

Panchayat Barai Kalyanpur. 2003–04. List of the Beneficiaries of Indira Awas Yojna. Reproduced in Singh (2009).

Omvedt, G. 2006. *Dalit Visions. The anti-caste movement and the construction of an Indian identity*. Hyderabad, India, Orient Longman.

Percy-Smith, J. 2000. Introduction: the contours of social exclusion, J. Percy-Smith (ed.), *Policy Responses to Social Exclusion: Towards inclusion?* Milton Keynes, UK, Open University Press.

Rodgers, G., Gore, C. and Figueiredo, J. 1995. *Social Exclusion: Rhetoric reality responses*. Geneva, ILO.

Sangari, K. 1995. Politics of diversity: religious communities and multiple patriarchies. *Economic and Political Weekly*, Vol. 30, No. 52, pp. 3381–9.

Sedwal, M. and Kamat, S. 2008. Education and social equity: with a special focus on scheduled castes and scheduled tribes in elementary education, create pathways to access, Research Monograph 19, May. Paris, IIEP-UNESCO. http://lst-iiep.iiep-unesco.org/cgi-bin/wwwi32.exe/[in=epidoc1.in]/?t2000=028416/(100). (Accessed 15 March 2019.)

Sen, A. 2000. Social exclusion: concept, application, and scrutiny. *Social Development Bank*, No. 1(June), pp. 1–54.

Shah, G., Mander, H., Thorat, S., Deshpande, S. and Baviskar, A. 2006. *Untouchability in Rural India*. New Delhi, Sage.

Silver, H. 2007. The process of social exclusion: the dynamics of an evolving concept, Working Paper 95. Manchester, UK, Chronic Poverty Research Centre (CPRC). www.chronicpoverty.org (Accessed 15 March 2019.)

Singh, D. 2009. Can law overcome social exclusion of Dalit communities at village level? Two villages of Uttar Pradesh, India, MA Research Paper submitted to the Graduate School of Development Studies, International Institute of Social Studies, Erasmus University, Rotterdam, Netherlands.

Srinivas, M. N. 1966. *Social Change in Modern India.* New Delhi, Orient Longmans.

Thapar, R. 1979. *Ancient Indian Social History: Some interpretations.* New Delhi, Orient Longmans.

Thorat, S. 2007. Caste, social exclusion and poverty linkages – concept, measurement and empirical evidence, paper presented at PACS Programme poverty conference, New Delhi.

---. 2008. Social exclusion in the Indian context: theoretical basis of inclusive policies. *Indian Journal of Human Development*, Vol. 2, No. 1, pp. 165–81.

---. 2009. *Dalits in India: Search for a common destiny.* New Delhi, California, London and Singapore, Sage.

Thorat, S. and Attewell, P. 2007. The legacy of social exclusion: a correspondence study of job discrimination in India. *Economic and Political Weekly*, 13 October, pp. 4141–5.

Thorat, S. and Lee, J. 2003. Caste discrimination and food security programs, mimeo, Indian Institute of Dalit Studies.

Thorat, S. and Newman, K. S. 2007. Caste and economic discrimination: causes, consequences and remedies. *Economic and Political Weekly*, 13 October, pp. 4121–4.

Truong, T., Wieringa, S. and Chhachhi, A. 2006. *Engendering Human Security: Feminist perspectives.* London and New Delhi, Zed Press and Women Unlimited.

UNDESA. 2010. *Report on the World Social Situation 2010: Rethinking Poverty*, ST/ESA/324. New York, UNDESA. www.un.org/esa/socdev/rwss/docs/2010/fullreport.pdf (Accessed 15 March 2019.)

CHAPTER 12
TRANSFORMATIONS NECESSARY TO 'LEAVE NO ONE BEHIND': SOCIAL EXCLUSION IN SOUTH ASIA

Gabriele Koehler and Annie Namala

South Asia: manifestations and magnitude of social exclusion

The South Asian governments have each endorsed the UN 2030 Agenda which, as we know, commits them to 'leave no one behind' and enable 'a life of dignity'. The eight countries together represent about a quarter of the world's population on only 3 per cent of the world's land surface, making this the most densely populated geographical region in the world. Such high population density, coupled with an extremely skewed distribution of resources, as well as frequent natural and human-made disasters, would create pressures even on the most well-endowed and equitable of societies.

However, to exacerbate the situation, the region is beset with inherent structural socio-economic inequities which this chapter will attempt to sketch. These result in extremely high levels of income poverty and disparities in human development indicators, and may be contributors to the region's persistent violent conflicts, such as those in Afghanistan and parts of India. Poor voice of and accountability to the socially excluded, weak rule of law and its capture by the elite, and high levels of corruption weaken the role of the state, which in each of the countries is structurally underfunded (Bonnerjee, 2014*a*, 2014*b*). The region's inherent structural inequalities and systemic social exclusion processes fundamentally challenge and threaten to derail the achievement of the Sustainable Development Goals (SDGs) – unless the very active and well-coordinated civil society across South Asia were to succeed in 'claiming' the goals, a point discussed towards the end of the chapter.

The national indicators in South Asia shown in **Table 12.1** may help to convey some of the challenges.

Social exclusion in South Asia

Table 12.1 South Asia – selected national indicators

	Afghanistan	Bangladesh	Bhutan	India	Maldives	Nepal	Pakistan	Sri Lanka
Socio-economic indicators								
Population Undernourished, % (FAO, 2015)	26.8	16.4	n/a	15.2	5.2	7.8	22	22
Under-5 mortality rate per 1000 (WHO, n.d.)	70	34	34	43	8.5	35	81	9
Population below the poverty line, % (Actualitix, 2016; World Bank, n.d.a)	35.8 (2011)	31.5 (2010)	23.7 12.0 – (2012)	21.9 (2011)	No data available	25.2 (2010)	22.30 (2005)	6.70 (2012)
Inequality-adjusted HDI, rank out of 187 countries (UNDP, 2016a)	166	141	136	127	114	142	149	65
Gender inequality index (UNDP, 2016b)	0.667	0.520	0.477	0.530	0.312	0.497	0.546	0.386
Gender ratios (UNDESA, 2017)	106	105	101	106	106	104	106	104
Maternal mortality per 100,000 live births (UNICEF ROSA, 2015)	396	176	148	174	68	258	178	30
Primary school enrolment, % of cohort (World Bank, 2015a)	29	90	85	92	94	96	73	98
Secondary School enrolment (World Bank, n.d.b, UNICEF, n.d.)	49% Revised to 54% (2013)	54% Revised to 54% (2012)	78% Revised to 78% (2013)	71% Revised to 71% (2012)	NA Revised to NA	67% Revised to 67% (2013)	38% Revised to 38% (2013)	99% Revised to 99% (2013)
Governance indicators								
Corruption Perception (Transparency International, 2016)	169	145	27	79	95	131	116	95
Voice and Accountability (World Bank, 2015b)	16%	31%	46%	61%	30%	33%	27%	36%
Rule of law (World Bank, 2015b)	2%	27%	70%	56%	35%	27%	24%	60%

314

	Afghanistan	Bangladesh	Bhutan	India	Maldives	Nepal	Pakistan	Sri Lanka
Tax to GDP ratio (latest available year) (World Bank, n.d.c, n.d.d; Taxmann, 2018; Economy Watch, 2019)	7.6% (2015)	8.5% (2015)	13.8% (2015)	11% (2015-16)	19.5% (2014)	16.7% (2015)	10.5% (2015)	12.4% (2015)

Compiled by the authors from the sources given.

In the following sections, the chapter discusses the main vectors that create exclusions in South Asia (Köhler and Keane, 2006). Gender is the most striking form of exclusion in most of the region. It emanates from deeply embedded patriarchal power relations, and while this is a global phenomenon, it appears especially predominant in this region. The most manifest expressions are the gender ratio and maternal mortality rates – among the worst globally.

This is overlaid with the caste system, an additional hierarchical structure of unequal economic power and embedded political and social privileges; power and privileges increase as the group's location moves 'up' the system. Obligations and duties increase as the group's location moves 'downward' in the hierarchy, with those positioned at the perceived bottom – the Dalits – being the worst affected (Bennett, 2006; Gardener and Subrahmanian, 2006; Hooper, 2003; Kurian and Singh, ch. 11).

An additional vector of exclusion is derived from language, or ethnicity and cultural identity communities – indigenous peoples; in India, the latter groups are referred to as 'tribal' (Roy, 2014).

Social exclusion in South Asia is also directly associated with faith. The region is home to a large diversity of population across various faiths – with large Hindu, Muslim and Buddhist communities and smaller Sikh, Jain, Parsi and Christian groups. In each country, the larger religious groupings dominate the minorities, which in the low-income groups in most instances have manifestly worse human development outcomes.

In addition, we could compile a far more extensive list of social exclusion vectors characterizing the region, including class or income quintile, occupational group, location, age, ability and disability, health condition, sexual preference, the condition of menstruation, citizenship status, and even appearance and looks (Koehler and Namala, 2013;[113]

---

[113] In a series of workshops the authors conducted under UNICEF auspices between 2006 and 2009 in Afghanistan, Bangladesh, Maldives, Nepal and Pakistan, the participants contributed an ever-widening list of vectors of social exclusion, based on each group's and country's specific experiences.

also see UNICEF ROSA, 2016, which has developed an indicator of equity around a number of factors). Other factors resulting in discrimination and oppression include widowhood, orphanhood and intellectual capacity (Hanlon et al., 2011). However, we limit the discussion in this chapter to gender, caste and faith, and their intersections; for India, it will include some pointers on ethnicity-based ('tribal') exclusions.

Examples and data to reflect inequalities and disadvantages of the socially excluded communities in this section are disproportionately drawn from India, owing to the better availability of government and civil society data.

Gender-based exclusion

Despite much progress in recent decades, gender equality remains an enormous challenge. Across the planet, in different 'cultures', economic situations and political systems, women experience personal discrimination, wage gaps, low parliamentary representation, and gender-based violence which is played down or goes hidden altogether (Razavi, 2007; CSW, 2015; Esquivel, 2016; UN Women, 2018). In South Asia, gender-based social exclusion is all-pervasive and underwrites all the other forms of exclusion.

In India, gender-based exclusion and violence is observed in its most existential form: female foeticide (Sen, 1990). Female foetuses and girl babies are deprived of their very life (see the gender ratios in **Table 12.1**). Women and girls are systematically subjected to sexualized violence in the form of brutal, often fatal, rape attacks. In India, more than 30 per cent of the women in the age group 15–49 years report having faced physical or sexual violence in their lifetime (India, 2015–16). In parts of Nepal, the Hindu practice of *chauphadi* forces women and girls to spend days of menstruation in animal sheds, as they are considered 'polluting' (Gurung, 2013; Upadhyay, 2017). Though forbidden by law since 2005, the practice continues. It too is an existential assault: apart from the emotional brutality, women and girls die of cold, smoke, snake bites and infections (Budhathoki and Safi, 2019). In Sri Lanka, some Muslim communities continue to practise child marriage (Muslim Personal Law Reforms Action Group, 2019).

Women and girls are given less access to food, to health services, are excluded from education opportunities, and in low-income and income poverty settings are exploited even more than men and boys, with excruciating time budgets. They are disadvantaged in paid work. Women are saddled with the triple burden of responsibility for care work in the home, maintaining social relations, and enduring work in the economy outside the home that is low-skilled and systemically underpaid. As a result, girl children and women in low-income households have more health issues and significantly lower educational attainment than their male relatives. They are rendered powerless in the home, the community and the general political system. According to an OECD estimate, on average women in India spend 6 hours per day on unpaid work, compared with just 36 minutes by men (Ferrant et al., 2014).

Table 12.2 illustrates this for India, where the body mass index and anaemia indices of women from ethnic minorities (Scheduled Tribes, ST), the disadvantaged castes (Scheduled Castes, SC), and other disadvantaged castes (other backward castes, OBC) compare extremely unfavourably with the national average.[114]

Caste-based exclusion

Caste-based exclusion derives from Hinduism (Kurian and Singh, Chapter 11), and as this is the earliest of the region's organized faiths, its concepts permeate the cultures of the entire region, even where Buddhism or Islam subsequently became the predominant or majority faith. The caste system has seeped into every religion, and affects daily lives across the region, a fact rarely acknowledged.[115] The caste system along with patriarchy defines the social, economic and political framework of privileges and disadvantages of different population groups in the region. These two factors also influence all existing and emerging power relationships and their consequences. Even the more modern systems of governance, the executive and judiciary are influenced by the mindset of caste and patriarchy.

In Hinduism, privileges and disprivileges are associated with one's hereditary caste; those at the perceived 'top' end of the caste system enjoy respect and privileges, while those at the perceived 'bottom' end face social exclusion, violence and poverty (Appasamy et al., 1995; Roy, 2014; Kurian and Singh, Chapter 11). The notion of 'untouchability' is the most direct expression of the system of caste-based exclusion – in its extreme form, it denies any interface between the so-called 'lower' castes and dominant groups. Some of these

---

[114] The terminology of the Indian government is of itself indicative of discrimination and exclusionary mindsets.

[115] See for instance BDERM et al. (2012) on social exclusion in Bangladesh, a predominantly Muslim country where we would not expect casteism.

practices have officially been addressed through legislation, or are receding in connection with economic development, or general social change. Nevertheless, the caste system remains an intricate element in Hindu society, and since caste is portrayed as hereditary, casteism is a form of racism.

Exclusion based on faith

In India, the interplay of identity, equity and security is at the core of the socio-economic and political processes of exclusion, not only of women and of the Dalit caste, but also of Muslims (Basant and Shariff, 2010).

In Nepal and India, low-income Muslim communities have the lowest health and education outcomes (Koehler, 2014). Gender-based oppression is magnified many times in the case of Muslim women; it was reported in India that for large number of Muslim women the only safe space – in terms of both physical protection and protection of identity – is within the boundaries of their home and community. Everything beyond the walls of the 'ghetto' is seen as unsafe and hostile – markets, roads, lanes and public transport, schools and hospitals, police stations and government offices. This observation however overlooks intra-household violence and discrimination against women and girls (see for instance Munjial and Kaushik, 2013).

In Pakistan Christians are a minority, recurrently featuring persecution. The persecution and death sentence of a Christian woman on grounds of alleged blasphemy is one well-documented example (Bhatti, 2018).

Across South Asia, faith-based social exclusion has many more manifestations. For example, the constitutions in Bhutan and the Maldives have not accorded citizenship to children born to parents who happen not to follow the local majority version of the dominant faith.

Intersectionality of exclusions

Another decisive dimension in social exclusion is intersectional exclusion. Exclusions do not occur on linear lines. Instead, the different vectors interact with each other, and multiply and magnify their impact on the affected individual or community. Thus, in most of South Asia, gender-based exclusion compacts with other forms of exclusion (for examples see Bennett, 2006; Kabeer, 2010; World Bank, 2013; Chapters 9 and 11, this volume). For example, the exclusion of an indigenous adolescent girl living with a disability from education or health services is multilayered, and the exclusions she faces reinforce each other. The barriers are made even more intense by geographical inaccessibility, income poverty and other vectors of exclusion. Similar parallels on the intersectionality of multiple vectors of social exclusion are observed for almost all socially excluded communities. It then follows logically that multiple and complex strategies and resources are essential in ensuring that 'no one is left behind' and the SDGs are actually achieved in substance.

Social exclusion impacts

This section illustrates the effects of these exclusionary practices on employment and income-earning opportunities, and as an outcome, on poverty. It then looks at the effect of social exclusion on access to public services, on violence, and on internalized forms of exclusion.

Economic exclusion in production and consumption

Economic exclusion is primarily evident as exclusion from secured incomes and decent work in general, and specifically the exclusion from many occupations; it is also shown in lack of access to land titles, financial resources or market transactions.

In both India and Nepal, the Dalit community is limited to a set of defined occupations. These include manual scavenging, skinning and leather work, sewage and drainage work, and work related to death and cremation. Most of these professions are considered 'polluting' in Hindu religious practice, because they are associated with blood and dirt. That is the pretext for stigmatizing the work. It is underpaid, or not paid at all.

Through the interlinkages between caste and occupations, the poverty of those at the ascribed bottom of the caste hierarchy is embedded into the caste system. In Nepal, for example, the landless tend to be members of the Dalit caste (Khatiwada and Koehler, 2014). Privileged and well-paying professions are closed to people from lower castes or occupational groups, and even market-based transactions such as selling commodities become difficult. A detailed empirical study of India (Shah et al., 2007) illustrated the many layers of this economic exclusion. It showed that members of the Dalit caste are denied work as agricultural labourers, not touched when the employer pays wages, receive lower wages for the same work, and are not employed in house construction.

Another set of discriminations – or even outright physical violence and murder – is the lack of access to resources and assets (Shah et al., 2007; Kurian and Singh, Chapter 11), such as being denied access to irrigation facilities, access to fishing ponds/grazing lands, or not being not allowed to sell or buy milk to/from cooperatives, and more generally being prevented from selling products in local markets.

Unemployment rates are reportedly higher among these communities: the unemployment rate in the age group 15–59 years was 18 per cent among SCs and 19 per cent among STs compared with 14 per cent among the general population (India, 2011).

A particularly pernicious form of exclusion is the continuing practice of manual scavenging (the practice where human beings manually remove human excreta from dry toilets and dispose them in waste dumps). It is an extreme form of a caste-based obligatory occupation, considered a polluted occupation, and continues in many communities, despite being banned by public policy since 1993.[116] In response to public pressure in light of the continued practice and criticism of the poor and indecisive policy implementation, the Indian Parliament passed new legislation in 2013, the Prohibition of Employment as Manual Scavengers and Their Rehabilitation Act, 2013. The Act recognizes the link between manual scavengers and disadvantaged communities, and views manual scavenging as violative of their right to dignity (Lawyers Collective, 2013). However, despite progress, manual scavenging persists in India.

A study in Delhi in 2006–07 found that private companies, when recruiting for senior positions, rarely judge the 'suitability' of a candidate on formal qualifications alone. Almost every responding manager interviewed agreed that they ask their candidates about their family background (Jodhka and Newman, 2007). Another study (Thorat and Newman, 2010) found that the chances of a Dalit or Muslim candidate being called for interview for a job in the corporate sector were significantly less than for those from the so-called upper castes with exactly the same CVs.

In Nepal, the picture is similarly dire. Two surveys (ILO, 2005; Samata Foundation, 2014) found that 42 per cent of the Dalit population was engaged in ascribed traditional occupations – blacksmith work (20 per cent), tailoring (19 per cent), leatherwork (16 per cent), goldsmith work (5 per cent), copper/bronze work (5 per cent), earth-digging (5 per cent), sweeping and cleaning (5 per cent), ploughing,

---

116 India prohibited manual scavenging through the Employment of Manual Scavengers and Construction of Dry Latrines (Prohibition) Act, 1993.

musical instrument playing (3 per cent each), human waste disposal (2 per cent) and carcass disposal (1 per cent) (ILO, 2005, p. 27). Other 'traditional' caste occupations include midwifery, cremation of the deceased, disposal of carcasses, and the disposal of human waste (ILO 2005, p. 31). Commercial sex work is also a profession thrust upon women of the Dalit community (ILO, 2005, p. 31).

Those engaged in marketing produce found many systemic obstacles, including the sheer 'inability to participate in the market due to caste' (ILO, 2005, p. 37). They cannot sell food items, and so-called upper-caste people reportedly hesitate to frequent shops owned by Dalits. They were also excluded from transportation facilities (ILO, 2005, p. 37). In rural areas in Nepal, Dalits are not employed as teachers, as parents would allegedly be reluctant to enrol their children if they were. In some cases, Dalits are not employed as domestic help or in restaurants and shops because of their 'untouchable' status (ILO, 2005, p. 40).

For India, the disadvantaged castes and other marginalized groups have been prohibited from entering some restaurants/hotels, private health care clinics, cinema halls, and are denied barber services, laundry or carpenter services. Tailors refuse to take their measurements, and potters refuse to sell them pots. Other forms of discriminatory treatment included separate seating or distinct eating utensils in hotels/restaurants, no seating or last entry in public transport, or discrimination in private clinics (Shah et al., 2007).

A similar constricting and oppressive situation affects members of the Muslim faith in India. The majority of Muslims in low-income settings tend to be self-employed, pushing them into ethnic economic enclaves (Das, 2008). Sengupta and colleagues (2008) found that Muslims experienced the lowest level of decline in poverty (2.9 per cent) between 1993–94 and 2004–05, with 95 per cent employed in the informal sector in 2004–05. Market-level discrimination is reflected in the poor representation of Muslims in public employment – in the bureaucracy, police, judiciary and so on. The Government of India set up the Ministry of Minority Affairs in 2006 to address minority communities in education, economic development and institution-building. The recommendation of the government programme on minorities (India, 2006) made it mandatory for selection committees to include representatives of minority communities.

Muslim presence in the private sector was found to be even more dismal (India, 2006). While economic liberalization has enhanced growth, people of Muslim faith have been displaced from traditional occupations, trade and business, and experience increased poverty levels. The home-based occupations where Muslim women are conventionally engaged are characterized by low wages, poor working conditions, and the absence of social security or insurance benefits. It is also probable that the push back into home-based work is connected to discrimination in the public sphere, poor education and technical skills, and lack of access to credit facilities. Jeemol Unni (2010) empirically showed that the highest proportion of home-based, self-employed women among all socially vulnerable groups is in the Muslim community (56 per cent). Very similar processes and outcomes are observed for the Muslim community in Nepal (Bennett, 2006).

Poverty and social exclusion

There is a direct causal link between social exclusion, the lack of decent work, and poverty. People living in poverty almost invariably are members of an excluded community. Acts of deliberate political or economic discrimination and exclusion, and the power related to social exclusion, are used to deny access to employment, physical assets, finance and markets (Kabeer, 2010; Koehler and Namala, 2013; World Bank, 2013; Kurian and Singh, Chapter 11; more generally see Spicker, Chapter 3). As a direct consequence, socially marginalized groups systematically fall under the poverty line (Thorat and Newman, 2010). In parallel, social and physical violence against marginalized groups reinforces their exclusion. These processes moreover contribute to the transmission of poverty and powerlessness from one generation to the next. In Nepal, studies show that people from so-called lower castes remain in poverty because of restricted access to resources, notably land and access to financial capital, as well as soft resources such as information, and access to training and technology (ILO, 2005, p. 36).

The human rights of the socially excluded groups are violated routinely and systematically. As a result, these groups constitute the poorest sections in each society, and their human development outcomes as a group fall far below the national averages (***Tables 12.2*** and ***12.3***).

Table 12.2 Multi-dimensional poverty index (MPI) across social groups, India

	MPI	% of MPI poor population
ST	0.482	81.40%
SC	0.361	65.80%
OBC	0.305	58.30%
Others	0.157	33.30%

Source: OPHI (2010).

Table 12.3 Poverty ratio by social groups, India, 2011–12

Social group	Rural	Urban	Total
ST	45.3	24.1	43.0
SC	31.5	21.7	29.4
OBC	22.7	15.4	20.7
Others	15.5	8.1	12.5
All	25.4	13.7	22.0

Source: Panagaria and More (2013), based on National Sample Survey Organisation (NSSO), Government of India.

The proportions of enterprises owned by people from SCs (11.4 per cent) and STs (5.4 per cent) are far below their population proportion. Their share is even less in the real estate business (SC: 7.5 per cent, STs: 3.6 per cent) and insurance services (SC: 7.1 per cent and STs: 2.7 per cent). Of the 3.27 million women-owned establishments, SC women own only 12.18 per cent and ST women only own 6.97 per cent (NCDHR, 2017).

Throughout South Asia, forced labour and modern slavery are a direct form of economic oppression, with an estimated 18 million persons affected in India, 2.1 million in Pakistan and 1.5 million in Bangladesh (ILO et al., 2017).

An interesting observation in this connection is that the share of Dalits among the 855 employees of the UN system in Nepal, including its specialized agencies – the UN system is the largest employer among external agencies in the country – was negligible, at less than half a per cent (0.47 per cent) in 2002 (ILO, 2005, p. 27).

In recent years, social exclusion and outright physical violence, including murder, based on political affiliation or perceived violations of faith-based tenets have become visible in other countries of the region, for example in Bangladesh, the Maldives and Pakistan.

Exclusion from public services and spatial exclusions

There is a continued process of girl children and the disadvantaged castes and faith groups being excluded from access to basic public services. In delivering health or education services, for example, professionals treat children differently depending on their social background.

In India, some doctors refuse to touch patients they consider as lower caste. Village water points are segregated, and Dalit women cannot collect water from the Brahmin section of the village (Shah et al., 2007). Similar manifestations of exclusion are recorded for Nepal (Bennett, 2006; ILO, 2005). According to a 2005 survey, 38 per cent of Dalits hesitate to enter temples; around 46 per cent have been prohibited from entering temples; and 35 per cent have reportedly been forced to wash their own dishes at hotels, restaurants and tea-stalls (ILO, 2005, p. 22). This has been observed in non-formal educational classes; community meetings; birth, wedding and funeral functions; community feasts or cultural programmes; local community-based training in health, sanitation, agriculture, cottage industries and other income-generating activities (ILO, 2005, p. 22). An outcome of such forms of discrimination is documented for India, which shows the divergent body mass indices for different communities (***Table 12.4***).

Table 12.4 Intersectional inequalities: hunger and nutrition outcomes for women in India (2015-2016)

	ST	SC	OBC	Others	All India
Women with body mass index below 18.5	31.7	25.3	22.9	17.8	22.9
Anaemia among women	59.9	55.9	52.2	49.8	53.1

Source: IIPS and ICF (2017).

Discrimination in education equally illustrates the tenacity of the issue (***Tables 12.5*** and ***12.6***). The Indian midday school meals scheme for example has been in place since 1995 – for over 20 years. However, a 2003 study (550 villages across five states) revealed massive discrimination against children from disadvantaged castes: more than one-third of the government schools in the scheme showed caste-based discrimination. The practices included making these children sit separately, serving them last, not serving them second helpings, not allowing these children to touch the food of or serve others, in an insulting gesture dropping the food on the plate of these children, and in addition, verbally abusing them. There have been protests about the appointment of cooks from the Dalit communities, with the dominant community forcing schools to dismiss Dalit cooks (Thorat and Lee, 2006). In 2005, the Supreme Court of India issued an Act prescribing a warm (cooked on site) meal for all children in all public schools; in 2017, this decision was complemented by a decision to expand the right to a cooked lunch also in Madrasa schools run by mosques and not part of the government school system (Koehler, 2017b).

Table 12.5 Inequalities in literacy rates in India (7 years and above)

	Male	Female	Total	Gender gap
All India	80.9	64.6	73.0	16.3
Scheduled Castes	75.2	56.5	66.1	18.7
Scheduled Tribes	68.5	49.4	59.0	19.1
Literacy gap between SC and All India	5.7	8.1	6.9	
Literacy gap between ST and All India	12.4	15.2	14.0	

Source: India (2011). Census 2011, Govt of India

Table 12.6 Gender inequalities in India: drop-out rates by school grade

Level	All India			SC			ST		
	Boys	Girls	Total	Boys	Girls	Total	Boys	Girls	Total
1–V Primary	21.2	18.3	19.8	17.7	15.4	16.6	31.9	30.7	31.3
1–VIII	39.2	32.9	36.3	42.4	34.4	38.8	49.8	46.4	48.2
1–X	48.1	46.7	47.4	51.8	48.0	50.1	63.2	61.4	62.4

Source: India (n.d.)

The Indian Government's *Sachar Report* (2006) on the situation of the Muslim community also presented school-related findings. Factors that hinder Muslim children in their education include the 'communal' content of school textbooks: Muslim children find no representation of their community in the school textbooks. Schools are culturally hostile, and Muslim children experience an atmosphere of marginalization and discrimination.

Spatial exclusion is another manifestation of exclusion. Across rural South Asia, people tend to live in segregated habitations, where sections of a village are reserved for a particular caste or religious community, and access to water is also regimented (***Table 12.7***). This limits the radius of personal movement, the access to resources, the quality of public services accessible, and economic and social opportunities (Shah et al., 2006). Across South Asia, ethnic communities – tribal minorities – are particularly disadvantaged by their location in areas that have become remote, because infrastructure is deliberately not developed. These areas are difficult to reach, and generally underserved by public services.[117]

Table 12.7 Unequal access to water and sanitation for all

Household amenity	2011			Variance	
	SC	ST	All India	SC %	ST %
Tap drinking water	41.28%	24.44%	43.5%	2.5%	19%
Toilet within the house	33.86%	22.64%	47.0%	13%	24%

Source: India (2011, house-listing data).

With regard to the Muslim community in India, surveys found that social, cultural and interactive spaces in India could be very daunting to this group (India, 2006). They carry the double burden of being labelled 'anti-national' and 'being appeased' at the same time. They are looked upon with suspicion, not only by fellow citizens but also by public institutions and governance structures. Many felt that the media tend to perpetuate the stereotypical image of Muslims. Muslims reported discrimination in public places, housing and education – identity in public spaces was constructed because of the difference in attire. Muslim members have complained of impolite treatment in marketplaces, hospitals, schools, on public transport and so on,

---

[117] As the World Bank (2013, pp. 70, 74) points out, child mortality rates for Adivasi communities in India are far higher than those of the country on aggregate.

and find it difficult to get housing in non-Muslim residential areas, to register their children at good educational institutions, and to access scholarships.

Social exclusion and violence

Violence is central to social exclusion: structural violence, direct violence, but also – less open – cultural violence (Galtung, 1969; Kurian and Singh, Chapter 11). Social exclusion perpetuates and is used as a justification for violence.[118] The concealed nature of such violence, embedded in relationships produced by direct and cultural violence, fuels structural violence, a continuous process in itself. Violence against socially excluded groups is a daily experience across South Asia, at its most extreme in the civil conflicts experienced in the recent past in Sri Lanka, parts of Pakistan and India, in Nepal, and for more than 30 years in Afghanistan.

Personal and community-level violence is a daily experience for many people in the region, notably women, excluded castes, ethnic groups and minority faiths. Such violence against Dalits and Muslims has emerged as a major point of concern in India. Public floggings and violence against Dalit youth in Una, Gujarat over the alleged killing of a cow raised national uproar among the community. Violence against Dalit communities in India is rampant, but often not recognized despite the fact that there are daily cases of rape and murder (*Tables 12.8* and *12.9*). The Quint recorded 86 cases of mob violence and lynching, particularly against Muslim men, since 2015 (Quint, 2018).

The double issue of gender and caste-based violence was documented in a study of violence against 500 Dalit women (Irudayam et al., 2006 study on four states of India, table 8). Dalit women were accused of lacking sexual integrity and hence seen as 'available' by dominant-caste men; violence was used as a means to reinforce their considered low-caste identity when they tried to share common or public resources like water and grazing land. Violence was considered justified as a means to prevent them from questioning any injustice on the basis of caste, or when they improved their economic positions and tried to move forward economically. Thus, violence against Dalit women was closely linked to their ascribed 'low-caste' status and social exclusion. Despite the depth of (horrifying) evidence of almost daily caste and gender-based violence in India (see e.g. International

---

118 This is palpable in the discussion of research findings from two Indian villages in Chapter 11.

Dalit Solidarity Network et al., 2009), policy-makers as well as the general public were seemingly taken totally by surprise by – and finally took some interest in – violence against women after the Delhi rape case of 2012, and the girl child rape and murder in 2018.

Table 12.8 Crimes against Dalit women

Nature of crime	2014	2015
Rape – Indian Penal Code (IPC) section 376	2,388	2,541
Attempt to rape (IPC 376, 511)	104	91
Outrage modesty (IPC 354)	2,742	3,150
Sexual harassment (IPC 354 A)	896	1,369
Assault with intention to disrobe (IPC 354 B)	174	178
Stalking (IPC 354 D)	130	142
Kidnap and abduction for marriage (IPC 366)	469	501
Acid attack (IPC 326 a)	2	3
Attempt to acid attack (IPC 326 b)	3	0
Voyeurism (IPC 354 C)	20	26
Insult to modesty (IPC 509)	126	151
Others	1,522	1,435
Total	8,576	9,587

Source: NCRB (2018).

On top of the actual violence, there is the issue of accessing justice – those violated or their family members are frequently and almost systemically obstructed in reporting the case, notably in the violence against socially excluded Dalit and tribal communities. **Table 12.9** shows the low conviction rates in cases of violent crimes – less than 30 per cent.

Table 12.9 Crimes against SCs registered under the Prevention of Atrocities Act

Nature of crimes	2013	2014	2015
Cases registered	39,408	47,064	45,003
Murder	676	704	707
Attempt to murder	n/a	420	547
Rape	2,073	2,233	2,326
Pending trial	118,773	127,341	140,340

Nature of crimes	2013	2014	2015
Trial completed	18,202	17,712	17,012
Convictions	4,334	5,102	4,702
Acquittals	13,868	12,610	12,310
Conviction rate	23.8%	28.8%	27.6%
Pending cases	84.7%	85.3%	86.9%

Source: NCRB (2018).

The subjective element in social exclusion

Exclusion can be internalized. For example, it is reported that Dalit mothers teach their daughters not to wear colourful clothes, and not to enter the homes of Brahmins (Shah et al., 2006). Dalit young people are hesitant to apply for employment in non-traditional occupations – although this has changed in recent years, notably in urban settings, with the spread of new professions in the IT-based sectors, such as call centres and computing.

In Nepal too, where Dalits have poor educational outcomes, to some degree this has been attributed to 'the belief among a large proportion (59 per cent) of Dalits that their children are discriminated against at school' (Gurung et al., 1999, p. xix, cited in ILO, 2005, p. 22), so some families do not enrol their children in school, in order to avoid discrimination against them. In Nepal, menstrual exclusion – *chaupadi* – mentioned above is practised within families against their own wives and daughters.

In sum

Provisions and programmes to address social exclusion have not resulted in eliminating its hold and power, because it has not been accompanied by structural change. Processes of exclusion reassert themselves as coercive powers. Across South Asia, the processes of social exclusion result in extremely low human development outcomes. In terms of hunger, under-5 malnutrition and mortality, maternal mortality and illiteracy, Afghanistan, India, Pakistan and Nepal have among the worst-performing social indicators globally, and have the most skewed social indicator outcomes for gender, ethnicity, language and faith (UNICEF ROSA, 2016).

An inventory of South Asian policy responses

The processes of social exclusion mapped out above occur at the personal, interpersonal and community levels. However, what is crucial for the *policy* level is whether it is possible, and if so how, to contribute to transforming attitudes and behaviours, prevent violence both open and hidden, materially improve social services delivery, and most centrally, fundamentally change economic structures. This necessitates first, understanding such processes; second, gauging their impact; and third, designing and implementing policies that will help tackle the issue.

Public policies to redress social exclusion and the poverty it generates have been in place in South Asia for decades, and experienced a surge from 2005 to 2010 (Koehler and Chopra, 2014; Koehler 2017*b*). Despite the risk of romanticizing these policy innovations, they merit a discussion in connection with a search for public policies that are designed to aid social inclusion. A critique of the policies follows.

The policies include a conventional mix of policy interventions, ranging from affirmative action such as quotas – called reservations (reserved places, for example in educational institutions), to efforts in education and health services provision, to social transfers. Nepal, partly as a reaction to overcoming the decade of civil war associated precisely with social exclusion and poverty, has developed an especially elaborate set of social policies to address groups excluded in that society (Khatiwada and Koehler, 2014).

Table 12.10 lists a sample of social policies in place in countries in South Asia.[119] One way they can be classified is by their objectives. A first set of efforts address the social situation, such as hunger, health, education and public infrastructure.[120] A second set of policies is aimed at insecurities around employment and access to assets. A third category of public policy aims at poverty reduction. Several of these policies address social exclusion and intersecting inequalities as supporting objectives. A fourth set of policies is directly designed to address social exclusion, such as policies and economic incentives in the form of categorical stipends (scholarships specifically for girls or Dalits) or grants (such as child benefits or old age pensions)

---

[119] This inventory is limited to policies adopted by governments, and includes donor-funded initiatives only when they are integral to government policy.

[120] Several chapters in this volume (Kumar, ch. 9 and de Wit, ch. 10) explore Indian government policy regarding housing, another important and often under-analyzed policy domain.

and affirmative action using legal mechanisms such as quotas and reserved places, but some of the other three categories do also – at the conceptual level – address social inclusion.

Table 12.10 Overview: selected public policy programmes in South Asia

Policy domain	Programme examples	Social inclusion angle
i) Policies addressing the basic social situation		
Food and nutrition: price subsidies	Bangladesh, India	
Education: universal primary education as a right	Bangladesh, India, Nepal	Gender
Health: access to universal basic health services	India, Nepal	
Drinking water and sanitation measures: improved access	India	
ii) Policies addressing socio-economic insecurity		
Employment schemes for decent work	Bangladesh, India, Nepal	Gender
Youth employment drives	Nepal	Age
Tribal land and commodity rights	India	Ethnicity
Micro-credit/micro-asset schemes	Bangladesh, Nepal	Gender
Urban renewal	India	Poverty

Policy domain	Programme examples	Social inclusion angle
iii) Social assistance policies and programmes addressing poverty		
Food-security related	Bangladesh, India, Nepal	Poverty
Income poverty-related	Bangladesh, India, Nepal, Pakistan, Sri Lanka	Gender (in Pakistan)
Child benefit	Nepal	Age, caste
Conflict, emergency-related, recovery-related	Nepal	Caste
iv) Policies for voice and social inclusion		
Tools for social inclusion (grants)	Bangladesh, India, Nepal	Gender, caste
Affirmative action legislation	India, Nepal	Gender, caste, ethnic, religious equality
Right to information	Bangladesh, India, Nepal	
Legal instruments to address exclusion practices/constitutional directives banning caste practices	India, Nepal	
Local self-governance provisions	India	
Judicial reform	India	

Sources: revised and updated from Chopra (2014) and Koehler (2017b).

Some examples illustrate this. With respect to *gender*, as the most visible and widespread form of discrimination, exclusion and oppression across South Asia, several governments have designed and are implementing programmes with a gender-inclusive lens. Frequently cited is the Secondary School Stipend in Bangladesh, which accords a scholarship to girl students if they remain in school, unmarried, and have satisfactory school attendance and grades till age 18. In terms of outcomes, the programme, in place since the early 1990s, is recognized as one of several factors in girls' increased school attendance in the country. The micro-credit schemes, notably of the Grameen Bank, are exclusively for women participants.[121] In Nepal, the government adopted a policy of universal access to secondary schooling, although there is no particular effort to support girls. In Pakistan, some NGOs are escorting girls to school; in India, there have been bicycle schemes to facilitate girls reaching their school. School sanitation programmes are key, since adolescent girls need privacy, especially during menstruation.

At the political level, in India, a number of policies have been introduced to address the caste system. They include protective measures at the level of legislation, such as the abolition of manual waste scavenging; reservations (quotas) in education, employment and political representation, and measures designed to address economic inclusion. India has quotas for women's representation in local governance, where one-third to half of the seats are reserved for women.[122] In the Mahatma Ghandi National Rural Employment Guarantee Act (MGNREGA), there is a quota for women's employment, and worksites are meant to provide some form of child supervision to make it easier for mothers to apply for work. Some states in India have introduced girl child grants in the form of a savings account opened in a girl's name upon her birth, which is paid out at age 18 if the girl remains in school and does not marry before that age (Chopra, 2014, p. 201; Kurian and Singh, Chapter 11).

Regarding age and caste, a child grant introduced in Nepal in 2009 currently covers roughly half a million children – all under-5 children in the Karnali zone, the country's five poorest districts, and under-5 children of the disadvantaged Dalit caste and in low-income households in the remainder of the country. In 2016 the programme was extended to become universal in earthquake-affected districts. While the benefit amount is minute (NPR 200, or one-eighth of the poverty line), the grant is encouraging birth registration, thus making children more visible as citizens (Koehler, 2017*a*). School scholarships are available in Nepal for children from disadvantaged castes (Khatiwada and Koehler, 2014).

Regarding faith-based exclusion, there are special budget allocations for SC communities under the Scheduled Caste Sub Plan, for Tribal communities under the Tribal Sub Plan, and for Muslim

---

[121] For a critical review of the adverse social and gendered impact of this and other micro-credit schemes, see Mader (2015).
[122] Kurian and Singh in Chapter 11 show how this modality is however undermined in practice.

and other religious minority communities under the Prime Minister's 15-Point Programme (Government of India, various years).

A critique of the South Asian policy responses

The many public policy efforts, adopted, notably in the years 2005–12, across South Asia are impressive in terms of declared ambitions and objectives, and demonstrate public concern. For this, they are invaluable. However, the policies are conventional and ultimately conservative as opposed to genuinely transformative. Critique is necessary, and ranges from the shortcomings at the design and implementation level, to pinpointing the structural faults.

As outcome disparities persist, it is clear that the policies are not sufficient: they do not touch the structural, power-driven causes of social exclusion (on this, see Roy, 2014; in general also see Razavi, 2016). At times, they play out to actually intensify social exclusion and poverty (World Bank, 2013; Kurian and Singh, Chapter 11). To be effective, from an *operational* point of view, policies would need to be more comprehensive, to operate on multiple levels, to be adequately and consistently publicly funded, and to have strong and genuinely independent accountability and redress mechanisms.

From a *political* point of view, they would need to actually unseat the existing power relations – an entirely different proposition.

To start with the most obvious, incoherent fiscal policy and inadequate public *resources* (see Table 12.1 for tax to GDP ratios) hollow out the effectiveness of policies designed to enable social inclusion, such as incentives in the form of cash transfers, or affirmative action (quotas and reserved places) which need financial support for their implementation and continuous monitoring. Most of the programmes are too shallow financially to make a difference to households. Benefit levels are very small, and not sufficient to make a dent. The Bangladesh secondary school stipend is an exception. The Indian policy to allocate special budgets for SCs and STs under the Scheduled Caste Sub Plan and the Tribal Sub Plan initiated in the 1970s continues to be neglected or diverted, and the situation is similar with the special funds allocated to Muslim minority communities through the 15-point Prime Minister's Programme for their development. The fiscal budget under the current Government of India appears to be cutting all the key social programmes (Mander, 2015; Safi, 2017), showing their vulnerability to regime change.

At the *design level*, there are many omissions, owing to insensitivities, or to the lack of voice and force of the communities concerned (see Kurian and Singh, Chapter 11). For example, a key vector of social exclusion across the region – religious faith – remains untackled in the social programmes of South Asia, with few exceptions. In the arc of poverty stretching across northern South Asia, social exclusion of Muslim communities is coupled with gender-based exclusion. There is a double element here. One is the oppression of women and girls within and by the communities themselves, most visible in Afghanistan and the northern border areas of Pakistan, where girl children are deprived of schooling and health services, and women do not have personal or property rights – this is one reason why the Pakistan Benazir Income Support Programme (Gazdar, 2014) is an important effort. The other is the discrimination against Muslim communities in those regions or countries where they are in the minority – but there are few approaches to address faith-based exclusion.

In a different way, some forms of inclusion programme may have unintended effects of reinforcing and cementing social exclusion, by identifying a group as belonging to a particular caste, living with HIV/AIDS, practising a particular faith, or speaking a minority language. Accessing services or transfers earmarked for groups singled out by particular characteristics may be stigmatizing. As one example: the emphasis in public works schemes on including women has had the effect that in several states in India, and in several public works schemes in Nepal, women are the primary workers, because men prefer other types of work, or out-migrate. The labour in public works schemes is almost entirely in construction, which is not at all mechanized, and has extremely harsh physical conditions with exposure to accidents, extreme heat and physical exertion. Workplaces have not been created to provide more pleasant forms of work.[123] Women, who face multiple burdens of reproduction, of care work for children, the elderly and sick in their families, of housework, and of unpaid work on any family assets, are then burdened in addition with construction work. Thus, the well-intentioned quota for women backfires, exposing them to yet another form of exploitation.

At the *implementation* level, another set of obstacles rears its head. Adequate mechanisms are not put in place to translate constitutional provisions. For example, although the abolition of

---

123 On alternative proposals for public work schemes, see Kurian and Singh's survey findings.

the notion of untouchability was proclaimed under Article 17 of the Indian constitution in 1950 – almost seven decades ago! – little public education or debate in society has taken place, and few grievance redress mechanisms have been put in place to abolish this crime (see Roy, 2014). Little attention is given to implementing laws against specific forms of caste-based practices – an example is the 'prohibition of manual scavenging' which was banned via an Act in 1993 – 25 years ago! – but continues to this day, in practice by both private agencies and government bodies.

Poor implementation of policies and legislation is also caused by a lack of interface between federal and state or district-level bodies. This hinders the delivery of targeted interventions. That situation is exacerbated, obviously, in situations where non-state actors have hollowed out governance. In terms of party politics, many programmes and policies are beholden to political constellations in the government, and can be upended when there is a change of regime. This is currently especially visible in India, where a conservative and Hindu–upper caste government has replaced the more left-wing United Progressive Alliance coalition government (Ghosh, 2015; Kurian and Singh, Chapter 11).

At the structural level, the policies are monocausal. Instead, policies need to be multipronged, recognizing that social exclusions are multilayered and interlocking, and 'occur on multiple axes at once ... policies that release just one of these axes of deprivation (such as improved access to education) will not unleash the grip of others' (World Bank, 2013, p. 52). There are correlations between exclusions in one dimension with exclusions in other dimensions (Rodgers et al., 1995).

Most central, though, is the issue that the policies do not address power relations. Access to economic resources, incomes and assets, and to political power is not put in question. Often, instead of upsetting the power structure, there is elite capture. This can be in the government machinery more abstractly, or in the direct relationship at the delivery point of a policy or programme. Government decisions to address social exclusion – which in principle is banned constitutionally across the region – can easily be weakened, or undermined completely. This is illustrated poignantly for India, for example in Thorat and Newman (2010) and Kurian and Singh (Chapter 11), or for Nepal in Bennett (2006). Elite capture at the local level undermines inclusionary approaches at the delivery point, for example by obscuring information on entitlements, or undermining service delivery (Kurian and Singh).

All of these factors are doubly strong in their impact on the women and children of excluded communities, most palpably on girl children, who often experience discrimination even within their own family and community.

In summary, the current array of public policy measures addressing social exclusion scratches the surface only. The policies in no way suffice to tackle social exclusion and poverty, and would not even if design and implementation were more effective. They would need to go far beyond the current policy mix of affirmative action using legal mechanisms such as quotas and reserved places, or economic incentives such as categorical grants. They are merely palliatives.

The policies do not unseat deep-rooted resentment against particular identity groups. There is thus also a need for explicit, stand-alone social inclusion policy which would include awareness-raising not just on the outcomes of exclusion, but on the right to information, action by the media,[124] policies on language and labelling, legal action against acts of discrimination and violence. There is a need for community and personal-level action to bring about fundamental behaviour change. A lack of empowerment of the socially excluded directly, and of civil society organizations that could genuinely voice their interest, reinforces processes of social exclusion at the local and government level. Coalition-building is important (Rodgers et. al., 1995; DeWit, Chapter 10), but is becoming increasingly difficult in times when human rights and civil society autonomy are under threat globally and in the region.

Proposals for social inclusion policies

Far more radical policies would be required to crack the multiple intersections of social exclusion and poverty, and the power relations that create them. Nevertheless, the policy packages are important steps towards awareness of the right to social inclusion. Hence, to the extent that they are claimed and fought over, they can have transformative potential, if supported by civil society and other progressive movements – nationally and internationally.

---

[124] On the role of media, and new tools such as soap operas as vehicles of behaviour change, see the discussion in World Bank (2013, p. 202).

Civil society responses

Social exclusion and disadvantages have always been and continue to be contested. Anti-casteism movements were prevalent even prior to the Indian independence movement. The socially excluded communities, based on their own strength, the policy environment and available support from the larger society, have confronted the system. While there have been larger social reformative efforts and processes led by the conscience of the larger society, the leadership and agency of the communities themselves is also evident. These are often not recorded, misrecorded or lost from memory. Various efforts were under way during the independence movement; a prominent name in this regard is Dr B. R. Ambedkar, who was instrumental in inserting positive provisions into the Constitution of India.

Over the past two or three decades across South Asia, civil society organizations have emerged representing socially excluded communities, often in the form of community-led organizations (CLOs). Some of these CLOs are also engaged in public policy research and advocacy, tracking and monitoring social policies and provisions, and networking and building capacities.

Responses from young people

Many young people from Dalit and Tribal communities in India have been able to access higher education owing to the policies and provisions of reserved places, scholarships, residential hostels and so on. However, these programmes are poorly implemented, and frequently the state goes back on its promises and withdraws provisions. Further, students on these schemes are harassed and humiliated. Student bodies of SC, ST and other marginalized communities have emerged in Indian universities, and they are standing in student elections, protesting against the violations of their rights and entitlements. Alliances are also being built with other student bodies.[125] The death of Rohith Vemula from Hyderabad Central University in India in 2016 triggered student protests across the country.

Other examples include campaigns against manual scavenging, action against triple *talaq* by Muslim women, efforts by the tribal

---

125 Jignesh Mewani from Gujarat and Chandrasekar Azad from Uttar Pradesh have emerged as the faces of Dalit youth in the public and political sphere in recent times.

communities to implement the Forest Rights Act, and efforts of persons with disability to promote access.

Engagement with the United Nations

The United Nations can play a role as a normative anchor to support inclusion policies. Historically, we can refer back to the work of the UN Subcommission on the Promotion and Protection of Human Rights, a subsidiary body of the former Commission on Human Rights and a precursor to UN Human Rights Council, which in 1947 began work on the exclusion of national or ethnic, religious and linguistic minorities. One of its successes was the Declaration on the Rights of Persons Belonging to National or Ethnic, Religious and Linguistic Minorities of 1992 (UN HRC, 2017).

An important stepping stone, with specific implications for social exclusion as practised in South Asia, was the World Conference against Racism, held in Durban in 2001. That conference emphasized that 'poverty, underdevelopment, marginalization, social exclusion and economic disparities are closely associated with racism, racial discrimination, xenophobia and related intolerance, and contribute to the persistence of racist attitudes and practices which in turn generate more poverty' (UN WCAR, 2001, para. 18; also see UN HRC, 2009). Though the Durban conference did not recognize caste-based exclusion as a form of racism, the subsequent General Recommendation 29 of the International Convention on the Eradication of Racial Discrimination (CERD) in 2002 brought it within the purview of 'other forms of discrimination akin to racism'. As a result of persistent pressure by the Dalit rights movement and other human rights groups, its processes produced recommendations that can be used constructively to address all manifestations of social exclusion.

Community-led organizations therefore engage with the UN bodies in-country and globally in pursuit of their rights, compiling and submitting data and evidence to the concerned UN bodies. Periodic civil society reports are submitted to the various committees at the Office of the High Commissioner for Human Rights (OHCHR).

Public advocacy

Community-led organizations are also conscious of the need to build public awareness and public opinion against social exclusion and discrimination in their countries. For India, progressive civil society has developed a five-pronged approach to address social exclusion and promote social inclusion, dubbed the '5Rs' – summarized as recognition, respect, representation, reparation and reclamation (*Table 12.11*). This approach is based on the systematic study and observation of the experiences of exclusion, on strategies adopted by members of socially excluded communities, and on government strategies. The approach is built on the principles of social equity, and integrated with the rights-based approach. It clearly goes beyond charity, patronage and development to emphasize the need for 'social equity' to promote equality.

Table 12.11. The 5-Rs framework for social inclusion

Recognition	Naming the social groups that are excluded.
	Recognizing the root causes of social exclusion.
	Recognizing the form and nature of social exclusion.
	Recognizing the magnitude of the issue in terms of population groups, development inequalities, participation inequalities and so on.
Respect	Respecting the identity and culture, and practices of the excluded groups.
	Ensuring dignity when rights and entitlements are implemented.
	Respecting the contribution and leadership of the socially excluded communities in national growth and development.
Representation	Proportionate representation in various social and public spaces.
	Proportionate representation in leadership and decision-making spaces.
	Representation of concerns and issues in dialogues, policies and provisions.
Reparation	Adequate and effective legislative and other measures to address social disadvantages.
	Adequate and effective legislative and other measures to address economic disadvantages.
	Adequate and effective legislative and other measures to promote social inclusion.
	Updated measures to meet the dynamic process of social exclusion–inclusion.

Reclamation	Public education for promoting social inclusion.
	Formal and informal public spaces for social interface across excluded and dominant sections.
	Active social inclusion measures based on experiential learning.
	Cultural and social interface based on mutual respect and dignity.

Source: Centre for Social Equity and Inclusion (CSEI), Delhi, 2017.[126]

This framework was used in preparing the India Common Country Assessment, 2017 in preparation for the UN Development Assistance Framework (UNDAF, 2018–2022).[127] Building on the 2030 Agenda, discussions were held with groups that have faced social exclusion – Dalits, Muslims, people living with disability, the LGBTQI community, nomadic tribes, migrants, women, single women, orphans, fisherfolk – in the preparation of the country-level UN Sustainable Development Framework. The 5-Rs framework indicates the equity and inclusion measures necessary to ensure they are not left behind while achieving the SDG 2030 agenda. It could be adapted to specific campaigns and demands by civil society organizations in other countries in South Asia.

The UN 2030 Agenda for Sustainable Development and social inclusion – 'anchors' for South Asian policy development?

Social exclusion is unacceptable, and as we know, 'exclusion is not immutable'. Abundant evidence demonstrates that social inclusion can be 'planned and achieved', but it is also clear that it takes time (World Bank, 2013). The UN 2030 Agenda for Sustainable Development offers a political opportunity to rethink and scale up social policy and social inclusion policies, since its aspirations include 'transformation' and the demand to leave no one behind.

With respect to social inclusion, the most concrete policy proposal of the 2030 Agenda (United Nations, 2015) calls for universalizing social protection, in the form of introducing social protection floors to ensure access to health, child benefits, old age pensions and some income security during periods of unemployment – for all (UN

---

[126] CSEI developed this methodology and uses it as a framework in its capacity-building work. Note by the authors.

[127] The Sustainable Development Framework has in its full title 'Leave No One Behind – Reaching the Furthest Behind First', which, in India, is abbreviated as LNB-RFBF. CSEI organized a consultation with the most marginalized sections in the CCA preparation. See UN Country Team India (2017).

DESA, 2018). Arguably, however, a universalist approach will not be able to tackle social exclusion unless there is a provision for special measures to ensure that socially excluded individuals, households and communities are compensated for the particular disadvantage they experience, and receive particular support to claim their rights (Köhler and Keane, 2006). Special efforts are necessary, because equality and justice cannot be achieved without measures that can help groups overcome their disadvantages. Such 'social equity measures' may include additional resources, affirmative action, representation, quotas and other interventions.[128]

Moreover, social inclusion policy needs to be integrated into other policies, the most important of which are to ensure decent productive work (SDG 8) and land rights (SDG 1.4)[129] so as to address the root causes of income poverty and hunger. Other areas that need to have a compensatory element include policies to ensure access to health services, education, water and sanitation, energy, and economic infrastructure.

The remit will therefore be for legislation and policy practice to step up to the 2030 Agenda commitment to transformation and inclusion, and fill the policy gaps in that Agenda. For South Asia, this would mean fundamentally revising and improving policies for social inclusion.

One useful driver for this could be the periodic reporting to the Committee on Economic, Social and Cultural Rights (ICESCR), the Convention on the Elimination of all Forms of Discrimination against Women (CEDAW), the Convention on the Rights of the Child (CRC), the Convention on the Eradication of Racial Discrimination (CERD) and the Convention on the Rights of Persons with Disabilities (CRPD) – to name a representative set of human rights instruments. They do put normative pressure on governments. For example, the special rapporteurs on the topic of discrimination based on work and descent, Yozo Yokota and Chin-Sung Chung, in accordance with Resolution 2005/22 adopted in the 57th session of the Subcommission

---

128 A frequent critique of social equity measures is that they appear to impinge on equality. Reserved places is an often-cited example in India, sometimes decried as reverse discrimination, with current generations being punished for their parents' and grandparents' acts of social exclusion.

129 SDG 1.4: 'By 2030, ensure that all men and women, in particular the poor and the vulnerable, have equal rights to economic resources, as well as access to basic services, *ownership and control over land and other forms of property, inheritance, natural resources, appropriate new technology and financial services*, including microfinance' (italics by the authors).

(2005), sent out questionnaires to all the member states of the United Nations, national human rights institutions, UN bodies and specialized agencies, and NGOs. The ensuing report recommended the Human Rights Council undertake studies on 'work and descent based discrimination' (Yokota and Chung, 2007). Subsequently, the special rapporteurs drafted the 'Principles and guidelines for the effective elimination of discrimination based on work and descent' (Yokota and Chung, 2009). In 2017, the OHCHR developed a new *Guidance Tool on Descent-Based Discrimination: Key challenges and strategic approaches to combat caste-based and analogous forms of discrimination* (OHCHR. 2013, 2017; IDSN, 2017).

An additional push can come from the voluntary reviews which countries are invited to present to the ECOSOC High-level Political Forum, in tune with the 2030 Agenda. In 2017, forty-four countries presented their reviews. From South Asia, they included Afghanistan, Bangladesh, India, the Maldives and Nepal (https://sustainabledevelopment.un.org/hlpf). With some progressive political pressure, a thorough, rights-based follow-up discussion on these submissions could be instrumentalized to address poverty and social exclusion.

The socially excluded communities in South Asia are critically engaging in the SDG agenda, particularly the Dalit-led civil society organizations and community-led organizations. The National Campaign on Dalit Human Rights (NCDHR) and the Asia Dalit Rights Forum (ADRF) are examples. An Asian Parliamentarians Forum is also an important space in this regard. SDG processes at the national and regional levels need to engage with these bodies while framing strategies and monitoring mechanisms. Asia Pacific Regional Civil Society Engagement (APRCEM), supported by the UN regional commission ESCAP, is an example of the civil society–UN interface at the regional level. Similar bodies for engagement can also be initiated at the South Asian level. Ensuring space for and participation of socially excluded civil society in these forums and processes is essential.

But this is not enough. The power relations need to be addressed – which the 2030 Agenda avoids (see Telleria, Chapter 4). To *eradicate* poverty and 'leave no one behind' – ensure universality and social inclusion – is a different proposition requiring more radical (albeit pacifist) action. The excluded in many South Asian countries are highlighting their issues and demand for equality and justice through various available procedures. However, the lack of accountability to the socially excluded thwarts their efforts. Greater attention is necessary to include rightful demands for resources, voice, accountability and justice to promote greater equality in economic, social and political power relations.

Acknowledgement

Some sections of this paper reproduce or build on an unpublished discussion paper by Koehler and Namala (2013).

References

Appasamy, P., Guhan, S., Hema, R. Majumdar, M. and Vaidyanathan, A. 1995. Social exclusion in respect of basic needs in India. G. Rodgers, C. Gore and J. Figueiredo, *Social Exclusion: Rhetoric, reality, responses.* Geneva, IILS, pp. 237–49.

Actualitix. 2016. Population below poverty line by country. https://en.actualitix.com/country/wld/population-below-poverty-line.php (Accessed 11 April 2019.)

Daneil, E., Johns, H. and Nikarthil, D. 2017. Progress towards inclusive sustainable development in India: a study of Dalits and Adivasis in 2030 Agenda. Asia Dalit Rights Forum. https://gcap.global/wp-content/uploads/2018/11/Dalit-Shadow-Report-2017.pdf (Accessed 23 March 2019.)

Basant, R. and Shariff, A. 2010. Introduction. R. Basant and A. Shariff (eds), *Handbook of Muslims in India*, New Delhi, Oxford University Press, pp. 1–26.

BDERM (Bangladesh Dalit and Excluded Rights Movement), Bangladesh Dalit and Excluded Women Federation (BDEWF) and Nagorik Uddyog (Citizen's Initiative). 2012. The human rights situation of Dalits in Bangladesh. Joint NGO Submission related to Bangladesh for the 16th Universal Periodic Review session, 22 April–3 May. https://lib.ohchr.org/HRBodies/UPR/Documents/Session16/BD/JS7_UPR_BGDS16_2013_Jointsubmission7_E.pdf (Accessed 18 March 2019.)

Bennett, L. 2006. Unequal Citizens: Gender, caste and ethnic exclusion in Nepal. World Bank and UK Department for International Development. http://documents.worldbank.org/curated/en/745031468324021366/pdf/379660v20WP0Un00Box0361508B0PUBLIC0.pdf (Accessed 28 May 2017.)

Bhatti, H. 2018. Supreme Court acquits Aasia Bibi, orders immediate release. *Dawn*, 30 October. www.dawn.com/news/1442396/supreme-court-acquits-aasia-bibi-orders-immediate-release (Accessed 7 January 2019.)

Bonnerjee, A. 2014*a*. Fiscal space in South Asia: evidence for the welfare state. G. Koehler and D. Chopra (eds), *Development and Welfare Policy in South Asia*, London, Routledge, pp. 39–61.

---. 2014b. 'Social sector spending in South Asia: a mixed bag. G. Koehler and D. Chopra (eds), *Development and Welfare Policy in South Asia*, London, Routledge, pp. 185–97.

Budhathoki, A. and Safi, M. 2019. Mother and two boys suffocate in Nepal's latest 'period hut' tragedy. *Guardian*, 10 January. www.theguardian.com/global-development/2019/jan/10/mother-and-two-boys-suffocate-in-nepal-latest-period-hut-tragedy (Accessed 14 January 2019.)

Chopra, D. 2014. Welfare, development and rights in South Asia. G. Koehler and D. Chopra (eds), *Development and Welfare Policy in South Asia*, London, Routledge, pp. 198–211.

Commission on the Status of Women (CSW) 2015. Implementing the Beijing Platform For Action. Political Declaration o. The Occasion O. The Twentieth Anniversary o. The Fourth World Conference on Women. www.unwomen.org/-/media/headquarters/attachments/sections/csw/59/declaration-en.pdf?la=en&vs=4833 (Accessed 7 April 2019.)

Das, M. B. 2008. Minority status and labour market outcomes: does India have minority enclaves? Policy Research Working Paper Series 4653. Washington DC, World Bank.

Economy Watch. 2019. Tax burden % of GDP for all countries. http://economywatch.com/economic-statistics/economic-indicators/Tax_Burden_Percentage_GDP/ (Accessed 4 April 2019.)

Esquivel, V. 2016. Power and the sustainable development goals: a feminist analysis. *Gender and Development*, Vol. 24, No. 1, pp. 9–23.

FAO (Food and Agriculture Organization of the United Nations.) 2015. *Regional Overview of Food Insecurity-Asia and the Pacific: Towards a food secure Asia and the Pacific.* Rome, FAO.

Ferrant, G., L. M. Pesando, K. Nowacka. 2014. Unpaid care work. The missing link in the analysis of gender gaps in labour outcomes, December 2014. OECD Development Centre. www.oecd.org/dev/development-gender/Unpaid_care_work.pdf (Accessed 4 April 2019.)

Galtung, J. 1969. Violence, peace and peace research. *Journal of Peace Research*, Vol. 6, No. 3, pp. 167–191.

Gardener, J. and Subrahmanian, R. 2006. Tackling social exclusion in health and education: case studies from Asia. Summary report. DFID Asia. https://gsdrc.org/document-library/tackling-social-exclusion-in-health-and-education/ (Accessed 11 April 2019.)

Gazdar, H. 2014. Political economy of reform: social protection reform in Pakistan. G. Koehler and D. Chopra (eds), *Development and Welfare Policy in South Asia*. London, Routledge, pp. 148–63.

Ghosh, J. 2015. India's rural employment programme is dying a death of funding cuts. www.networkideas.org/news-analysis/2015/02/indias-rural-employment-programme-is-dying-a-death-of-funding-cuts/ (Accessed 24 May 2017.)

Gill, T. 2007. Making things worse: how caste blindness in Indian post-tsunami disaster recovery has exacerbated vulnerability and exclusion, report. Dalit Network Netherlands (DNN).

Gurung, J. B. et al. 1999. The Condition of Dalits (Untouchables) in Nepal: Assessment of the Impact of Various Development Interventions. Lalitpur, TEAM Consult.

Gurung, S. 2013. Chaupadi: a social evil. *EGEP 2012 Winter Open Forum,* Vol. 1, pp. 86–92. www.dbpia.co.kr/Journal/ArticleDetail/NODE07136652 (Accessed 14 January 2019.)

Hanlon, J., Barrientos, A. and Hulme, D. 2011. *Just Give Money to the Poor. The Development Revolution from the Global South.* Boulder, Colo., Kumarian Press.

Hooper, E. 2003. Review of social exclusion in selected countries in the Asia region, mimeo. London, UK Department for International Development (DFID).

IDSN (International Dalit Solidarity Network). 2009. United Nations Principles and Guidelines for the Effective Elimination of Discrimination Based on Work and Descent. A Comprehensive Legal Framework to Eliminate Caste Discrimination Globally. Draft. http://idsn.org/uploads/media/UN_Principles_And_Guidelines_-_IDSN.pdf (Accessed 14 January 2019.)

–––. 2017. Landmark UN guidance tool on caste discrimination launched in Kathmandu, news, 31 March. http://idsn.org/landmark-un-guidance-tool-caste-discrimination-launched-kathmandu/ (Accessed 18 March 2019.)

IDSN, Cordaid, Justice and Peace Netherlands, National Campaign on Dalit Human Rights and Feminist Dalit Organisation Nepal. 2009. Violence against Dalit women, briefing note prepared for the 11th session of the Human Rights Council. www.dalits.nl/pdf/HRC-11_briefing_note_-_Violence_against_Dalit_Women.pdf (Accessed 18 March 2019.)

ILO (International Labour Organization) Nepal. 2005. Dalits and Labour in Nepal: Discrimination and Forced Labour, Series 5. www.ilo.org/wcmsp5/groups/public/@asia/@ro-bangkok/@ilo-kathmandu/documents/publication/wcms_112922.pdf. (Accessed 4 April 2019.)

ILO, International Organization for Migration (IOM) and Walk Free Association. 2017. Global estimates of modern slavery, forced labour and forced marriage. www.ilo.org/wcmsp5/groups/public/@dgreports/@dcomm/documents/publication/wcms_575479.pdf (Accessed 24 March 2019).

India. 2005. Guidelines for implementation of Prime Minister's New 15 Point Programme for the Welfare of Minorities. www.minorityaffairs.gov.in/sites/default/files/pm15points_eguide.pdf (Accessed 18 March 2019.)

–––. 2006. *Social, Economic and Educational Status of the Muslim Community of India: A report (Sachar Report).* New Delhi, Prime Minister's High Level Committee Cabinet Secretariat, Government of India. www.minorityaffairs.gov.in/sites/default/files/sachar_comm.pdf (Accessed 19 March 2019.)

---. 2009. Government's New 15-point Programme for the Welfare of Minorities. New Delhi, Ministry of Minority Affairs, Government of India. www.minorityaffairs.gov.in/sites/default/files/15pp-english.pdf (Accessed 18 March 2019.)

---.2011. Census 2011. New Delhi, Government of India.

---. 2012. Press note on poverty estimates, 2009–10. New Delhi, Planning Commission.

---. 2017. National Family Health Survey 4, 2015–16. New Delhi, Ministry of Health and Family Welfare, Government of India. http://rchiips.org/nfhs/NFHS-4Reports/India.pdf (Accessed 1 January 2019.)

---. various years. National Sample Survey Organisation (NSSO). New Delhi, Ministry of Statistics and Programme Implementation (MOSPI), Government of India. www.mospi.gov.in/national-sample-survey-office-nsso (Accessed 18 March 2019.)

---. 2016 n.d. Educational statistics at a glance. New Delhi, National Institute of Educational Planning and Administration, Ministry of Human Resource Development (U-DISE, MHRD), Government of India. http://udise.schooleduinfo.in/ (Accessed 14 January 2019.)

International Institute for Population Sciences (IIPS) and ICF. 2017. National Family Health Survey (NFHS-4), 2015-16: India. Mumbai: IIPS.

Irudayam, A., Mangubhai, J. and Lee, J.G. 2006. *Dalit Women Speak Out: Violence against Dalit women in India, Vol. I: Study Report*. Chennai, India, National Campaign on Dalit Human Rights (NCDHR). http://idsn.org/wp-content/uploads/user_folder/pdf/New_files/Key_Issues/Dalit_Women/dalitwomenspeakout.pdf (Accessed 18 March 2019.)

Jodhka, S. S. and Newman, K. 2007. In the name of globalization: meritocracy, productivity and the hidden language of caste. *Economic and Political Weekly*, Vol. 42, No. 41, pp. 4125–32.

Kabeer, N. 2010. Can the MDGs provide a pathway to social justice. The challenges of intersecting inequalities. Sussex, UK, IDS. http://www.ids.ac.uk/files/dmfile/MDGreportwebsiteu2WC.pdf

Khatiwada, Y. R. and Koehler, G. 2014. Social policy in a nascent welfare state. G. Koehler and D. Chopra (eds), *Development and Welfare Policy in South Asia*. London and New York, Routledge.

Koehler, G. 2017a. The 2030 Agenda and eradicating poverty: new horizons for global social policy? *Global Social Policy*, Vol. 17, No. 2, pp. 1–7.

---. 2017b. The politics of rights-based, transformative social policy in South and Southeast Asia. *International Social Science Review*. Vol. 70, Number 4. pp.105 - 126.

Koehler, G. and Chopra, D. (eds). 2014. *Development and Welfare Policy in South Asia*. London and New York, Routledge.

Koehler, G. 2014. Approaching developmental welfare states: a 'welfare geography' of South Asia. G. Koehler and D. Chopra (eds), *Development and Welfare Policy in South Asia*. London and New York, Routledge, pp. 25–38.

Köhler, G. 2009. Policies towards social inclusion. *Global Social Policy*, Vol. 9, No. 1, pp. 24–29.

Köhler, G. and Keane, J. 2006. Social policy in South Asia: towards universal coverage and transformation for achieving the Millennium Development Goals. Report for UNICEF ROSA. https://www.researchgate.net/publication/260348416_Social_Policy_in_South_Asia_Towards_Universal_Coverage_and_Transformation_for_Achieving_the_Millennium_Development_Goals

Köhler, G. and Namala, A. 2013. Social exclusion and government policy approaches to inclusion: reflections on the South Asia experience, paper for RC19: Research Committee on Poverty, Social Welfare and Social Policy. International Sociological Association (ISA), Budapest, 22–24 August. www.asszisztencia.hu/casm2/upload/111/A-0111.pdf (Accessed 18 March 2019.)

Lawyers Collective. 2013. New law abolishing manual scavenging. lawyerscollective.org/wp-content/uploads/2013/09/Report-on-new-MS-Act.pdf (Accessed 10 January 2019.)

Mader, P. 2015. *The Political Economy of Microfinance: Financializing poverty*. London, Palgrave Macmillan.

Mander, H. 2015. Modi government: one year of dismantling the welfare state. *Hindustan Times*, 20 May. www.hindustantimes.com/ht-view/modi-government-one-year-of-dismantling-the-welfare-state/story-QTxNQWLK0bEDxMnwZl7vTO.html (Accessed 18 March 2019.)

Munjial, M. and p. Kaushik, 2013. Muslim women and minority rights in India. Mainstream Weekly, Vol L1, No12, March 9, 2013

Muslim Personal Law Reforms Action Group. 2019. Muslim women's demands on reforms to the Sri Lankan Marriage and Divorce Act (1951), January. https://mplreforms.com/demands/?fbclid=IwAR3uxo3Ry04yqGhH8OKhZMfJdtdoqjdpYNiVj01z9z4Bo-xAlhOLfD2MAY8 (Accessed 18 March 2019.)

NCDHR (National Campaign on Dalit Human Rights). 2017. Progress towards inclusive sustainable development in India: a study of Dalits and Adivasis in 2030 Agenda. http://www.ncdhr.org.in/wp-content/uploads/2018/12/293284207ADRF-report-for-web.pdf (Accessed 24 March 2019.)

NCRB (National Crime Records Bureau). 2018. Crime in India. New Delhi, Government of India. http://ncrb.gov.in/ (Accessed 1 January 2019.)

OPHI (Oxford Poverty and Human Development Initiative). 2010. India country brief. www.ophi.org.uk/wp-content/uploads/Country-Brief-India.pdf (Accessed 10 January 2019.)

Panagaria, A. and More, V. 2013. Poverty by social, religious and economic groups in India and its largest states, 1993–94 to 2011–12. http://indianeconomy.columbia.edu/sites/default/files/working_papers/working_paper_2013-02-final.pdf (Accessed 10 January 2019.)

Quint. 2018. Hunted: India's lynch files. www.thequint.com/quintlab/lynching-in-india/ (Accessed 10 January 2019.)

Razavi, S. (ed.). 2007. *Gender and Social Policy in a Global Context: Uncovering the gendered structure of 'the social'*. London, Palgrave Macmillan.

———. 2016. The 2030 Agenda: challenges of implementation to attain gender equality and women's rights. *Gender and Development*, Vol. 24, No. 1, pp. 25–42.

Rodgers, G., Gore, C. and Figueiredo, J. (eds). 1995. *Social Exclusion: Rhetoric, reality, responses.* Geneva, ILO IILS.

Rogers, D. S. and Baláz, B. 2016. The view from deprivation: poverty, inequality and the distribution of wealth. A. Cimadamore, G. Koehler and T. Pogge (eds), *Poverty and the Millennium Development Goals: A critical look forward.* London, Zed, pp. 45–82. http://bora.uib.no/bitstream/handle/1956/15276/Cimadamore%20et%20al%20MDGs%20text%20with%20cover.pdf?sequence=1 (Accessed 18 March 2019.)

Roy, A. 2014. The doctor and the saint. Preface to B. R. Ambdekar. *The Annihilation of Caste.* London and New York, Verso.

Safi, M. 2017. 'Risking lives of mothers and children': India condemned for cuts to benefits. *Guardian*, 30 May. www.theguardian.com/global-development/2017/may/30/india-risking-lives-of-mothers-and-children-cuts-to-maternal-benefits (Accessed 18 March 2019.)

Samata Foundation 2014. Benchmarking the draft UN Principles and Guidelines on the Elimination of (Caste) Discrimination based on Work and Descent. Kathmandu, Samata. www.samatafoundation.org/wp-content/uploads/2017/09/Benchmark-study_nepal-report.pdf (Accessed 18 March 2019.)

Sen, A. 1990. More than 100 million women are missing. *New York Review of Books*, 20 December. www.nybooks.com/articles/1990/12/20/more-than-100-million-women-are-missing/ (Accessed 18 March 2019.)

———. 2000. Social exclusion: concept, application, and scrutiny. Manila, ADB, June. https://think-asia.org/bitstream/handle/11540/2339/social-exclusion.pdf?sequence=1 (Accessed 18 March 2019.)

Sengupta, A., Kannan, K. p. and Raveendran, G. 2008. India's common man: who are they, how many are there, and how do they live? *Economic and Political Weekly*, Vol. 43, No. 11, pp. 49–63.

Shah, G., Mander, H., Thorat, S. Deshpande, S. and Baviskar, A. 2007. *Untouchability in Rural India.* New Delhi, Sage.

Silver, H. 1995. Reconceptualizing social disadvantage: three paradigms of social exclusion. G. Rodgers, C. Gore and J. Figueiredo, 1995. *Social Exclusion: Rhetoric, reality, responses.* Geneva, IILS, pp. 57–80.

Taxmann. 2018. India's Tax to GDP ratio needs to be improved, 24 January. www.taxmann.com/budget/t21/indias-tax-to-gdp-ratio-needs-to-be-improved.aspx (Accessed 11 April 2019.)

Thorat, S. and Lee, J. 2006. Dalits and the right to food – discrimination and exclusion in food related government programmes. Working paper, vol. 1, no. 3. New Delhi, Indian Institute of Dalit Studies. www.dalitstudies.org.in/download/wp/0603.pdf (Accessed 18 March 2019.)

Thorat, S. and Newman, K. (eds). 2010. *Blocked by Caste: Economic discrimination in modern India.* New Delhi, Oxford University Press

Transparency International. 2016. Corruption Perception Index. www.transparency.org/news/feature/corruption_perceptions_index_2016 (Accessed 18 March 2019.)

United Nations. 2000. United Nations Millennium Declaration. Resolution adopted by the General Assembly. A /RES/55/2. New York, United Nations.

---. 2015. *Transforming our World: the 2030 Agenda for Sustainable Development.* www.un.org/ga/search/view_doc.asp?symbol=A/RES/70/1&Lang=E (Accessed 18 March 2019.)

---. 2017. Rights of persons belonging to national or ethnic, religious and linguistic minorities. Annual report of the United Nations High Commissioner for Human Rights and reports of the Office of the High Commissioner and the Secretary-General. Promotion and protection of all human rights, civil, political, economic, social and cultural rights, including the right to development. 27 February–24 March. http://reliefweb.int/sites/reliefweb.int/files/resources/G1643400.pdf (Accessed 18 March 2019.)

UN Country Team India. 2017. India: Common Country Assessment 2017, final draft 15 March, shared by A. Namala.

UN DESA. 2010. *Analysing and Measuring Social Inclusion in a Global Context.* New York, United Nations. www.un.org/esa/socdev/publications/measuring-social-inclusion.pdf (Accessed 28 May 2017.)

---. 2017. *World Population Prospects. The 2017 Revision.* https://esa.un.org/unpd/wpp/Download/Standard/Population/ (Accessed 18 March 2019.)

---. 2018. *Report on the World Social Situation 2018: Promoting inclusion through social protection.* www.un.org/development/desa/dspd/report-on-the-world-social-situation-rwss-social-policy-and-development-division/2018-2.html (Accessed 18 March 2019.)

UNDP. 2016a. Human Development Index. New York, United Nations.

---. 2016b. Gender Inequality Index. New York, United Nations.

UNESCO. 2015. An indicative review of UNESCO's work on social inclusion. http://unesdoc.unesco.org/images/0024/002431/243129e.pdf (Accessed 28 May 2017.)

UNICEF. n.d. Secondary education. https://data.unicef.org/topic/education/secondary-education/ accessed 4.4.2019

UNICEF ROSA 2016. *Statistical Pocketbook South Asia.* Kathmandu, UNICEF Regional Office South Asia (ROSA).

UN OHCHR (Office of the High Commissioner for Human Rights). 2004. Discrimination based on work and descent. Sub-Commission on Human Rights Resolution 2004/17, Geneva. www.ohchr.org/Documents/HRBodies/HRCouncil/RegularSession/Session11/A-HRC-11-CRP3.pdf (Accessed 18 March 2019.)

---. 2009. Final report of Mr Yozo Yokota and Ms Chin-Sung Chung, Special Rapporteurs on the topic of discrimination based on work and descent. Human rights bodies and mechanisms. New York, Human Rights Council, A/HRC/11/CRP.3, 18 May. www.ohchr.org/Documents/HRBodies/HRCouncil/RegularSession/Session11/A-HRC-11-CRP3.pdf (Accessed 18 March 2019.)

---. 2013. Guidance note of the Secretary-General on Racial Discrimination and Protection of Minorities. www.ohchr.org/Documents/Issues/Minorities/GuidanceNoteRacialDiscriminationMinorities.pdf (Accessed 18 March 2019.)

---. 2017. Guidance tool on descent-based discrimination: key challenges and strategic approaches to combat caste-based and analogous forms of discrimination. UN Network on Racial Discrimination and Protection of Minorities. www.ohchr.org/Documents/Issues/Minorities/GuidanceToolDiscrimination.pdf (Accessed 14 January 2019.)

Unni, J. 2010. Informality and gender in the labour market for Muslims: has education been a route out of poverty? R. Basant and A. Shariff (eds), *Handbook of Muslims in India*. New Delhi, Oxford University Press, pp. 221–34.

UNRISD. 2005. *Gender Equality: Striving for justice in an unequal world.* Geneva, UNRISD

UN WCAR (World Conference against Racism). 2001. Declaration. www.un.org/WCAR/durban.pdf (Accessed 18 March 2019.)

UN Women. 2018. *Turning Promises into Action: Gender equality in the 2030 Agenda for Sustainable Development.* New York, UN Women. www.unwomen.org/en/digital-library/publications/2018/2/gender-equality-in-the-2030-agenda-for-sustainable-development-2018#view. (Accessed 25 March 2019).

Upadhyay, P. 2017. Menstruation pollution taboos and gender based violence in Western Nepal. *NEHU Journal*, Vol. 15, No. 2, pp. 101–11.

WHO (World Health Organization). n.d. Child mortality data. www.childmortality.org/index. https://www.who.int/gho/child_health/mortality/en/. (Accessed 25 March 2019.)

World Bank. 2013. *Inclusion Matters. The foundation for shared prosperity.* Washington DC, World Bank. https://openknowledge.worldbank.org/handle/10986/16195 (Accessed 19 March 2019.)

---. 2015*a*. School enrolment, primary, 19702017. Washington DC, World Bank. https://data.worldbank.org/indicator/SE.PRM.NENR (Accessed 11 November 2017.)

---. 2015*b*. Worldwide Governance Indicators. Washington DC, World Bank.

---. n.d.*a*. Poverty Headcount ratio at national poverty lines (% population). Washington DC, World Bank.

---. n.d.*b*. Gross enrolment ratio, secondary, both sexes, 1970–2017. Washington DC, World Bank. https://data.worldbank.org/indicator/SE.SEC.ENRR (Accessed 19 March 2019.)

---. n.d.*c*. Tax revenue (% of GDP). https://data.worldbank.org/indicator/ GC.TAX.TOTL.GD.ZS

---. n.d.*d*. Tax revenue (% of GDP). https://databank.worldbank.org/ data/reports.aspx?source=2&series=GC.TAX.TOTL.GD.ZS&country= (Accessed 4 April 2019).

Yokota, Y. and Chung, C.-S. 2007. Prevention of discrimination. Final report of the Special Rapporteurs on the topic of discrimination based on work and descent. www.indianet.nl/pdf/PreventionOfDiscrimination.pdf (Accessed 14 January 2019.)

---. 2009. Principles and guidelines for the effective elimination of discrimination based on work and descent.

Human rights conventions and declarations

Convention on the Elimination of all Forms of Discrimination against Women (CEDAW). www.ohchr.org/EN/ProfessionalInterest/Pages/CEDAW.aspx

Convention on the Rights of the Child (CRC). www.ohchr.org/EN/HRBodies/ CRC/Pages/CRCIndex.aspx

Convention on the Rights of Persons with Disabilities (CRPD). www.ohchr. org/EN/HRBodies/CRPD/Pages/CRPDIndex.aspx

International Convention on the Eradication of Racial Discrimination (CERD). www.ohchr.org/EN/ProfessionalInterest/Pages/CERD.aspx

International Covenant on Economic, Social and Cultural Rights. www.ohchr. org/EN/ProfessionalInterest/Pages/CESCR.aspx

UN Declaration on the Rights of Indigenous Peoples. www.un.org/esa/ socdev/unpfii/documents/DRIPS_en.pdf

UN Declaration on the Rights of Persons Belonging to National or Ethnic, Religious and Linguistic Minorities. General Assembly resolution 47/135, 18 December 1992. www.ohchr.org/Documents/Publications/ GuideMinoritiesDeclarationen.pdf

Notes on the contributors

Editors

Gabriele Koehler, lead editor, is a development economist trained in Germany, and a senior research associate affiliated with the UN Research Institute for Social Development (UNRISD), Geneva. She is a former UN official, with over 25 years of experience, and a former Senior Fellow of the Academic Council of the UN System (ACUNS). Her research and advocacy work focuses on the UN development agenda and human rights, and on social and economic policy, notably social protection. She is on the governing board of the UN Association of Germany.

Alberto D. Cimadamore is CROP scientific director, professor of theory of international relations at the University of Buenos Aires, and researcher at the National Council of Scientific and Technological Research of Argentina (currently on leave). He holds a Ph.D. in international relations from the University of Southern California (USC), Los Angeles. His publications focus on the political economy of poverty, international development and regional integration.

Fadia Kiwan is the chairperson of the Scientific Advisory Committee of MOST, at UNESCO. She holds a doctorat d'état in comparative politics from Paris1-Sorbonne and a certificat d'aptitude au professorat de l'enseignement du second degré (CAPES) in philosophy and psychology from the Lebanese University. Her research focuses on public policies in a comparative perspective, especially in the field of policies on women's inclusion in the Arab states. She has been the director general of the Arab Women Organization (AWO) since June 2018.

Pedro Manuel Monreal Gonzalez is a programme specialist, Sector for Social and Human Sciences, UNESCO Paris, and member of the secretariat of MOST. He holds a Ph.D. in economics from the University of Havana. His research interests include social inclusion, the research– policy-making nexus, and Small Island Developing States (SIDS).

Contributors

Nelson Antequera Durán holds a Ph.D. in anthropology from the National Autonomous University of Mexico. His current position is associate researcher of the Centro AGUA–UMSS, Cochabamba, Bolivia.

His main research interests include cultural diversity, social inclusion, water, climate change and development in Andean societies.

Judith Audin is a researcher at the French Centre for Research on Contemporary China (CEFC, Hong Kong) and an associate researcher at CECMC (Paris). She is the chief editor of the journal *China Perspectives*. She holds a Ph.D. in political science from Sciences Po, Paris. Her research interests include power relationships at the neighbourhood level, an ethnographic study on urban residents' committees in Beijing, and the ethnography of post-industrial transformation (Shanxi, Datong). Her current research focuses on abandoned places and contemporary ruins in China.

Joop de Wit is a political anthropologist retired from but still associated with the International Institute of Social Studies of Erasmus University (ISS). The Hague, as associate professor in public policy and development management. He taught in the fields of governance, policy and political science, and his research is on urban poverty and governance issues, decentralization, participation and the (formal but especially informal) interfaces between poor communities, local government, politicians and the state. A recent book is *Urban Poverty, Local Governance and Everyday Politics in Mumbai* (2017).

Enrique Delamonica is senior statistics specialist (child poverty and gender equality) at UNICEF Headquarters, New York. He has held senior positions in social policy in UNICEF Nigeria and the Latin America and Caribbean Regional Office. He is a CROP fellow, and holds a Ph.D. in economics from the New School for Social Research, New York. His research focuses on equity and discrimination, child poverty, poverty reduction and human development strategies, social protection, financing social services, and the impact of macroeconomic trends on child welfare.

Aldrie Henry-Lee is a professor of social policy and university director at the Sir Arthur Lewis Institute of Social and Economic Studies (SALISES), University of the West Indies (Mona Campus), Jamaica, West Indies. She holds a Ph.D. in sociology from the University of the West Indies, and has conducted research and published in the areas of poverty, deviance, social protection and children's rights.

Ashok Kumar is professor of physical planning, School of Planning and Architecture, New Delhi, India, with a Ph.D. from the University of Liverpool, UK. He trained as a geographer and a city planner, and his research focuses on spatial justice and equity.

Rachel Kurian is senior lecturer in international labour economics at the International Institute of Social Studies, Erasmus University, Rotterdam, Netherlands. Her research focuses on economic reforms and labour, plantation labour, trade unions, child labour, elderly protection, gender politics and women's rights, poverty and social exclusion. Her recent publications include *Class, Patriarchy and Ethnicity on Sri Lankan Plantations: Two centuries of power and protest* and *Natesa Aiyar and Meenachi Ammal: Pioneers of trade unionism and feminism on the plantations* (both with Kumari Jayawardena, 2016).

Annie Namala is co-founder and executive director of the Centre for Social Equity and Inclusion (CSEI), Delhi. She is also co-convener of the Wada Na Todo Abhiyan (national campaign on governance accountability) (WNTA), working on poverty and social exclusion. She has over two decades of experience in community mobilization, policy and advocacy in India, working with marginalized communities to end caste-based discrimination, strengthen community-led organizations (CLOs) and promote social equity and inclusion among youth from vulnerable communities.

Gilbert Siame is a lecturer and researcher at the Department of Geography and Environmental Studies, and director, Centre for Urban Research and Planning, University of Zambia. He holds a doctorate from the University of Cape Town in South Africa. His research interests and projects include urban informality, urban sustainability, climate change and cities, urban governance, transdisciplinary research methods, and the interface of planning theory and practice in the global South.

Deepak Singh is a grassroots worker and development consultant whose research and experience has focused on the empowerment of marginalized communities in South and South-East Asia, including Dalits, Tribal communities and women's rights, challenging their exclusion and discrimination, and improving their livelihood, food and security needs.

Paul Spicker is an emeritus professor of Robert Gordon University, Scotland, and a CROP fellow. He works as a consultant on social welfare, and has done work for a range of agencies at local, national and international levels. His research includes studies related to benefit delivery systems, the care of older people, psychiatric patients, housing management and local anti-poverty strategy. His published work, mainly focusing on poverty, social security, policy analysis and the theory of social policy, includes eighteen books and some ninety academic papers.

Juan Telleria holds a Ph.D. in philosophy from the University of the Basque Country (UPV/EHU). He is a postdoctoral researcher at the HEGOA Institute for Cooperation and Development Studies, UPV/EHU, researching questions of development, identity and power.

ibidem.eu